THE
COMMUNICATOR'S
COMMENTARY

THE COMMUNICATOR'S COMMENTARY SERIES

THE COMMUNICATOR'S COMMENTARY

MATTHEW

MYRON S. AUGSBURGER

LLOYD J. OGILVIE, GENERAL EDITOR

THE COMMUNICATOR'S COMMENTARY SERIES, Volume 1: *Matthew.*
Copyright © 1982 by Word, Inc.
All rights reserved. No portion of this book may be reproduced in any form whatsoever, except for brief quotations in reviews, without written permission from the
publisher.

The Bible text in this series is from The New King James Bible, New Testament,
copyright © 1979 by Thomas Nelson, Inc., Publishers. All rights reserved. Used
by permission. Brief Scripture quotations within the commentary text are also from
The New King James Bible, New Testament, unless otherwise identified, as follows:
NIV, from *The Holy Bible, New International Version,* copyright © 1978 by New York
International Bible Society, used by permission; TLB, from *The Living Bible, Paraphrased*
(Wheaton: Tyndale House, Publishers, copyright © 1971, used by permission); NASB,
from *The New American Standard Bible,* copyright © 1960, 1962, 1963, 1968, 1971, 1972,
1973, 1975 by the Lockman Foundation, used by permission; KJV, from The Authorized
King James Version.

Library of Congress Cataloging in Publication Data
Main entry under title:

The Communicator's commentary.

   Includes bibliographical references.
   Contents: v. 1. Matthew / Myron S. Augsburger.
   1. Bible. N.T.—Commentaries—Collected works.
I. Ogilvie, Lloyd John.   II. Augsburger, Myron S.
BS2341.2.C65   225.7'7   81–71764
ISBN 0–8499–0154–5 (v. 1) regular edition   AACR2
ISBN 0–8499–3800–7 (v. 1) deluxe edition
ISBN 0–8499–3274–2 (v. 1) paper

Printed in the United States of America

1 2 3 9 AGF 9 8 7 6 5 4 3 2 1

Contents

Editor's Preface

God has called all of His people to be communicators. Everyone who is in Christ is called into ministry. As ministers of "the manifold grace of God," all of us—clergy and laity—are commissioned with the challenge to communicate our faith to individuals and groups, classes and congregations.

The Bible, God's Word, is the objective basis of the truth of His love and power that we seek to communicate. In response to the urgent, expressed needs of pastors, teachers, Bible study leaders, church school teachers, small group enablers, and individual Christians, the Communicator's Commentary is offered as a penetrating search of the Scriptures of the New Testament to enable vital personal and practical communication of the abundant life.

Many current commentaries and Bible study guides provide only some aspects of a communicator's needs. Some offer in-depth scholarship but no application to daily life. Others are so popular in approach that biblical roots are left unexplained. Few offer impelling illustrations that open windows for the reader to see the exciting application for today's struggles. And most of all, seldom have the expositors given the valuable outlines of passages so needed to help the preacher or teacher in his or her busy life to prepare for communicating the Word to congregations or classes.

This Communicator's Commentary series brings all of these elements together. The authors are scholar-preachers and teachers outstanding in their ability to make the Scriptures come alive for individuals and groups. They are noted for bringing together excellence in biblical scholarship, knowledge of the original Greek and

Hebrew, sensitivity to people's needs, vivid illustrative material from biblical, classical, and contemporary sources, and lucid communication by the use of clear outlines of thought. Each has been selected to contribute to this series because of his Spirit-empowered ability to help people live in the skins of biblical characters and provide a "you-are-there" intensity to the drama of events of the Bible which have so much to say about our relationships and responsibilities today.

The design for the Communicator's Commentary gives the reader an overall outline of each book of the New Testament. Following the introduction, which reveals the author's approach and salient background on the book, each chapter of the commentary provides the Scripture to be exposited. The New King James Bible has been chosen for the Communicator's Commentary because it combines with integrity the beauty of language, underlying Greek textual basis, and thought-flow of the 1611 King James Version, while replacing obsolete verb forms and other archaisms with their everyday contemporary counterparts for greater readability. Reverence for God is preserved in the capitalization of all pronouns referring to the Father, Son, or Holy Spirit. Readers who are more comfortable with another translation can readily find the parallel passage by means of the chapter and verse reference at the end of each passage being exposited. The paragraphs of exposition combine fresh insights to the Scripture, application, rich illustrative material, and innovative ways of utilizing the vibrant truth for his or her own life and for the challenge of communicating it with vigor and vitality.

It has been gratifying to me as Editor of this series to receive enthusiastic progress reports from each contributor. As they worked, all were gripped with new truths from the Scripture—God-given insights into passages, previously not written in the literature of biblical explanation. A prime objective of this series is for each user to find the same awareness: that God speaks with newness through the Scriptures when we approach them with a ready mind and a willingness to communicate what He has given; that God delights to give communicators of His Word "I-never-saw-that-in-that-verse-before" intellectual insights so that our listeners and readers can have "I-never-realized-all-that-was-in-that-verse" spiritual experiences.

The thrust of the commentary series unequivocally affirms that God speaks through the Scriptures today to engender faith, enable adventuresome living of the abundant life, and establish the basis of obedient discipleship. The Bible, the unique Word of God, is unlimited in its resource for Christians in communicating our hope to others. It is our weapon in the battle for truth, the guide for ministry, and the irresistible force for introducing others to God. In the New Testament we meet the divine Lord and Savior whom we seek to communicate to others. What He said and did as God with us has been faithfully recorded under the inspiration of the Spirit of God. The cosmic implications of the Gospels are lived out in Acts and spelled out in the Epistles. They have stood the test of time because the eternal Communicator, God Himself, communicates through them to those who would be communicators of grace. His essential nature is exposed, the plan of salvation is explained, and the Gospel for all of life, now and for eternity is proclaimed.

A biblically rooted communication of the Gospel holds in unity and oneness what divergent movements have wrought asunder. This commentary series courageously presents personal faith, caring for individuals, and social responsibility as essential, inseparable dimensions of biblical Christianity. It seeks to present the quadrilateral Gospel in its fullness which calls us to unreserved commitment to Christ, unrestricted self-esteem in His grace, unqualified love for others in personal evangelism, and undying efforts to work for justice and righteousness in a sick and suffering world.

A growing renaissance in the church today is being led by clergy and laity who are biblically rooted, Christ-centered, and Holy Spirit-empowered. They have dared to listen to people's most urgent questions and deepest needs and then to God as He speaks through the Bible. Biblical preaching is the secret of growing churches. Bible study classes and small groups are equipping the laity for ministry in the world. Dynamic Christians are finding that daily study of God's Word allows the Spirit to do in them what He wishes to communicate through them to others. These days are the most exciting time since Pentecost. The Communicator's Commentary is offered to be a primary resource of new life for this renaissance.

This volume, *Matthew*, is written by one of the leaders of today's biblical resurgence. Myron Augsburger is a world-recognized scholar, preacher, and teacher. His numerous books have opened the rich treasures of the Bible for countless readers. Dr. Augsburger has had a distinguished career as lecturer, evangelist, and preacher, as president of Eastern Mennonite College, and as adjunct professor for several seminaries.

Matthew's Gospel is vividly portrayed in this commentary. The arrangement of the exposition introduces us to Christ the King and the adventure of living in His Kingdom. My prayer is that you will discover, as I have, new insight and inspiration as you communicate with the King and seek to communicate the joy of His reign and rule in the minds and hearts of people today.

LLOYD OGILVIE

Introduction

The Gospel of Matthew holds first place in all extant witnesses to the text of the four Gospels. Standing first, it forms the link between the Old Testament and the New. However, most scholars today are agreed that the Gospel of Mark is the earliest of the synoptic Gospels, and that the writers of Matthew and of Luke had access to Mark's Gospel as an aid in their writing. Matthew, however, was responsible for an earlier collection of the sayings of Jesus called the *logia*. In the actual writing of the Gospel of Matthew this provided the basic content material.

History provides witness to a previous form of Matthew's Gospel, as the earlier Gospel, written in Hebrew or Aramaic from the setting of the Jewish community. Papias, bishop of Hierapolis about A.D. 140, said, "Matthew composed his history [logia; sayings] in the Hebrew dialect and everyone translated it as he was able."[1] About A.D. 185, Irenaeus wrote, "Matthew, indeed, produced his gospel written among the Hebrews in their own dialect whilst Peter and Paul proclaimed the gospel and founded the church in Rome."[2] And Pantaenus, A.D. 195, was reported to have found in India "the Gospel of Matthew in Hebrew."[3] Origin identified the *logia* as by Matthew, "the same that was once a publican, but afterwards an apostle of Jesus Christ, who having published it for the Jewish converts, wrote it in the Hebrew."[4]

Matthew is the bridge from the Old Testament to the New, the basic source for the relationship between the Old and New Covenants. In this Gospel there are sixteen statements, "That it might be fulfilled which was spoken by the prophet saying. . . ." This is significant for: (1) here we have classic examples of the New Testament use of the Old Testament, (2) it helps us recognize that the Christ events, His birth-death-rising again, are a fulfillment of the total sweep of salvation history which Oscar Cullmann calls *Heilsgeschichte;* and (3) it helps us to understand the identification in the Gospel of Matthew with Hebraic history and tradition. Matthew relates the whole of salvation history to its culmination in the person of Christ, moving from an ethnocentric to a Christocentric faith in God.

As one of the three synoptic Gospels, Matthew has its own unique characteristics. As Bacon and other writers have shown, the story of Jesus' life is interspersed with five great discourses: (1) Righteousness, in 5:1–7:29, (2) Missions, in 9:35–10:42, (3) Kingdom, in 13:1–58, (4) Church, in 18:1–35, and (5) Eschatology, in 24:1–25:46. These five discourses have been called the "five books" of Matthew and are the major presentations in the Gospel of the teachings of Jesus. Krister Stendahl sees these five books, always concluding with a similar identifying formula, as the outline for the Gospel itself. He finds reasons to identify this Gospel with the history of Israel, suggesting a conscious identification with the five books of Moses. However, as shown by Jack Kingsbury, this may do violence to Matthew's own pattern of systematizing the materials from Jesus' ministry.

It is without question that we owe our knowledge of the substance of our Lord's teachings to Matthew, for it is supremely the Teaching Gospel. William Barclay says in the introduction to his commentary on Matthew, "Broadly speaking, to Mark we owe our knowledge of the events of Jesus' life; to Matthew we owe our knowledge of Jesus' teaching."[5] And Matthew presents (1) Jesus' radical claims to discipleship, to obedience to God's will; (2) Jesus' own life as a model for these high ethical demands; and (3) Jesus' emphasis on the church as the community of faith in which the ethic is lived.

The material of Matthew, the accountant, was very systematic in composition. Special attention is given to money, with two parables dealing with financial transactions found only in this Gospel (Matt. 18 and 20). He also notes financial details in Judas' betrayal and the bribing of the guards at the sepulcher. As a systematizer, he arranged the material in the Gospel in ways which make it easy to grasp and even memorize units; enabling greater retention of sections, especially important when there was a limited amount of "printed" material available for the Christian church. For example: the "Sermon on the Mount" is found in three consecutive chapters rather than spread throughout the Gospel as in Luke. This is true also of the grouping of miracles in chapters 8 and 9, of the listing of parables in chapter 13, and of the teachings in chapters 21 through 25.

In the earliest days, the Christian church had a strong oral tradition. From the death and resurrection of Christ (around A.D. 30) to the earliest of Paul's letters (to the Thessalonians, around A.D. 50), we have no documents. A "Rule of Faith" provided a new Christological approach to the Old Testament Scriptures. The writing of the Gospels came later. Perhaps Matthew's Hebrew *logia* were first; contemporaneous with Paul's writings, to be followed by Mark between A.D. 60 and 65, then the Greek composition of Matthew was written, as we know it, in the late or middle 60s, prior to the destruction of Jerusalem.

Since the publication of *The Messianic Secret* by M. Wrede in 1901, the school of form criticism has sought to gain an understanding and interpretation of the significance of this oral tradition. Form criticism regards the Gospels not as biographies but as confessional material of the Jesus story. The purpose of the Gospels, alike for all four, is the portrayal of Jesus as the Messiah. Simply stated, form criticism is the study of the oral tradition, of the preliterary stage of the Jesus-tradition. A later work by K. L. Schmidt, *Der Rahmen der Geschichte Jesu*, in 1918, interpreted Mark, the earliest writer, as providing a framework to which the oral traditions of Jesus' life and teachings were attached. This is known as redaction criticism, the attempt to separate out the writer's redactional work. Popularized by Bultmann, it has largely determined the approach of the less conservative scholars.

Redaction criticism is not the approach I have followed in writing this commentary. Holding an evangelical theology with a more conservative approach, I believe in an inspiration of the Scripture by the Holy Spirit who provides us with a correct statement of Jesus' life and teachings from the context of His own ministry. This is not to say that the Holy Spirit dictated a revelation of material, but that He guided the writer in the research of oral tradition and in the selection of materials for composing a Gospel of our Lord that is authentic and trustworthy in all details. Nor does this mean that the Holy Spirit preempted the writer's personality or style in research and writing, nor that He excluded from the writer possible perspectives gained from His work in the Christian church following Pentecost. Rather, we recognize the promise of Christ that the Holy Spirit would be the Guide into all truth. Therefore, my approach gives first consideration to the primary setting of Jesus' teachings in the historical setting of His life and ministry.

It is significant to compare Matthew with the other synoptic Gospels. Mark, the shortest and no doubt the earlier of the Gospels in their present forms, has 661 verses. Matthew has 1,068 verses and Luke is the longest with 1,149 verses. Matthew, with his concern for content, reproduces at least 606 of Mark's verses, while Luke reproduces 320. There are some 55 verses of Mark which Matthew does not reproduce, but of them Luke reproduces 31. This leaves only 24 verses in the Gospel of Mark not reproduced in either Matthew or Luke. Between the two of them they reproduce 637 of Mark's verses.

In Matthew and Luke there is much more material than Mark supplies, and, comparing the two, there are some 200 verses of this additional material that are almost identical. This similarity has led scholars to see a common sourcebook of the teachings of Jesus which does not now exist. To designate this source scholars use the letter "Q" from the German word for source, *Quelle*. As a handbook of the teachings of Jesus, "Q" provided a source from which the synoptic writers drew material. It might have been the manuscript which Papias refers to as Matthew's collection of the sayings of Jesus in the Hebrew tongue. We cannot affirm more regarding "Q" than the internal evidence. There are several hundred verses which appear in Matthew and Luke but are not in Mark. A study of Matthew's and Luke's use of Mark also shows those usages in all three Gospels which point toward a common source. Whether "Q" is the early collections of Jesus' sayings by Matthew, or whether it is material gathered and written by some other person remains unknown.

Matthew expands Mark at both ends, adding new materials. While he follows Mark's sequence in chapters 3 through 4 and 12 through 28, he rearranged Mark's materials in chapters 5 through 11. He groups material according to theme or type and uniquely presents Jesus' teachings in five major units with a similar concluding formula (7:28–29, 11:1, 13:53, 19:1, and 26:1). Luke says that many had written of the things "fulfilled among us, just as they were handed down to us by those who from the first were eyewitnesses" (Luke 1:1–2 NIV). While the early church was producing writings about Jesus from oral tradition, the Spirit of God motivated and inspired particular writers to provide an authentic word of the Person and teachings of Jesus Christ which has come down to us in the four Gospels.

Tasker explains, "The differences between Matthew and Mark may equally well be explained on the supposition that the Gospel of Matthew retains details originally handed down by the apostle of that name, and that the Gospel of Mark often draws upon Peter's reminiscences."[6]

The proposal that Matthew was written basically for the Jewish community needs to be critically examined. Some claim that Jesus introduced the Kingdom to the Jewish community but, upon their rejection, the Kingdom was postponed to a future time; i.e., the millennial reign. This theory is advocated by persons who hold a dispensationalist theology with a theory of the postponement of the Kingdom. The teachings on the Kingdom are consequently seen as nonapplicable to the church but are given for the future millennial age. An advocate of this position, C. I. Scofield, states that the Sermon on the Mount is legal language, and that it is not for the present day but for the millennial age. He then contradicts himself, stating that all of the spiritual teachings of Jesus in the Sermon on the Mount for the church-age can be found in the Epistles.[7] In contrast, E. Stanley Jones calls the Sermon on the Mount "the Christian's working philosophy of life."[8]

This issue is answered when we read the Gospel of Matthew under the larger rubric of *Heilsgeschichte;* i.e., salvation history. Rather than having been written to the Jewish community to offer hope of a future kingdom for them, the Gospel shows the emergence of the people of God in the Judaic tradition; a people which extends beyond the Jewish community to the Gentiles and to the whole world.

As evidence of this interest in the larger world, we call attention to the repeated references to Gentiles. The lineage of Jesus includes various Gentile persons. Following His birth He was visited by Gentile sages from the East. To protect His life from Herod, His parents took Him to Egypt. Upon His return He did not live or grow up in Jerusalem, the heart of Judaism, but in Nazareth of Galilee, called Galilee of the Gentiles. Early in His ministry, Jesus accepted the Gentile Centurion and ministered to him, saying that He had found greater faith in this Gentile than in the Judaic community (chap. 8). In the same context Jesus stated that "many will come from the east and west, and sit down with Abraham, Isaac, and Jacob in the kingdom of heaven." (Matt. 8:11). The Kingdom of heaven transcends national lines, and the superior loyalty to God forms the basis of judgment upon the "subjects of the Kingdom" who, although of Israel, are not men of faith.

In chapter 12, verse 50, it becomes clear that Jesus not only moves the meaning of the Kingdom beyond the Judaic community, but He also moves the mission of the Kingdom beyond family ties. His emphasis on "whoever does the will of My Father" lays the meaning of Kingdom membership open to other than the Judaic community. Jesus took His disciples to Caesarea Philippi, the border where the Judaic people met the people of the Gentile world, to ask the disciples the question, "Who do men say that I . . . am?" (16:13 f.). In this context He stated that He would build His church in the world. The Kingdom is for a people of faith rather than for those of a particular religious lineage. The people to whom the Kingdom is given is His church, a fellowship of both Jew and Gentile. Jesus' exposure of the unbelief of the Judaic religious leaders should not be construed as a rejection of the Jewish people as such. On the contrary, in the new covenant "He Himself is our peace, who has made both one, and has broken down the middle wall of division between us . . . so as to create in Himself one new man from the two, thus making peace" (Eph. 2:14–15).

The people of God emerged from the Judaic tradition, but expanded to include the Gentiles, reaching out into all the world. Rather than reading the Gospel of Matthew as a Jewish book for a Jewish people, we may recognize it as a book written in the Jewish context to show the roots and origins of the Messianic faith. It moves from the tribal to the universal. A view which would apply the teachings of Jesus basically to a millennial period does as much violence to the integrity of Jesus' ministry as factors in redaction criticism appear to do in attributing words of Jesus to the early church.

A significant emphasis in Matthew is the "church." In all of the synoptic Gospels, the concept of church as *ekklesia* is found only in Matthew. Jesus introduced the church, in response to Peter's confession, as the ultimate redemptive purpose of the Christ. It was when He introduced it that Jesus also told His disciples of His coming death and resurrection. The church was to be an expression of the new covenant of the people of God in contradistinction with the Judaic tradition of the continuing expression of the people of God. Jesus' selection of the twelve was a deliberate symbol that He was constituting a new Israel, and this people of faith were the true heirs of salvation history.

As the early church wrestled with the acceptance of the Gentiles into the Jewish church, James, the brother of our Lord and leader of the church, affirmed that God "visited the Gentiles to take out of them a people for His name." He based his belief on the prophetic word from Amos 9:11: "After this I will return and will rebuild the tabernacle of David which has fallen down. I will rebuild its ruins, and I will set it up, so that the rest of mankind may seek the Lord, even all the Gentiles upon whom My name is called, says the Lord who does all these things. Known to God are all His works from the beginning of the world" (Acts 15:14, 16–18).

As further evidence that Matthew was not written primarily for the Jew, we note the inclusion of materials which are direct confrontations with the Jews. Beginning with John's denunciations in chapter 3, we move to Jesus' conflicts with the Jewish community (chapters 9, 12, 15, 16, 21) and especially the pointed denunciations in chapter 23. Furthermore, the Gospel of Matthew was not written until A.D. 65 to 70, late enough in the experience of the early church that the gospel had already been extended to the Gentiles. The early church had ratified the acceptance of "uncircumcised" Gentiles into the church as full participants in the people of God (Eph. 2:11–22).

It seems far more appropriate to affirm Matthew as authentically expressing the acts of God in salvation history. He is showing the movement of God's unfolding revelation through the history of God's acts in the Judaic community to the introduction of the new covenant by and in the person of Jesus Christ. The church is not "parentheses" in salvation history as we await the Kingdom of God, but is rather the expression of the activity of the Kingdom of God in the world. It is this Kingdom which penetrates all nations, Jew and Gentile, to extend the grace of God to all people.

The extensive use of this Gospel in liturgy and teaching in early church history supports this interpretation. From the second century on, it has been the most frequently quoted book of the Gospels by the church in her worship, in her ethical teaching, and in her discipline. For instruction of new converts it has served as a manual for the life and mission of the church. The Gospel creates a new community built on the heritage of Israel's faith, a community which is heir of the true meaning of God's revelation in history fulfilled in Himself.

My own appreciation of Matthew is enhanced by its place in the Anabaptist heritage of the sixteenth century which is the background and theological conditioning of the Mennonite Church. It was under the evangelical preaching of Huldrich Zwingli, the reformer in Zurich, in his expositions of Matthew, that Conrad Graebel and Felix Manz became "born-again" disciples. These men, who worked with Zwingli, later separated over their Christological hermeneutic and in January of 1525 began a Free Church movement. Their emphasis on the meaning of Christology in conversion, discipleship, ethics, and church discipline drew heavily from the teachings of Jesus in this Gospel.

While exegesis deals with meaning, preaching deals with significance for life. My attempt throughout this commentary is to interface exegesis with proclamation. While the exegesis is not always explicit, it has conditioned the writing which points the way for application to our contemporary needs.

Matthew, the Gospel of *Heilsgeschichte*, is the Gospel of the King and His Kingdom. With the Apostle Peter we say, "Thou art the Christ, the Son of the Living God." And we also hear the words of the Master, "All authority is given unto me in heaven and in earth; go ye therefore and make disciples of all nations. . . ."

NOTES

1. Eusebius, *Ecclesiastical History*, tran. C. F. Cruse, III, 89, p. 127.

2. Ibid., V, 9, p. 187.

3. Ibid., V, 10, p. 190.

4. Ibid., VI, 25, p. 245.

5. William Barclay, *The Gospel of Matthew*, 2 vols. (Edinburgh: St. Andrew Press, 1963), 1:xii.

6. R. B. G. Tasker, *The Gospel According to St. Matthew*, Tyndale New Testament Commentary Series (Grand Rapids, Wm. B. Eerdmans, 1979), p. 14.

7. C. I. Scofield, *Scofield Reference Bible* (New York: Oxford Univ. Press, 1945), footnote on Matthew 5.

8. E. Stanley Jones, *The Christ of the Mount* (Nashville: Abingdon, 1966), p. 11.

An Outline of Matthew

I. The Person of the King: 1:1—4:25
   A. The Lineage and Birth of the King: 1:1–25
   B. The Safety and Development of the King: 2:1–23
   C. The Announcement of the King: 3:1–17
   D. The Testing and Ministry of the King: 4:1–25
II. The Message of the King: 5:1—7:29
   A. The Attitude of Disciples: 5:1–48
   B. The Character of Disciples: 6:1–34
   C. The Integrity of Disciples: 7:1–29
III. The Authority of the King: 8:1—9:38
   A. Authority for a New Community: 8:1–22
   B. Authority to Call Disciples: 8:23—9:13
   C. Authority to Proclaim the Good News: 9:14–38
IV. The Ministry of the King: 10:1—12:50
   A. The Ministry to the World: 10:1–42
   B. The Ministry Duly Attested: 11:1–30
   C. The Ministry Divinely Affirmed: 12:1–50
V. The Parables of the King: 13:1–58
   A. Parable of the Sower: 13:1–23
   B. Parable of the Weeds: 13:24–30, 36–43
   C. Parable of Small Beginning: 13:31–35
   D. Parables of Kingdom Value: 13:44–46
   E. Parable of the Net: 13:47–50
   F. The Parable of Life Itself: 13:51–58
VI. The Compassion of the King: 14:1—15:59
   A. The Account of John's Martyrdom: 14:1–12

B. Jesus' Compassion and Power: 14:13–36
C. Compassion and the Law: 15:1–39
VII. The Confession of the King: 16:1—20:34
    A. Distinguishing the New Community: 16:1–23
    B. Discipleship and God's Power: 16:24—17:23
    C. Priorities of the New Community: 17:24—18:35
    D. Covenant in Marriage: 19:1–15
    E. Eternal Life: 19:16–30
    F. The Greatness of God's Grace: 20:1–34
VIII. The Presentation of the King: 21:1—23:39
    A. Jesus' Entry into Jerusalem: 21:1–17
    B. Jesus' Teaching on Faithfulness: 21:18–46
    C. Jesus' Teaching on God's Claims: 22:1–22
    D. Jesus' Interpretation of Messiah's Role: 22:23–46
    E. Jesus' Woes upon False Leaders: 23:1–39
IX. The Predictions of the King: 24:1—25:46
    A. The Sweep of History to the End of the Age: 24:1–14
    B. The Destruction of Jerusalem and Tribulation: 24:15–28
    C. The Affirmation of Jesus' Parousia: 24:29–35
    D. Jesus' Instructions to Be Prepared: 24:36—25:30
    E. The Ultimate Judgment of the Nations: 25:31–46
X. The Suffering of the King: 26:1—27:66
    A. Jesus' Awareness of His Impending Death: 26:1–16
    B. Jesus' Celebration of the Passover: 26:17–30
    C. The Gethsemane Vigil: 26:31–46
    D. Betrayal, Arrest, and Trial: 26:47–68
    E. The Suffering Servant Stands Alone: 26:69—27:14
    F. The Mockery of the Savior: 27:15–31
    G. The Crucifixion and Death of Christ: 27:32–56
    H. The Burial and Securing of the Tomb: 27:57–66
XI. The Victory of the King: 28:1–20
    A. Jesus Is Risen from the Dead: 28:1–8
    B. Jesus Appears to His Followers: 28:9–10
    C. The Guards Are Bribed: 28:11–15
    D. Jesus Commissions His Followers: 28:16–20

CHAPTER ONE

The Person of the King

Matthew 1:1—4:25

The expectation of the remnant, or the faithful in Israel, was the coming of the Messiah. He would be the Deliverer-King, a Savior to release Israel from its oppression, reconstituting the people as the Kingdom of God. The Book of Matthew is written in the historical context which, while understanding this expectation on the part of Israel, also understood a new interpretation of that Kingdom as was being experienced and taught in the early church.

By the time the Gospel of Matthew was written, thousands of Jewish believers constituted the church, including hundreds of priests from the Jewish community who had been converted to faith in Jesus Christ as risen Lord and now participated in His Kingdom. This church, including Gentiles from many parts of the Mediterranean world, understood its mission as the pronouncement of the gospel of the Kingdom of God.

For forty days after His resurrection, Jesus had appeared to His disciples, discussing with them things relating to the Kingdom of God (Acts 1:3). When the disciples asked Him whether He was now going to restore the Kingdom to Israel (v. 6), Jesus told them to leave it with God, saying instead, "You will receive power when the Holy Spirit has come upon you; and you will be witnesses to Me in Jerusalem, and in all Judea and Samaria, and to the end of the earth" (Acts 1:8). The movement of the missionary church in the Book of Acts follows this outline. There are various references to the ministry of the church and its mission as declaring the gospel of the Kingdom of God (Acts 20:25; 28:31).

The Gospel of Matthew was written with a focus on the King

and His Kingdom, interpreting the new understanding of the messianic role. Significantly, the concept of the Kingdom appears fifty-five times in the Gospel of Matthew. Thirty-three references refer to "the Kingdom of Heaven," a phrase which is found only in Matthew, but understood in the Jewish community as the rule of God. Matthew is the bridge from the old covenant to the new covenant. He introduces the Christ and His Kingdom as the fulfillment of the messianic prophecies of the Old Testament.

His approach to the way of salvation is a call to repentance for entry into the Kingdom, to a commitment of one's self to the King as His follower. In Luke salvation is described as a call to be a disciple of Jesus Christ. In Mark salvation is described as taking up the cross in identification with Jesus Christ. In the Gospel of John salvation is spoken of as a new birth, a new beginning, as abiding in Christ as the branch abides in the vine, of belief or faith that commits one's self to Jesus as Lord. Matthew uses language that relates the rule of Christ to people's lives. This means that the life of faith is to recognize Jesus as Lord and ourselves as His subjects. Faith is to confess Him as King of kings, and to commit ourselves to Him as the expression of our highest loyalty.

Matthew begins his Gospel by introducing the King himself, Jesus Christ (*Kristos*, Messiah).

THE LINEAGE OF THE KING

1 The book of the genealogy of Jesus Christ, the Son of David, the Son of Abraham:

2 Abraham begot Isaac, Isaac begot Jacob, and Jacob begot Judah and his brothers.

3 Judah begot Perez and Zerah by Tamar, Perez begot Hezron, and Hezron begot Ram.

4 Ram begot Amminadab, Amminadab begot Nahshon, and Nahshon begot Salmon.

5 Salmon begot Boaz by Rahab, Boaz begot Obed by Ruth, Obed begot Jesse,

6 and Jesse begot David the king.

David the king begot Solomon by her who had been the wife of Uriah.

7 Solomon begot Rehoboam, Rehoboam begot Abijah, and Abijah begot Asa.

8 Asa begot Jehoshaphat, Jehoshaphat begot Joram, and Joram begot Uzziah.

9 Uzziah begot Jotham, Jotham begot Ahaz, and Ahaz begot Hezekiah.

10 Hezekiah begot Manasseh, Manasseh begot Amon, and Amon begot Josiah.

11 Josiah begot Jeconiah and his brothers about the time they were carried away to Babylon.

12 And after they were brought to Babylon, Jeconiah begot Shealtiel, and Shealtiel begot Zerubbabel.

13 Zerubbabel begot Abiud, Abiud begot Eliakim, and Eliakim begot Azor.

14 Azor begot Zadok, Zadok begot Achim, and Achim begot Eliud.

15 Eliud begot Eleazar, Eleazar begot Matthan, and Matthan begot Jacob.

16 And Jacob begot Joseph the husband of Mary, of whom was born Jesus who is called Christ.

17 So all the generations from Abraham to David are fourteen generations, from David until the captivity in Babylon are fourteen generations, and from the captivity in Babylon until Christ are fourteen generations.

Matt. 1:1–17

In Jewish history the most natural and essential way to begin the story of a man's life is to give his genealogy. This passage, which might appear uninteresting, is of great importance in Jewish history. Josephus, the great Jewish historian, writing his own autobiography, began with his personal pedigree. King Herod the Great was despised by the pure-blooded Jews because he was half Edomite. As a consequence, Herod destroyed official registers so that others could not prove a more authentic pedigree than his own!

Matthew begins by calling this "The Book of the Genealogy of Jesus Christ," a common phrase among the Jews when giving reference to the record of a man's lineage.

During a preaching mission in India in 1969, I learned of a young Hindu man who came to Christ by reading the first chapter of Matthew. When asked what there was about the genealogy which led to his conversion, he stated that for the first time he had found a religion which is actually rooted in history in contrast to the mythology of Hinduism and Buddhism. Matthew roots his Gospel in history, beginning with the lineage of the King. It is the lineage of salvation history, of *Heilsgeschichte*. This salvation history expresses the acts of God in history, His unfolding of a revelation of Himself, having chosen the people of Israel as the channel through whom He would bring the Messiah as Savior for the world.

Matthew's first reference is to Jesus Christ as "the Son of David," a reference to the royal kingly line; and as "the Son of Abraham," a reference to the line of promise or line of grace. Matthew begins his genealogy with Abraham, the man who was called the friend of God, the father of the way of faith, showing that Jesus fulfilled Israel's hopes.

We are reminded in verse 2 of the many occasions in the Old Testament when God identified Himself as the God of Abraham, of Isaac, and of Jacob. A personal friend of mine, Dr. Robert Lamont, for twenty years pastor of the First Presbyterian Church in Pittsburgh, Pennsylvania, once gave me the following very stimulating sermon outline to elaborate the significance of this Old Testament reference: He is the God (1) of differing personalities; (2) of varying circumstances; and (3) of succeeding generations.

The lineage of Jesus is presented in three sections with fourteen periods for each. This distinctive grouping has a functional purpose. The three groupings correspond to the three great stages of Jewish history. The first stage is the history from Abraham to David, a stage which moves from the call of faith to the period in which David welded Israel into a nation. The second stage covers the history of Israel down to the exile in Babylon, a stage which deals with the interplay between man and God, exposing man's unfaithfulness and the consequent captivity. Interspersed with the captivity was the prophetic word of judgment, of grace and of hope. The third stage carries the history of Israel from the Babylonian captivity to the birth of Jesus Christ. It shows how the salvation history continued through a remnant of the faithful, focusing on the family of faith through which God entered the world in the Incarnation, in Jesus of Nazareth.

The summation in verse 17 marks off fourteen generations from Abraham to David, fourteen from David to the captivity, and fourteen from the captivity to the coming of Christ. This use of generations is a teaching method on the part of Matthew to help persons grasp and memorize this sweep of history. Actually, the listings are not harmonized with Luke's list, nor with the Old Testament accounts.

Rahab appears much later in the line than in the Old Testament account (v. 5). In comparing 1 Chronicles 3 with the genealogical listing in Matthew, we discover that in verse 8 Matthew skips across several persons we might call generations (i.e., Joash, Amaziah, and Azariah). Matthew goes from grandfather to grandson in moving from Josiah to Jeconiah (v. 11). He moves from Shealtiel to Zerubbabel as though this is father and son (v. 12), while 1 Chronicles 3:19 and Ezra 3:2 together state that while these are in a close family lineage, Shealtiel is actually Zerubbabel's uncle.

This suggests that Matthew's use of generation is not as literalistic as ours when we go from father to son, but rather that it is a method he used to mark off periods of time in salvation history. We need to leave this part uninterpreted (how Zerubbabel carries on the lineage of his uncle Shealtiel) with awareness that in the Old Testament, to safeguard a heritage and lineage in family experience, it was not unknown for a man to have his brother or his brother's son carry on his inheritance and lineage in the stream of history.

Prominence is given to four women who are named in the Messiah's lineage. William Barclay says, "It is not normal to find the names of women in Jewish pedigrees at all. Woman had no legal rights; she was not regarded as a person, but as a thing."[1] The presence of these names in the lineage of Christ is a significant affirmation of woman. When God created man He "created man in His own image, in the image of God he created him; male and female he created them" (Gen. 1:27, NIV), a biblical witness to equality.

But why mention these women in contrast to Sarah? First, all four were aliens, Gentiles. Second, three of four were suspected of adultery. Including these women in the lineage of Christ highlights the message of divine grace. God forgave and accepted persons in the lineage of Christ whose history was clouded, men and women. The fact that these particular women are named makes clear that God in grace does not discriminate against persons because of past mistakes. Verse 3 refers to Tamar, of whom Judah begot Perez and Zerah. Tamar was actually Judah's daughter-in-law, and the conception of these sons from Judah took place in an immoral relationship outside of the bonds of matrimony. In verse 5 we find Rahab, who is spoken of as the harlot of Jericho in Joshua 2:1–7. Tradition tells us that she later became the wife of Joshua. In verse 5 Ruth is included, who was not Jewish, but was a Moabitess, a special expression of God's grace in that the Law said, "No Ammonite or Moabite . . .

may enter the assembly of the Lord" (Deut. 23:3, NIV). And fourthly, Uriah's wife, Bathsheba, the mother of Solomon is included—the woman whom David seduced, and whose husband Uriah he afterwards killed in an attempt to cover his sin. The presence of these four persons in the lineage of the King emphasizes a genealogy of grace.

Through this lineage God fulfills His promise to Abraham that, in his seed, all the earth would be blessed; that the "Earth Blesser," the Messiah, would come through the seed of Abraham. Also, Matthew is showing Jesus as born of Mary and not begotten by Joseph, evident in verse 16.[2] An outline for this passage can be expressed in four basic points. It is a genealogy that demonstrates: (1) a faith rooted in history, (2) a faith expressing God's grace, (3) a faith recognizing divine providence, (4) a faith which focuses on the Messiah.

THE BIRTH OF THE KING

18 Now the birth of Jesus Christ was thus: After His mother Mary was betrothed to Joseph, before they came together, she was found with child of the Holy Spirit.

19 Then Joseph her husband, being a just man, and not wanting to make her a public example, was minded to put her away secretly.

20 But while he thought about these things, behold, an angel of the Lord appeared to him in a dream, saying, "Joseph, son of David, do not be afraid to take to you Mary your wife, for that which is conceived in her is of the Holy Spirit.

21 "And she will bring forth a Son, and you shall call His name JESUS, for He will save His people from their sins."

22 Now all this was done that it might be fulfilled which was spoken by the Lord through the prophet, saying:

23 "Behold, the virgin will be with child, and will bring forth a Son, and they will call His name Immanuel," which is translated, "God with us."

24 Then Joseph, being aroused from sleep, did as the angel of the Lord commanded him and took to him his wife,

25 and did not know her till she had brought forth
her firstborn Son. And he called His name JESUS.

Matt. 1:18–25

The story of Jesus' birth is told in a beautiful and simple style. There are matter-of-fact statements about the most mysterious aspects of the conception of Jesus. The Incarnation took place by the agency of the Holy Spirit in the life of a young woman referred to as a virgin. The passage tells us that Mary was betrothed to Joseph, and that they had not consummated their marriage in sexual relationship. It refers to Joseph as her husband, yet in the angel's message Joseph is addressed as Son of David and urged not to hesitate to go through with his marriage to Mary, who is referred to as his wife.

To understand this one must recognize that in Jewish marriage there were three steps. The first step was the engagement, a contract arranged by family members who determined whether the couple would be well suited for each other and for a future marriage. Second, there was the betrothal, the public ratification of the engagement, with a period of one year for the couple to become known as belonging to each other, but not having the rights of living together as husband and wife. The only way a betrothal could be terminated was by a divorce. In Jewish law there is a phrase which states that a young woman whose fiancé dies during the period of betrothal is called "a virgin who is a widow." Mary and Joseph were in the second stage in the account of this text. The third stage is the marriage proper, which took place at the end of the year of betrothal.

It was during the year of their betrothal that Mary made known to Joseph that she was with child by the miraculous act of God. Joseph is referred to as a just man with special love and consideration for Mary. Confronted with the problem of his betrothed being pregnant, he contemplated how to end the betrothal in a divorce. He sought ways to do it privately rather than to expose her publicly. In his careful contemplation, the angel of the Lord appeared to Joseph with a message from God.

This passage of Scripture on the character of the man, Joseph, provides an outline for a message on "parentage which God affirms." This should be placed alongside an understanding of Mary and her character in the moving presentation called "The Magnificat" (Luke 1). The outline from Matthew would suggest the following five points:

he was a man (1) of justice, v. 19; (2) of discretion, v. 19; (3) of piety, v. 20; (4) of obedience, v. 24; and (5) of self-discipline, v. 25.

The same section deals strikingly with the Incarnation. The birth of the King is referred to in three ways: (1) Jesus Christ, the Messiah, v. 18; (2) Jesus, the Savior, v. 21; and (3) Immanuel, meaning "God with us," v. 23. *Christ* is the Greek form of the Hebrew word for Messiah. "Jesus," or "Joshua," means "Yahweh is salvation." *Immanuel,* from Isaiah 7:14, speaks of the deliverance of Yahweh, a deliverance so striking that the mother would call her child Immanuel, *"God with us."*

In verse 22 is a statement frequently used by Matthew: *"that it might be fulfilled which was spoken by the Lord through the prophet, saying. . . ."* It ties the old covenant with the new and ties the events of which Matthew is writing to salvation history. The Old Testament contains many statements referring to the coming of the Messiah. Beginning with Genesis 3:15, it is expressed again in God's promise to Abraham (Gen. 22:18). He is predicted by Moses as the prophet which was to come (Deut. 18:18), referred to by Balaam in Numbers 24:17, by David in numerous Psalms, and by Isaiah, Micah, and other of the prophets, all of whom present a Savior, a Redeemer, and a King.

Here Matthew selected a passage from Isaiah which states that the birth of the Messiah would come through a young woman, and that His name would be called Immanuel, God with us. Matthew quotes Isaiah as saying, *"Behold, the virgin will be with child, and will bring forth a Son."* Scholars point out that in Isaiah there is no absolute evidence that the Hebrew word which is translated "virgin" by the King James version means an unmarried person. It may only be a reference to a young woman, but in Matthew the word *parthenos* is interpreted as virgin. From this passage and the account in Luke 1, the doctrine of the virgin birth of Christ is affirmed. Other New Testament passages dealing with the Incarnation should be seen in relation to this passage with a high Christology interpreting for us the meaning of Incarnation. Such references include the Gospel of John 1:1–18; Philippians 2:5–11; Colossians 1:15–19; Hebrews 1:1–13; 1 Timothy 3:16; 1 John 1:1–3; and others. These are theological presentations of the mystery of Incarnation wherein the eternal Christ came into the world as Jesus of Nazareth.

The doctrine of the virgin birth is the biblical affirmation that God actually became man; that God entered the world in the person of Jesus of Nazareth. We do not argue that this Jesus of Nazareth must be divine because of His unusual birth, being born of a virgin, but rather we affirm that God actually came into the world by a virgin birth and thus God became man. The Apostle's Creed, the most universally accepted Christian creed, states that He was "born of the Virgin Mary." In the Nicene Creed we read that Jesus Christ was "very God of very God . . . and was made man."

Should one have a problem believing in the virgin birth, other questions relating to the Incarnation must be answered as to how the eternal God actually became man. Matthew affirms that Jesus Christ was born of the Virgin Mary. He also affirms that He was conceived by the Holy Ghost, which means that in some miraculous way the Holy Spirit ushered the life of the eternal Christ into the body of Mary and here a person was conceived and born who is the one true expression of God and the one expression of true man. This person was able to say, "He that hath seen me hath seen the Father" (John 14:9, KJV).

In Greek literature Virgil wrote about the plight of humanity and the need for a new type of person to help man out of his predicament. Such a person, he said, would need to be a virgin-born person who was half god and half man. Pagan mythology had stories of intercourse between a god and a woman or a goddess and a man, the offspring being a "hero" of legend. The New Testament passage is not the story of any such half god and half man but is rather the expression of Incarnation. This affirmation of faith is that God came to us in Jesus of Nazareth so that we may know authentically what God is like. Dr. Karl Barth has said, "Either Jesus Christ was actually God, or we do not have a full revelation yet."

The Incarnation is God's greatest affirmation of humanness. In the Incarnation God demonstrated that He could become human without becoming sinful. Humanness and sinfulness are not synonymous. Sinfulness is the perversion of the truly human, the perversion of the *Imago Dei* (the image of God) in which we were created. Salvation is, among other things, the restoration of the truly human in our lives, the correction of perversion so that we may be persons who express again the image of God.

Following is an outline on the Incarnation from this passage: Jesus was (1) conceived by the Holy Spirit, 1:18–20; (2) confirmed by the Holy Angel, 1:20–21; and (3) contextualized by the Holy Scriptures, 1:22–23.

Accepting the direction which God gave him in a dream, Joseph

29

claimed Mary as his wife. As stated in verse 25, Joseph did not enter into marital relations with her until after the birth of Jesus. In God's providence, the conception of Jesus by the Holy Spirit must have taken place near the end of the year of the betrothal so that, with Joseph now taking Mary to be his wife, the development of her pregnancy and the birth of their child was safeguarded from public reproach.

Years later, Jewish leaders reacted to Jesus' judgments that they were not true to the heritage of Abrahamic faith by saying, "We be not born of fornication." Their defense is seen by some as a reference to Jesus' own birth. From the nature of the account here in Matthew, it does not seem likely that Joseph and Mary suffered such accusations. God, in His providence, arranged this experience in a way which remains a beautiful expression of sanctity and love. The Holy Spirit, the same divine creative Agent who brooded over chaos and brought order at the dawn of creation morning, who acted in the creation of the first man and the first woman, was the divine Agent who ushered the life of the eternal Christ into the body of Mary for the miracle of the ages known as the Incarnation.

Thus the God who created man in the beginning from nothing, who created woman from man without the agency of man or woman, now created Jesus of Nazareth through Mary without the agency of a man. The sanctity of this passage rests on our acceptance of the divine act through the Holy Spirit as the Agent who brought the Incarnation to pass.

THE KING IS BORN

1 Now after Jesus was born in Bethlehem of Judea in the days of Herod the king, behold, wise men from the East came to Jerusalem,

2 saying, "Where is He who has been born King of the Jews? For we have seen His star in the East and have come to worship Him."

3 When Herod the king had heard these things, he was troubled, and all Jerusalem with him.

4 And when he had gathered all the chief priests and scribes of the people together, he inquired of them where the Christ was to be born.

5 And they said to him, "In Bethlehem of Judea, for thus it is written by the prophet:

6 *'And you, Bethlehem, in the land of Judah,*
Are not the least among the rulers of Judah;
For out of you will come a Ruler
Who will shepherd My people Israel.'"

7 Then Herod, when he had secretly called the wise men, determined from them what time the star appeared.

8 And he sent them to Bethlehem and said, "Go and search diligently for the young Child, and when you have found Him, bring back word to me, that I may come and worship Him also."

Matt. 2:1–8

Jesus was born in Bethlehem of Judea, a small town five miles south of Jerusalem, previously called Ephrath. It was here that Jacob had buried Rachel and had set up a pillar in memory of her (Gen. 48:7). It was here that Ruth had lived when she married Boaz (Ruth 1:22). More significantly, Bethlehem was the home of David (1 Sam. 16:1–13) and it remained in the history of Israel as uniquely the City of David. It was from the City of David that the Jewish community expected David's greater son to be born; from this city they expected God's appointed Messiah. The prophet Micah is quoted by Matthew predicting that Bethlehem would be the city from which the Deliverer would come (Micah 5:2).

Bethlehem means "house of bread." It is situated in a fertile country area, built above the fields on a grey limestone ridge some 2,500 feet in elevation. One of the early fathers, Justin Martyr, A.D. 150, who came from the district near Bethlehem, relates that Jesus was born in a cave near the village of Bethlehem. His words have perpetuated the traditional view that when Joseph and Mary found that the inn was full they were granted lodging in a cavelike stable under the inn, in which setting Jesus was born.

On numerous occasions it has been my privilege to visit this site where through the years different edifices have been built. The Roman Emperor Hadrian attempted to desecrate the place by building a shrine to the heathen god Adonis. But under Constantine a church was built on the site, and to the present time this is the Church of the Nativity. A unique element of this church is that the door to enter is exceedingly low so that everyone who enters needs to stoop. But the tourist is usually disappointed in entering the room under the altar, known as the cave, for it has been so enshrouded with religious symbols that it has lost the simplicity of the site of the birth of our Lord. It is from Luke's account that we learn that when the Lord of glory came to earth He was born in a stable, cradled in a manger, sheltered among the beasts of the earth (Luke 2).

Matthew tells us that Jesus was born in Bethlehem, the City of David, emphasizing the royal lineage. His emphasis is clearly focused on the kingly lineage of the Chirst even in the lowly circumstances of His birth. Again, the quotation from the Old Testament prophet is the bridge from the old covenant to the new and a further testimony to salvation history, the fulfillment of God's plan predicted through the ages by His prophets.

THE WITNESS OF THE WISE MEN

9 When they had heard the king, they departed;
and behold, the star which they had seen in the East
went before them, till it came and stood over where
the young Child was.

10 When they saw the star, they rejoiced with
exceedingly great joy.

11 And when they had come into the house, they
saw the young Child with Mary His mother, and fell
down and worshiped Him. And when they had opened
their treasures, they presented gifts to Him: gold,
frankincense, and myrrh.

12 And being warned by God in a dream that they
should not return to Herod, they departed for their
own country another way.

Matt. 2:9–12

It is believed that the magi came from Persia and were a tribe of priests. Herodotus says that the magi were originally a tribe of Medians who had tried to overthrow the Persian empire but failed and became among the Persians a priestly tribe much like the Levites in Israel. These magi became the teachers of the Persian kings and were skilled in philosophy and science. They were known as men of holiness and wisdom and were interpreters of dreams.

As was common in those ancient days, such men of science and wisdom studied the stars, believing in astrology. They held that a man's destiny was influenced or settled by the star under which he was born. If some spectacular phenomenon appeared in the heavens, it impressed them that God was breaking into the natural order and announcing some special event. Much speculation has been made as to what brilliant star these ancient magi saw; whether it was some supernova, or whether it was a brilliant comet such as Halley's Comet, or whether it was a brilliant conjunction of planets such as Saturn and Jupiter. At least the Scripture tells us that there was a brilliant star that appeared, and the magi, seeing this star, were convinced of an act of God in which the entry of a great king was being heralded to the world.

There was a general expectation in the world at that time of an imminent messianic announcement. This is found in the writings of Josephus, the writings of wise men in the Middle East and in Greece and in the writings of Roman historians. It is reflected in the writings of Virgil, the Roman poet, in what is known as the Messianic Eclogue, where he even hailed Augustus the Roman Emperor as the savior of the world. At the time Jesus Christ was born there was a general expectation of an act of God to bring a person into the world who would deliver man from his bondage and limitations.

The magi represent Gentiles coming from distant areas of the world to worship the Christ. In view of our thesis that Matthew presents the gospel of salvation history, introducing the Son of God as King of kings, as a ruler of a new Kingdom which extends far beyond the borders of national Israel, we note that at the very beginning of the Gospel there is a relationship to the Gentiles.

Apparently the wise men took some length of time after the birth of Christ to arrive at Bethlehem. There is no indication that they found Jesus in the stable or in the cave. It may have been all of two years until they actually arrived and found the young child, Jesus. At least we discover that Herod's attempt to destroy Christ included all of the boy children two years and under. In verse 11 we read that *"when they had come into the house, they saw the young Child with Mary His mother."* This reference of finding them in a house, and reference to a young child rather than to a babe are further indications of the elapsed time from the birth of Christ until the occasion when the magi arrived.

As a Christmas message from the experience of the magi, a suggested outline follows: (1) they worshiped in light of the star, vv.

2, 9–10; (2) they worshiped in light of the Scripture, vv. 5–6; and (3) they worshiped in the presence of the Savior, v. 11.

Or another approach is from the perspective of God's acts in revelation: (1) God's witness in nature, vv. 2, 9–10; (2) God's witness in the Word, vv. 4–6; and (3) God's witness in confrontation, vv. 11–12.

Or, perhaps more simply, the theme of Christmas with the awareness that "wise men still seek Him." It is Christmas, a Christ-mass for us, if with the wise men (1) we have followed, (2) we have found, (3) we have fellowshiped.

The story includes a striking confrontation with Herod, the king in Judea. The magi, searching for one born to become King of the Jews, challenged Herod's rule. Half Jew and half Idumaean, Herod had been governor from 47 B.C., and in 40 B.C. he had received the title of king. In power for four decades, he was called Herod the Great—a great ruler in keeping order, a great builder whose works included the building of the temple in Jerusalem, a great manager who supplied from his own reserves to help the Jewish people in famine. But he was also a man of great suspicion, and in his older years became known as "a murderous old man." He murdered his wife, Mariamne; his mother, Alexandria; his oldest son, Antipater; as well as his sons Alexander and Aristobulus. Augustus, the Roman Emperor, once said that it was more safe to be Herod's pig (in Greek, *hus*) than Herod's son (in Greek, *huios*). Approaching his death, Herod had a group of elite citizens of Jerusalem arrested and imprisoned, with orders that the moment he died they were to be killed so that some tears would be shed when he died.

On hearing of the wise men, the crafty king sent for them to inquire about their mission. Upon their inquiry as to where the Messiah was to be born, Herod called the chief priests and the scribes, experts in the Scripture. These theological scholars were able to tell him that the Anointed One, according to Micah 5:2, would be born in Bethlehem. Cunningly, Herod sent the wise men to Bethlehem, instructing them that with success they were to bring him word so that he might also bring homage to the newborn king!

Pagan kings with a limited sign had come to seek the Messiah, while persons who were exposed to the truth of God's acts in history failed to take seriously the coming of their own Messiah. These aristocratic theologians, leaders of the Jewish community, were threatened by the coming of the Messiah who would displace them in the religious order as Herod was threatened over being displaced in the political order.

A suggested outline in developing this interplay is as follows: (1) the faith of the nonethnic (the magi); (2) the nonfaith of the ethnic (Jewish scholars); and (3) the nonfaith before evidence (Herod and the chief priests).

The providence of God continues, for as the magi left the confusion of the city of Jerusalem they were again able to behold the star. When they came to the house and found Mary with the young child, they worshiped Him. This act of worship is in contrast to the hostile attitudes of Herod and of the indifferent attitudes of religious leaders.

The wise men presented gifts in the form of gold, frankincense and myrrh (2:11). It is from this reference to three gifts that the legend developed that there were three magi. Legend has also made them kings, and has given them names: Caspar, Melchior, and Balthazzar. Marco Polo told of a Persian village from which, the villagers claimed, the wise men had begun their journey. The gifts that were presented probably had no symbolic intent but were simply gifts fit for a king. They are illustrative. First, gold is a gift for a king, and Matthew is introducing a King who is to rule not by force but by love, to express His will not with a crown but with a cross. Second, frankincense is said to be a gift for a priest, a sweet perfume used in temple sacrifice. Jesus, as King of kings, rules men on behalf of God, but as Priest He ministers on behalf of men to God. And third, myrrh is said to be the gift for one who is going to die. Early on the morning of the third day after Jesus' crucifixion, the women came to the tomb bringing spices such as this to anoint the body of Jesus.

As the next note concerns the flight into Egypt, it is more relevant to see that God, in His providence, arranged adequate resources through these three gifts from the magi for Joseph and Mary to make the journey to Egypt. They were not a wealthy couple and had traveled from Galilee to Bethlehem for the tax registration where the child was born. Now the flight to Egypt for his protection was made possible in God's providence by these unique and costly gifts.

In verse 12 we have a warning to the magi given by God in a dream. This dream exposed the subtle plan of Herod, so they departed to their own country. They apparently went east to the Jordan and north and east to Persia without going back to Jerusalem.

35

THE FLIGHT INTO EGYPT

13 And when they had departed, behold, an angel
of the Lord appeared to Joseph in a dream, saying,
"Arise, take the young Child and His mother, flee to
Egypt, and stay there until I bring you word; for Herod
will seek the young Child to destroy Him."
14 When he arose, he took the young Child and
His mother by night and departed into Egypt,
15 and was there until the death of Herod, that it
might be fulfilled which was spoken by the Lord
through the prophet, saying, *"Out of Egypt I have
called My Son."*

Matt. 2:13–15

Joseph again received a message from God, through a dream instructing him to take the child Jesus and His mother and flee into
Egypt. The instruction is very explicit that Herod would seek to take
the child's life and that they were to stay in Egypt until God gave
them the next word of direction. Previously, the reference stated
that the wise men found Mary and the child in the house, with no
reference to Joseph. During the day Joseph may have been at work
in Bethlehem at his trade as carpenter. However, the fact that
God gives the communication to Joseph in a dream emphasizes the
solidarity of the family, the responsible role of Joseph as the husband and head of the family and the realism in which the birth of
Christ is a part of the normal family life experience of Joseph and
Mary.

We could develop from the accounts of the nativity an outline
on "The Angel-of-Care in God's Providence": (1) announcing His
sanctity (1:18–25); (2) assuring His safety (2:13–15); and (3) achieving
His security (2:19–23).

The flight to Egypt was not especially unusual for a Jewish family.
Through the history of Israel, in numerous times of persecution, Jewish people sought refuge in Egypt. In every city in Egypt there was
a colony of Jews. As a consequence, Joseph and Mary had no problem
finding associations amidst their own people for the brief period of
living in Egypt.

In the early church, pagan philosophers such as Celsus attacked
Christianity by describing Jesus as both an illegitimate child and as

one who lived in Egypt and learned the sorcery and magic of the Egyptians. But Matthew makes clear that Jesus went to Egypt as a little child and that He returned from Egypt as a child.

There are a number of stories, or legends, regarding experiences Joseph, Mary and the child Jesus had on the flight to Egypt. But these are legends, not documented by the Scriptures, and we exegete here the text itself. Significantly, Matthew again ties the new covenant with the Old Testament Scripture: "Out of Egypt I have called my Son" (Hos. 11:1). In the original statement, Hosea was referring to God's act of delivering the nation of Israel from their bondage in the land of Egypt. God's salvation history moves from the people of Israel to faithful Israel, to the remnant and to the servant of God in Jesus of Nazareth; thus Matthew applies this reference to Jesus Himself. The full text says, "When Israel was a child, I loved him, and out of Egypt I called my Son" (NIV). Matthew projects this passage forward to the birth of God's Son rather than backwards to the exodus of the people of Israel from the land of Egypt.

HEROD'S SLAUGHTER OF THE CHILDREN

16 Then Herod, when he saw that he was deceived by the wise men, was exceedingly angry; and he sent forth and put to death all the male children who were in Bethlehem and in all that region, from two years old and under, according to the time which he had determined from the wise men.

17 Then was fulfilled what was spoken by Jeremiah the prophet, saying:

18 *"A voice was heard in Ramah,*
   Lamentation, weeping, and great mourning,
   Rachel weeping for her children;
   And she would not be comforted, because they
      are no more."

Matt. 2:16–18

Herod was a master assassin, but here he needed to identify the destined child. The Scripture says he felt tricked by the wise men, and in his anger he acted to remove the life of any child born to be king. Having inquired of the wise men as to when they had first seen the star and begun their journey, he concluded that he needed to kill all the children the age of two years and under. According to Barclay, the small population of Bethlehem would mean that between twenty to thirty children would have been executed in the town. Including the border areas, the number must have been twice that. His attitude that he wished to eliminate the Christ was the same as that which was expressed much later when Jesus stood before Pilate with the crowd crying, "Crucify Him; we have no king but Caesar."

Once again Matthew quotes from the Old Testament, of Rachel weeping for her children, refusing to be comforted for they were not (Jer. 31:15). Jeremiah was speaking primarily of Jerusalem being led into captivity, leaving the land where Rachel lay buried, and in a figure of speech he sees Rachel as the land of God's promise, weeping for her children who should be there but are not. Matthew uses this Old Testament passage in a new setting, focusing the hopelessness in Bethlehem, for its hope for the future died with the death of its children. God, in His providence, had led Joseph and Mary and the child Jesus from Bethlehem, and we are reminded that hope in God's providence is the answer to the hopelessness of man's perversity.

JESUS AT HOME IN NAZARETH

19 But when Herod was dead, behold, an angel of the Lord appeared in a dream to Joseph in Egypt,

20 saying, "Arise, take the young Child and His mother, and go into the land of Israel, for those who sought the young Child's life are dead."

21 And he arose, took the young Child and His mother, and came into the land of Israel.

22 But when he heard that Archelaus was reigning in Judea instead of his father Herod, he was afraid to go there. And being warned by God in a dream, he turned aside into the region of Galilee.

23 And he came and dwelt in a city called Nazareth, that it might be fulfilled which was spoken by the prophets, "He will be called a Nazarene."

Matt. 2:19–23

Once again, divine instruction led Joseph, and he took Jesus and His mother, Mary, and returned to Israel. Again, he was instructed by God in a dream not to stay in Judea, and he journeyed on to Galilee. From these various communications we can discern something of the character of Joseph. He was evidently a man of great reverence who meditated and prayed to discern the will of God. With that sensitivity, God could communicate with him and know that he would understand. These instances are confirmation of Joseph's integrity and piety as the kind of man to whom God would entrust His Son.

Upon Herod's death, the kingdom he had ruled was divided into three parts. The Romans did not allow the power that Herod had held to go on unbroken. Herod anticipated this and divided the kingdom, leaving a part to each of his three sons. Judea was left to Archelaus, Galilee was left to Herod Antipas, and the northeast region beyond Jordan was left to Philip. Archelaus, who succeeded his father, Herod, in Judea, attempted to continue the pattern of his father and began his rule with the slaughter of three thousand influential people. Augustus granted him only the rank of ethnarch; then in A.D. 6 he was removed and banished. It was this pattern of violence that led Joseph to go on from Judea to Galilee. There Herod Antipas reigned with a more tolerant and peaceful pattern.

Joseph and Mary returned to their home community of Nazareth, Matthew says, *"that it might be fulfilled which was spoken by the prophets, 'He will be called a Nazarene.' "* The mystery is that Matthew presents an insoluble problem because there is no such text in the Old Testament. It might be suggested that Matthew is drawing from the Old Testament outline regarding a Nazirite, who is a person uniquely set aside by vows of service to God. He may be referring to Judges 13:5, "The child shall be a Nazirite" (KJV), or to Isaiah 11:1 where the word for "sprout" or "branch" (KJV) is similar to the word for Nazarene. Here Matthew designates him as a Nazarene, not from the standpoint of the vows, but from the standpoint of his living and growing up in Nazareth.

Nazareth is in Galilee of the Gentiles, a designation which supports the thesis that the book of Matthew shows God's salvation history as moving through Judaic history to become a gospel for the world, a gospel of the Kingdom which is open to all peoples. This theme runs throughout the Book of Matthew to its culmination in the words of the risen Christ, "Go ye therefore and make disciples of all nations."

Interestingly, Nazareth is only about six miles from the hometown of Jonah, the prophet who was called to carry the gospel to the Gentile Ninevites. Jesus' home being in Nazareth fits into the larger meaning of God's gospel of grace for the world and frees Him from the provincialism that would tie His message to only the Jewish community.

Nazareth is not to be thought of as a backwoods community, but was on the trade routes of the world. Located in the north of Israel, it was a town which lay in the hills of the southern part of Galilee, on the major trade routes which carried the news of the world. All one needed to do was to climb the hills of Nazareth to have a view of the world. Off to the west one could view Mt. Carmel and beyond the blue waters of the Mediterranean Sea. Here ships came and went from Rome, and from Rome to the ends of the earth. One could look to the foot of the hills and see one of the greatest roads in that part of the Roman world, leading from Damascus to Egypt and on into Africa. This was one of the great caravan routes, one which Abraham probably used in his business of operating a caravansary. It had been followed three centuries earlier by Alexander the Great and his legions. On this road, called "the way of the south," Jesus, as a boy, could have observed and met travelers of many nations. The second road came through this community from Telmius on the sea to the west, traveling on to Tiberias and the eastern frontiers of the Roman Empire. On this road the caravans from the east moved to the coast on the west, while the Roman legions moved from the coast into the eastern frontiers. Thus Jesus was brought up in a town where the traffic from the ends of the earth moved through His sphere of life.

Jesus' boyhood days exposed him to the cultures and philosophies of people of all nations. This must have enhanced his conviction that the Kingdom of God was for people of all nations. It is probably true as well that Galilee was the one place in Palestine where a new teacher could readily be heard. This setting helped focus Jesus' message, not on a revival of Judaistic religion as it was known in Jerusalem, but on God's grace for all people, from a base in Capernaum where the gospel could be heard by the peoples of all lands. Matthew quotes the striking prophetic statement, "The people who sat in darkness saw a great light, and to those who sat in the region and shadow of death light has dawned" (4:16). Here is the good news of God's grace, the gospel for the world.

JOHN'S ANNOUNCEMENT OF THE KING

1 In those days John the Baptist came preaching in the wilderness of Judea

2 and saying, "Repent, for the kingdom of heaven is at hand!"

3 For this is he who was spoken of by the prophet Isaiah, saying:

"The voice of one crying in the wilderness:
'Prepare the way of the LORD,
Make His paths straight.'"

4 And John himself was clothed in camel's hair, with a leather belt around his waist; and his food was locusts and wild honey.

5 Then Jerusalem, all Judea, and all the region around the Jordan went out to him

6 and were baptized by him in the Jordan, confessing their sins.

7 But when he saw many of the Pharisees and Sadducees coming to his baptism, he said to them, "O brood of vipers! Who has warned you to flee from the wrath to come?

8 "Therefore bear fruits worthy of repentance,

9 "and do not think to say to yourselves, 'We have Abraham as our father.' For I say to you that God is able to raise up children to Abraham from these stones.

10 "And even now the ax is laid to the root of the trees. Therefore every tree which does not bear good fruit is cut down and thrown into the fire.

11 "I indeed baptize you with water to repentance, but He who is coming after me is mightier than I, whose sandals I am not worthy to carry. He will baptize you with the Holy Spirit and fire.

12 "His winnowing fan is in His hand, and He will thoroughly purge His threshing floor, and gather His wheat into the barn; but He will burn up the chaff with unquenchable fire."

Matt. 3:1–12

John the Baptist burst upon the Jewish scene like a flaming voice from God. He came preaching in the wilderness of Judea, acclaimed by the people as a prophet of God. The uniqueness of his prophecy was the announcement of the coming of the Christ. His message was a call to repentance, a genuine renewal of piety, but in the context of preparation for the Kingdom of heaven. In this sense his confrontation with Pharisees, Sadducees, publicans and soldiers had sociopolitical implications; a new kingdom was being announced.[3]

Here again Matthew quotes the prophet Isaiah, thereby bridging the old covenant to the new inbreaking of the messianic age. The quote from Isaiah clearly focuses on the messianic age: *"The voice of one crying in the wilderness: 'Prepare the way of the Lord.' "*

The description of John introduces him as a unique and bold prophet. In being clothed with camel's hair and a leather belt, even his appearance marked him as a man of the wilderness rather than a man of the courts and the streets. His diet of the locust-bean and wild honey was good food, but it was the rough diet of a man who lived close to earth and nature. Like Elijah in his spirit and power, John broke the comfortable silence of humanism with a word from Yahweh. Significantly, this inbreaking of a special message from God comes not from the synagogues or the temple schools but from a man whose schooling was in his walk with God.

John's message was focused on the very center of Jewish faith, for the call to repentance meant turning away from sin and turning toward God. He was a stern realist regarding right and wrong, calling for public confession and integrity in daily life. His message is given in Luke 3:10–14: share with the needy, bear fruit of integrity, do not extort money, be content with your wages. He saw himself as only a slave for the coming Messiah (v. 11), yet he was the voice to prepare the way—lifting the valleys of poverty that embitter, lowering the hills of pride and wealth, smoothing the rough road of social injustice, trying to show others that the Kingdom was at hand. To repent meant to live the life that God means for us to live.

John seems to have introduced a baptism with water as a unique symbol of "repentance for the remission of sins" (Mark 1:4). Scholars have wrestled with the relationship of this baptism to that with blood in the initiatory rites of the Essene community, as well as with proselyte baptism highly regarded by the School of Hillel. But John was not creating a new religious structure. Rather, he was announcing the coming of the King. Baptism for John was a symbol of repentance, a symbol of cleansing from sin and turning away from the old life to a new life.

In verses 5 and 6 we read that *"Jerusalem, all Judea, and all the region around the Jordan went out to him and were baptized by him in the Jordan, confessing their sins."* It is evident first, that his ministry was understood and respected, for the people came from Jerusalem and from the total region to John's ministry. Second, it is evident that his baptism was understood as a baptism of repentance, for the people were baptized, *"confessing their sins."*

The boldness of John is evident in his addressing the religious leaders who came to him, describing them as a brood of vipers. The picture is as though they fled judgment like snakes from a field on fire. John requires of them *"fruits worthy of repentance."* In verse 9 he attacks their claim to identity with Abraham by traditional or ethnic associations. God's children are children of faith as was Abraham, rather than people with simply an ethnic or traditional relationship. Here again, the Gospel of Matthew points beyond the Jewish community to an understanding of God as bringing His message of grace through Abraham and his Jewish descendants, a message for the whole world.

John's words in verse 10 are a special word of judgment corresponding to the judgments of the Old Testament prophets. He said that God would cut off Israel for their unbelief and called for persons to return to a life of faith. John was a herald of reform, introducing a movement which would touch every level of society: the religious, ethical, social, and political.

We here note the character of John the Baptist as the forerunner of the Messiah. In the light of the testimonies of the Scripture: (1) John was the witness of the Messiah (John 1:6–8); (2) John understood his place in relation to the Messiah (John 1:19–23); (3) John announced the Christ as the Lamb of God (John 1:29–30); (4) John was a voice of transition from the old covenant to the new (Matt. 1:11–14); (5) John accepted his role with humility, stating, "He must increase, but I must decrease" (John 3:30); (6) John was a fearless preacher before men of whatever rank in society (Mark 6:20); (7) John's witness of the Christ was recognized by the people, for they said, "John performed no sign, but all the things that John spoke about this Man were true" (John 10:41).

John announced the baptism with the Spirit and the baptism with fire as superior to his baptism with water. The word "baptism" means to be brought under the control of a superior power or influence. There are five uses of the term "baptism" in the New Testament. There is the baptism with water, which symbolizes being initiated into the church or being brought under the influence of the covenant community. Second, there is the baptism with the Holy Spirit, which means to be brought under the control and influence of the presence of the Spirit of God. Third, there is the baptism with suffering, which means to be brought under the influence of a suffering, purging experience. Fourth, there is the baptism with fire, which means to be brought under the influence of a judging, refining, searching experience. And fifth, there is the baptism into the Body of Christ (1 Cor. 12:13), which means to be brought under the control of the Head of the church which is Jesus Christ, and to be made a part of His Body.

In verse 11, John speaks of the baptism *with* the Holy Spirit and *with* fire in a relationship which seems to hold grace and judgment together. Baptism with the Spirit has to do with the gift of divine presence, and the baptism with fire has to do with a judgment experience which God's presence brings to bear upon persons who are not open to Him. These two baptisms are of redeeming love and of righteous fear.

This is the first use of the term "baptism with the Holy Spirit." John said that he baptized *with* water, meaning that John was the agent, and that with which he baptized was water. In a similar way he refers to the Christ as the one who will do another kind of baptizing, and that with which He would baptize would be the Holy Spirit. Simply interpreted, this means that Jesus is the one who does the baptizing with the Spirit, and the baptism is the Holy Spirit Himself. What one receives in the baptism with the Holy Spirit is the gift of the Holy Spirit from the Master.

The emphasis is on the baptism *with* the Spirit or *in* the Spirit. This is not to be read as baptism *of* the Spirit, as though it is something the Holy Spirit does. The baptism is the gift of the Spirit Himself. There are things which the Holy Spirit does for us and we can properly speak about the regeneration *of* the Holy Ghost, the illumination *of* the Spirit, the fruit *of* the Spirit, the gifts *of* the Spirit, the anointing *of* the Spirit, etc. But when we refer to the baptism we must speak of the baptism *with* the Holy Spirit.

There are at least five ways in which the Christian church has spoken of the baptism with the Spirit through the centuries. The first is the historical interpretation, which is to say that the Holy Spirit was given on the Day of Pentecost to the church, that He has been in the church ever since, and that we share in the Spirit as we share in the church. The second is the Wesleyan interpretation which relates the baptism with the Spirit to sanctification, affirming that beyond the initial experience of grace and justification by faith, there is a second work of a baptism with the Spirit for sanctification. A third interpretation may be called the R. A. Torrey interpretation, which relates the baptism with the Spirit as a special enduement for power to witness which is to be sought and experienced in the life of the believer. Fourth, there is the charismatic interpretation which relates the baptism with the Spirit to gifts or manifestations, associating these gifts with the expression of the baptism itself. Fifth, there is the relational interpretation which sees the baptism with the Holy Spirit as the occasion in which Christ gives the Holy Spirit to dwell in the life of one who takes Him as Lord. While there is truth in all of these interpretations, the relational interpretation seems to be the most satisfactory.

JESUS' BAPTISM OF IDENTIFICATION

13 Then Jesus came from Galilee to John at the
Jordan to be baptized by him.

14 But John tried to prevent Him, saying, "I have
need to be baptized by You, and are You coming to
me?"

15 And Jesus answered and said to him, "Permit
it to be so now, for thus it is fitting for us to fulfill
all righteousness." Then he allowed Him.

16 And Jesus, when He had been baptized, came
up immediately from the water; and behold, the
heavens were opened to Him, and He saw the Spirit
of God descending like a dove and alighting upon Him.

17 And suddenly a voice came from heaven, saying,
"This is My beloved Son, in whom I am well pleased."

Matt. 3:13–17

The baptism of Jesus has been difficult to interpret. Why did the Son of God need to be baptized? John's baptism was a call to repentance; it was an introduction to the new Kingdom. When Jesus came to the Jordan and asked John to baptize Him, John tried to dissuade Him. John stated that he needed what Jesus could give him rather than that Jesus needed anything from John. However, Jesus responded that it should be done *"to fulfill all righteousness."*

For thirty years Jesus had lived in Nazareth, awaiting the time when the Father would direct Him to begin His public ministry. His act of being baptized by John was a complete and full identification with the Kingdom that John was announcing. Baptism symbolized the turning from the old to the new. Jesus' baptism was His own symbolic act of identification with the new, of participation in the Kingdom of God. Jesus' use of the word "righteousness" is significant, for righteousness is the word which denotes right relationship. Jesus' act of being baptized was a witness to the rightness of His relationship in the Kingdom and to His right relationship with God, the sovereign of this Kingdom.

A second symbolic happening with Jesus' baptism was the descending of the Spirit of God upon Him. As John said in his witness, "I saw the Spirit descending from heaven like a dove, and He remained upon Him. And I did not know Him, but He who sent me to baptize with water said to me, 'Upon whom you see the Spirit descending, and remaining on Him, this is He who baptizes with the Holy Spirit' " (John 1:32–33). John was granted the visual symbol of the Spirit of God lighting on Jesus in the fashion of a dove alighting—the assurance that this was the King coming in His Kingdom. But the Spirit came as a dove, not as a lion upon "the Lion of the Tribe of Judah" in power, but with dovelike meekness.

The third certification is the voice from heaven which John heard at the baptism. The voice said, *"This is My beloved Son, in whom I am well-pleased."* The statement has two phrases, each a quotation from the Old Testament. In Psalm 2:7, a psalm which described the Messiah as the coming King, we read, "You are my Son" (NIV). In Isaiah 42:1, the description of the suffering servant, we read, "in whom I delight" (NIV). At Jesus' baptism He is given this divine confirmation from the Father, a word of His being and His behavior, of His acceptance and His approval. The person of the King is now introduced as the Son of God!

A suggested outline for a message on Jesus' baptism of identification is as follows: (1) the Sign, the act of baptism; (2) the Spirit, the presence of God; and (3) the Sonship, attested by the voice from heaven (3:13–17). He is identified with the Kingdom, with the Spirit and with the Father.

THE TESTING OF THE KING

1 Then Jesus was led up by the Spirit into the wilderness to be tempted by the devil.

2 And when He had fasted forty days and forty nights, afterward He was hungry.

3 And when the tempter came to Him, he said, "If You are the Son of God, command that these stones become bread."

4 But He answered and said, "It is written, 'Man shall not live by bread alone, but by every word that proceeds out of the mouth of God.'"

5 Then the devil took Him up into the holy city, set Him on the pinnacle of the temple,

6 and said to Him, "If You are the Son of God, throw Yourself down. For it is written:

'He will give His angels charge concerning you,'
and,

'In their hands they will bear you up,
Lest you dash your foot against a stone.'"

7 Jesus said to him, "It is written again, *'You shall not tempt the Lord your God.'"*

8 Again, the devil took Him up on an exceedingly high mountain, and showed Him all the kingdoms of the world and their glory.

9 And he said to Him, "All these things I will give You if You will fall down and worship me."

10 Then Jesus said to him, "Away with you, Satan! For it is written, 'You shall worship the Lord your God, and Him only you shall serve.'"

11 Then the devil left Him, and behold, angels came and ministered to Him.

Matt. 4:1–11

Immediately following the baptism of Jesus and the divine manifestations of His Sonship, Matthew and Luke give us the account known as the Temptations of Christ. Jesus is now to enter publicly into His work of introducing men and women to the Kingdom of God, calling them into fellowship with God. The question facing Him was that of how He should fulfill this task.

The word "tempt" as used in this passage is the translation of the Greek word *peirazein*. It carries the basic meaning "to test." Such testing is a necessary part of life in revealing the true mettle of a man. William Barclay quotes the Jewish saying, "The Holy One, blest be His name, does not elevate a man to dignity until he has first tried and searched him; if he stands in temptation then he raises him to dignity."[4] Jesus had His sense of vocation tested with the choice between God's Kingdom and Satan's.

A classic illustration of testing is found in the story of God's testing Abraham (Gen. 22), in which God asked that he give his only son, Isaac, the son whom he loved, as a sacrifice to Jehovah. In Abraham's act of obedience he demonstrated the absolute commitment of his life to God and His will.

Similarly, the testing of Jesus is the demonstration of His full commitment to His Father. John writes of Jesus that "He did always those things which pleased the Father." This testing experience became the inaugural passage by which Jesus entered His ministry. While the devil was an agent in the testing, the choice was as much to rise as to fall.

The setting tells us that He was actually driven by the Spirit into the wilderness for this testing; that He spent forty days without food, wrestling with the issues in His calling to messianic ministry. Jesus had just come from the Jordan River where He had been baptized. Between the Jordan and Jerusalem, about thirty miles away, was a large wilderness area of jagged and warped landscape. The hills to the south ran right out to the edge of the Dead Sea, dropping down 1200 feet into the lowest spot on earth, with intense heat and emptiness. Here in this wilderness area Jesus walked alone with God, pondering and praying over His mission, and was attacked by the devil with the suggestion of alternate ways in which He might achieve His goal. Satan's temptations were self-serving approaches to the ambitions of life, while Jesus' answer and pattern was the way of sacrificial love which led to the cross.

In this account of the testing of Jesus we are given one of the most intimate glimpses into His inner life. Since Jesus was alone in the wilderness, it is His own story as He recounted it to His disciples. The drama is not only an expression of His vigorous mind but it reflects the intensity of the struggle with all of its subjective elements. It is a spiritual autobiography. Jesus, in the many temptations that followed, such as that at Caesarea Philippi when He needed to ask

Peter as an agent of temptation to get behind Him, or the searching temptations in the Garden of Gethsemane to bypass the cross, always responded in a manner consistent with the basic decisions made in the testing in the wilderness.

Significantly, testing comes to us at our points of power or ability, urging us to use those powers for our own self-aggrandizement. The tempter's approach was to say, *"If You are the Son of God . . .,"* perhaps as a suggestion of doubt over the witness at baptism. But the use of a first-class condition in the Greek language would suggest that it be translated, *"Since you are God's Son. . . ."* This means that the temptation was not primarily to focus doubt on the question of His Sonship but rather, in view of the voice from heaven affirming Him as God's Son, to use this privilege for His own self-interests. On occasions of sprirtual blessing, we are tested as to whether we will use spiritual privilege for the will of God and His glory or for our own self-interests.

The tempter attacked Jesus from three different angles. First was the temptation to turn the stones into bread, that is, to use His powers selfishly. There is an inference that He could become a "bread Messiah," a king who would use His power to meet man's material needs and thereby secure his service in His Kingdom.

Christ's commitment to the will of God is seen in His response: *"It stands written,"* in the force of the Greek word *gegraptai.* Jesus' quote is taken from Deuteronomy 8:3, "Man shall not live by bread alone, but by every word that proceeds out of the mouth of God." It is from Israel's experience in the wilderness, when they were fed by the miraculous hand of God but taught that the deeper meanings of life are more than to satisfy the hungers of the body.

The second temptation was to make Jesus a wonder-worker and thereby attract people to follow Him. The tempter projected Him into a vision of standing atop the temple on Mount Zion. At the corner where the Royal Porch and Solomon's Porch met was a drop of 450 feet into the Valley of the brook Kidron. A rabbinical tradition reads, "When the King Messiah reveals Himself, then He comes and stands on the roof of the Holy Place." This means to appear from above, miraculously introducing His national leadership. Satan's temptation suggested that Jesus stand atop that pinnacle and leap down and, by landing unharmed, present Himself to the multitudes as a wonder-worker. To support his temptation, Satan quoted from the Old Testament, "He will give His angels charge concerning you, in their hands they will bear you up, lest you dash your foot against a stone" (Ps. 91:11–12).

The tempter used Scripture, but took it out of context and bent it to his own advantage. Unless one is honest with the Bible, interpreting it in its context and historic meaning, an application can be a perversion of the Scripture. Christians sometimes fall prey to seeking proof-texts to back up an idea of their own rather than to be honest with the Holy Scripture. But Jesus knew the Scripture well, and said, *"It is written again,"* with a direct answer to Satan's temptation, *"you shall not tempt the Lord your God."* Jesus understood the Word and, discerning the devil's misquote, was true to the meaning of God's Word.

Jesus' quote from Deuteronomy 6:16 makes clear that faith is not attempting to see how far one can go in pushing God to answer our wishes. Faith is an attitude that opens one's will to God, that allows God to fulfill His own will through one's life. Faith that can respond more to signs and wonders than to the Word of God is not authentic faith. Jesus refused the way of becoming a wonder-worker to gain national leadership. He was not cultivating people's faith in wonders but faith in God Himself. Jesus' miracles were unselfish expressions which served the good of others and glorified God rather than miracles for His own self-interest.

The third temptation focused directly on Jesus' ultimate mission. He had come to seek and to save the lost, to reconcile men to God. The vision of the world that He came to save moved before Him, and the voice of the tempter said, *"All these things I will give You if You will fall down and worship me."* The tempter was suggesting that Jesus take another route to win the world than the way of the cross. But Jesus knew that He could not defeat evil by compromising with evil. Jesus' decision was to be faithful to God and His calling, to follow the way which inevitably led to the cross. Jesus' response to this temptation was abrupt and pointed: *"Away with you Satan! For it is written, 'You shall worship the Lord your God, and Him only you shall serve,' "*

Upon this direct confrontation the devil left Jesus. However, it was not the end of the temptations in Jesus' life. Another of the synoptic writers says, "he departed from Him until an opportune time" (Luke 4:13). Note that it was *after* Jesus had overcome the temptations that angels came and ministered to Him. He was true to His calling. He had rejected the thought of becoming an economic Messiah, turned from being a miraculously introduced national leader, and refused the quest for political power. The first would not answer

man's deepest needs, the second was out of harmony with the character of God, and the third would have led Him away from God's
redemptive mission.

In a world in which the dominant religion is secularism and the
lifestyle is materialism, we need to be discerning to understand God's
Word, and above all, we need to obey His Word. Christianity, in
the words of William Temple, "is the most materialistic religion in
the world"; it is not a mystical or pietistic retreat from life, but is a
call to responsible living in society. This very strength tests us. We
are to hold belief and behavior together, to relate salvation and ethics
equally to the person of Christ, to constantly interface the redemptive
and the ethical. With this thesis the following outline is suggested
for the development of a message on the nature of temptation: (1)
to make religion material by giving priority to man's material wishes;
(2) to make religion social by giving priority to the social dimensions
of human life; and (3) to make religion political by seeking to achieve
goals by alignments with the principalities and powers which influence this world.

Jesus' victory over the tempter is the basis for our victory as disciples
of Jesus Christ. We stand in fidelity to One who has already defeated
Satan and we know that Satan can be defeated repeatedly in our
lives as we identify with the power of Christ. It is with this awareness
that James writes, "Resist the devil and he will flee from you" (4:7).
In the Book of the Revelation we read that the brethren overcame
their accuser "by the blood of the Lamb and by the word of their
testimony" (Rev. 12:11).

It is also significant to note that Jesus is the only person who knows
the full weight of temptation, in that He is the only person who
never surrendered or yielded Himself to the temptation of Satan.
To say that He knows the full intensity of temptation is to recognize
that for us who have been tempted and yielded, the intensity of
the temptation terminates at the moment we surrender. As one has
said, "Desire is utopian until it is satisfied." For example, if a storm
should sweep through a woods leaving in its trail many broken trees,
we might ask, which trees know the full brunt of that storm? Obviously only the ones still standing know the full intensity of what
passed over them. Those that broke under the onslaught of the storm,
from that point on, did not experience further the intensity of the
storm.

Or, to illustrate another way, suppose one of us got into the boxing ring with Muhammad Ali and in a few seconds were flat on the mat, out for the count. After coming to in the locker room (if we did!), we might look up and say, "That fellow can really punch." But we would not really know. If one of us should walk into the boxing ring with Muhammad Ali and stand our ground for fifteen rounds and walk off on our own feet and then say, "That fellow can really punch," obviously we would know the full meaning of what we were saying. When we walked into the ring, so to speak, with Satan, in short order we had surrendered to his temptation and sinned. But Jesus Christ stepped into that ring and took everything Satan could hurl into Him, all the way to the cross, and even in death Jesus never cracked once. Jesus alone knows the full weight of temptation! Thus the writer to the Hebrews can say, "We have not an high priest which cannot be touched with the feeling of our infirmities; but was in all points tempted like as we are, yet without sin" (Heb. 4:15, KJV).

The temptation of Christ and His victory authenticates His person for our faith, assures our freedom in relation to the tempter, and affirms God's acceptance of His atoning work, for He did not die on the cross for His own sins but for ours.

THE INAUGURATION OF THE KING'S MINISTRY

12 Now when Jesus had heard that John had been put in prison, He departed to Galilee.

13 And leaving Nazareth, He came and dwelt in Capernaum, which is by the sea, in the regions of Zebulun and Naphtali,

14 that it might be fulfilled which was spoken by Isaiah the prophet, saying:

15 *"The land of Zebulun and the land of Naphtali,*
The way of the sea, beyond the Jordan,
Galilee of the Gentiles:

16 *The people who sat in darkness saw a great light,*
And to those who sat in the region and shadow
of death
Light has dawned."

17 From that time Jesus began to preach and to say, "Repent, for the kingdom of heaven is at hand."

Matt. 4:12–17

A transition is now made from John the Baptist to the proclamation of the Messiah Himself. John had been the herald of the King, announcing the coming of the King and His Kingdom. John's fearless preaching and his ethical integrity in holding men accountable led to his arrest and imprisonment. The arrest of John, which inevitably led to his execution (Mark 6), focused the attention of society upon the new teacher of righteousness who emerged upon the scene in Galilee.

An outline for this passage could well focus on two points: (1) the context of His ministry and (2) the content of His ministry.

The context is Galilee, with Jesus' deliberate move from Nazareth to Capernaum by the sea. The move placed Him in both a social and religious center to the north of the Sea of Galilee. For its size, Galilee had a dense population. Josephus said there were 204 villages in this region with no fewer than 15,000 people. Of these people he said that they "have never been destitute of courage," but a people open to new ideas and movements. Not only did Jesus begin His ministry in a setting where many people might hear Him, but His move to Capernaum from Nazareth was a breaking of the ties with His home and community.

The reference that this is Galilee of the Gentiles is significant for our thesis that Matthew shows the movement of the gospel from the Jewish community to the Gentile nations and to the world.

The content of the King's message is stated briefly in verse 17. Jesus preached the same message which John the Baptist had been announcing. His message is stated succinctly: *"Repent, for the Kingdom of heaven is at hand."* The word "preach" is translated from the Greek word *kērussein*, which means the herald's proclamation. Preaching is an announcement with both certainty and authority. For many people today the word "preach" has negative connotations. Dr. Donald Miller has said that "One of the signs of the 20th century is the statement, 'don't preach at me.'" But the atheist Voltaire once said of John Brown of Haddington, "Yon's the man for me; he preaches as though Christ Himself was at his very elbow."

The word from the Master is to repent. This message, as heard from John the Baptist, was a message to turn about, to turn from our own ways to God's ways. Repenting or converting is always a change of direction. It is not first a moralistic change, but is first of all a change in the orientation of one's self. Since the development of the science of psychology, conversion is understood as a change of identification and self-image, a decision to identify our lives with Jesus Christ. The moralistic changes follow, for they are the implication of letting God be God in one's life. If we are to be participants in the Kingdom of heaven, then we are to live by the rule of the King.

The Kingdom is central in Jesus' teaching. Although it will come in its full glory in the future, it is already breaking into our midst. The Kingdom is the rule of Christ, and Luke adds the remarkable story of Jesus' words in the synagogue at Nazareth, where He read from Isaiah 61:1–2 a brief description of the character of the Messiah's mission. For us, the Kingdom is the doing of God's will on earth; it is sharing His mission, it is participating with the Master as disciples, as persons who live under the direction of the King. Later He introduces the church as the fellowship of disciples who evidence the rule of Christ, or the reality of the Kingdom. And later still, Paul uses the term "body of Christ" to show that the church becomes the visible expression on earth of the ascended Christ.

THE CALLING OF DISCIPLES

18 And Jesus, walking by the Sea of Galilee, saw two brothers, Simon called Peter, and Andrew his brother, casting a net into the sea; for they were fishermen.
19 And He said to them, "Follow Me, and I will make you fishers of men."
20 And they immediately left their nets and followed Him.
21 And going on from there, He saw two other brothers, James the son of Zebedee, and John his brother, in the boat with Zebedee their father, mending their nets. And He called them,
22 and immediately they left the boat and their father, and followed Him.

Matt. 4:18–22

Jesus' strategy was to develop a disciple community, to call a group of associates who would be with Him and learn from Him. A disciple is one who both identifies with and learns from his master. Jesus began by calling Peter and Andrew, a report which is here given very briefly. In the Gospel of John we learn that Andrew, who had been a disciple of John the Baptist, upon meeting Jesus, first went and found his brother, Simon, and brought him to Jesus (John 1:41–42). Jesus called them both to follow Him as disciples. "Simon" is the Greek form of the Hebrew "Simeon," just as "Andrew" is a Greek name, suggesting the less provincial nature of the region of Galilee.

Matthew states that Jesus said to them, *"Follow Me, and I will make you fishers of men."* He was moving these men from their occupation as fishermen to recognize the vocation to be disciples, heralds of the good news. Like the rabbis, Jesus trained disciples, but, unlike the rabbis, He called them not to be scholars but to be heralds of the Kingdom. It is impressive that *"they immediately left their nets and followed Him."* There was something magnetic and authoritative about the claims of Jesus Christ upon these men.

Jesus next called the two brothers, James and John, sons of Zebedee, from their occupation of fishing, asking them likewise to follow Him. In view of the reference to several of these men as having been disciples of John the Baptist, it would appear that they knew something about the Christ prior to this occasion when Jesus called them to come follow Him. If so, no doubt they had discussed the implication of relating to this new teacher. At least the reference in Matthew tells us that upon Jesus' call, they immediately followed Him.

These four make up the inner circle of Jesus' larger group of disciples. They were average men, individualists, not the bravest nor the easiest to work with. Peter was impulsive and headstrong, Andrew was homespun and supportive, James and John were ambitious and called "sons of thunder"; yet they were willing to change, to identify with Christ and become heralds of the Kingdom of God.

For teachers to have disciples was not unusual in Jesus' day. Earlier, Socrates had had his disciples, inviting them to follow him and learn of goodness and virtue. The rabbis of Jesus' day had disciples who studied and learned at their feet. But there is a difference between Jesus' calling of disciples and the approach of the rabbis. Jesus called them, rather than waiting for them to come and apply to study with Him. Jesus was a younger teacher in the discipling role than were the rabbis traditionally. Jesus was discipling people by being with them, modeling His truth rather than simply teaching them the Law. Jesus did not graduate His disciples as did the rabbis, for a disciple of Jesus Christ remains a disciple. Jesus called disciples who would in turn disciple others. He called them to be *"fishers of men."* Their mission was not so much teaching and admonishing people in the Law as it was to invite others to become fellow-disciples in the Kingdom of Christ.

THE METHOD OF HIS MINISTRY

23 And Jesus went about all Galilee, teaching in their synagogues, preaching the gospel of the kingdom, and healing all kinds of sickness and all kinds of disease among the people.

24 And His fame went throughout all Syria; and they brought to Him all sick people who were afflicted with various diseases and torments, and those who were demon-possessed, epileptics, and paralytics; and He healed them.

25 And great multitudes followed Him—from Galilee, and from Decapolis, Jerusalem, Judea, and beyond the Jordan.

Matt. 4:23–25

Jesus' strategy was to tour Galilee, teaching in the many synagogues. This itinerant pattern of teaching took the message of the Kingdom to the people. The center of the religious life of each Jewish community was the synagogue, the most important institution in their life, and the primary center of their education. In fact, to this day, it is recognized that the synagogue pattern through the Babylonian captivity was the development of one of the finest educational systems in history. Wherever there was a Jewish community there was a synagogue. While the temple existed as the place where ritual sacrifices were made to God, the synagogue was the place of preaching and teaching. Synagogues were the popular religious colleges of the day. If anyone had ideas to share, the synagogue was the place to begin.

Jesus went to the synagogue with His message. He did not crawl off in a corner, but dared to lay His message of the Kingdom open before each religious center in the villages of Galilee. The structure of the synagogue service gave Him this privilege. In addition to the periods of prayer, the readings from the Law and the prophets, there was a third aspect of their service in which individuals had the privilege of addressing the assembly, followed by an opportunity for discussion. Jesus used the open door of the synagogue to share the gospel of the Kingdom.

Jesus not only preached and taught; the record says that He healed all kinds of sicknesses and diseases among the people. His ministry was one of restoring people to wholeness. The man who preached radical change, who announced the Kingdom, was performing deeds of mercy. He healed and restored common people to wholeness and elevated them to a sense of worth. He restored their spiritual well-being as He preached and their physical well-being as He administered healing. Verse 24 adds to the list of sicknesses the problems of demon-possession and crippling limitations. His ministry overcame ignorance, religious formalism, disease, and demonic attacks; it was a ministry designed to liberate and enable people to be their best in the grace of God.

In the synagogue at Nazareth, as Luke reports, Jesus read from the Scroll of Isaiah, from the place where it is written, "The Spirit of the Lord is upon me, because he hath anointed me to preach the gospel to the poor; He hath sent me to heal the brokenhearted, to preach deliverance to the captives, and recovering of sight to the blind, to set at liberty them that are bruised, to preach the acceptable year of the Lord" (Luke 4:18–19, KJV). Just as Jesus was led of the Spirit into the wilderness to be tested, so the Spirit of the Lord anointed Him for a ministry that would bring liberty and fulfillment to persons in the grace of God.

We are told in verse 24 that His fame went throughout all of Syria and the people came to Him. This account shows that early in the ministry of Christ His word was not confined to the Jewish community. His message included Gentiles from the very beginning. The saving acts of God are not limited to ethnic Judaism but are extended to all the world. If Matthew's Gospel is said to have a special communication for the Jewish community, it must be seen as showing them that the gospel is for the Gentiles as well as the Jews.

Matthew concluded this section to show how popular the ministry of Jesus Christ actually was. We read in verse 25 that great multitudes followed Him from Galilee, from Decapolis, the free Greek cities across the Sea of Galilee to the east (largely Gentile), from Jerusalem and Judea and from "the region across the Jordan"(NIV). This description is an affirmation of Jesus' popularity as a teacher. He attracted people from all over the land of Palestine to both learn from Him and to be healed by Him. The ministry of Christ was not carried on in a quiet, secret way but in complete openness and candor before the total society and the world.

Matthew thus completes the first section of his Gospel, having introduced the person of the King by showing His universal appeal. The King is presenting a Kingdom that is for all people, Jew and Gentile, who will come into the fellowship of God through the gospel of grace. His appeal is not to one ethnic group only nor to one given culture. Having begun His ministry among the Jews, but in Galilee of the Gentiles, it is made apparent that His appeal is universal.

An outline for this section could be a discussion of the character of His ministry: (1) teaching in the synagogues; (2) preaching the gospel of the Kingdom; and (3) healing diseases.

Jesus touched persons at their point of need and from that point of need led them to the experience of faith. The gospel of the Kingdom is the good news by which we may live in the fellowship of the King.

An outline for the total section from verse 12 through 25 on the ministry of Christ shows: (1) the inauguration of Jesus' ministry in Galilee of the Gentiles; (2) the strategy of His ministry of making disciples; and (3) the character of His ministry with its universal appeal.

Matthew has prepared the reader for the next section, the Sermon on the Mount. Great crowds followed Jesus, from which He withdrew and began to teach His disciples. In chapter 4 we have seen: (1) Jesus' rejection of popular messianic expectations; (2) Jesus' call to openness to the Kingdom of God; (3) Jesus' creation of a disciple community; and (4) Jesus' ministry to the needy. The climax is significant, for the man who announced the Kingdom of God and called for radical change is not functioning with the violence of the zealot but is healing, casting out demons, performing deeds of mercy. The stage is set for a sermon to interpret the lifestyle of the Kingdom.

NOTES

1. Barclay, *Gospel of Matthew*, 1:7.

2. Bruce Metzger, "The Text of Matthew 1:16," in *Studies in the New Testament and Early Christian Literature* (Leiden: E. J. Brill, 1972), pp. 21–22.

3. John Howard Yoder, *The Politics of Jesus* (Grand Rapids: Eerdmans, 1972), p. 29.

4. Barclay, *Gospel of Matthew*, 1:56.

CHAPTER TWO

The Message of the King

Matthew 5:1—7:29

The Sermon on the Mount has been called by Oswald Dykes "The Manifesto of the King." It is an outline of behavior for the citizens of the Kingdom. As one of many messages by Jesus, it presents important moral or ethical teachings. It is not a message on salvation as is John 3, neither is it on the work of the Holy Spirit as in John 16. Rather, it is a message on a lifestyle for the "new creation"— those who are born of the Spirit. It outlines the kind of life which is expected of the "new community." However, it is not a legalistic formula, but rather this message calls the members of the kingdom to faith in every area of life.

Matthew presents Jesus as Messiah of Word and Deed. Eduard Schweizer says, "Matthew's most important contribution is undoubtedly his composition of the Sermon on the Mount, and his incorporation of it in his Gospel."[1] The sermon, as recorded by Matthew, may incorporate excerpts of numerous messages that Jesus gave, recalled by Matthew under the guidance of the Holy Spirit to give us an authentic presentation of the teachings of Jesus.[2] But Plummer says, "The theory, however, that it is entirely made up of short utterances cannot be sustained."[3] It is a coherent, orderly sermon. The Sermon on the Mount is not to be thought of as a New Torah. While Jesus is the fulfillment of a long line of preparation, He is the culmination of God's revelation, and He, as "God with us," is the ultimate expression of the will of God. As such, He introduces what John H. Yoder calls "The Messianic Ethic."[4]

Matthew is the Gospel of the teachings of Jesus. He might have chosen to have written an epistle to the church of His time, but by the guidance of the Spirit He wrote a Gospel.

Matthew has been called the Five-fold Gospel, because of the five major presentations of Jesus' teachings. As has been pointed out, these are sometimes referred to as five books, and are outlined as follows: (1) 5:1—7:29, on Righteousness; (2) 10:5–10:42, on His Mission; (3) 13:3–13:52, on His Kingdom; (4) 18:3–18:35, on His Church; and (5) 23:1—25:46, on His Parousia. In this section we are studying the first of the five, the message, or "book," on righteousness. Through the years scholars have recognized in this sermon a collection of Jesus' teachings as a manual for the catechism of the church. But Jesus' original purpose in giving this "Sermon" would mean that we should regard it as The Way of Discipleship.

It is not easy to outline the Sermon on the Mount, lest one do it a disservice. In my earlier book *The Expanded Life,* I examined the Beatitudes as an outline for the interpretation of the sermon. In an exposition of Matthew, Hobbs interprets the Sermon from the perspective of citizens of the Kingdom, noting in the three chapters respectively (1) the quality of the citizens; (2) the function of the citizens; and (3) the motive of the citizens.[5] John W. Miller sees the materials of the sermon as carefully arranged to "deal in sequence with the major spheres of life: our personal life, our life with others, our relation to God, and the various problems confronting us as we seek to act upon Christ's teachings in our daily life."[6] For this study we shall follow the theme of discipleship, noting Jesus' emphasis on ethics or morality and his presentation of righteousness toward God as expressed in justice toward man. Lest this be taken as a legalistic formula, we should recognize that Jesus' call to love requires us to determine the service of love in each instance, an approach which makes this sermon applicable for all time.

The message was given primarily to His disciples, although doubtless the crowd listened as He introduced the nature of Kingdom living. The setting was on the mountainside somewhere near the Sea of Galilee, perhaps to the north of the sea but very possibly on the slopes of the "Horns of Hattin."

THE DISCIPLES' JOY: THE BEATITUDES

1 And seeing the multitudes, He went up on a
mountain, and when He was seated His disciples came
to Him.

2 And He opened His mouth and taught them, saying:

3 "Blessed are the poor in spirit,
For theirs is the kingdom of heaven.

4 Blessed are those who mourn,
For they shall be comforted.

5 Blessed are the gentle,
For they shall inherit the earth.

6 Blessed are those who hunger and thirst for righteousness,
For they shall be filled.

7 Blessed are the merciful,
For they shall obtain mercy.

8 Blessed are the pure in heart,
For they shall see God.

9 Blessed are the peacemakers,
For they shall be called sons of God.

10 Blessed are those who are persecuted for righteousness' sake,
For theirs is the kingdom of heaven.

11 "Blessed are you when they revile and persecute you, and say all manner of evil against you falsely for My sake.

12 "Rejoice and be exceedingly glad, for great is your reward in heaven, for so they persecuted the prophets who were before you.

Matt. 5:1–12

Matthew is the teaching Gospel, and it presents Jesus as the Teacher. The context shows that, pressed by the crowds, Jesus withdrew to teach—an act which let those who were most sincerely interested gather to listen. *"When He was seated"* expresses the symbol of the rabbi who sat to teach, a phrase similar to our references to a professor's chair. It designates this message as a presentation of the essence of Jesus' teaching. The double phrase, *"He opened His mouth and taught them"* has special significance in the Greek. It is used of an oracle or of intimate teaching, making clear that Matthew wants us to see the sermon as the summary or the essence of Jesus' teachings. Barclay says this phrase should be translated, "This is what he used to teach them."[7] In an emphasis on evangelical faith, it is important that we not only recognize God's saving grace but also His transforming grace; both His forgiving grace and His enabling grace. In our fear of works-

righteousness we have minimized "the righteousness which is from
God by faith" (Phil. 3:9). T. W. Manson says,

To divorce the moral teaching of Jesus from His teaching as a whole is
thus to make it practically useless: it is also to make it theoretically unintelligible. For all the moral precepts of Jesus, in the last resort, flow from a
single principle which is not of itself moral but religious; and the understanding of any part of the ethical teaching demands a grasp of the whole religious
context in which it has its place.[8]

The context of Christian ethics is that of the coming of the Kingdom
of God. For people of faith, the Kingdom is coming and will always
be coming, as we pray "Thy Kingdom come, Thy will be done."
While it is coming wherever and whenever God is ruling, it will
ultimately come in its fullness in the *Parousia* (the second coming of
Christ). To make it solely a present happening would minimize its
greatness, and to make it only a future happening would destroy
the meaning and authority of Jesus' present Lordship. Yoder says,

Men may choose to consider that kingdom as not real, or not relevant, or
not possible, or not inviting; but no longer may we come to this choice in
the name of systematic theology or honest hermeneutics. At this one point
there is no difference between the Jesus of *Historie* and the Christ of *Geschichte*,
or between Christ as God and Jesus as Man, or between the religion of
Jesus and the religion about Jesus, (or between the Jesus of the Canon and
the Jesus of history). No such slicing can avoid His call to an ethic marked
by the cross, a cross identified as the punishment of a man who threatens
society by creating a new kind of community leading a radically new kind
of life.[9]

The beatitudes should be thought of as be-attitudes. This is, in
reality, a deeper-life sermon. A comparison with Luke's account and
with the teachings of Jesus in such stories as the Pharisee and the
Publican (Luke 18:10–14) or of the Good Samaritan (Luke 10:30–37)
will help avoid a tendency to regard the sermon legalistically. Here
Jesus is probing the inner being, raising the question of motive. As
has often been said, the larger question in ethics is not what a person
does but why he does what he does. And motive is the source from
which our acts issue. As C. H. Dodd has pointed out, "The ethics
of the sermon on the mount are the absolute ethics of the Kingdom
of God."[10]

In presenting this sermon, Jesus called for a change in the thinking of the people about the Kingdom of God. He rejected the more popular messianic expectations and outlined the creation of a new covenant community of God's people, a disciples' community. In contrast to the revolutionary zealots preparing persons for guerrilla war, He prepared disciples in grace and sent them out in missions of healing.

Blessed are the poor in spirit—the humble—for theirs is the Kingdom. Barclay calls this "the supreme blessedness." The Greek word *makarios,* which is translated "blessed," is difficult to translate into English. It incorporates the meaning of wholeness, of joy, of well-being, of a holistic peace expressed by the Hebrew word *shalom.* The word describes a condition of inner satisfaction expressed by Jesus in John 14:27: "My peace I give unto you: not as the world giveth, give I unto you" (KJV). The poor in spirit are those who, in absolute poverty of spirit, are solely dependent upon God. Such persons have no confidence in their own successes or achievements, for they enjoy the gift of God's acceptance and fellowship.

Blessed are those who mourn—those who care deeply—for they shall be comforted. The Greek word used for "mourn" is the strongest word in that language for mourning; it is the word used to designate mourning for the dead. To mourn is to care deeply, to know godly sorrow for sin, to be deeply concerned about the evil in the world and to know the meaning of suffering because of the sin, injustice, and perversion in society. Jesus assures such of the comfort of God, for in this realism one draws near to God and God in turn draws near to him. There is a direct relationship between the word for "comfort" and the word describing the Holy Spirit as the Comforter for the believer (John 14:16). As we live with a repentant spirit we open ourselves to the presence of God. The psalmist wrote, "A broken and a contrite heart, O God, thou wilt not despise" (Ps. 51:17, KJV).

Blessed are the gentle—the meek—for they shall inherit the earth. And it is the meek person who does enjoy or receive the deepest satisfaction from God's created order. Meekness is not weakness; rather it is the gentle spirit, the disciplined or controlled spirit. In Greek the word for meek, *praus,* is an ethical word. Aristotle spoke of meekness as the mean between anger and indifference. It is a word that denotes self-control, but also means genuine humility. There is progress from the reference to the "poor in spirit" to the reference in the second beatitude on caring deeply, to this third beatitude on the "meek." The pride of the rabbis was in learning; of the Greeks, in intellect;

63

and of the Romans, in power. But it is only the humble who can receive, who can learn or be taught, who can accept forgiveness, who can walk in grace, who can live in love.

Blessed are those who hunger and thirst for righteousness—those who seek God—for they shall be filled. "Righteousness" means right-relatedness, and Jesus' emphasis is not on right-relatedness with Torah but on right-relatedness with God! The Apostle Paul, in Philippians 3:9, contrasts the righteousness of the Law and the righteousness that is "through the faith of Christ" (kjv); i.e., in Christ we have an actual righteousness, an actual right-relatedness with God. In Matthew 6:1–8 Jesus shows the difference between religious rites and genuine hunger for God. His statement of "hungering and thirsting" reminds us of the words of the psalmist, "As the hart panteth after the water brooks, so panteth my soul after thee, oh God" (Ps. 42:1, kjv). This longing for God is a longing to see God's kingdom established in His people, who then practice justice themselves.

Blessed are the merciful, for they shall obtain mercy. The disciple is a follower of Christ because he has been called and accepted by God. Having thus received mercy, he becomes in turn a channel to convey mercy to others. One who truly understands the freedom of being forgiven will share the same release with others. On the other hand, one who refuses to forgive "breaks down the bridge over which he himself would pass." James writes, "He shall have judgment without mercy, that hath shewed no mercy" (James 2:13, kjv). Jesus illustrated this in the story of the unforgiving debtor who, having been forgiven ten million dollars, was unwilling to forgive another man a mere twenty dollars! Jesus followed His model prayer by showing a direct relationship between experiencing God's grace and expressing God's grace.

The word "mercy" must be seen in its historic and positive meaning. Jesus' use of the word is based on the Hebrew word *chesedh,* used frequently in the Old Testament to express the unique quality of the everlasting mercy of Jehovah. The word carries the meaning of identification in the suffering of others, of going through something with another, of entering into another's problem with understanding and acceptance. And this is what God did for us in Christ; identifying with humanity and suffering on behalf of our sin.

Blessed are the pure in heart—those of integrity—for they shall see God. The word "pure" means unmixed, without alloy. Blessed are those with unmixed motives. Throughout the Gospel of Matthew

Jesus speaks of this integrity of commitment: "No one can serve two masters. . . . You cannot serve God and mammon" (6:24); the narrow way leads to life and the broad way leads to destruction (7:13); "Not everyone who says to Me, 'Lord, Lord,' will enter the kingdom of heaven, but he who does the will of My Father who is in heaven" (7:21). One is reminded of Kierkegaard's conviction, *Purity of Heart is to will one will:* a call for unmixed motives that seek only the will of God. This is the way of the disciple and the reward is that such *"shall see God."* The inference and requirement is that only such actually see Him.

This beatitude calls us to the most exacting self-examination. Perhaps we need to examine our motives in religious exercises more than in any other area. How easy it is to cover selfish ambition with the cloak of religious service. Throughout the sermon Jesus raises the issue of motive, asking that we serve not for the praise of men, not for conventional respectability, but with integrity of heart. It has been said that in religious service there are three temptations: the first, the temptation to shine; the second, the temptation to whine; and the third, the temptation to recline.

Blessed are the peacemakers, for they shall be called sons of God. The Greek word used for "peacemakers" means the founders of peace. Bruce Metzger points out that the emphasis is on the verb "make."[11] In chapter 7, verses 1–6, Jesus gives us qualifications of the peacemaker. But above all He personified this peace in Himself. Paul writes in Ephesians 2:14–17, "For he is our *peace,* who hath made both one, and hath broken down the middle wall of partition between us . . . for to make in himself of twain one new man, so making *peace;* and that he might reconcile both unto God in one body by the cross, having slain the enmity thereby: and came and preached *peace* to you which were afar off, and to them that were nigh" (KJV). The message of peace is the message of the gospel; for people find peace within themselves and among themselves as they enter right-relatedness with God in Christ. Such persons are known in society as *"the sons of God."* The word peace, *shalom* in the Hebrew, is not a negative state; it denotes not simply the absence of evil, but is a positive word which has to do with the well-being of another, seeking for him the highest good. Consequently, being a peacemaker is to work for right relations between persons, all persons. The Christian church has a calling which will separate the children of God from people of violence and war, a calling to work for peace and well-being among men.

Blessed are those who are persecuted for righteousness' sake, for theirs is the kingdom. The progress from one beatitude to the next is obvious here. Being a peacemaker by practicing justice and love and living by Kingdom standards is initiating a confrontation with society which can be taken as a judgment. To will God's will is to be different from those who will their own will. This is the way of the cross in which God's will cuts across the will of humanity. The Kingdom is breaking into time, calling persons to be disciples of Christ, living by His mercy and love. The response of humanity is either repentance and faith, or rejection and persecution. The King Himself came as the "suffering servant," as one who identified with humanity in its problems without altering His own relation with the Father, thereby calling us to the Kingdom of the Father. This confrontation led to the cross, a fact which led Paul to say, "Yea, and all that will live godly in Christ Jesus shall suffer persecution" (2 Tim. 3:12, KJV).

Blessed are you when they revile and persecute you . . . for My sake. This beatitude is often merged with the preceding one. However, it has the direct focus of persecution for the person of Christ. One can stand for religious ideals or for moral principles and be accepted in a society that is pluralistic. However, when one affirms that in Christ alone we are truly related to God, the very exclusiveness of this claim subjects one to persecution. And this is our message: "There is none other name under heaven given among men, whereby we must be saved" (Acts 4:12, KJV).

Later Jesus informed His disciples that they would be persecuted because of identification with Him. Is it not strange that in most universities we can speak freely of Freud, or of Marx, but cannot find open discussion of Christ and His teachings? In the first centuries of the Christian church the disciples met emperor worship with the words, "Caesar is not Lord; Jesus Christ is Lord." And to this day the issues of nationalism, of secularism, and of materialism confront us with the same issue. These principalities and powers are not Lord; Jesus is Lord. Notice how Jesus picks up this issue near the conclusion of the sermon in chapter 7, verses 21–23, in a manner which interfaces word and deed. The witness to His Lordship is expressed in our being His servants.

In summary of this review of the beatitudes, we see, as Dr. Richard C. Halverson says, that "the way of the Kingdom of God is antithetical to the way of our contemporary culture."[12] God says, *"Blessed are the poor in spirit,"* but we say blessed are the achievers. God says, *"Blessed* are those who mourn," but we say blessed are the self-fulfilled. Jesus says, *"Blessed are the meek,"* but we say blessed are the powerful. Jesus says, *"Blessed are those who hunger and thirst after righteousness,"* but we say blessed are the unrestrained. Jesus says, *"Blessed are the merciful,"* but we say blessed are the manipulators. Jesus said, *"Blessed are the pure in heart,"* but we say blessed are the uninhibited. Jesus said, *"Blessed are the peacemakers,"* but we say blessed are the strong. Jesus said, *"Blessed are those who are persecuted for righteousness' sake,"* but we say blessed are the expedient. Jesus said we are blessed when persecuted for His sake, but we say blessed are the aggressors. Jesus challenges the very selfishness that determines so much of our social behavior.

THE DISCIPLE'S INFLUENCE

13 "You are the salt of the earth; but if the salt loses its flavor, how shall it be seasoned? It is then good for nothing but to be thrown out and trampled under foot by men.
14 "You are the light of the world. A city that is set on a hill cannot be hidden.
15 "Nor do they light a lamp and put it under a basket, but on a lampstand, and it gives light to all who are in the house.
16 "Let your light so shine before men, that they may see your good works and glorify your Father who is in heaven.

Matt. 5:13–16

Jesus followed the beatitudes with two designations or symbols of the disciple: salt and light. Both are very expressive, both designate a service beyond itself, and both are important in human experience. The Romans of Jesus' day had a statement, "There is nothing more useful than sun and salt."[13] But Jesus addresses these symbols as characteristics of His Kingdom members in society. These two symbols refer to the enriching and preservative influence of the Christian in the world and to the influence or witness the Christian shares of Christ.

"You are the salt of the earth" suggests at least three things: purity, preservation, and flavor. Salt in the Roman world symbolized purity—

no doubt from the process of using sea water and the sun to acquire the salt. Roman soldiers were often paid in salt, the basis for the word "salary." Jesus' use of the symbol of salt to describe the disciple emphasizes the call and influence of purity the Christian brings to society. But salt was also a preservative in a day without refrigeration. This meaning is expressed in Jesus' warning about salt that has lost its savor (Luke 14:34–35). Meat spoiled unless it was salted. Similarly, the Kingdom member is a preserving element in society.

Salt loses itself in service to the object that is being salted or preserved, which is the third aspect of the meaning of this symbol—flavor. When salt is applied to food properly, it is not so that one can taste the salt, but so that the food itself tastes more authentically as it should. As salt makes the food more "foodier," the disciple as the salt of the earth makes the earth more authentically as it should be. Our role in society is not to be over against it so much as it is to enrich or purify the social order, making it more truly a realm of blessing for humanity. Such enriching persons are the salt of the earth.

"You are the light of the world." The light is a symbol of radiance, of openness, of joy compatible with the "blessedness" expressed in the beatitudes. There is nothing secretive about the Christian commitment or way of life. The disciple is described as a light to the world, an influence for openness and honesty, for acceptance and love. This is not a call to monasticism, to a retreat from life; but a call to manifest the joy of fellowship with God as a witness to the world. As Tasker says, "The disciples must not hide themselves, but live and work in places where their influence can be felt."[14]

While a light is to be seen, serving as a guide for travelers, it is basically to be of service. The disciples are lights in the world, not calling attention to themselves but pointing the way of God. They obtain their light from the One who is the Light of the world. This visibility and service is expressed by Jesus in two illustrations: the city on the mountain and the candle placed on the lampstand. The light dispels darkness simply by being present. As one has said, "It does little good to curse the darkness; one should light a candle." And the motive is to illuminate the way of God for others, that by seeing our good works they may glorify God. For this light to be seen we live openly in the midst of the world as disciples of Christ, a visible witness of the rule of Christ or of the presence of the Kingdom of God.

THE DISCIPLE'S HERMENEUTIC

17 "Do not think that I have come to destroy the
Law or the Prophets. I have not come to destroy but
to fulfill.

18 "For assuredly, I say to you, till heaven and earth
pass away, one jot or one tittle will by no means pass
from the law till all is fulfilled.

19 "Whoever therefore breaks one of the least of
these commandments, and teaches men so, he will be
called least in the kingdom of heaven; but whoever
does and teaches them will be called great in the
kingdom of heaven.

20 "For I say to you, that unless your righteousness
exceeds the righteousness of the scribes and Pharisees,
you will by no means enter the kingdom of heaven.

Matt. 5:17–20

Jesus introduces a basic element of hermeneutics, biblical interpretation. While affirming the continuing relevance and authority of
the Old Testament Scriptures, He introduces a new level of interpretation. Jesus Himself is the fulfillment of the revelation or self-disclosure
of God. He says that He did not come to destroy the Law or the
Prophets but to fulfill them; that is, to make their meaning full, or
complete *(plērōsai)*. Throughout the sermon we discover what it means
for Jesus to "fill full" the meaning of Scripture. While the whole
Bible is the Word of God written, inspired by the Spirit and an
infallible rule for faith and practice, our task still remains to understand and interpret it in a manner consistent with its own claims.
To do so means that we recognize the nature of God's unfolding
revelation and see its fulfillment in Christ. From this perspective we
do not see the Bible as a "flat book," but rather, we recognize levels
between the Testaments. All that the Old Testament says about God
is revealed more clearly in Christ. The Bible is God's Word written
and Jesus Christ is God's Word personified, actualized, for "the Word
was made flesh, and dwelt among us" (John 1:14, KJV).

Significantly, Jesus identifies His teaching with the Old Testament
Scriptures and affirms their timeless authority. He calls us to faithfulness to even the least of God's commandments; yet he avoids a legalism that focuses on the letter of the Law in the fashion of the scribes
and Pharisees. Rather, He calls the disciple to the spirit of the Law.

Paul speaks of our new life in the Spirit as one in which "the righteousness of the law [is] fulfilled in us, who walk not after the flesh, but after the Spirit" (Rom. 8:4, KJV). Jesus made clear early in His message that He is interpreting the spirit of Scripture, that is, revealing its basic intent. For example, we have Jesus' interpretation of the Sabbath in the words, "The sabbath was made for man, and not man for the sabbath" (Mark 2:27, KJV). As such, the Scripture is an authority that will not pass away without all being fulfilled.

In the Jewish community the standard of God was laid down for all time in the Torah, the Law of God. Schools of interpretation had hedged in the Law, with safeguards against infringement. In Jesus' day the debate was between two such schools: those of Hillel and of Shammai. There were 613 commandments, rules, traditions and examples without number, which made the Law a confusing exercise for the mind and a burden for the conscience.

When the Jews referred to the Law, they meant either the Ten Commandments or the first five books of the Old Testament, or, by referring to "the Law and the Prophets," they meant the whole of Old Testament Scripture, or they meant the Oral Law. The Oral or Scribal Law was the most common in Jesus' day. Jesus cut through the traditions and legalistic interpretations and disclosed the broad principles of the Law from which he interpreted its basic intent. This intent was not to focus on the righteousness of the Law but on the need for righteousness with God. Paul says that "Christ is the end of the law for righteousness to every one that believeth" (Rom. 10:4, KJV). He does not say that Christ is the end of the Law, as is often misquoted, for the Law still serves to show us our sin, our sinfulness, and to show us our need of the Savior (Rom. 7). But the Law is no more than a pointer, a reminder of our need for the righteousness of God. To answer this need, Christ is the end of the Law *for righteousness.* He is the "end" to which the Law pointed.

THE DISCIPLE'S SPIRIT

21 "You have heard that it was said to those of
old, *'You shall not murder,'* and whoever murders will
be in danger of the judgment.
22 "But I say to you that whoever is angry with
his brother without a cause will be in danger of the

judgment. And whoever says to his brother, *'Raca!'* will be in danger of the council. But whoever says, 'You fool!' will be in danger of hell fire.

23 "Therefore if you bring your gift to the altar, and there remember that your brother has something against you,

24 "leave your gift there before the altar, and go your way. First be reconciled to your brother, and then come and offer your gift.

25 "Agree with your adversary quickly, while you are on the way with him, lest your adversary deliver you to the judge, the judge hand you over to the officer, and you are thrown into prison.

26 "Assuredly, I say to you, you will by no means get out of there till you have paid the last penny.

Matt. 5:21–26

This section introduces us to some of the more important ethical teachings of Jesus in the New Testament. Having just affirmed the abiding authority of the Law, Jesus now makes His own pronouncements. *"You have heard that it was said"* to the Mosaic generation, *"but I say to you . . . !"* He uses the emphatic first person. This places the declaration of Christ on the highest level of authority, on the level of the ultimate prophet of God, the Messiah who is prophet, priest and King. His words, *"but I say to you . . ."* express His authority as Lord of the Scriptures. A rabbinical principle held that some authority must confirm the dictum of every teacher.[15] But Jesus acted on His own authority, and gave the Scriptures their full meaning. Note that the words, *"It has been said,"* do not correspond to the words, *"It stands written"* (gegraptai) which Jesus used when appealing to the authority of Scripture. This implies that what Jesus was actually confronting was the wrong interpretation or inference of the scribes in their use of Scripture.

This section begins a series of six issues from the Law which Jesus interpreted, giving the full word of God on these matters. The first is the prohibition against killing. The Law had said that if you take another's life yours is to be taken in return (Lev. 24:17), which is the legal or external balance. But Jesus says anything that leads to killing is wrong. It is not only the act that is to be avoided but the attitude of ill-will.

71

In his work *Stride Toward Freedom,* Martin Luther King admonished his people "to avoid not only violence of deed but violence of spirit." He reflects the teaching of Jesus from this section. To be angry with one's brother brings one to judgment. To call one *"raca,"* stupid, or empty-headed, may bring one before the Sanhedrin or supreme court; and to hold one in contempt, calling him a worthless fool or outcast, places one in danger of "hellfire." The disciple is to have the highest regard for his fellow man, to respect the sanctity of human life and to meet differences by the practice of love. There is no justification for men to destroy human life—it is always sin and when it happens it is a consequence of sin. This teaching strikes at the very base of a power-dominated social order which often sacrifices lives for the achievement of its goals.

Jesus teaches that anything that leads to killing is sin, and He calls His disciples to be free from anger. While one may say he has never killed, Jesus asks about the inner attitude of anger and hate, of destructive words and hostility. Anger wounds others and also warps the spirit of the one immersed in the feeling of wrath or indignation. We need to understand our feelings to be honest about them, but we must resolve anger in other ways than focusing on personalities with destructive attitudes toward them. Paul writes, "If you are angry, don't sin . . ." (Eph. 4:26, TLB). Anger is a temporary madness and its expression has no place in the community of disciples.

Jesus answers the human problems by asking His followers to take the initiative in reconciliation. He teaches that the problem of human estrangement is so serious that one should even interrupt his worship to go on a mission of reconciliation when this is brought to mind. At a communion service in the South Pacific Islands, a man kneeling at the altar to receive the emblems suddenly got up and moved to the back of the auditorium with an agitated expression. Later he rejoined the communicants and participated in the sacrament. When asked, following the service, about his action, he revealed that he had seen the man kneeling at the other end of the altar rail who had killed his father. He was so angry in his spirit that he could not partake of the emblems until God enabled him to experience a forgiving spirit. Just so, Jesus elevates reconciliation with one's brother to a greater importance than religious rites. And the ministry of reconciliation was ultimately expressed by the Master who, while we were enemies, died for us.

THE DISCIPLE'S COVENANT

27 "You have heard that it was said to those of old, *'You shall not commit adultery.'*

28 "But I say to you that whoever looks at a woman to lust for her has already committed adultery with her in his heart.

29 "And if your right eye causes you to sin, pluck it out and cast it from you; for it is profitable for you that one of your members perish, and not that your whole body be cast into hell.

30 "And if your right hand causes you to sin, cut it off and cast it from you; for it is profitable for you that one of your members perish, and not that your whole body be cast into hell.

Matt. 5:27–30

The second issue Jesus takes from the old commandments is *"You shall not commit adultery."* He fills it full of meaning by saying, *"But I say to you . . ."* whoever looks to lust is guilty of an adulterous heart. Jesus wants His community free from anger and killing; so likewise, He wants it free from lust and adultery. The word "adultery" means "marriage breaker"; it has to do with violating one's covenant. This passage is addressed to the married in its primary meaning, although the teaching on pure thoughts and high regard for the personage of others is a valid secondary interpretation. Married or single, purity calls us to the highest regard for others, to see them as persons and not as bodies to be used for our pleasure. However, marriage is a covenant between two people for life, and adultery is to violate that covenant. Jesus expects His disciples to keep covenant in both deed and attitude. When two persons covenant to be husband and wife, for one to entertain thoughts of relating sexually to someone other than the spouse, makes that one guilty of breaking covenant. Such would have committed adultery against the spouse, if even only in thought. This is the highest standard of fidelity in marriage! Jesus is saying that not only is the act of immorality sin, but the inner desire for immoral experiences is sin as a violation of covenant.

Verses 29 and 30 emphasize how seriously the disciple is to regard this problem. Anything that leads to lust should be given up. One regards sin so seriously as to prefer to lose an eye or a hand rather than to lose one's self in sin. We should understand these statements attitudinally, just as the previous injunction is addressed to our thoughts and attitudes. This means taking literally the basic intent of the passage, rather than physically removing the eye. The loss of one eye or one hand cannot in itself prevent a lustful look or thought. The word-picture is to emphasize deliberate, decisive action in dealing with our propensity to sin. As Tasker writes, "Jesus is expressing in metaphorical language the all-important truth that a limited but morally healthy life is better than a wider life which is morally depraved."[16]

This passage has special relevance for us in our sensual culture. Sexual interests and stimulation are promoted freely in advertising as well as in social life. The so-called sexual revolution has led to more openness about sexual expressions, but to less meaning. The current pseudo-freedom is a compensation for the loss of security of personhood and a quest for the pride of sensual achievement. Reinhold Niebuhr, in his critique of pride, sees it expressed at two levels: the pride in superiority or power, and the pride in sensuality.[17] While the sensual, in God's order, can be an ecstatic aspect of the love in which two people give themselves completely to each other in the marriage covenant, it can be perverted into selfish gratification and exploitation of another.

Jesus' teachings oppose the perverted social order's freedoms expressed in fornication, adultery, group sex, group masturbation, and homosexuality. Infatuated with orgasm, moderns want to justify deviant sex-patterns that achieve this experience so long as "no one is hurt." But it is improper to alter God's created plan which subordinates sex to the larger meaning of the completeness of personality in which masculinity and femininity complement each other in the fulfillment of personhood made possible by this covenant association. The sinful conduct of fornication, the use of pornography, the selfish practice of masturbation beyond adolescent awakening, the practice of homosexuality which avoids adjustments of relating to the complementing aspects of heterosexuality, and affairs on the part of the married for the vanity and thrill of conquest, are all brought under judgment by Jesus' teachings. He calls His disciples to live in a real world of sexual responsibility.

THE DISCIPLE'S MARRIAGE COMMITMENT

31 "Furthermore it has been said, *'Whoever puts away his wife, let him give her a certificate of divorce.'*

32 "But I say to you that whoever divorces his wife, except for sexual immorality, causes her to commit adultery; and whoever marries a woman who is divorced commits adultery.

Matt. 5:31–32

The sacredness of marriage is emphasized in this prohibition against divorce. This third example of Jesus' interpretation of Jewish laws is directly related to the second. The problem of lust and the breakdown of commitments are evils that undermine marriage. The Law had given permission for a man to put away his wife, but he was to give her a bill of divorcement, freeing her (Deut. 24:1). Again Jesus says, *"But I say unto you . . ."* and prohibits divorce by making it clear that it is a breaking of covenant, an act of unfaithfulness or adultery to the covenant made with one's partner.

This appalling social evil, advocated by some as a necessary step for self-fulfillment, is one of the greater social problems of our society. It is now reported that, in America, one out of four marriages undergoes separation and in some areas of the country one out of two. However, note that where the family attends church regularly it is one out of forty, and in families with daily devotional life it is one out of four hundred! The loss of moral integrity, the inability to find continuing meaning in the disciplines of commitment, the selfishness that militates against covenant, and the constant promotion of the sensual at the expense of the holistic sharing that should characterize marriage—all serve to destroy the marriage relationship. Love, when fully understood, is opening one's self to another completely and it can succeed only where trust and fidelity are present. This faithfulness in commitment is a complement to the highest level of human personality, which is moral responsibility.

In this passage, Jesus, by implication, is elevating the status of women. In rabbinic prayers, men thanked God daily for not having been born a Gentile, a slave, or a woman. In Jesus' time, women had such limited rights that a man could divorce his wife by simply stating it several times in front of witnesses and by giving her a written statement. Jesus is here correcting this practice, emphasizing the dignity and worth of women and men equally by calling each to the highest covenant in their marriage.

While this basic teaching appears in Mark 10:11–12 and in Luke 16:18, only Matthew includes the exception found in verse 32. Some scholars would suggest that this is not genuine scripture, but I concur with those who hold that there is insufficient ground to alter this reading. As Hobbs says, "An analysis of the very nature of marriage makes this a reasonable statement in keeping with the divine nature of the marriage relationship."[18] It does not appear that we should interpret the reference to moral lapse in this passage as an event that happened prior to the actual marriage, during the long period of engagement in the Jewish wedding practice. Taken strictly as the verse stands in the teaching in Matthew 19:9, the phrase *"except for sexual immorality" (mē epi pornia)* means unfaithfulness after marriage. Schweizer comments that this means "continual infidelity rather than a single act of adultery." This verse is saying that a disciple is not bound to continue in a marriage relationship where the spouse lives in continued unfaithfulness. But even so, the breakup of the marriage is a breaking of covenant and rarely are the elements that lead step-by-step to a break so clearly one-sided that the other partner can be counted the innocent party. Jesus is basically saying that the marriage commitment is binding for life, the only exception being a state of immorality which has already broken covenant.

This teaching is focused primarily on fidelity to the marriage covenant. It is saying in essence that, while what one does with a third party is sin, the basic sin is what one has done to the spouse. This is a most serious sin—adultery, the breaking of covenant. When this has happened and the partner is remarried, this has such finality about it, God said in Deuteronomy 24:4 that the man may not return to the estranged-remarried wife. What a price!

The question of what God does in forgiving grace for such persons has not found an easy answer in the church. A divorced and remarried person has sinned in the adultery that broke the former marriage. Jesus said, "What . . . God hath joined together, let not man put asunder" (Matt. 19:6, KJV). And yet man has done so, sinning, and there is no other way to regard such a break than as sinful. But the remarriage means that the person has a responsibility in this new relationship and new family which cannot be taken lightly. He is a polygamist—in serial fashion. God accepts repentant people where they are as implied in 1 Cor. 7:20–24, and asks for a Christian commitment never again to commit adultery but to live faithfully in the new marriage, which is a gift of God even after former failures. This is not easy and persons in such tangles will always live with the influence of those broken relationships and failures. They need the understanding and prayerful help of the community of disciples. It will always be true that "the way of transgressors is hard" (Prov. 13:15, KJV).

THE DISCIPLE'S HONESTY

33 "Again you have heard that it has been said to those of old, 'You shall not swear falsely, but shall perform your oaths to the Lord.'

34 "But I say to you, do not swear at all: neither by heaven, for it is God's throne;

35 "nor by the earth, for it is His footstool; nor by Jerusalem, for it is the city of the great King.

36 "Nor shall you swear by your head, because you cannot make one hair white or black.

37 "But let your 'Yes' be 'Yes,' and your 'No,' 'No.' For whatever is more than these is from the evil one.

Matt. 5:33-37

The disciple is to be honest and trustworthy, making the swearing of an oath unnecessary. One's yes is to mean yes, and one's no is to mean no. Whatever is needed beyond this is because there is evil, for where there is honesty and trust there need be no more words. Much of what Jesus taught was basically believed already by the Jews. On murder and adultery Jesus interpreted the Law, but on divorce and oaths He corrected Jewish tradition. They held that "the world stands fast on three things: on justice, on truth, and on peace." However, as their Law permitted the oath, the Jewish community had developed a hierarchy of values for swearing, a pattern which made some statements more binding than others. Jesus' statement on this fourth issue is *"Swear not at all,"* which was a call for return to respect for Jehovah and a refusal to take His name in vain. In this sense it was a prohibition of profanity. But the basic intent of Jesus' statement was to address the use of the Lord's name in oaths.

The practice of swearing the oath in our society is an illustration of bringing the Lord into an issue to make it binding. Associated with this is the accepted condemnation of perjury. Jesus calls for honesty without the oath. This is the background for the stance of Mennonites, Quakers, and others who have refused the oath in business or in court and who choose instead to "affirm" (see James 5:12). Jesus taught that swearing is unnecessary, irreverent, and ineffective in that it does not really change anything. The critical issue is truthful speech. Jesus wants His community of disciples to practice truth in relation to society and especially among themselves. Truthfulness is the expression of inner security and of integrity.

THE DISCIPLE'S FREEDOM

38 "You have heard that it has been said, *'An eye for an eye and a tooth for a tooth.'*
39 "But I tell you not to resist an evil person. But whoever slaps you on your right cheek, turn the other to him also.
40 "And if anyone wants to sue you and take away your tunic, let him have your cloak also.
41 "And whoever shall compel you to go one mile, go with him two.
42 "Give to him who asks you, and from him who wants to borrow from you do not turn away.

Matt. 5:38–42

The calling of Christ in this fifth issue frees one to live by His direction. We are free from having our behavior determined by the way we are treated. Jesus says, *"Do not resist injury,"* or, *"Do not resist the one who injures you."* The disciple is to live by the higher law of love and thereby respond to the treatment he receives from others in a manner reflecting the freedom and love of Christ. This love was ultimately expressed by Jesus on the cross, where He expressed the deepest love to His enemies and extended forgiveness to all. Peter writes, "For even hereunto were ye called: because Christ also suffered for us, leaving us an example, that ye should follow his steps" (1 Pet. 2:21). His teaching prohibits retaliation and prescribes the way of love.

The teaching of this section is one of the more unique ones in Jesus' affirmations. Again He says, *"It has been said,"* and follows with the words, *"But I tell you not to resist. . . ."* Eduard Schweizer says,

"The actual content of Jesus message is nothing unprecedented. Almost all of His sayings have parallels in Judaism; only the call to love one's enemies cannot be found in the same blunt terms. What is unprecedented is this *'But now I . . .'* something utterly new."[19] It is evidenced by a reading of Leviticus 19:18.

This passage contains the essence of the Christian ethic, and is the distinguishing characteristic of Christian conduct. It is clearly taught by Paul in Romans 12, in various statements. "Recompense to no man evil for evil. Provide things honest in the sight of all men. If it be possible, as much as lieth in you, live peaceably with all men. Dearly beloved, avenge not yourselves, but rather give place unto wrath: for it is written, Vengeance is mine; I will repay, saith the Lord. Therefore if thine enemy hunger, feed him; if he thirst, give him drink: for in so doing thou shalt heap coals of fire on his head. Be not overcome of evil, but overcome evil with good" (vv. 17–21, kjv).

John Miller divides this section into four principles relating to four major dimensions of life: "one from the realm of inter-personal relations ('If any one strikes you on the right cheek turn to him the other also'), another from the realm of jurisprudence ('If any one would sue you and take your coat, let him have your cloak as well'), a third from the realm of politics ('If any one forces you to go one mile, go with him two miles'), and a fourth from the realm of business ('Give to him who begs from you, and do not refuse him who would borrow from you')."[20]

Hans Küng writes that Jesus' position is revolutionary: love for enemies instead of their destruction, unconditional forgiveness rather than retaliation, readiness to suffer rather than use force, and blessing for peacemakers instead of hymns of hate and revenge. "Jesus did not set in motion a social/political revolution; what He set going was a non-violent revolution, emerging from man's heart, from a radical change in man's thinking, from a conversion."[21]

The most important element in this passage is the strategy that moves from negativism to a positive course of action. The disciple is to be free for God and for his fellow man who needs him. The principle is in the opening lines of this section. *"Do not set yourself against the person who wrongs you."* Turning the other cheek is not a surrender but a strategy of operation. This act is to take the initiative in behaving in the freedom of Christ and His love.

Previous mention was made of a hermeneutical principle which recognizes the progressive nature of God's revelation. In contrast to the "flat-book" view of the Bible, this principle recognizes God's confrontation of man at different levels, moving man forward until "in the fulness of time God sent His Son," the One in whom the full will of God is known. This One could say, "But I say unto you." This speaks to a progress through the Old Testament toward Christ.

Jesus referred to the oldest law in the world, an eye for an eye and a tooth for a tooth. The law is known as the *Lex Talionis,* and is parochially referred to as tit for tat. It is not only to be found in the Old Testament but is found in the Code of Hammurabi, the earliest known code of laws, which originated between 2285 and 2242 B.C. But it also became a part of the Old Testament, appearing in Exodus 21:23–25, in Deuteronomy 19:21, and in Leviticus 24:20, as well as being suggested in Genesis 4:23–24.

In early times vengeance was a part of life, and if a man of one tribe wounded a man of another, the result was revenge by the tribe of the wounded man on the members of the tribe of the offender. God's intent in the law of *"an eye for an eye"* was to limit vengeance. Early in God's revelation His higher ethic was being introduced in placing a limitation on vengeance. But now Jesus gives the highest expression of God's will and, rejecting revenge, He calls us to act in love. While there are glimpses of this mercy in the Old Testament (as in Lev. 19:18, "Thou shalt not avenge, nor bear any grudge against the children of thy people," KJV), the new emphasis in Jesus' teaching is that we are to love our enemies.

A suggested outline for the larger passage (5:38–48) can highlight three essential elements of its basic intent. Christian freedom (1) elevates others above one's self (5:39, 43–45); (2) elevates personalities above material (5:40–42); and (3) elevates behavior above bargaining (5:46–47). This is a fulfillment of the teaching in Deuteronomy 15:7–11, that God's people are to be ready to help the needy. But the prophetic role is for us to apply this passage to our own times to the issues of materialism, status-seeking, power mania and violence, both in private life and in social ethics.

Eduard Schweizer asks some penetrating questions: "What does it mean to resist not evil when I receive my draft notice? Does it mean that I comply without resisting, or does it mean, that, in order to avoid being forced to resist as a soldier, I resist the draft? Does it mean that I must not resist an evil system that exploits the poor and the weak, and thus participate in exploitation, or does it mean that I must in fact resist so as not to participate?"[22] The disciple of Christ must be true to his new citizenship in the Kingdom of heaven, a Kingdom of peace after the model of the Sermon on the Mount. We must recall Jesus' words that the citizens of His Kingdom are like salt to the earth, light to the world and yeast in the loaf; the minority which influences the whole but never dominates it, which lives by the higher ethic of love even at the cost in one's own life of the way of the cross.

THE DISCIPLE'S COMPASSION

43 "You have heard that it has been said, *'You shall love your neighbor* and hate your enemy.'

44 "But I say to you, love your enemies, bless those who curse you, do good to those who hate you, and pray for those who spitefully use you and persecute you,

45 "that you may be sons of your Father who is in heaven; for He makes His sun rise on the evil and on the good, and sends rain on the just and on the unjust.

46 "For if you love those who love you, what reward have you? Do not even the tax collectors do the same?

47 "And if you greet your brethren only, what do you do more than others? Do not even the tax collectors do so?

48 "Therefore you shall be perfect, just as your Father in heaven is perfect."

Matt. 5:43–48

Jesus' teaching on loving our enemies is introducing a new element into ethical behavior. A Jewish scholar, C. G. Montefiore, is to have said, "This is the central and most famous section" of the Sermon on the Mount. It is one of the most difficult as well as the most unique passages. This is not the natural course of action for man. Only the disciple who has been born of the Spirit, who knows the enabling grace of Christ, can live by this standard. It is the extension of Christ's love, not of natural affection as *erōs* or *phileō*, but of *agapē*, a love which is an act of the will more than of the heart. Such love is not primarily something you feel but something you do, opening your life in the spirit of Christ even to your enemy. Such love includes the entire life, disposition, word, act and intercession.

In verse 45 Jesus bases His call to love on the very nature and practice of the Father, who, in perfect love, without respect of persons, treats enemies and friends alike in His gracious providence. The next two verses, 46 and 47, call us to the higher ethic of positive love. Jesus says that to treat others as they have treated us is to behave at the same level as the sinners about us who do not experience the transforming grace of Christ. Perhaps the injunction in verse 47 is as difficult as any: to be gracious to those who are not our brethren, who are not of our group! This needs to be heard as a corrective admonition for all whose denominational prejudice, in-group bias, or whose cozy security in a primary fellowship keeps them from being a light to the world. Jesus removes all of the fences; He breaks down the walls. He shows us that loving enemies is of God and sharing God's Kingdom is to share His way of love. Such are the sons of the Father in heaven, such are godly men (v. 45).

The commandment to be perfect in the same way our Father is perfect is to be seen in this context of love. His perfect love is without discrimination; our love is to be open to all people, friends and enemies. We should not read the word "perfect" as a philosophical or moralistic perfection. As Bruce Larson has said of moralistic perfectionism, "It will drive you up the wall. You can't be all right and be well!" The Greek word is *teleios,* a word which carries the meaning of culmination, of maturity, of achievement in function. We were created in the image of God, and having perverted this image in sin we are re-created in grace and predestined "to be conformed to the image of his Son" (Rom. 8:29, KJV). The goal of the disciple is to live in this perfection, this *teleios,* this extension of the love of Christ. It is an active word and, in context, means that our love must be all-inclusive as God's is all-inclusive.

The teaching of this section deals first of all with one's personal relationships. A person does not alter these principles of love when relating to others in the larger social group or in international relationships. For many of us, this passage is a clear basis from the teachings of Jesus for Christian pacifism. Consequently, those of us who take this position are conscientiously opposed to participation in war, any war, and choose the vocation of nonresistant redemptive love. Recognizing that a nation will have an army to protect its commitments, the disciple has the option of remaining free from the nation's course of action in war so that the community of the King can serve in an alternate course of loving service that will help "overcome evil with good." He seeks to be salt to the earth in showing a better way of arbitration. To take such a stance, the disciple must share the deepest meaning of love in the way of the cross, as demonstrated by Jesus. We don't have to live; we can die.

We must recognize Jesus' fundamental point: only the person who places his confidence entirely in God can learn to renounce his own security and encounter his neighbor openly. Schweizer says, "And when he encounters his neighbor thus—with the compassion of God himself—he will no longer need to kill in order to live; no longer need to guard his heart with half-truths or oaths; no longer maintain his cause by vengeance—by returning blows or going to court—or carry the day for his own party by vilifying the enemy."[23]

Whether the reader is pacifist or not, the total Christian Church faces the ethical issues of nuclear warfare. Since August 6, 1945, when the first atomic bomb was dropped on Hiroshima, all of history was changed. As Albert Einstein said, "The loosing of the atoms has changed everything except the way we think." Unfortunately, in the evangelical church we have failed to come to grips adequately with this issue. The bomb that destroyed Hiroshima was small, capable of destroying 100,000 people; but we now have nuclear weapons capable of destroying 10 million people! And between the United States and the Soviet Union we have arsenals of 50,000 nuclear warheads, and plans for 10,000 more in this decade. And still we have persons, even preachers, advocating national security by amassing more weapons than Russia—a position which cannot win, for if we amass the larger number we simply add to the threat of the opposition needing to strike first. Dr. Paul Warnke, former director of the U.S. Disarmament Agency, speaking on the arms race at Princeton, New Jersey, on September 27, 1980, said, "A nuclear war could not be limited and no one would be the winner." With this, all informed persons on this issue appear to agree. The evangelical church needs to awaken to its responsibility to be peacemakers, to help the world find deliverance from living by a balance of terror. Jesus' principle, put in contemporary terms, means that there is no security where the survivability of the other side is threatened.

THE DISCIPLE'S MOTIVE IN GIVING

1 "Take heed that you do not do your charitable deeds before men to be seen by them. Otherwise you have no reward from your Father who is in heaven.

2 "Therefore, when you do a charitable deed, do not sound a trumpet before you as the hypocrites do in the synagogues and in the streets, that they may have glory from men. Assuredly, I say to you, they have their reward.

3 "But when you do a charitable deed, do not let your left hand know what your right hand is doing,

4 "that your charitable deed may be in secret; and your Father who sees in secret will Himself reward you openly.

Matt. 6:1–4

Having called the disciple to be mature in love, Jesus then turned to the matter of motive in the disciple's lifestyle. He showed that even right things can be done with wrong motives. Jesus used three basic examples to make His point and in doing so selected the three most important demonstrations of religious devotion in Judaism: almsgiving, prayer, and fasting. In each instance Jesus condemned service with ulterior motives, for the praise of men or for selfish benefits. He emphasized service for the sake of righteousness, that is, fellowship with God. If our aim is to gain the world's rewards, we can no doubt win or receive them, but in so doing we miss the eternal dimension of reward from God. That which the world rewards is of the world and that which God rewards is of the Kingdom of heaven. Persons who function primarily for the praise of men should know that when they have received this, they have their "pay" or reward in full; they have what they wanted (6:2, 5, and 16). The word translated "have" in verse 16 is the word in Greek which is used in payment of bills; in receiving glory from men the payment has been made in full. But when we serve for the praise of God we will receive His blessing in full, although not for outward notice. It is proper to live for the reward of a good conscience and peace with God.

The question of motive challenges much of contemporary Christian activity, including one-upmanship, competition for bigness, assurances that God blesses the faithful with material bonanzas or with health and healing, etc. We are not to bargain with God in quest of a deal that if we do our part He will grant particular rewards. Contemplation of personal advantage stands in opposition to service in the spirit of Christ. The wording of this reference to "your Father who is in heaven" is uniquely Matthean. It carries with it the connotation of majesty and greatness and highlights the contrast between serving merely for the praise of men or for the glory of God.

One of the difficult phrases here is the statement, *"let not thy left hand know what thy right hand doeth"* (KJV). Probably a current proverb, in the context of doing charitable deeds, it implies a secrecy about deeds of kindness rather than acting to impress others. This was not an unknown practice, for the Jews had what was called "the Chamber of the Silent" for those who for some reason wanted to be completely anonymous in their giving. In reading this proverb it is worth noting that it is your own left hand that is not to know what your own right hand is doing; it is not the other person's. The expression may simply mean that we are to avoid all scheming or planning for our own advantage in human attention. One does not give with strings attached. One gives in complete trust when the gift is in the spirit of love, and gives for the good in the experience itself rather than for personal benefits resulting from the gift.

THE DISCIPLE'S PRAYING

5 "And when you pray, you shall not be like the hypocrites. For they love to pray standing in the synagogues and on the corners of the streets, that they may be seen by men. Assuredly, I say to you, they have their reward.

6 "But you, when you pray, go into your room, and when you have shut your door, pray to your Father who is in secret; and your Father who sees in secret will reward you openly.

7 "But when you pray, do not use vain repetitions as the heathen do. For they think that they will be heard for their many words.

8 "Therefore do not be like them. For your Father knows the things you have need of before you ask Him.

Matt. 6:5–8

Prayer is opening one's life to God. It is inviting Him to act in our lives. Prayer is not overcoming God's reluctance, it is being willing to accept His will in our lives. Prayer moves the hand of God by giving Him the moral freedom to do in our lives what He has been wanting to do. God, in His sovereign practice, does not impose His will upon us. Consequently, He can function in our lives in accordance with the degree of freedom we surrender to Him. Prayer is therefore relational; it is not merely a psychological exercise of self-fulfillment, nor is it a mental review of God's principles, nor is it coercing God; rather, it is a free personality inviting the Personage of heaven to share with us.

To expose the hypocritical motive of praying to be seen of men, Jesus refers to the style of Jewish praying, which was to stand in the synagogues and corners of the streets for human notice and praise. He again says they have their reward; they received what they were asking for. The style is like that described in a newspaper report of a religious service, which, in referring to the prayer, said, "The finest prayer ever offered to a Boston congregation!" In contrast, Jesus says that the prayer to God is to be addressed to Him in the secrecy of heartfelt communion. Second, He says that we are to avoid repetition, for prayer is neither to impress God nor man, especially since God knows us so completely that He already knows all of our needs. Should we ask, if He knows our needs, why pray? It is because He waits to move until we recognize Him and His will. Prayer is relationship, not entreaty. Prayer is fellowship, not impression. Someone has said that "Power in prayer is not measured by the clock any more than power in preaching."

THE DISCIPLE'S MODEL FOR PRAYER

9 "In this manner, therefore, pray:
Our Father in heaven,
Hallowed be Your name.
10 Your kingdom come.
Your will be done
On earth as it is in heaven.
11 Give us this day our daily bread.
12 And forgive us our debts,
As we forgive our debtors.

13 And do not lead us into temptation,
But deliver us from the evil one.
For Yours is the kingdom and the power and
the glory forever. Amen.

Matt. 6:9–13

The beauty of this prayer, called the Lord's Prayer, has been honored in both spoken word and in music. Across the lines of culture and language, the Lord's Prayer has served as the model for Christians to approach God. No liturgy is complete without it and no prayer can surpass the scope of meaning contained in its simplicity. Placed here at the center of the Sermon on the Mount, it is a focus of faith. It is a liberating expression before God. It is faith in action, focused on the future rather than on a restoration of the past. His Kingdom is to come now, His will is to be done now, for piety is not our works but is God working in and through us.

The prayer includes an invocation that is threefold, with three petitions in the body of the prayer. Numerous scholars hold the belief that the doxology was added in the early part of the second century. But with the Matthean account we include the doxology as an essential part of the prayer. It may be divided into three sections of emphasis: (1) the honor that worship accords to God; (2) the humility that recognizes our dependence upon God; and (3) the hope which the rule of God creates. As a model prayer, it calls for more attention than this suggested outline offers.

The use of "our Father" means that we are members of a community. "Father" is a designation that witnesses to personal concern, and the phrase *"which art in heaven"* (KJV) is a Jewish expression found twenty times in Matthew as a title for the Father-God. To reverence His name is to worship. For His Kingdom to come means to experience the full reign of God now, a desire for the fulfillment of divine purpose. For His will to be done is a response of the disciple confessing that it will be done in us. The request for bread focuses on that which will sustain us for the coming day. The confession of debts is in relation to our sins or debts owed to God. To forgive, as we forgive, is to recognize that God cannot renew those who stubbornly cling to grudges, thus defying His extension of grace. The prayer to be delivered from the evil *one* is a recognition that we will not totally escape temptation, nor delight in temptation, but we will ask God to deliver us when we are being tempted. The Kingdom is His, and has priority for us; the power is His and sustains our trust and respect, for it is ultimately in His power that we serve; and the glory is His forever, and is the ultimate end or meaning of our creation and purpose. It is of interest here that the second petition of the Jewish Kaddish reads, "May He establish His Kingdom in your lifetime and in your days and in all the ages of the whole house of Israel soon and in the near future."

THE DISCIPLE'S CALL TO FORGIVE

14 "For if you forgive men their trespasses, your
heavenly Father will also forgive you.
15 "But if you do not forgive men their trespasses,
neither will your Father forgive your trespasses.
Matt. 6:14–15

Our attitude toward others is an indication of our attitude toward God. One cannot affirm openness to God and His will and then pervert the communication of God's grace to others. Also in chapter 18 Matthew shares some very searching words from Jesus on forgiveness. This is not to be construed as legalism, but as the question of sincerity in our sharing the spirit of Christ. The grace of forgiveness is to care more about a person than about what he has done. This is illustrated in the story of the prodigal son in which the Father was able to move beyond the issue to the person. He wasn't "up tight" over the sin of the son; he cared more about the son than about what he had done. God forgives because He loves us. He isn't "up tight" over our sins, for, in His love, He cares more about us than about what we have done.

Forgiveness means to release another, to give up our power-play by keeping something we can hold over another. Forgiveness is to take one's thumb off of another, so to speak, and grant him freedom. Such forgiveness is difficult; it is costly, for it means that the offended one resolves the hurt by love and releases the offender without making him suffer. If one hurts you and you hurt that person back, then say that you will forgive, you haven't really forgiven because you "settled the score" by retaliation first, then offered to call it quits. Forgiveness means that the innocent one resolves his own indignation toward an evil and releases the offender. The forgiving one carries his own wrath on another's sin rather than making the other one feel it. The ultimate expression of this forgiveness took place at Calvary where God carried His own wrath on our sin and extended to us the freedom of forgiveness. It is not some mystical, hard-to-believe aspect of the Christian faith, but it is something built into the fabric of human relationships. Scarcely a day goes by but that each of us needs to extend this kind of forgiveness in some degree to another, and to receive such forgiveness from another.

To carry grudges or bitterness warps the spirit of the unforgiving one. How much better it is to release the offender than to burn up psychic energy carrying resentment and bitterness. The story is told of a bishop, in the days before the automobile, driving to church in his horse and buggy. He tied the horse, went into the service and several hours later came out to leave. Untying the horse, he climbed into the buggy, calling to the horse to go. To his surprise the wheels were dragging and the horse could not pull the buggy. Looking back, he saw that someone had piled the buggy full of rocks. Wrapping the lines around the post, he unloaded the rocks, unwrapped the lines, and drove off home. Some twenty years later there was a knock at his door one evening, and three middle-aged men were standing there, nervously asking to speak with him. He invited them in, and after fidgeting for sometime while engaging in small talk, one finally said, "Bishop, do you remember one Sunday morning when there were rocks in your buggy . . . ?" Whereupon the bishop threw his head back and laughed, "Do you men mean to tell me that you've been carrying those rocks around all of these years? Why, I threw them out twenty years ago and forgot about it!"

THE DISCIPLE'S MEDITATION OR FASTING

16 "Moreover, when you fast, do not be like the hypocrites, with a sad countenance. For they disfigure their faces that they may appear to men to be fasting. Assuredly, I say to you, they have their reward.

17 "But you, when you fast, anoint your head and wash your face,

18 "so that you do not appear to men to be fasting, but to your Father who is in secret; and your Father who sees in secret will reward you openly.

Matt. 6:16–18

In the opening words of this section, Jesus assumes that fasting is a part of religious exercise. However, His teaching shows that fasting is not to be a ritual, done by the calendar, but is a voluntary time of meditation, of drawing near to God. Fasting as an exercise is to deprive one's self of the normal and pleasant performances of life for the sake of personal enrichment. The more obvious form of fasting is in dieting, and may have health benefits as well. But the purpose is to transcend distraction or sensual gratification for the sake of enhancing meditation. Sexual abstinence on the part of a married couple for a time may be a form of fasting. Or for youth to forego certain pleasures in sports or recreation for a period for the sake of a spiritual retreat may be another form of fasting.

Whatever the form may be, Jesus' emphasis is to avoid a ritual practice for merit in the eyes of others. Instead, we are to fast for the sake of spiritual enrichment. But even in the exercise, we should beware of using fasting as a sign of superior piety. Neither should we assume that fasting, any more than prayer, is a way of impressing God or of somehow entreating or coercing God to answer a request. Fasting for "power with God" is not to somehow "pressure" Him to act; rather it is to be more objective in discerning the will of God and to be able to rightly claim His presence and His answer.

In verse 17 Jesus uses the emphatic "you" to say that in contrast to the way in which hypocrites fast to impress people, *you,* when *you* fast, do so in the proper manner. The next phrases ask that we go about our daily normal toiletry; put on our perfume or after-shave lotion and go about life in our normal spirit. Fasting has its own values for the person fasting and they are not found in impressing people. In addition to the value of meditative reverence in fasting, Barclay lists five values in fasting that show the abiding benefits of this practice: (1) the value of self-discipline, (2) the release from slavery to habit, (3) the preservation of the ability to do without things, (4) the positive value for health, and (5) the enhancement of our appreciation of things.[24]

THE DISCIPLE'S GOAL

19 "Do not lay up for yourselves treasures on earth,
where moth and rust destroy and where thieves break
in and steal;

20 "but lay up for yourselves treasures in heaven,
where neither moth nor rust destroys and where
thieves do not break in and steal.
21 "For where your treasure is, there your heart will
be also.

Matt. 6:19–21

Jesus answered the question of rewards by speaking of treasures
in heaven. Of course there is a reward for following righteousness;
otherwise, we ask, "Why be good?" To what end does one follow
righteousness? The reward is not material, or tangible. Worldly values
are corruptible and the plaudits of the crowd are soon gone. But
the values of the Kingdom continue with the Kingdom. A clear conscience and a free and joyous spirit are present rewards. The Kingdom
is eternal, and the Kingdom member is sharing eternal life, a quality
of life that is eternal.

Gathering earthly treasures is not a great enough cause by which
to structure a philosophy of life. Earthly treasures offer no long-range
security, for moths destroy, deterioration ruins, and thieves break
through the walls and steal. Rather, the treasures of the eternal life
are the securities that remain. Such *"treasures in heaven,"* as Jesus called
them, were understood in His day to be matters of character. They
are the development of a godly personality, of minds that can enjoy
the great thoughts of God and His creation, of hearts that transcend
selfishness by loving. Such treasures have heavenly meaning and will
abide forever.

Jesus concludes this section with a reference to the importance of
our goals. He introduces a formula which is as real as life: where a
man's treasure is, there his heart is. If everything a person values is
on earth, then his values will also be earthly. But when one's goals
are set on the eternal will of God, his values reflect the same. And
this applies to both short-range and long-range goals. In fact, the
long-range goals are very important in offering direction for short-
range goals. In game hunting, one has two sights on the gun barrel,
a near one and a far one at the end of the barrel so that when these
two are lined up on the rabbit or deer, there is a successful shot.
So it is in life; one needs the distant sight as well as the one close
in, and keeping them in line assures consistency and success. To
use another figure, when one is in love he is drawn to the person
of that love. The result, in both thought and practice, is the contem-

plation of the object of love. That which is first in our affection is first in our thoughts.

THE DISCIPLE'S INTEGRITY

> 22 "The lamp of the body is the eye. If therefore your eye is good, your whole body will be full of light.
> 23 "But if your eye is bad, your whole body will be full of darkness. If therefore the light that is in you is darkness, how great is that darkness!
> 24 "No one can serve two masters; for either he will hate the one and love the other, or else he will hold to the one and despise the other. You cannot serve God and mammon.
>
> *Matt. 6:22–24*

The thrust of this section is singleness of purpose. Verses 22–23 are simple but vivid imagery, meaning that a "single" eye is one with clear vision while an eye with astigmatism produces a blurred vision. The eye is the window by which light registers on the body or perception is brought to the mind. If the window is clear the effect is good, but if it is distorted or dirty the light is hindered. Jesus is saying that the light which gets to a man's heart depends upon the spiritual state of the individual. An eye clouded with lust, envy or covetousness leads to improper behavior. An eye that is clear in singleness of purpose, loving and generous toward others, adds light and joy for all in its range. The Greek word translated "single" has the meaning of generous. It is often associated with liberality and is used in various New Testament passages in connection with sharing material resources (James 1:5, Rom. 12:8).

With this understanding, verse 24 follows the theme which Jesus has introduced. The statement that no man can serve *two* masters is self-evident. Jesus said in John 8:34, "Whosoever committeth sin is the servant of sin" (KJV). Jesus confronts us with the decision as to which master we will serve in the words, *"You cannot serve God and mammon."* "Mammon" is a Chaldean word for the money-god. It is a word which speaks of the systems of materialism which are so very dominant in human experience. The disciple is to give undivided loyalty to the Master; mammon is to take a very inferior place.

Jesus is not teaching a withdrawal from the material world. Rather, He calls for a decision which is necessary for His disciples to live freely in the world. Christianity is a materialistic religion in that it takes creation seriously. The Christian does not withdraw into monasticism, but, in a clear decision which confesses Christ's rule, the disciple pursues the course of stewardship. However, this is no easy answer to materalism, for New Testament stewardship means that we belong entirely to God, that we have no rights of our own and that we are managers of His possessions. We must always ask, "What does the Master want me to do with a property or an opportunity?"

THE DISCIPLE'S TRUST

25 "Therefore I say to you, do not worry about your life, what you will eat or what you will drink; nor about your body, what you will put on. Is not life more than food and the body more than clothing?

26 "Look at the birds of the air, for they neither sow nor reap nor gather into barns; yet your heavenly Father feeds them. Are you not of more value than they?

27 "Which of you by worrying can add one cubit to his stature?

28 "And why do you worry about clothing? Consider the lilies of the field, how they grow: they neither toil nor spin;

29 "and yet I say to you that even Solomon in all his glory was not arrayed like one of these.

30 "Now if God so clothes the grass of the field, which today is, and tomorrow is thrown into the oven, will He not much more clothe you, O you of little faith?

31 "Therefore do not worry, saying, 'What shall we eat?' or, 'What shall we drink?' or, 'What shall we wear?'

32 "For after all these things the Gentiles seek. For your heavenly Father knows that you need all these things.

33 "But seek first the kingdom of God and His righteousness, and all these things will be added to you.

34 "Therefore do not worry about tomorrow, for
tomorrow will worry about its own things. Sufficient
for the day is its own trouble."

Matt. 6:25–34

This section begins with the word "therefore," a word which is a
bridge, tying this section to the one just preceding. Someone has
said that when we see the word "therefore" we should see what it
is there for! Jesus is emphasizing that, having decided to serve one
Master, it follows that we perform the duties of obedience. As servants, we look to our Master for His care and trust Him for our
well-being. This call to trust God is an answer to the human tendency
to worry. We find it easier to feel secure with things that we can
control and, when something is beyond our control, we worry. But,
when we have found the greater security in God, we can trust Him
for our needs. Christ calls us to give up our limited securities for
the greater security in His grace.

Jesus presents evidence that worry is *irreverent*, for it fails to recognize
the God who gave us life and is sustaining it. Worry is *irrelevant*; it
does not change things, nor does it help us in coping with problems.
And worry is *irresponsible*; it burns up psychic energy without using
it to apply constructive action to the problem. Jesus used the birds
of the air to illustrate freedom from anxiety, the lilies of the field
to illustrate freedom from status-seeking, and the grass of the field
to illustrate our need to assess priorities. Interspersed with His illustrations are His admonitions. In verse 27, He says that by worry we
cannot add to our span of life; we may even limit it! In verse 32,
He contrasts the way of the members of the kingdoms of this world
with the way of the children of the Father.

The basis of our trust is confidence in the King. We believe that
God is the primary actor on the stage of history. We trust His sovereign providence, believing that He is holding back the end, the final
judgment of history, for the sake of His work of grace. When we
are truly Kingdom members, having been born into the Kingdom
by the Spirit, it follows that our highest purpose is "the kingdom
of God and His righteousness." This concentration on doing God's
will is the positive answer to worry, but it is also and primarily a
direction for positive action as a lifestyle. But even in reading verse
33 the tendency to worry emerges, for we ask about the meaning
of the clause, "all these things will be added to you." To ask at

once how material these things are is a reaction which exposes our materialism. The passage calls us to seek first the Kingdom and leave the secondary matters to His providential care. Jesus concludes by saying that we are to live one day at a time. The problems of each day are sufficient for the present. We are to face given problems in faith and not invite additional concerns.

THE DISCIPLE'S RESPECT

1 "Judge not, that you be not judged.
2 "For with what judgment you judge, you will be judged; and with the same measure you use, it will be measured back to you.
3 "And why do you look at the speck that is in your brother's eye, but do not consider the plank that is in your own eye?
4 "Or how can you say to your brother, 'Let me take the speck out of your eye'; and look, a plank is in your own eye?
5 "You hypocrite! First remove the plank from your own eye, and then you will see clearly to take the speck out of your brother's eye.
6 "Do not give what is holy to the dogs; nor cast your pearls before swine, lest they trample them under their feet, and turn and tear you in pieces.

Matt. 7:1–6

Respect for others is an indication of one's own self-understanding. The awareness of the complexity of our own lives and the limitations of our own nature should help us to be more considerate and understanding of others. This does not mean that, by an attitude of acceptance toward others, we are thereby endorsing their practice. But we can be discerning without being judgmental. The approach of love is to use personal power or privilege to benefit another. And the sanctity of service is realized only as we serve another in the way which that person wishes to be served, else, in serving in the way we wish to serve them, we are actually determining or controlling their lifestyle. In fellowship with another we affirm the worth of the other personality without copying or subscribing to his total life pattern. Hence, to build the community of the Kingdom, Jesus asks

His disciples to avoid censoriousness, to avoid prejudgment or prejudice, to refrain from sterotyping persons which thereby limits their possibilities for fulfillment.

The old adage says, "Do not judge your neighbor until you have walked in his shoes." This is a valid statement as far as it goes. But Jesus extends the statement to simply say, "Don't judge." Judgment is actually an ego trip. We usually judge others to make ourselves feel better. One who develops a judgmental attitude estranges himself from others, hinders the spirit of fellowship and creates a reaction of judgment in return. In verse 2 the words *"measured back to you"* are literally, "added to you." The word "added" is from the same Greek word as used in 6:33. Having just spoken about our not being anxious about things, this passage, in context, focuses on the temptation to be envious of those who have "things" which we may desire. It condemns the ease with which we become judgmental of successful persons.

The very interesting illustration in verses 3 to 5 also reveals something of Jesus' humor. Although we never read of Jesus laughing, it is impossible to think that One whose joy in life was so complete did not laugh freely with His disciples. But there are indications of His humor in various statements, such as the picture of a person with a beam in his eye trying to pick a speck of sawdust out of his brother's eye. Recall also Jesus' words when told that Herod was asking about Him: "Go tell that fox. . . ." Or again, when He described scribes and Pharisees as straining a gnat out of their tea but swallowing a camel—head, tail, and all! The illustration in this passage shows how ridiculous it is for us to judge others and fail to judge ourselves honestly.

There are numerous reasons why we should refrain from judging others. In the first place, we only know in part and never fully understand all of the issues involved or the motives of the person. Second, we cannot be completely impartial, for we have emotional identifications that are often subconscious which affect our judgment and make us critique others at the feeling level. Third, only God is competent to judge another in His holiness and understanding. Thus James writes, "Who are you to judge another?" (4:12). However, verse 5 does not leave us to escape the discernment that will help another. We are to first judge ourselves and find the correction which God's grace can achieve, then we will be able to take the speck out of the brother's eye. The refusal to be judgmental does not mean a refusal to be helpful. But helping one's brother at his point of need must be done with a spirit of grace and understanding.

The word-pictures in verse 6 are not easy to interpret. They evidently mean that we should not handle the pearls of the Gospel carelessly or present truths of grace to persons who will only seek to destroy them. Both dogs and swine, considered unclean in the culture which Jesus shared, were symbols of negation. Furthermore, the Jewish community regarded the Gentiles as dogs and acted condescendingly toward them. But the early church used this verse to mean discrimination in the fellowship with respect to pseudobelievers and followers of the various religions of the Roman Empire. The *Didache*, the first book of the Christian church on "service order" from around A.D. 100, includes this statement, "Let no one eat or drink of your Eucharist except those baptized into the name of the Lord, for, as regards this, the Lord has said, 'Give not that which is holy unto dogs.'" Basically the passage is a call for discernment in relating to others.

The passage offers a balance for the teaching against judging. One who works for peace, who is a peacemaker, will use discretion in relating to persons.[25] Further, in preaching or sharing the gospel we should use discrimination as to what to share and how much to share, depending upon the attitude and receptivity of the hearers. An overexposure of sacred things to persons unprepared to receive them can create an adverse reaction.

THE DISCIPLE'S FAITH

7 "Ask, and it will be given to you; seek, and you will find; knock, and it will be opened to you.

8 "For everyone who asks receives, and he who seeks finds, and to him who knocks it will be opened.

9 "Or what man is there among you who, if his son asks for bread, will give him a stone?

10 "Or if he asks for a fish, will he give him a serpent?

11 "If you then, being evil, know how to give good gifts to your children, how much more will your Father who is in heaven give good things to those who ask Him!

12 "Therefore, whatever you want men to do to
you, you also do to them, for this is the Law and
the Prophets.

Matt. 7:7–12

The walk with God is a walk of prayer, a life in fellowship. And
as we pray we need to understand the kind of God to whom we
are praying. It is this knowledge which undergirds our faith, for faith
is not a blind wish; it is response to evidence. The more we understand
God the more our faith is developed. It has been said that it is better
to have a small faith in a great God than a great faith in a small
God. The threefold emphasis on prayer in this section is answered
by the statement in verse 11 about the goodness of God. The comparison is made between the good deeds sinful men do for their children
and the goodness of the Father toward His children in response to
their prayers. The words *"how much more"* add the dimension of contrast. This same teaching is found in Luke 11:9–13, where Jesus says,
"How much more will your heavenly Father give the Holy Spirit
to those who ask Him!"

The threefold command to ask, seek, and knock is both command
and invitation. These words are present imperatives in the Greek
which mean continuous action. Ask and keep asking. This may suggest persistent effort, but more likely it is the recognition that we
need to continually come to God. We should not think that, having
asked once, we are presumptuous to ask again. In fact the progression
suggested in the words "ask," "seek," "knock" may suggest growing
awareness of our dependence upon God.

Jesus follows with two illustrations from the relationship of father
and son. These are lifted from well-known Jewish arguments on the
nature of prayer. This fact gives us insight on Jesus' own synagogue
education and also on His ability and strategy of identifying whenever
He could with the proper emphasis in Jewish faith. A father whose
son has asked him for bread will not respond with a stone, nor,
when asked for fish will instead give him a serpent or an eel—something unclean and forbidden in his diet. This is to say, with these
illustrations, that a father won't mock a son in his requests. He concludes with, *"How much more will your Father who is in heaven give good
things . . . !"*

The word "therefore" in verse 12 is a bridge which makes this
remarkable verse a conclusion to what has just preceded. In essence,

Jesus is saying that what God wants to see in our lives He initiates by the things He is already doing for us! He is doing for us what He wants us to do. This is the theological base for the "Golden Rule." And Barclay says, "With this commandment the Sermon on the Mount reaches its summit and its peak. This saying of Jesus has been called 'the capstone of the whole discourse.' "[26] This statement is no doubt the best known of Jesus' teachings and is the highest level of His ethical teaching.

There is no problem in finding parallels to this statement from a negative approach. In the fourth century B.C. an Athenian wrote, "Whatever angers you when you suffer at the hands of others, do not do to others."[27] And Rabbi Hillel said, "Whatever is displeasing to you do not do to your neighbor." Or, in the book of Tobit, we read, "What thou thyself hatest, to no man do" (Tob. 4:16). This negative aspect can be found in other religions as Buddhism and Confucianism. Confucius said, "What you do not want done to yourself, do not do to others." But Jesus placed this ethical principle in the positive form. He made it a model for action, a marching order for the disciple: *"Whatever you want men to do to you, you also do to them."* This, He said, *"is the Law and the Prophets,"* which is to say, that this is the fulfillment of the will of God as revealed in the Old Testament Scriptures.

THE DISCIPLE'S SELECTIVITY

13 "Enter in at the narrow gate; for wide is the gate and broad is the way that leads to destruction, and there are many who go in through it.
14 "Because narrow is the gate and difficult is the way which leads to life, and there are few who find it.

Matt. 7:13–14

Life is made up of decisions, and decisions reveal the inner nature of a person. One makes decisions out of the inner conditioning that is determined by goals and priorities. Setting goals and establishing priorities are our responsibility. Man, as a free moral agent, is responsible for his own decisions; he is accountable to God for this responsibility. For the disciple, the most crucial decision was made when he became a disciple of Jesus Christ. But that is not the final decision;

one keeps making decisions that are consistent with this commitment to discipleship. Conversion to Christ is a change of direction from our way to His way, but following conversion or change of direction, we still need to decide at which level we will live our lives. We will live either at a level of magnanimity or at a level of mediocrity. Describing the latter, Peter Marshall said, "We are like people all suited out in deep-sea diving gear marching bravely to pull out plugs in bath tubs."

There are three very significant contrasts which Jesus presents in the last part of this sermon, and this section presents the first of these. They are (1) the broad and narrow way, (2) bad and good fruit, and (3) doing and failing to do the will of God. The first, the narrow way and the broad way, is a contrast between the abundant life, which Jesus offers, and the way of selfishness, which has no restraints. Jesus said, "I am come that [you] might have life, and . . . have it more abundantly" (John 10:10, KJV). But the abundant life is not without discipline. One only achieves abundance by the disciplines that condition it. Bishop Fulton Sheen said, "The difference between a river and a swamp is that the river has borders and the swamp has none." To have the freedom of playing a piano one must go through the discipline of achievement. One does not have freedom to do a thing just because no one is telling you that you cannot. Freedom comes through participation. This calls for selectivity, because while you are doing one thing you can't be doing another. When one says yes to Christ he must also say no to other things so that he can be true to the yes.

The gate is narrow in that it is demanding, for it requires faith, discipline, and integrity. The resulting character is the expression of "willing one will," of recognizing one Master, of having an "eye that is single," of walking with the Master as a disciple. The broad road, in contrast, has no demands of loyalty, integrity, discipline or character. Howard Skinner, a friend who was the musician with me in a number of evangelistic missions, made an interesting comment on this text. Talking with me about where the narrow way is in relation to the broad way, he remarked, "It is not over at the edge, separated by distance from the broad way, but is right smack in the middle of the broad way, just headed in the other direction." The narrow way is right in the middle of the broad stream of humanity, but headed in the opposite direction.

THE DISCIPLE'S DISCERNMENT

15 "Beware of false prophets, who come to you in sheep's clothing, but inwardly they are ravenous wolves.

16 "You will know them by their fruits. Do men gather grapes from thornbushes or figs from thistles?

17 "Even so, every good tree bears good fruit, but a bad tree bears bad fruit.

18 "A good tree cannot bear bad fruit, nor can a bad tree bear good fruit.

19 "Every tree that does not bear good fruit is cut down and thrown into the fire.

20 "Therefore by their fruits you will know them.

Matt. 7:15–20

While we are to exercise the moral discernment which is introduced earlier in the sermon, Jesus now stresses the dimension of religious discernment. The warning against pseudoprophets was readily understandable to Jesus' audience. There had been many false prophets in their history, and Jeremiah and Ezekiel especially were outspoken against them (Jer. 6:14, Ezek. 22:28). By the time Matthew was writing this Gospel, the significance of this warning was even more evident in the early church, for they were confronted with Gnosticism and with the legalists of the circumcision. Paul referred to this with deep concern in Acts 20:29. He also pointed out to the Corinthians that ecstatic utterances did not always mean that the prophet was being guided by the Spirit. He wrote to the Thessalonians that they were to test the spirit of a prophet (1 Thess. 5:20–21).

Actually, in the Old Testament, the true prophet was in the minority. Jesus warned His disciples that they should be discerning and not accept everything that is presented under the guise of being the gospel. The description of such apostates coming in sheep's clothing but being ravenous wolves is to show the danger of the influence of a false prophet. More harm is done to the Christian church from within than by persecution from without. Vance Havner has said (in his inimitable style), "More harm has been done to the church by termites on the inside than by woodpeckers on the outside!" Zephaniah wrote of false prophets in Israel: "Her princes within her are roaring lions; her judges are evening wolves; they gnaw not the bones

till the morrow. Her prophets are light and treacherous persons"
(3:3–4, KJV).

Jesus' second word-picture is to contrast the good tree and its good
fruit and the bad tree and its evil fruit. He emphasizes the impossibility of an evil tree bearing good fruit—we never mistake a tree seeing
its fruit. Discernment by the disciples is emphasized in his conclusion;
"By their fruits you will know them." In the *Didache*, there is instruction
on how to discern the claims of prophets who were itinerant in the
church. If a claimant was a true prophet he was highly regarded
and his freedom safeguarded. But there were specific guidelines to
discern a false prophet who was "a trafficker in Christ." He was to
remain one day and perhaps two if necessary, but if he stayed three
days he was a false prophet. He was to ask for nothing but his food
and if he asked for money he was a false prophet. All prophets claim
to speak in the Spirit, but the early church had a test: they were to
be known by their character. "Every prophet that teacheth the truth,
if he do not what he teacheth is a false prophet. If an itinerant comes
to a congregation and wishes to settle there he is to secure a trade
and work that he may eat." Significantly, this makes clear that the
discernment of a false prophet is not only with regard to heretical
words but includes the failure to live by the principles of discipleship.

Teaching is false when it claims salvation without discipleship.
Teaching is false when it offers grace as something separate from
God's gracious presence. Teaching is false when its emphasis on faith
does not include the fidelity that issues in ethical living. But teaching
is false when it emphasizes ethics as a saving way of life rather than
as the expression of the transforming work of the Spirit in us, the
dynamic of our salvation.

THE DISCIPLE'S OBEDIENCE

21 "Not everyone who says to Me, 'Lord, Lord,'
will enter the kingdom of heaven, but he who does
the will of My Father who is in heaven.
22 "Many will say to Me in that day, 'Lord, Lord,
have we not prophesied in Your name, cast out demons
in Your name, and done many wonderful works in
Your name?'

23 "And then I will declare to them, 'I never knew
you; depart from Me, you who practice lawlessness!'

Matt. 7:21–23

The Kingdom is not only words, it is expressed in deeds. The disciple is one who interfaces deed and word, for the deed demonstrates the word and the word interprets the deed. Jesus' words in this sermon are not to be passed off as an idealism, rather, they are to become the guideline for the disciples' life. They make us aware that we live only by and in His grace, that there is no ability of our own to behave this sermon without the enabling power of the Spirit. His call to obedience is evident and in this section Jesus makes clear that the deed verifies the word.

It is to be expected that the Master would extend the warning expressed in this section if He was at all serious about the content of His sermon. It is significant that Jesus combines words with "doing" five times in verses 17–19, and twice more in this section, verses 21–23. The false prophets are condemned, not on account of what they say, but on account of what they do or do not do. It is not the one who says *"Lord, Lord . . . , but he who does the will of My Father"* who is accepted by Christ. There is only one proof of love and that is obedience. And the attitude of obedience is sincere when it is evident in one's practice. Barclay says, "Faith without practice is a contradiction in terms, and love without obedience is an impossibility."[28]

It is not easy to discern the truth about practice in these days of mass media when words are the primary means of communication. There is need for a discerning community of brothers and sisters to be relating to (and with) those who are voices for the gospel. Communication is the responsibility of the church, the whole church, and at times we need to take action to call the church to clean up her act before the world. Jesus even says that many will have prophesied using His name, will have cast out demons in His name and will have performed wonderful works using His name, but they are not His disciples; He did not know them or own them! This awareness calls each of us to fidelity to Christ and faithfulness to His Word, to fellowship in a group of disciples and openness to the "binding and loosing" function of the believing community. The brotherhood

103

or fellowship of believers is not needed simply to inspire our piety or to excite our spiritual aptitudes, but is a community of counsel and discernment, of encouragement and guidance.

THE DISCIPLE'S CHOICE

24 "Therefore whoever hears these sayings of Mine, and does them, I will liken him to a wise man who built his house on the rock:

25 "and the rain descended, the floods came, and the winds blew and beat on that house; and it did not fall, for it was founded on the rock.

26 "And everyone who hears these sayings of Mine, and does not do them, will be like a foolish man who built his house on the sand:

27 "and the rain descended, the floods came, and the winds blew and beat on that house; and it fell. And great was its fall."

28 And it came to pass, when Jesus had ended these sayings, that the people were astonished at His teaching,

29 for He taught them as one having authority, and not as the scribes.

Matt. 7:24–29

A good sermon marches; it moves to a goal; it is going somewhere. As we listen to a message we are called to act by its conclusions. Jesus was a good speaker. His sermon moved to a conclusion that called for action. The choice is now with the hearers; having heard, they will or they will not do His will. His conclusion places upon the hearers the full authority of His message. He places the emphasis squarely on our hearing and doing "these sayings of Mine." It is no wonder that the people were astonished, for they discerned the authority with which He spoke. It was not simply the authority of the scholar, as the scribe who could quote at length from the fathers, but the authority of One who, on behalf of God, calls persons to act, to obey. He assured all hearers of the eternal benefits of this action.

The illustrations Jesus uses from building were most appropriate as a conclusion to His message. They came from His own knowledge of carpentry, for He had done such work with His parents. They were relevant in His land, for there were many valleys which were dry gulleys in summer but which, during the rains, became filled with torrents of rushing water. But above all, the illustration is appropriate to the nature of Christian discipleship, for we are building the character and spiritual achievements of the godly life as we walk with Him. Such building calls for a good and sure foundation and this was exactly what Jesus was providing.

Jesus gives special emphasis to the identification of His words with Himself. There is no sure foundation other than the King Himself. One cannot share the meaning or fellowship of the Kingdom without being personally related to the King. The Kingdom is happening wherever the King is in residence, wherever He is ruling. It is this spiritual transformation which makes Kingdom membership and Kingdom behavior a reality. Jesus said to Nicodemus that except a man be born of the Spirit, he can neither see nor enter the Kingdom of heaven (John 3:3, 5).

It is important to note that each of the five discourses in Matthew conclude with a similar formula as is found here in 7:28–29. This is evident in 11:1; 13:53; 19:1 and 26:1. As we review this sermon we should recognize that the One who promises us salvation does so with the authority that sets us free to live. It is essential for the community of Jesus to live by His words. We should recognize that Jesus uses "Law" in the sermon as an invitation to faith. His demands are perverted the moment they are divorced from the promises of Jesus Himself. It is He who grants us grace. He gives us a new heart, spoken of by the prophet Jeremiah as he anticipated the new covenant (Jer. 31:33–34). Jesus is not asking for a confession of faith so much as a conduct of faith.

Numerous scholars have taken an approach to this sermon which seeks to release the Christian from its high standards of performance. Eduard Thurneyson interprets the sermon as the self-proclamation of Christ. Wilhelm Herrmann and Rudolf Bultmann interpret the words of Jesus merely as a call to a new way of looking at the world, apart from the consideration of whether the actual deeds are possible. The Syriac Church Order shows how the sermon can be changed into wisdom literature and falsified, for example: "Love those who hate you and you will have no enemies." Even though the basic content of the sermon appears in Luke and its teachings appear also in the Epistles, the dispensationalists reject the application of the sermon to the present "church age" and see it as predictive of the standards for Christ's future Kingdom, i.e., the millennium. Lutheran Orthodoxy sees the sermon as a judgment because it cannot be fulfilled and regard it as serving similarly as the Law in exposing our sins; yet, they require of man mercy, purity of heart, peacemaking, acceptance of persecution and concrete actions that issue from the teaching of this sermon. One other classical approach is that of Luther, whose concept of the "two kingdoms" in which the Christian is said to live divides between that which is required of the disciple by virtue of his office and that which is required of him in his personal life. For him, since the order of the family, the church and the state is willed by the Creator, one must act in these contexts according to their appropriate rules. Consequently, this alters the application of the sermon in relation to social ethics and makes it basically restricted to individual ethics.

Eduard Schweizer says, "There is not the slightest hint of any realm where the disciple is not bound by the words of Jesus. The realm of family has been explicitly discussed in the sayings about adultery and divorce; the state, in the sayings about revenge and love for enemies." He asks, "Then is the left wing of the Reformation correct— and all movements down to the present that interpret the Sermon on the Mount as a realizable social program. Undoubtedly the demands of the Sermon on the Mount are really meant to be fulfilled; but through all that Jesus says there sounds the call to faith, and faith can only grow in total liberty." [29]

The Sermon on the Mount is an ethical guide that confronts all people with the higher will of God. It is expected of the disciple of Christ who lives by His grace and walks in the Spirit. Such have been born into the Kingdom and are the persons in whose lives the reign of Christ becomes visible in society. This is where the liberalism of Rauschenbusch's Social Gospel breaks down, for he sees the Kingdom as "society organized according to the will of God." The Kingdom is not general society, it is a regenerated society within society. It is the people of God as a covenant community of the committed.

NOTES

1. Eduard Schweizer, *The Good News According to Matthew,* tran. David E. Green (London: SPCK, 1978), p. 203.

2. Bruce Metzger, "The Sermon on the Mount: Aspects of Its Form and Content," *Central Baptist Seminary Journal* 1, no. 2 (October 1966).

3. Alfred Plummer, *An Exegetical Study on the Gospel According to St. Matthew* (London: R. Scott, 1928), p. 56.

4. Yoder, *The Politics of Jesus,* pp. 22–25.

5. Herschel H. Hobbs, *An Exposition of the Four Gospels: Matthew* (Grand Rapids: Baker, 1965), p. 58.

6. John W. Miller, *The Christian Way* (Scottdale, PA: Herald Press, 1969), p. 11.

7. Barclay, *Gospel of Matthew,* 1:82.

8. T. W. Manson, *The Teaching of Jesus* (Cambridge: Univ. Press, 1939), p. 286.

9. Yoder, *The Politics of Jesus,* p. 63.

10. C. H. Dodd, *The Bible Today* (Cambridge: Univ. Press, 1947), p. 84.

11. Metzger, "The Sermon on the Mount," p. 6.

12. Richard C. Halverson, in *Perspective* 31, no. 7 (March 28, 1979).

13. Plummer, *An Exegetical Study on . . . Matthew,* p. 71.

14. Tasker, *The Gospel According to St. Matthew,* p. 64.

15. Plummer, *An Exegetical Study on . . . Matthew,* p. 76.

16. Tasker, *The Gospel According to St. Matthew,* p. 69.

17. Reinhold Niebuhr, *The Nature and Destiny of Man* (New York: Charles Scribner's Sons, 1949), pp. 138–39.

18. Hobbs, *An Exposition of . . . Matthew,* pp. 66–69.

19. Eduard Schweizer, *The Good News According to Matthew,* p. 136.

20. Miller, *The Christian Way,* p. 59.

21. Hans Küng, *On Being a Christian* (New York: Doubleday, 1976), p. 190.

22. Eduard Schweizer, *The Good News According to Matthew,* p. 205.

23. Ibid., pp. 137–138.

24. Barclay, *The Gospel of Matthew,* 1:239–240.

25. See my book *The Expanded Life* (Nashville: Abingdon, 1972), pp. 90–95.

26. Barclay, *The Gospel of Matthew,* 1:276–277.

27. Eduard Schweizer, *The Good News According to Matthew,* p. 175.

28. Barclay, *The Gospel of Matthew,* 1:294.

29. Eduard Schweizer, *The Good News According to Matthew,* pp. 194–195.

CHAPTER THREE

The Authority of the King

Matthew 8:1—9:38

Deeds demonstrate the words and Matthew now presents the authority of Christ in deeds. The ten miracles reported in chapter 8 and 9 express Christ's authority over disease, over demons, over destructive forces of nature and over death. These miracles are credentials of the King.[1] Performed out of compassion, His deeds of love were for the well-being of the needy. Expressions of the divine will, they confirm the authority of the Christ.

The term "authority" appears numerous times in the Gospel. A contrast is drawn between the recognition of Jesus' authority by the Roman centurion and the attitude of the scribes and Pharisees who challenged the authority of Christ. Jesus expressed, in miracles, the uniqueness of the God-given authority of His messianic role.

The order in which these miracles are listed is of interest. They are recorded in three groups with three miracles in each group and a fourth miracle "sandwiched" into the story in the third group. The first group includes the healing of a leper, of a paralytic, and of Peter's mother-in-law, followed by teaching on discipleship. The second group includes stilling the storm, healing the demoniacs and healing another paralytic, followed by the call of Matthew to be a disciple. The third group includes the healing of the hemorrhaging woman, the raising of the dead daughter, the healing of the two blind men, and the healing of the dumb demoniac, followed by a preaching tour of Galilee. Matthew has grouped these miracles together for teaching purposes. It would seem that Mark gives the chronological order, while Matthew selects them for his own order and purpose. The new Prophet, of whom Moses spoke as a greater one to come, now appears, not only as a giver of oracles or new laws, but as a man of compassion and a performer of miracles. The Kingdom is where Jesus rules and His authority as King is certified by His deeds. The Kingdom is breaking into time and Jesus had the authority to say, "The Kingdom is among you."

The Authority over Leprosy

1 When He had come down from the mountain, great multitudes followed Him.
2 And behold, a leper came and worshiped Him, saying, "Lord, if You are willing, You can make me clean."
3 And Jesus put out His hand and touched him, saying, "I am willing; be cleansed." And immediately his leprosy was cleansed.
4 And Jesus said to him, "See that you tell no one; but go your way, show yourself to the priest, and offer the gift that Moses commanded, as a testimony to them."

Matt. 8:1–4

This miracle introduces the first group of three miracles showing the special compassion and authority by which Jesus was guided. Lepers were regarded as unclean; Gentiles were considered outside the people of God, and women were second-class persons in Jewish society. We could consequently title these three stories (1) "The Untouchable Leper," (2) "The Unacceptable Gentile," and (3) "The Unprofitable Woman"! But Jesus had the authority to transcend the bias of society and minister to each with compassion.

After Jesus came down from the mountain where he had delivered His sermon, Matthew says that great crowds followed Him and became witnesses to His deeds. Henry Alford says, "I conceive it highly probable that St. Matthew was himself a hearer of the Sermon, and one of those who followed our Lord at this time."[2] Matthew injects vividly the scene of a leper coming through the crowd and worshiping Jesus. One can almost see the crowd drop back, opening the way for the leper as people cried, "Unclean, unclean!" (see Mark 1:40–45 and Luke 5:12–16). In verse 2 we see (1) the manner of approach:

109

the leper worshiped in faith, affirming his belief that Jesus could, if willing, cleanse him. In verse 3 we see (2) the man of compassion, for Jesus reached out His hand and touched him, saying, *"I am willing; be cleansed."* In verse 4 we see (3) a man faithful to the Law while going beyond it, for He asked the leper to go to the priest and fulfill the requirements of the Law, *"as a testimony to them."* Jesus sought to avoid undue publicity, saying, *"Tell no one."*

Matthew says that Jesus reached out and touched the leper, defying the practice concerning lepers, for the Law had forbidden the touching of any such one (Lev. 13:45–46). Jesus acted with authority, not fearing the disease nor hesitating to be of service. Authority is not dominance, but is the deepest sense of security in truth and in relationship. A suggested outline for this passage is as follows: (1) the interchange of faith, vv. 1–2, (2) the interaction of compassion, v. 3, and (3) the interface with the Law, v. 4.

THE AUTHORITY OVER PARALYSIS

5 And when Jesus had entered Capernaum, a centurion came to Him, pleading with Him,

6 saying, "Lord, my servant is lying at home paralyzed, terribly tormented."

7 And Jesus said to him, "I will come and heal him."

8 The centurion answered and said, "Lord, I am not worthy that You should come under my roof. But only speak a word, and my servant will be healed.

9 "For I also am a man under authority, having soldiers under me. And I say to this one, 'Go,' and he goes; and to another, 'Come,' and he comes; and to my servant, 'Do this,' and he does it."

10 When Jesus heard it, He marveled, and said to those who followed, "Assuredly, I say to you, I have not found such great faith, not even in Israel!

11 "And I say to you that many will come from the east and west, and sit down with Abraham, Isaac, and Jacob in the kingdom of heaven.

12 "But the sons of the kingdom will be cast out into outer darkness. There will be weeping and gnashing of teeth."

13 And Jesus said to the centurion, "Go your way;

THE AUTHORITY OVER PARALYSIS

and as you have believed, so let it be done for you."
And his servant was healed that same hour.

Matt. 8:5–13

The story of "The Unacceptable Gentile" becomes one of the greater illustrations of faith. Calvin said, "This officer had been healed by God before his servant was healed by Jesus." The setting was in Capernaum, the unique city which Jesus had chosen for His base of operation, a city open to the trade movements of the world. Significantly, early in Jesus' ministry, the Gentile is seen coming to Him, and the interchange sets forth the priority of faith over nationality. God's compassion is for all men alike, based on faith in Him. In Luke's account (7:1–10) the centurion sent emissaries from the Jewish elders to entreat Jesus to help him, for they said the centurion *"was worthy."*

The centurion's approach is striking, not only in his humility, but in that he attests Jesus' authority by an illustration from his own command under the authority of Rome. He thereby recognized Jesus' authority as under the command of God, with resources and power commensurate with the command! The centurion states that he is a man "under" authority, recognizing that the extent of one's authority is determined by the authority over him. For the centurion, this meant that the authority of Rome, who was Caesar, was over him granting him authority. The meaning of his statement is, "I know how to obey, myself being under authority, and having others under me I know how servants obey."[3] By implication, seeing Jesus to be under God's authority, he extends the perimeters of Jesus' authority to all that God grants. There is in this a humble awareness that authority is given.

In this passage and in comparison with Luke 7:1–10 and John 4:46–54, recognition is given to the unique faith of the Gentile. Matthew emphasizes Jesus' words that Gentiles will be seated with Abraham, Isaac, and Jacob in the Kingdom of heaven. The Old Testament prophets refer to a coming eschatological banquet, at which the Messiah will include the Gentiles (Isa. 25:6; Mic. 4:2). Jesus affirms this anticipation in His comments regarding the faith of this Gentile centurion and adds His judgment on the unbelief of the children of Israel. Luke, in a different context, confirms Jesus' statement (Luke 13:28–29).

Without going to the man's home, Jesus simply said, *"Go your way;*

and as you have believed, so let it be done for you." The fact that the servant was healed that very same hour verifies Jesus' authority and also the centurion's faith.

A suggestion for this passage would be an outline as follows: (1) the request that overrides barriers, vv. 5–6; (2) the response that overwhelms the seeker, v. 7; (3) the results that His "oversight" achieves, vv. 8–9 and (4) the reality that occurs in confirmation of faith, vv. 10–13.

THE AUTHORITY OVER SICKNESS

14 And when Jesus had come into Peter's house,
He saw his wife's mother lying sick with a fever.
15 And He touched her hand, and the fever left
her. And she arose and served them.
16 When evening had come, they brought to Him
many who were demon-possessed. And He cast
out the spirits with a word, and healed all who were
sick,
17 that it might be fulfilled which was spoken by
Isaiah the prophet, saying:
"He Himself took our infirmities
And bore our sicknesses."

Matt. 8:14–17

The healing of Peter's wife's mother, according to Mark, was on the Sabbath day. Jesus had both taught in the synagogue and ministered in healing, and as He returned to the house, they told Him of the illness of Peter's mother-in-law. Jesus appears to have taken the initiative and reaching out His hand to the woman with the fever and healed her (Mark 1:31). The healing is both instantaneous and complete, for she arose and served them. Jesus made no distinction between women and men even though He often addressed men, holding them accountable for their responsibilities.

In these several verses we see (1) Jesus' choice to minister to the woman, (2) Jesus' compassion for all human need, and (3) Jesus' centrality in the service of discipleship. In developing this discussion, attention should be given to Jesus' attitude toward women. He does not regard women as "second-class," nor as inferior to men.

An interesting Old Testament account on the equality of women is the story of the five daughters of Zelophehad. When Moses was instructing the people of Israel as to how the Land of Palestine was to be divided when they would occupy it, he instructed them to assign the land by the process of the lot, and set restrictions that would keep a given plot of land in the posterity of a given family. The five daughters of Zelophehad came to Moses quiet concerned, saying that since their father had died in the wilderness and since they had no brother the inheritance would be lost. They as women wanted to receive the portion allotted to their father. Moses said he would need to inquire of the Lord on such a matter. In asking God he received the reply, "the daughters of Zelophehad are right. . . ." This may be the first equal-rights message in the Bible (Num. 27:1–9, NASB)!

This section concludes with Matthew's interpretation of Jesus' acts of healing as the fulfillment of Isaiah's statement about the Suffering Servant. The same evening, after the Sabbath had ended, the people of Capernaum flocked to Jesus with their sick relatives and friends (Mark 1:32). Jesus healed them—a witness to the authority of His words. Especially prominent was the casting out of demons. Mark included an account of such a deliverance having happened earlier in the synagogue, saying that the possessed man identified Jesus as the Holy One of God. Jesus commanded the spirits that they should not tell who He was! Matthew turns instead to the Old Testament for a reference which tied Jesus' acts of healing to the Messiah's role as the Suffering Servant.

The quotation in point is from Isaiah 53:4, *"He took up our infirmities and carried our sorrows"* (NIV). Some teach from this reference that our healing is in the atonement, certified similarly as is our forgiveness of sins. However, Matthew is quoting this passage as a fulfillment in the life and ministry of Jesus, not as being fulfilled at Calvary. As Ralph Earle says, "Physical healing is not involved in the atonement in the same sense as salvation is, but all blessings come to Christians now by way of the cross."[4] Alford sees this as fulfilling the Isaiah prophecy in that "the very act of compassion is . . . suffering with its object, and if this be true between man and man, how much more strictly so in His case who had taken upon Himself the burden of the whole sin of the world."[5] Jesus did not need to die for our healing; such is an act of the gracious providence of God.

He did need to die to taste the depth of man's sin and fulfill the justice of forgiving, of reconciling love, by participating in our sin problem to its depth.

THE AUTHORITY TO CALL DISCIPLES

18 Now when Jesus saw great multitudes about Him, He gave a command to depart to the other side.

19 And a certain scribe came and said to Him, "Teacher, I will follow You wherever You go."

20 And Jesus said to him, "Foxes have holes and birds of the air have nests, but the Son of Man has nowhere to lay His head."

21 And another of His disciples said to Him, "Lord, let me first go and bury my father."

22 But Jesus said to him, "Follow Me, and let the dead bury their own dead."

Matt. 8:18–22

Matthew's account that Jesus was surrounded by great multitudes emphasizes the success of Jesus' ministry. At the end of chapter 4 we saw that His fame had spread across all of Palestine and also across Syria. With such demands of the crowd, Jesus needed freedom to keep His priorities clear, so He commanded His disciples to take Him by boat to the other side of Galilee. The eastern shore was not as densely populated as the northern and western shores. As He was leaving, an impetuous scribe volunteered to follow Him as a disciple. Jesus' words in this section were an examination of the man's understanding and sincerity about discipleship.

The calling of disciples was a central aspect of Jesus' early ministry. He selected persons whom He would put through a very rigorous school of education for three years. As a college president, I would have given degrees to the twelve disciples upon their completion of such training. Under Jesus' teaching they were well educated even though not in letters or in the arts as we know them. In making disciples, Jesus took the initiative in calling them and His disciples remained in a serving relation to the Master.

The essential characteristic of the Christian life is discipleship. We learn from the Master and we identify with the Master. He is our Savior by virtue of being our personal Lord and as disciples, we live under His Lordship. Dietrich Bonhoeffer has said, "Only he who obeys truly believes, and only he who believes truly obeys."[6] It is not a "works-righteousness" to win God's approval, but is a response to His grace by which we are saved. The disciple is not working up to the cross; he has been to the cross for forgiveness and is working out from the cross, expressing the new life in Christ. The disciple regards Jesus as the model for ethical directives. To accept Christ is to accept the whole Jesus, what He *taught* and what He *modeled,* as well as what He *did* in dying for us on the cross.

In Jesus' answer to the scribe He tested the man's sincerity, for the disciple must give up earthly securities to know the greater inner security in the purpose of God. (See Luke's more extended account, 9:57–62.) In both passages Jesus refers to Himself as the Son of Man. This is the first time Jesus makes use of this expression in the Gospel of Matthew. It is used as a designation of Himself thirty-one times in Matthew, fourteen in Mark, twenty-five in Luke and thirteen in John.[7]

The second man who addressed Jesus is said to have been one of His disciples. The request, *"Let me first go and bury my father"* meant that he wished to remain with his parents until fulfilling their occupational expectations. This might have taken several years, and Jesus' mission was now! The words, *"Let the dead bury their own dead"* are a word-picture. They may mean to let the spiritually dead bury their physical dead. However, the meaning could be better expressed, "Let that which is a part of the dying order of the age die, and follow me." Jesus' call has priority. Jesus called disciples and asked them to put Him and His will above all else.

An outline for this section on The Call to Discipleship should include: (1) the test of sincerity, vv. 18–20; (2) the test of priorities vv. 21–22; and (3) the test of faith, vv. 23–27.

THE AUTHORITY OVER NATURE

23 And when He got into a boat, His disciples followed Him.

24 And suddenly a great tempest arose on the sea, so that the boat was covered with the waves. But He was asleep.

25 And His disciples came to Him and awoke Him, saying, "Lord, save us! We are perishing!"

26 And He said to them, "Why are you fearful, O

you of little faith?" Then He arose and rebuked the
winds and the sea. And there was a great calm.

27 And the men marveled, saying, "What kind of
Man is this, that even the winds and the sea obey
Him!"

Matt. 8:23–27

While crossing the Lake of Galilee a great storm swept down upon
them. The word "tempest" in the Greek is the word for earthquake
(seismos), emphasizing the violence of the storm. The boat is described
as becoming covered (imperfect tense) with the waves, yet Jesus *"kept
on sleeping"* (imperfect). In great fear the disciples came to Jesus and
awakened Him, crying, *"Lord, save us: we perish"* (KJV). Jesus first admonished the disciples about their fear, emphasizing their *"little faith."*
In so doing He recognized the faith they did have, and He rebuked
the storm in the same manner as He had rebuked demonic spirits.
To the amazement of the disciples, the wind ceased and the waves
were calm. They marveled at His authority, witnessing to the power
of the Creator over His creation (see Mark 4:36–41).

Several basic points need emphasis. The first is the disciples' fear,
stimulated by circumstances beyond their control. Some were skilled
seamen not unaccustomed to dealing with storms, which offers further
reason to believe this storm was especially severe. The second is
Jesus' instruction of faith, showing how that faith copes with problems beyond our power by engaging God's power. The third is Jesus'
authority over His creation, for God continues to act in creation history, the elements being subject to Him. The writer to the Hebrews
says that He sustains the world "by the word of His power" (Heb.
1:3). Also, of working on the Sabbath Jesus said that God has continued to work through history: "My Father worketh hitherto, and I
work" (John 5:17, KJV). In the purpose and will of God, there is no
area in which His presence and power cannot be felt, nor where it
will not make the decisive difference.

THE AUTHORITY OVER DEMONS

28 And when He had come to the other side, to
the country of the Gergesenes, there met Him two
demon-possessed men, coming out of the tombs,
exceedingly fierce, so that no one could pass that way.

29 And suddenly they cried out, saying, "What have
we to do with You, Jesus, You Son of God? Have
You come here to torment us before the time?"

30 And a good way off from them there was a herd
of many swine feeding.

31 So the demons begged Him, saying, "If You cast
us out, permit us to go away into the herd of swine."

32 And He said to them, "Go." And when they
had come out, they went into the herd of swine. And
suddenly the whole herd of swine ran violently down
the steep place into the sea, and perished in the water.

33 And those who kept them fled; and they went
away into the city and told everything, including what
had happened to the demon-possessed men.

34 And behold, then the whole city came out to
meet Jesus. And when they saw Him, they begged
Him to depart from their region.

Matt. 8:28–34

On the east side of the lake was the country of the Gergesenes,
where a city called Gergasha may have existed near the shore. But
scholars have not absolutely identified such a setting. Alford says
it was more likely Gadara, located about six miles from the shore.[8]
But it was hardly Gerasa, a town thirty miles southeast of the lake.
There is no need to place either the city or the herd of swine next
to the lake. In fact, verse 30 would suggest that there was some
distance. The primary aspect of the story involves the men who were
living among the tombs which were carved in the rocks or probably
above-ground crypts for the dead. These provided places where street-
dwellers could find some shelter. There is a problem in Matthew's
reference to two men, while Mark and Luke refer only to one. Some
hold that Matthew frequently tends to add to Mark's account, while
another quite satisfactory interpretation is that there were two men,
but that one was especially prominent in the confrontation. Mark
and Luke tell the story of the man called Legion (Mark 5:1–20; Luke
8:26–39). The men were so fierce that people were afraid to pass
near them.

The ancient world was obsessed with the problem of demons. They
blamed demonic influences for most diseases, including mental illness,
epilepsy and most physical illness. The Egyptians believed the body
to have thirty-six parts and that any one or all of them could be

possessed by demons. There were Jewish beliefs that demons were the result of fallen angels who had seduced mortal women (see Gen. 6:1–8). Whatever the source, the Gospel writers are pledged to the historic truth of these narratives and to the fact that Jesus Himself spoke of the personality and presence of demons.[9] The essential element in this story is not a debate about belief in demons, but that the demons knew who Jesus was. Their statement represents knowledge of the world beyond, of the person of Jesus Christ as the Son of God, and of their own coming judgment. James wrote, "The devils also believe, and tremble" (2:19, KJV).

In no way did Jesus evidence fear of the demonic. Rather, He took authority over them and ordered their departure from the men whom they held in bondage. It is important for us to realize that the devil, while his power may excel ours, is not a second God in the world and in no way does his power match that of God's. Furthermore, whatever the demons are as extensions of the devil's power or influence, they are not to be feared when we know Christ. In any comparison with Him they are puny, and can be overcome in the name of Christ!

The longer story is presented by Mark and adds to our understanding. The incident of the destruction of a herd of 2000 swine is one of the difficult elements of this passage. Perhaps the demons anticipated what would happen and found this to be a way of striking back at Jesus. Perhaps Jesus saw in this and in the suicide of the herd of swine an act of judgment, as they had petitioned Him not to judge or torment them before the time. Jesus acted in a manner consistent with His coming; He enacted a judgment upon all extensions of the satanic for He entered the strong man's house to bind the strong man (see Matt. 12:28–29). Perhaps Jesus saw in this action a confrontation with the people of the region, demonstrating that human life and well-being were far more valuable than the swine business. Or possibly it was to demonstrate, for the sake of the possessed men, that they were actually free, that the demons had gone into the swine and went with them to their destruction, freeing the men from the hellish powers that had bound them.

All of the city turned out to see what had happened. There is an impressive statement in Mark that, upon coming to Jesus, they saw the demoniac "sitting and clothed and in his right mind" (5:15). Here was their opportunity to recognize true values, the value of persons above the material, and to rejoice with those who were released and

healed. But the loss in their business, the destruction of the herd
of swine, was too great for them to see the movement of God in
their midst. Consequently, they made a choice between their way
of life and the person and ministry of Jesus; they entreated Jesus
to depart from them!

This is a graphic illustration of the choice between the values of
the Kingdom and the materialism of the world. The pigs had perished
and what did it matter to the people that two men were made whole
if their economy was now in recession? This is human selfishness
in its most blatant expression. But it is not foreign to our times,
for the needs of the Third World, the plight of the hungry and starv-
ing, do not appear to be as high on our agenda as safeguarding our
own economic privileges. And this is true of the church where we
speak so deliberately about "protecting our security" without a commensurate concern for the well-being of our brothers in other parts
of the world. I heard Bishop Zulu of Zululand say at Pretoria, South
Africa, "What is wrong with the Church today is that she has something else on her agenda which she has elevated above the will and
person of Christ."[10]

There are several possible approaches to an outline from this remarkable story. One could develop a treatise on liberation from bondage or on the impact of changed lives, for Mark tells us that the
healed man of Legion wanted to go with Jesus but the Lord sent
him back to share his freedom and faith with all in the city. Or,
one can develop a message around the actions relating to Jesus. A
suggested outline is that confrontation by Jesus means (1) knowing
Him authentically is to meet Him as the Son of God; (2) knowing
Him is to acknowledge what He can do (for the men whom others
feared now are gripped with the fear of Jesus' power); and (3) knowing
His action to deliver precipitates a choice (men continue to choose
between Jesus and pigs!).

THE AUTHORITY OVER PARALYSIS

1 And He got into a boat, crossed over, and came
to His own city.
2 And behold, they brought to Him a paralytic
lying on a bed. And Jesus, seeing their faith, said to
the paralytic, "Son, be of good cheer; your sins are
forgiven you."

3 And at once some of the scribes said within themselves, "This Man blasphemes!"

4 And Jesus, knowing their thoughts, said, "Why do you think evil in your hearts?

5 "For which is easier, to say, 'Your sins are forgiven you,' or to say, 'Arise and walk'?

6 "But that you may know that the Son of Man has power on earth to forgive sins"—then He said to the paralytic, "Arise, take up your bed, and go to your house."

7 And he arose and departed to his house.

8 But when the multitudes saw it, they marveled and glorified God who had given such power to men.

Matt. 9:1–8

Having been asked by the people of Gadara to leave, Jesus got into the boat and went to the north coast, to His residence at Capernaum, very likely with Simon Peter (implied in 8:14). This may account for the explicit details in Mark 2:1–12, as he related this story as told to him by Peter. Since it took place in Peter's house, he would have noticed in detail the breaking open of the roof so that the men could lower the paralytic in front of Jesus. Matthew omits these details, concentrating less upon the faith of the friends than upon the authority of Jesus to release the paralytic by forgiving his sins! Matthew does mention Jesus' recognition of their faith, but does so without graphic accounts of the way in which the men achieved their objective.

In this story is a remarkable presentation of The Healing of Forgiveness: (1) the action of faith is carried beyond physical healing, 9:2; (2) the affirmation of forgiveness focuses the central issue of well-being, 9:3–5; and (3) the authority to forgive sin is confirmed by God's grace of healing, 9:6.

Upon the man's healing which was a confirmation of Jesus' authority, the crowd stood in awe. The physical miracle confirmed the inner spiritual miracle of release from sin and guilt. Matthew's account is more brief than that of either Mark or Luke, emphasizing his concentration on the teaching and meaning of Jesus' acts. The account contrasts the attitude of the crowd in glorifying God for giving such power to men, with the attitude of the scribes or teachers of the Law who thought evil things in their hearts, for they thought of Jesus as a blasphemer.

Jesus again referred to Himself as "the Son of Man" (v. 6). The apocalyptic term, significant in Jewish writings, related directly to the Messiah. We read in Daniel 7:13 that the world will see "the Son of Man" coming with clouds. The unique element in this story is the evidence that the Kingdom of God is breaking into time; the King is here and He can forgive sin as the Son of God on earth! This aspect of the messianic mission was not fully understood by the people. But that something unusual and valid was happening had dawned upon them, for they said, "We have seen strange things today!" (Luke 5:26). Bengel writes, "The Son of Man, as God manifest in man's flesh, has on man's earth that power, which in its fountain and essence belongs to God in heaven."

THE AUTHORITY OVER OCCUPATION

9 And as Jesus passed on from there, He saw a man named Matthew sitting at the tax office. And He said to him, "Follow Me." And he arose and followed Him.

10 And so it was, as Jesus sat at the table in the house, behold, many tax collectors and sinners came and sat down with Him and His disciples.

11 And when the Pharisees saw it, they said to His disciples, "Why does your Teacher eat with tax collectors and sinners?"

12 But when Jesus heard that, He said to them, "Those who are well have no need of a physician, but those who are sick.

13 "But go and learn what this means: 'I desire mercy and not sacrifice.' For I did not come to call the righteous, but sinners, to repentance."

Matt. 9:9–13

The call of Matthew is in the context of his having been a tax collector. For Jesus to enjoy the hospitality of his home and friends sets the stage for Jesus to be known as a friend of publicans and sinners. His calling Matthew to be a disciple places the authority of Christ over occupation. We have one vocation as followers of Jesus and that is to be disciples. This vocation supplies the directive for choice of occupation as well as for the character of our work in an acceptable occupation. The first three Gospels refer to the calling of Matthew to follow Jesus. However, Mark and Luke refer to him as Levi. Only here do we have the designation "Matthew," suggesting that he had a direct relation to the writing of this Gospel. Matthew was at the "tax office" or the place of toll, and upon Jesus' call he arose and followed Him. He paid a unique price, for since a number of the other disciples were fishermen they could return to their nets, but for Matthew to leave his post meant "no turning back."

There was nothing secretive about Matthew's decision to be a disciple, for he openly invited his friends to his spacious home for a dinner with Jesus. They are referred to as publicans (tax collectors) and sinners (persons careless about ceremonial laws), and are set in contrast with the Pharisees who were the Separatists of Jesus' day (priding themselves in their righteousness). Jesus demonstrated love and acceptance by his willingness to sit down with sinners and associate with them. This is friendship evangelism, for we cannot win sinners to the Lord if we keep ourselves aloof from them.

The Pharisees were asking Jesus' disciples about His association with sinners, and when Jesus heard it, He answered His critics with two statements. First, *"They that are whole need no physician, but they that are sick"* (KJV) was Jesus' word that He came to save sinners. His mission opens the door to all, "For all have sinned, and come short of the glory of God" (Rom. 3:23, KJV). Second, Jesus called these religious persons to read their Scriptures, noting Hosea 6:6, that God desires mercy rather than sacrifices, a forgiving spirit more than legal demands or religious rites. The Master's conclusion was that He is calling the sinful to repentance—a word hard to hear for the self-righteous. Since Matthew was working for Rome, specifically for Herod, his friends no doubt included Gentiles, a factor which adds breadth to the meaning of Jesus' invitation to sinners.

An outline for presenting a meditation on Friendship Evangelism is suggested as follows: (1) Jesus asked persons of any walk to follow Him, vv. 9–10; (2) Jesus associated with sinners to win them to God, vv. 11–12; and (3) Jesus actualized the extension of God's mercy to all people, v. 13.

THE AUTHORITY OVER FASTING

14 Then the disciples of John came to Him, saying, "Why do we and the Pharisees fast often, but Your disciples do not fast?"

15 And Jesus said to them, "Can the friends of the
bridegroom mourn as long as the bridegroom is with
them? But the days will come when the bridegroom
will be taken away from them, and then they will
fast.

16 "No one puts a piece of unshrunk cloth on an
old garment; for the patch pulls away from the
garment, and the tear is made worse.

17 "Nor do people put new wine into old wineskins,
or else the wineskins break, the wine is spilled, and
the wineskins will be ruined. But they put new wine
into new wineskins, and both are preserved."

Matt. 9:14–17

The uniqueness of the announcement of the Kingdom is the presence of the King. Matters of religious rites now have a secondary
place as we relate to the Lord Himself. In His presence we rejoice
in fellowship rather than needing to seek His recognition by fasting.
The disciples of John the Baptist raised the question on fasting, for
they were of the old order as were the Pharisees. Jesus said of John
that there was none greater in the "old order" than John, who had
the privilege of announcing the Messiah, and yet the least person
in the "new order" has greater privilege than had John. In answer
Jesus spoke of the presence of the bridegroom, making it improper
for "friends of the bridegroom" to fast at a time of wedding. Jesus'
presence was a time for rejoicing, not for mourning or fasting (see
Isa. 54:5–10). The role of the bridegroom's friends at a wedding was
to go with Him to bring the bride.

The first inference to the coming Passion of Christ is expressed
here. With the reference to the bridegroom and implied wedding,
Jesus added the reference that He would be taken away from them.
John adds "[for] a little while" (John 16:16–21). From this time on
Jesus repeatedly referred to His coming death. He fully understood
the conflict between the will of man and the will of God. His death
on the cross was not an accident; it was an achievement. It was the
result of His faithfulness to the will of God in spite of the fact that
the will of man is counter to God's will.

A message from this passage could follow the theme, "Heralds
of the New Order," or "The New versus the Old." (1) In Christ
religion is not meritorious exercises, vv. 14–15; (2) in Christ religion
is not monitoring an old traditionalism, vv. 16–17a; (3) in Christ

religion is the miraculous inbreaking of a new order, v. 17b. In some degree this is "realized eschatology," for the new is happening. But, from the teachings of Jesus, we know there is more to come. It is evident that the old has run out, that it isn't worth patching in comparison to the new creation in Christ. This is the new age, and Jesus began His miracles by the miracle of wine (John 2)—an illustration of the wine of the new age fulfilling the prophecy of the time of our salvation (Isa. 12).

Two illustrations express this. The first, not putting a piece of unshrunk cloth into an old garment, is self-evident. He was not simply introducing a new code of laws, for laws alone, applied to the stresses of life, would tear persons apart. Nor is His ministry the pouring of new wine into old wineskins, for the vitality of the new life of love could not be contained or controlled by the old structures or institutionalism of their religious orders. Yet there is structure, for there are new wineskins for the new wine so that both are preserved. This is the challenge of new ideas. It includes a call to objectivity which frees one from prejudice and opens one's mind to the Spirit's guidance. This is a contrast "between the legal and the evangelic dispensations."[11] The new wine of Christian faith could not be poured into the old wineskins of Judaism. The Book of Acts demonstrates this fact, and the Letter to the Galatians interprets it from Paul's mission work.

THE AUTHORITY OVER LIFE

18 While He spoke these things to them, behold, a ruler came and worshiped Him, saying, "My daughter has just died, but come and lay Your hand on her and she will live."

19 And Jesus arose and followed him, and so did His disciples.

23 And when Jesus came into the ruler's house, and saw the flute players and the noisy crowd wailing,

24 He said to them, "Make room, for the girl is not dead but sleeping." And they laughed Him to scorn.

25 But when the crowd was put outside, He went in and took her by the hand, and the girl arose.

26 And the report of this went out into all that land.

Matt. 9:18–19, 23–26

The three consecutive stories in the group in which this is the first have the feeling of desperation in common: the ruler of the synagogue, the woman with a hemorrhage, and the blind men. In each instance the faith for healing is faith in Christ, not faith as a psychological influence that serves to induce healing. The two interlaced stories present Jesus as the Lord and Giver of life, the One who can restore and extend life, the One whose compassion reaches out to bless the suffering and afflicted. In answer to John the Baptist's question as to Jesus' messiahship, He said, "The blind receive their sight and the lame walk, the lepers are cleansed and the deaf hear, the dead are raised up and the poor have the gospel preached to them" (11:5). Such is the witness expressed in the accounts of Jesus' miracles presented here. His miracles were signs of the Kingdom.

An outline to develop the sections dealing with the raising of Jairus' daughter could be as follows: (1) the worship in the ruler's faith, v. 18; (2) the witness in the Master's faith, v. 19; and (3) the work that confirms faith, vv. 23–26.

Mark makes clear that Jairus was a ruler of the synagogue (5:21–43) as does Luke (8:40–56). Here we have an important witness to faith on the part of an Israelite which corresponds to the faith of the Gentile centurion told in an earlier story. In Matthew we have the distinctive feature that the ruler reported the death of the child immediately upon coming to Jesus, while in the other accounts she is in the *extremis*. This adds to our respect for the man's faith. In Jesus' ministry of restoring the young girl, there is a contrast between unbelief of those who *"laughed Him to scorn"* and the faith of Jairus. In Jesus' calling her to life, His fame is spread throughout the land.

We should not overlook the unique and positive act on the part of Jesus in response to the request by Jairus. Jesus arose immediately and followed him to minister to his daughter. There was no question on the part of Jesus that the Father had given him adequate authority to minister to this need.

THE AUTHORITY OVER HEMORRHAGING

20 And suddenly a woman who had a flow of blood for twelve years came behind Him and touched the hem of His garment;
21 for she said to herself, "If only I may touch His garment, I shall be made well."

22 But Jesus turned around, and when He saw her
He said, "Be of good cheer, daughter; your faith has
made you well." And the woman was made well from
that hour.

Matt. 9:20–22

The story of the woman with the *"flow of blood"* is reported by
each synoptic writer, described as an incident which happened while
Jesus was on the way to minister to Jairus' daughter. It is of interest
that, compared to Mark's lengthy account, Matthew told the story
with such brevity, but with such conciseness and clarity as to leave
out no significant aspect. The woman had suffered for twelve years,
and Luke, the doctor, added that she had spent all her living on
doctors! She came in the crowd as one person in need, resolved that
if she could only touch the hem of Jesus' garment she would be
healed. This act of faith was detected by Jesus (Luke adds that Jesus
perceived that virtue had left Him to heal) and He said to the woman,
"Be of good cheer, daughter; your faith has made you well." What gracious
words to one who, with an issue of blood, was considered unclean;
who had imposed herself as unclean into this setting, to then be
healed and graciously blessed by the Master!

The hymn writer caught the simple pathos of this scene: "She
only touched the hem of His garment, as to His side she stole; amid
the crowds that gathered around her, and straightway she was whole."
Points for our learning include (1) His goodness turns our problems
into occasions of hope, v. 20; (2) His greatness makes our needs seem
small, v. 21; (3) His graciousness makes our healing sure, v. 22.

In developing a message on physical healing we should be careful
to relate healing to the providence and will of God. That He can
heal is without question; that it is always His will to heal is another
question. We must seek to discern the will of God, that which will
be to His glory, as an authentic witness of His presence and purpose.
This witness often includes suffering with a spirit of trust in His
grace—often as important a witness to the character of the Kingdom
as healing. The ministry of healing is the church's privilege more
than her program. Willard Swartley says, "As Christians we are not
told to copy Jesus' miracles, but His sufferings and His self-giving
love (2 Pet. 2:21, 22)."[12] We may relate this to the healing of the
estrangement of our uncleanness, to the deliverance from our sinfulness and perversion, to release from our loneliness, as well as to
physical well-being.

THE AUTHORITY OVER BLINDNESS

27 And when Jesus departed from there, two blind men followed Him, crying out and saying, "Son of David, have mercy on us!"

28 And when He had come into the house, the blind men came to Him. And Jesus said to them, "Do you believe that I am able to do this?" They said to Him, "Yes, Lord."

29 Then He touched their eyes, saying, "According to your faith let it be to you."

30 And their eyes were opened. And Jesus sternly warned them, saying, "See that no one knows it."

31 But when they had departed, they spread the news about Him in all that country.

Matt. 9:27–31

This story is peculiar to Matthew and is told with his fondness for pairs. The men followed Him to the house, no doubt in Capernaum, and kept entreating Him, using the title *"Son of David."* In all three cases of healing the blind men in the Gospel of Matthew the title "Son of David" is used (15:22, 20:30). The title described Jesus in terms of the popular understanding of the Messiah. This account is the first occasion where Jesus is called Messiah. Inadequate though their understanding may have been, it was the highest designation in their minds and they respected Jesus as the anointed of God.

Jesus did not answer their shouts immediately. There were many blind people about, no doubt due to a lack of hygiene. With diseases carried by flies, and other insects, blindness was a common problem. Jesus tested their sincerity by waiting for their persistence and, even more so, by giving the response, *"Do you believe that I am able to do this?"* This question asked for confidence, not just intellectual assent. Upon their affirmation, Jesus said (Knox's translation), "Your faith shall not be disappointed." There was no word or act by which He commanded the healing. He let it happen as an evidence of the faith of the blind men. Upon their healing, Jesus "warned them" not to tell this around. No doubt He was already so pressed by the crowd wanting healing that it was difficult to share His message. But perhaps it expressed a concern, lest public recognition further arouse the malice of the Pharisees before His hour was come. But we read that when they departed *"they spread the news about Him in all that country."* The phrase *"news about him"* is an impressive word for our witness.

127

The healing of blindness appears in Scripture as a sign of God's sovereign power. We read in Isaiah, "I the Lord have called thee in righteousness, and will hold thine hand, and will keep thee, and give thee for a covenant of the people, for a light of the Gentiles; to open the blind eyes, to bring out the prisoners from the prison, and them that sit in darkness out of the prison house" (42:6–7, KJV). And again from Isaiah 61:1, the passage quoted by Jesus in the synagogue at Nazareth (Luke 4:18), we have the messianic expectation associated with deeds of mercy which include "recovery of sight to the blind."

An outline for this passage could well center on this messianic character of Jesus' mission of love: (1) Jesus' care has priority in the messianic claim, v. 27; (2) Jesus' conditions have precedence in the messianic healing, v. 28; (3) Jesus' concern is the uniqueness of the messianic identity, vv. 29–31. It is the Person who is important in God's expression of grace; the focus of faith is on Him. It is as Jesus encounters persons that He awakens faith from them.

THE AUTHORITY FOR EXORCISM

32 As they went out, behold, they brought to Him a man, mute and demon-possessed.

33 And when the demon was cast out, the mute spoke. And the multitudes marveled, saying, "It was never seen like this in Israel!"

34 But the Pharisees said, "He casts out demons by the ruler of the demons."

Matt. 9:32–34

The brevity of this account is not to minimize its significance. Barclay says that "there are few passages which show better than this passage does the impossibility of an attitude of neutrality towards Jesus Christ."[13] The crowds looked on Jesus with amazement as the anointed of God, while the Pharisees looked at Jesus with the accusation that He was in league with demonic forces, in opposition to their religious system. They were too prejudiced to see what the Spirit of God was doing in Jesus, and too proud to learn from Him.

This story is also peculiar to Matthew. The healing of the blind men took place in the house away from the crowd. In this story, as Jesus left the house, the mute demoniac was brought to Him and the miracle took place before the crowd. If these events happened in sequence as suggested, the "they" of verse 32 may well refer to the healed blind men, which would mean that the first memorable event of their new life was to witness a fellow sufferer made whole!

Again the messianic prophecies of Isaiah are being fulfilled in actions by Jesus, relating His ministry directly to salvation history (Isa. 29:18; 35:5). This makes the charge of the Pharisees even more self-condemnatory, for they did not understand their own Scriptures. Their charge was a repeated accusation and appears with more extended interchange in Matthew 12.

One could well develop a message from this passage on Jesus the Liberator, that: (1) messianic provision is one of grace, v. 32; (2) messianic power is one of liberation, v. 33a; (3) messianic presence is one initiating a decision, vv. 33b–34.

THE AUTHORITY FOR WHOLENESS

35 And Jesus went about all the cities and villages, teaching in their synagogues, preaching the gospel of the kingdom, and healing every sickness and every disease among the people.
36 But when He saw the multitudes, He was moved with compassion for them, because they were weary and scattered, like sheep having no shepherd.
37 Then He said to His disciples, "The harvest truly is plentiful, but the laborers are few.
38 "Therefore pray the Lord of the harvest that He will send out laborers into His harvest."

Matt. 9:35–38

This passage summarizes Jesus' ministry of compassion. It is a presentation of the compassionate Shepherd and a remarkably fitting transition to the next section of the Gospel. This section is introduced by a presentation of the threefold ministry of Jesus: teaching, preaching, and healing. Jesus, as a preacher, was a herald of God; His was the message of the Kingdom of God. The phrase *"gospel of the kingdom"* or good news of the kingdom, is a key for the understanding of the gospel message. The gospel of the kingdom is the good news of the rule of God amidst His people, now actualized in the Person and presence of Jesus Christ.

The implications of this message are that (1) the Kingdom happens wherever Jesus is ruling; (2) the Kingdom creates a dualism in society; and (3) the Kingdom calls us to decision in the world. As shown in the Sermon on the Mount, the message of the Kingdom is the word by which we can live by the rule and will of Christ. The reality of this Kingdom is not general "society organized according to the will of God" as set forth by the Social Gospel movement, but is the rule of Christ in His people amidst society. It is the people of God living by the will of God. Christ is calling forth the New Israel, and while the Kingdom is even yet to fully come, it keeps coming into our lives in the rule of God. The Social Gospel movement humanized the concept of the Kingdom, making it a sociological factor and missing the redemptive mission of the church. On the other hand, the dispensationalists have, in the large, postponed the application of Kingdom teaching for a future millennial period. But Jesus said, "Except a man be born of water and of the Spirit, he cannot enter into the Kingdom of God" now (John 3:5, kjv)! And Paul wrote, He has "translated us into the kingdom of his dear Son," now (Col. 1:13, kjv)! Again, "The kingdom of God is not meat and drink; but righteousness and peace and joy in the Holy Ghost" (Rom. 14:17, kjv). Paul actually described his ministry as preaching the gospel of the Kingdom of God (Acts 20:25; 28:31).

We have presented in verse 36 the compassion of the Shepherd, seeing the multitudes as sheep without a shepherd. This picture appears frequently in Old Testament passages. We should note Numbers 27:17, where Moses entreats God to lead Israel lest they be as sheep without a shepherd, and 1 Kings 22:17, where the prophet Micaiah saw Israel scattered as without a shepherd. From a negative or judgmental stance, the prophets spoke about false or evil shepherds who misled and misused God's people (Jer. 23 and Ezek. 34). Finally, in John 10 Jesus calls himself the Good Shepherd. Jesus was moved with compassion by the world's suffering and bewilderment, the latter being the weariness of people trying to find the peace of God through a maze of religious requirements.

The last picture Jesus uses in this section is that of the harvest. Sowing and reaping go on together. Jesus speaks of reaping the harvest of God's acts in salvation history. This is evident also in John 4:35–38 where, having referred to the fields white unto harvest, He tells the disciples that they are entering in upon other men's labors. The parallel passages (Luke 10:1–2 and Mark 6:34) emphasize the impor-

THE AUTHORITY FOR WHOLENESS

tance of this section, in that it appears in all four of the Gospels. The message to his disciples is clear: the harvest is great, the laborers are few. The admonition is to pray God to send out laborers into His harvest. The fact that it is God's harvest is the key which interprets the vision of need and the commission to follow. This is the transition to the next section, chapter 10, about sending out His emissaries.

One could teach from this passage with an emphasis on the harvest. Another approach would emphasize the Compassionate Shepherd as: (1) aware of human need, (2) aware of redemptive mission, and (3) aware of divine purpose.

NOTES

1.   Charles Erdman, *Commentaries on the New Testament Books: Matthew* (Philadelphia: Westminster, 1920), p. 64.

2.   Henry Alford, *The Greek New Testament*, vol. 1, *The Four Gospels* (Boston: Lee and Shepherd Pub., 1872), p. 76.

3.   Ibid., 1:79.

4.   Ralph Earle, *Matthew*, in *The Wesleyan Bible Commentary*, ed. Charles W. Carter, vol. 4 (Grand Rapids: Eerdmans, 1975), p. 44.

5.   Alford, *The Greek New Testament*, 1:82.

6.   Dietrich Bonhoeffer, *The Cost of Discipleship* (New York: Macmillan, 1960), p. 69.

7.   Beyond the Gospels the designation of Jesus as the "Son of man" is used in Acts 7:56, in Hebrews 2:6, and twice in the Revelation, 1:13 and 14:14. In the Old Testament it is used in the Psalms as equivalent to "man," in Ezekiel 2:1 as referring to the prophet, and in Daniel 7:13 with an apocalyptic meaning in relation to the Messiah. By using this term in addressing the scribe, Jesus is identifying Himself in the messianic role.

8.   Alford, *The Greek New Testament*, 1:84.

9.   Ibid., 1:80.

10.   At South Africa Christian Leadership Assembly, Pretoria, July, 1979.

11.   Alford, *The Greek New Testament*, 1:94.

12.   Willard Swartley, *Mark: The Way for All Nations* (Scottdale, PA: Herald Press, 1979), p. 101.

13.   Barclay, *The Gospel of Matthew*, 1:360.

CHAPTER FOUR

The Ministry of the King

Matthew 10:1—12:50

The King's ministry is the creation of a people of God. This section of Matthew which focuses on "mission" is the *second* of the *five presentations* of Jesus' teachings in Matthew. It actually begins with the preceding unit on the compassion of Christ (9:35–38), a transition passage to this section on ministry. The next three chapters are on the nature of Jesus' ministry, but His address on mission strategy, or principles of evangelism, comprises chapter 10 as "Teachings, Book Two."

Our premise for interpretation has been that Matthew's Gospel continues salvation history. It was written at a time when the gospel had spread to the known world, a time when it was an acknowledged fact that Gentiles shared in the church. This larger section presents the gospel as moving from the Jewish community to the world. Jesus' commission began with a directive to minister to "the lost sheep of the house of Israel" (10:6) and moved to their future witness before Gentiles (v. 18). It then moved beyond ethnic bounds (vv. 34–35) and beyond nationalism (11:23–30), beyond religious traditionalism (12:1–14), beyond sectarianism (12:21) and even beyond family groups (12:46–50).

Following a long tour of ministry teaching in the cities and villages, Jesus expanded His ministry through the selected disciples whom He had been instructing along the way. They were apprentices, for He had engaged them in fieldwork such as a twentieth-century seminary might outline. Jesus had presented His message of the Kingdom (Chaps. 5–7), then demonstrated the power and nature of His work as signs of the Kingdom (Chaps. 8–9). He was then ready to extend His ministry by appointing heralds of the Kingdom.

THE CALLING OF HIS MESSENGERS

1 And when He had called His twelve disciples
to Him, He gave them power over unclean spirits, to
cast them out, and to heal all kinds of sickness and
all kinds of disease.

2 Now the names of the twelve apostles are these:
first, Simon, who is called Peter, and Andrew his
brother; James the son of Zebedee, and John his
brother;

3 Philip and Bartholomew; Thomas and Matthew
the tax collector; James the son of Alphaeus, and
Lebbaeus, whose surname was Thaddaeus;

4 Simon the Canaanite, and Judas Iscariot, who also
betrayed Him.

Matt. 10:1-4

The prayer for God to send workers is followed immediately by
Jesus calling and sending the twelve. Prayer conditions us to the
will of God. As it prepares us to share with Him, God often uses
us to help answer our own prayers. Matthew says He called the
disciples *"to Him"* and, in Mark's account of Jesus' calling the twelve,
we read that "He ordained twelve, that they should be with him,
and that he might send them forth to preach" (Mark 3:14, KJV). Further,
He gave them power to perform the ministries of the Kingdom, extending His authority by placing these twelve under the authority
of the King.

Jesus created the twelve as a body of leaders, a symbol of the
reestablishment of God's covenant people. The similarity with the
creation of Israel as a nation under Moses led Paul Minear to say
that Jesus was deliberately creating the New Israel. This new people
of God was heir of what God had been doing in salvation history.
His authority as the Messiah is in the establishing of a new people
of God. Later called the church, "the body of Christ," it is the visible
expression of the Head of the church on earth.

This was a major step for Jesus, and He made His choices after a
night of prayer. These men would carry on His mission and extend
it into all the world. As we look at the persons, we see they are
ordinary men from the communities in which He ministered, and
they were a group with great variety of backgrounds and personalities.
Peter is named first and is often referred to as a leader in the twelve.

Next is his brother Andrew, then another set of brothers, James and John. Philip, the scholar, and Bartholomew come next, followed by Thomas, the man who wanted to be certain before acting. Matthew's designating him as the twin leads some scholars to suggest that he and Matthew were twin brothers. Matthew names himself the tax collector, a role which would have marked him a traitor to the Jewish community. He is the son of Alphaeus (Mark 2:14) and therefore brother to James the less. The same group included Simon the Canaanite whom Luke calls the Zealot, the nationalist. These men worked together as disciples! The others include James the son of Alphaeus, Thaddaeus, and finally Judas Iscariot. The designation "Iscariot" probably meant "from Kerioth," making him the only one of the twelve who was not from Galilee. Such a variety could not have worked together apart from their common commitment to Jesus. People of radical differences can discover how to love each other in the presence of Jesus.

THE COMMISSION OF HIS MESSENGERS

5 These twelve Jesus sent out and commanded them, saying: "Do not go into the way of the Gentiles, and do not enter a city of the Samaritans.

6 "But go rather to the lost sheep of the house of Israel.

7 "And as you go, preach, saying, 'The kingdom of heaven is at hand.'

8 "Heal the sick, cleanse the lepers, raise the dead, cast out demons. Freely you have received, freely give.

9 "Provide neither gold nor silver nor copper in your moneybelts,

10 "nor bag for your journey, nor two tunics, nor sandals, nor staffs; for a worker is worthy of his food.

11 "And whatever city or town you enter, inquire who in it is worthy, and stay there till you go out.

12 "And when you go into a household, greet it.

13 "And if the household is worthy, let your peace come upon it. But if it is not worthy, let your peace return to you.

14 "And whoever will not receive you nor hear your words, when you depart from that house or city, shake off the dust from your feet.

15 "Assuredly, I say to you, it will be more tolerable
for the land of Sodom and Gomorrah in the day of
judgment than for that city!

Matt. 10:5–15

This passage, with parallels in Mark and Luke, presents Jesus' strategy for evangelism: (1) He knew how to motivate and work people; (2) He had a plan that sent out teams of two members each; (3) He designed a prewitness before He would arrive in a village; (4) He kept the mission singular in focus; and (5) He enabled his disciples to make faith a possibility for people.

The commission was to go to the Jewish communities, not to the Gentile areas, for the message of the Messiah was first for the Jew. There would not be enough time for Jesus to cover all of the villages in Palestine with His ministry. But rather than to see this as discrimination against Gentiles, it may be read as a confrontation which challenged Jewish pride and called them to repentance. The message of the disciples was to be a clear extension of the Master's message: *"The Kingdom of heaven is at hand."* This announcement was to accompany all of their deeds, as emphasized by the words, *"as you go, preach."* As the role of the herald, preaching is mentioned here for the first time. The commission emphasizes that preaching needs the deed to confirm it and the deed needs preaching to explain it.

At the risk of seeming more sensational, it may be said that Jesus asked them (1) to do the impossible, v. 8; (2) to dare the impractical, vv. 9–10; and (3) to deliver the impartial, vv. 11–15.

The miracles mentioned in verse 8 are signs that the messianic age had dawned as well as evidence of the character of their mission. The limited resources, mandated in verses 9–10, recognize that poverty provides freedom to accept help, that having no purse or money is a clear symbol of no benefit from their ministry. The absence of an extra coat or sandals illustrated their direct relationship to the people they were serving. There are implications here for modern mission. If we mean to serve others, we must serve others as they need to be served and not as we predetermine to serve them, for the latter is not service but dominance. The important thing in evangelism is making faith in Christ an option—making faith a possibility for people. In doing so we respect their freedom while making them aware of their responsibility. The blessing of grace depends upon the receptivity of the hearer (vv. 12–15), and the messenger is to come as an agent of peace. The peace mentioned in verse 13 is the customary Eastern greeting of peace, *Shalom.* Stier said, "The spirit of these commands binds Christian ministers to all accustomed courtesies of manner in the countries and ages in which their mission may lie."[1]

THE ENCOURAGEMENT OF HIS MESSENGERS

16 "Behold, I send you out as sheep in the midst of wolves. Therefore be wise as serpents and harmless as doves.

17 "But beware of men, for they will deliver you up to councils and scourge you in their synagogues.

18 "And you will be brought before governors and kings for My sake, as a testimony to them and to the Gentiles.

19 "But when they deliver you up, do not worry about how or what you will speak. But it will be given to you in that hour what you will speak;

20 "for it is not you who speak, but the Spirit of your Father who speaks in you.

21 "And brother will deliver up brother to death, and a father his child; and children will rise up against parents and cause them to be put to death.

22 "And you will be hated by all for My name's sake. But he who endures to the end will be saved.

23 "But when they persecute you in this city, flee to another. For assuredly, I say to you, you shall not have gone through the cities of Israel before the Son of Man comes.

24 "A disciple is not above his teacher, nor a servant above his master.

25 "It is enough for a disciple that he be like his teacher, and a servant like his master. If they have called the master of the house Beelzebub, how much more will they call those of his household!

26 "Therefore do not fear them. For there is nothing covered that will not be revealed, and hidden that will not be known.

Matt. 10:16–26

Jesus was a realist and, in sending out His apostles, He told them what to expect. A study of Mark 13 and Luke 10 and 12 may suggest that not all of this teaching was given at a single time. However, it could have been, as Alford asserts, and then repeated on other occasions such as the sending out of the seventy (Luke 10).[2] Just as Jesus at times dropped in words of His coming death before it was understood by the disciples, so here He may have let His mind run on to their future mission to the larger world and the persecution foretold in verses 18 and following.

Albert Schweitzer based his hypothesis on the words of Jesus in verse 23, holding that Jesus expected the Kingdom of God to arrive in society before the disciples returned from their mission to the cities in the surrounding area, thus experiencing His first disappointment. He then saw the crucifixion as Jesus' last disappointment. In my opinion, the reference in verse 23 is hardly speaking to the *Parousia* or Second Coming of Christ, but likely to His coming to those cities in an open declaration of the messianic mission. However, we do not read of the disciples having been persecuted on this particular mission, but much later. Tasker says it "is best understood with reference to the coming of the Son of Man with triumph immediately after His resurrection."[3]

In comment on Schweitzer's *Quest for the Historical Jesus*, John Howard Yoder says the concept of a set date for a future coming which failed to arrive and became a disappointment "is foreign to the Biblical mind. Thus the concept that the specific character of Jesus' ethic was conditioned upon the imminence for Him of a purely future end of human history is likewise unthinkable."[4] Yoder supports this by showing that "the movement in the development of New Testament literature was from the resurrection message to the Lordship proclamation which had cosmic significance, to the body of material on the work and words of Jesus; not away from filling out the history of Jesus' humanity."[5] It was not an abstract Christ but a real Jesus, the God-Man who commissioned and sent out His disciples as apostles or itinerant evangelists.

The apostles, or itinerant evangelists, were sent out as sheep amidst wolves and a sheep cannot defend itself; all it can do is bleat to be heard. Consequently they needed to be wise as serpents, that is, prudent, and harmless as doves, that is, sincere. The next verses outline persecution at various levels as a normal part of the life of the disciple. Solidarity with Jesus means suffering from those who are against Jesus.

The reference to local "councils" of the Sanhedrin is clear; "governors" meant Roman provincial governors, and "kings" no doubt mean

Herodian princes who were often given this title (vv. 17–18). Jesus makes them aware of both Jewish and Roman opposition.

In verse 20 Jesus injects a unique word about the Holy Spirit. The Spirit will be with the disciples to guide them in the declaration of faith in times of persecution. The intensity of persecution is stressed, for families will be divided and the closest family ties will be broken over loyalty to Jesus. Note that persecution is spoken of in verse 18 as *"for My sake,"* in verse 22 as *"for My name's sake,"* and in verse 25, by implication, it is for the Master's sake. Jesus concludes this section with a pun on Beelzebub as head of the demonic family, affirming that He is Himself the head of His disciples. This is a deliberate word speaking to the continued criticism by the Pharisees, who were saying that Jesus was working miracles by demonic power (John 8:48).

There is a remarkable nugget in verses 24–25a where Jesus shows the relation between disciple and master, between scholar and teacher. A disciple learns from and identifies with his teacher. The servant is not over his master. While the primary meaning is that the disciples should not expect a better lot than their Master, the relation of student to teacher is a similar inference. Jesus calls disciples to continue to learn from Him, to continue to follow Him, to continue to serve Him. The phrase could well be translated, *"It is enough for the scholar that he should be as his teacher."* The teacher is a model of the truth that is being shared. Having served in college administration for fifteen years, I found that this became a very important principle of Christian education. Teachers are not simply passing on to others content in the field of knowledge, but they should model what they teach, demonstrating how to integrate faith with life and learning, and modeling the spirit and character the student is to achieve. And students achieve maturity of education when the wholeness of their personal lives reflect this character.

THE FREEDOM OF HIS MESSENGERS

27 "What I tell you in the darkness, speak in the
light; and what you hear in the ear, preach on the
housetops.
28 "And do not fear those who kill the body but
cannot kill the soul. But rather fear Him who is able
to destroy both soul and body in hell.

29 "Are not two sparrows sold for a copper coin?
And not one of them falls to the ground apart from
your Father's will.
30 "But the very hairs of your head are all
numbered.
31 "Do not fear therefore; you are of more value
than many sparrows.

Matt. 10:27–31

Freedom is known in the fear or reverence of God. One is not free simply because a particular action is not forbidden, but one is free insofar as he is liberated to perform that action. One is not free to play a violin well unless he has been taught how to play the violin. So, one is not free to share the things of God unless instructed in them. And in this section Jesus emphasizes the freedom of His disciples in preaching the good news, for there is to be nothing secretive or hidden about the announcement of the Kingdom.

There is a question in verse 28 as to who it is that we are to fear. On the one hand we are told not to fear those who can kill only the body but not the soul; that is to say, don't fear the persecutor and the harm he can do to the body. But the next phrase says we are to fear *"Him who is able to destroy both soul and body in hell"*! A. B. Bruce notes that most commentators say that this refers to God, but he takes issue with it, holding that this refers to the tempter who works in the persecution to "buy one off" or capture one. W. C. Allen says this means to "fear the wrath of God against unfaithfulness to Him, for He can destroy both soul and body in Gehenna." The contrast between the two sentences in this verse emphasizes the second of these interpretations. As in Luke 12:3–7, our Heavenly Father is the correct object of our fear, for throughout Scripture God alone is sovereign over life and death, temporal and eternal. The next verse answers this issue with the emphasis on the fear, whereby we reverence God (note further James 4:12).

Jesus' basic argument for freedom from fear is the goodness and providence of God. Two sparrows are sold for a copper coin, an *assarion*, worth about one cent in our money, yet the heavenly Father takes note of them to the extent of providential care. In answer to the question of His taking care of us, Jesus says that even the hairs of our heads are numbered. Providence is God's interest and care over the smaller details of our lives. It is in direct contrast to the deistic view which holds that God created the world and set it on its course and we should not think that He pays attention to each of us individually! Jesus said that He does care for each, that we, being so much more valuable than sparrows, should rest in this faith, free from fear.

THE CONFESSION OF THE MASTER

32 "Therefore whoever confesses Me before men, him I will also confess before My Father who is in heaven.

33 "But whoever denies Me before men, him I will also deny before My Father who is in heaven.

34 "Do not think that I have come to bring peace on earth. I did not come to bring peace but a sword.

35 "For I have come to *set a man against his father, a daughter against her mother, and a daughter-in-law against her mother-in-law.'*

36 "And *'a man's foes will be those of his own household.'*

37 "He who loves father or mother more than Me is not worthy of Me. And he who loves son or daughter more than Me is not worthy of Me.

38 "And he who does not take his cross and follow after Me is not worthy of Me.

39 "He who finds his life will lose it, and he who loses his life for My sake will find it.

Matt. 10:32–39

Jesus Christ is the most divisive Person in the world. When we know about Him we are either for Him or against Him. While He sent His disciples on a mission with which they were to use the Semitic greeting *Shalom*, "peace to you," Jesus told them that He came not with peace for the earth but with a sword. This reference is to be understood in context as a reference to division or persecution. While the Messiah had been announced as the Prince of Peace in Isaiah's prophecy (9:6), a new element is introduced with the Messiah as an agent of division. It should be understood that when God confronts us in the person of Christ it is not by a law or philosophy from which we can select parts which we accept and reject others. When confronted with a Person we must either accept or reject Him.

When we are confronted by Christ, life's basic issues are at stake. We are "playing for keeps." People shove God out of their lives because they have other gods, because He interferes with what they want, yet ultimately it is because the way of Christ is too demanding. He divides between religion and relationship, transforming the former by the latter; between the secular and the sacred, sanctifying the former by the latter; and between the temporal and the eternal, enlarging the former by the latter. We are called to live for two worlds, for the eternal overlaps the world of time. If we should gain this world alone we would have only this world!

And as a suggestion for an approach to this text, Christ is the great divide between the Kingdom of heaven and the kingdoms of the world (32–34), between the church and society (35–37), and between the saved and the unsaved (38–39). When the *Titanic* sank in 1912, in the office of the Cunard Line in New York City there was a board listing names of passengers in only two columns, and they were headed "saved" and "lost."

The central point in the first two verses of this section is our relation to Jesus (32–33). The open confession of Christ will be honored by His act of vouching for us to the heavenly Father; while an open denial will receive a consequent denial before the heavenly Father. The centrality of Christ in the life of the disciple becomes a divisive element in human relations, even in the intimate relations of family life.

The conclusion of this section presents the claims of discipleship. The focus is on one's relation to Jesus Himself: (1) to be worthy of Christ we are to put Him first in all family relations (v. 37); (2) to be worthy of Christ we are to take up His cross and identify with Him, to accept the scandal of identification with Him (v. 38); (3) to be worthy of Christ we are to choose Him and His life rather than selfishly preserving our own way of life (v. 39). The paradox is that finding the selfish satisfaction of life means to lose life and miss its larger fulfillment, but losing one's own interests for the sake of Christ is to find life.

There are numerous ways in which one can develop the concepts of the gospel, of the Christ, and of decision. There is division because of Him, decision because of Him, and declaration because of Him. Christ divides between us and (1) loyalty to the world, vv. 32–33; (2) preferences of family relations, vv. 34–37; and (3) pursuit of status in a self-centered occupation.

THE REWARD OF SERVING CHRIST

40 "He who receives you receives Me, and he who
receives Me receives Him who sent Me.

41 "He who receives a prophet in the name of a
prophet will receive a prophet's reward. And he who
receives a righteous man in the name of a righteous
man will receive a righteous man's reward.

42 "And whoever gives one of these little ones only
a cup of cold water in the name of a disciple, assuredly,
I say to you, he will by no means lose his reward."

Matt. 10:40–42

A striking aspect of this passage is Jesus' identification with His
own. One is reminded of Jesus' words to Saul on the Damascus Road,
"Saul, Saul, why persecutest thou me?" (Acts 9:4 KJV). At the close
of Matthew's Gospel the risen Christ sends out the disciples with
the words, "And, lo, *I am with you alway,* even unto the end of the
world" (28:20, KJV). In this section Jesus states that the person receiving
the messenger, the one providing hospitality, is, in fact, doing a service
for Christ; he is in effect receiving Him. In the days of the sixteenth-
century Reformation when there was a price on the head of Menno
Simons, a "Free-Church" leader, persons who dared to offer hospitality were arrested and in at least one case executed. Of such, Jesus
says, the reward is commensurate with the service of the messenger.
We are a team, and the supporting players are participants with the
lead players. The church is a symphony rather than a series of solo
recitals. We do together what no one person can do alone.

Giving a cup of cold water in the name of a disciple means that
the simplest deed in discipleship of Christ will receive the Lord's
recognition. And this is applicable in many areas of life, for there
is a difference between giving a cup of cold water and giving that
cup of cold water in the name of discipleship to Christ, or in the
name of Christ. There is a difference between teaching a class and
doing so in the name of Christ; between filling an office and doing
so in the name of Christ; between working at a job and doing so
in the name of Christ. In concluding this section we should note
that life in the church is understood in this passage as discipleship
(v. 42).

This section stresses the identifications of Jesus for effective mission:
(1) Jesus identifies with the Father, v. 40; (2) Jesus identifies with

His disciples, v. 42; and (3) Jesus identifies the reward of service, v. 42. This section, verses 24–42, is Jesus' teaching in preparation for persecution. We are (1) to fear God more than men, vv. 26–31; (2) to confess Christ openly before men, vv. 32–33; (3) to accept the separation of discipleship, vv. 34–39; and (4) to serve compassionately in the name of Christ, vv. 40–42. The community of disciples is given authority from Jesus.

THE MESSIAH'S ANSWER FOR JOHN THE BAPTIST

1 And it came to pass, when Jesus finished commanding His twelve disciples, that He departed from there to teach and to preach in their cities.

2 Now when John had heard in prison about the works of Christ, he sent two of his disciples

3 and said to Him, "Are You the Coming One, or do we look for another?"

4 Jesus answered and said to them, "Go and tell John the things you hear and see:

5 "The blind receive their sight and the lame walk, the lepers are cleansed and the deaf hear, the dead are raised up and the poor have the gospel preached to them.

6 "And blessed is he who is not offended because of Me."

7 And as they departed, Jesus began to say to the multitudes concerning John: "What did you go out into the wilderness to see? A reed shaken by the wind?

8 "But what did you go out to see? A man clothed in soft garments? Indeed, those who wear soft clothing are in kings' houses.

9 "But what did you go out to see? A prophet? Yes, I say to you, and more than a prophet.

10 "For this is he of whom it is written:
'Behold, I send My messenger before Your face,
Who will prepare Your way before You.'

11 "Assuredly, I say to you, among those born of women there has not risen one greater than John the Baptist; but he who is least in the kingdom of heaven is greater than he.

12 "And from the days of John the Baptist until

143

now the kingdom of heaven suffers violence, and the violent take it by force.

13 "For all the prophets and the law prophesied until John.

14 "And if you are willing to receive it, he is Elijah who is to come.

15 "He who has ears to hear, let him hear!

16 "But to what shall I liken this generation? It is like children sitting in the marketplaces and calling to their companions,

17 "and saying:

'We played the flute for you,
And you did not dance;
We mourned to you,
And you did not lament.'

18 "For John came neither eating nor drinking, and they say, 'He has a demon.'

19 "The Son of Man came eating and drinking, and they say, 'Look, a gluttonous man and a winebibber, a friend of tax collectors and sinners!' But wisdom is justified by her children."

Matt. 11:1–19

The transition in the opening statement of this section which moves from Jesus' commissioning of the twelve to His own tour of ministry through Galilee is a continuation of the thrust of the entire section (10:1–12:50). The passage presents the messianic claims of Jesus. According to Luke, John's disciples came with his question in the context of the miracle at Nain where Jesus raised the widow's son. Consequently, Jesus' fame went throughout all Judea and the surrounding region (Luke 7:18–35).

John, imprisoned in the fortress of Machaerus by the Dead Sea, having been arrested by Herod the tetrarch of Galilee, was forced to draw his conclusions from fragments of information. He sent several of his disciples to Jesus to ask, "Is it thy coming that was foretold, or are we to wait for someone else?" (Knox). Matthew has this happening to set the stage for Christ's interactions with the Pharisees which follow in this section.

While John was asking for "proof" of Jesus' messiahship, Jesus, instead of offering proof, gave him evidence. The walk of faith most often means to accept evidence in the place of proof. God is His own proof and faith will not stop short of coming to God Himself.

The evidence which Jesus gave was that the prophet's words were being fulfilled (Isa. 35:5, 61:1), that the messianic age had dawned with the Messiah's activities. Jesus' statement focused His authority to reinterpret the messianic expectation, saying, *"Blessed is he who is not offended because of Me."* We can develop from this section some basic observations on the grace of God in Christ: (1) grace is at work in miraculous changes; (2) grace is being announced; and (3) grace is its own evidence, vv. 4-6.

The end of the old age has arrived, the new age is dawning. The *eschaton,* announced by the prophets, is not about to dawn; it has dawned (Isa. 34; 61:5-7). The new age is being manifested by word and deed. Yet miracles evoke both faith and doubt, for faith is personal response to evidence. In these verses (2-6) we see (1) John's desire for certainty about the Messiah. The doubt may not have been about our Lord's mission but about His way of manifesting the mission. What kind of Messiah is He since He has not toppled the powers of the political and religious orders? The idea of the Suffering Servant was not primary in John's perception. But it may be that John's intent in his question was to press Jesus to be more open about His messiahship. We see (2) Jesus' description of what is happening, for the Spirit's work in community incorporates Isaiah 35:6-7. Jesus is emphasizing a different aspect of messiahship than that which was the popular concept. And we see (3) Jesus' declaration of confidence in His self-understanding, for ultimately miracles are not the important point but rather the Person of the Christ.

Jesus pays a remarkable tribute to John, saying that He was *"more than a prophet"* (vv. 7-11). While God's prophets in history were great, John was the greatest. While they predicted the messianic age, John stood at the threshold of the new age! He was more than a prophet in that he lived at the dawn of the crisis period of history. Of this, C. G. Montefiore, himself a Jew and not a Christian, said, "Christianity does mark a new era in religious history and in human civilization. What the world owes to Jesus and to Paul is immense; things can never be, and men can never think, the same as things were, and as men thought, before these two great men lived."[6] The inbreak of the Kingdom of Christ, which John only saw at its dawning, but which went beyond John, caused Jesus to say that the *"least in the kingdom of heaven is greater than he."* This is because John did not experience the full work of Christ, the meaning of His death on the cross, His resurrection and His ascension (see Luke 7:34-35; 16:16; Mark

9:11–13). We should note especially (1) the tradition of the prophet, vv. 7–9; (2) the testimony of John's prophetic role, v. 10; and (3) the transition to new Kingdom realities, v. 11.

The last part of this section (vv. 12–19) gives us the new interpretation of the messianic age. *First,* the focus of tension is over the Kingdom of heaven (v. 12). Jesus may have meant violent men oppose it; exposing the negativism of the scribes and Pharisees toward the Kingdom. However, this is not an easy verse to interpret and some commentators see this as a declaration that the Kingdom had to be introduced by radical acts of exorcism and healing as a part of its inbreaking rather than as a loving message of peace and mercy. But Luke's expression that "everyone storms his way into the Kingdom," may clarify what Jesus actually meant, that the Kingdom was being entered by desperate persons. Persons with intense interest and deep need pressed their way into the Kingdom. *Second,* the fulfillment of prophecy is not readily understood (vv. 13–15). The common expectation that the messianic age would be announced by a return of Elijah was interpreted by Jesus to mean "in the spirit of Elijah," and the fulfillment of Malachi 4:5 was introduced in John. *Third,* the formula of Jesus' ministry was disregarded by his people (vv. 16–19). He said the people were acting like domineering children who blame their companions for being spoilsports.

The statement by Jesus, made in irony, says of the people who were so "wise" in their criticism, *"Wisdom is justified by her children."* The scene is of children playing in the street, crying "spoilsports, spoilsports." "We wanted to play at weddings," shouted the boys, for the round dance at weddings is done by men; "We wanted to play at funerals," shouted the girls, for the mourner's dirge is done by women. The use of the word *kathamenois* places the children in roles of passive spectators; those playing the flute left to their playmates the more strenuous exercise, and they did not comply. Jesus said that God sent His messengers, but all the people did was to criticize. They said that the Baptist was a madman because he fasted when they wanted to make merry. They said that Jesus should be separate when He ate with sinners. All that these people wanted to do was to play childish games while missing the Kingdom!

A biographical message on John should include the following: (1) John had a proper understanding of himself, John 1:19–23. (2) John had a clear sense of mission, in John 3:30 he said of Jesus, "He must increase, but I must decrease." (3) John had a spiritual certainty that radiated, John 5:31–33; as William James said, "Lives based on having are less free than lives based on doing or on being." (4) John had a reputation for righteousness, Mark 6:20, for he was heard and feared by Herod. (5) John was an effective witness to the truth, John 10:41, for the people said, "All the things that John spoke about this Man were true." It was said by John Wesley, "Get on fire and they'll come and watch you burn."

THE MESSIANIC JUDGMENT OF THE CITIES

20 Then He began to upbraid the cities in which most of His mighty works had been done, because they did not repent:

21 "Woe to you, Chorazin! Woe to you, Bethsaida! For if the mighty works which were done in you had been done in Tyre and Sidon, they would have repented long ago in sackcloth and ashes.

22 "But I say to you, it will be more tolerable for Tyre and Sidon in the day of judgment than for you.

23 "And you, Capernaum, who are exalted to heaven, will be brought down to Hades; for if the mighty works which were done in you had been done in Sodom, it would have remained until this day.

24 "But I say to you that it will be more tolerable for the land of Sodom in the day of judgment than for you."

Matt. 11:20–24

The judgments of Jesus are expressed as pity. The word translated "woe" could well be translated "alas," a word of sorrow and pity more than of anger. The passage is a sharp warning over the unbelief of Chorazin, Bethsaida, and Capernaum. The comparative symbols suggest that God's judgments are conditioned by the amount of opportunity to understand the will of God which a given people may have experienced. The warning is with three perceptions: (1) responsibility, v. 20, as seen in the call for their repentance; (2) accountability, vv. 21–22, as they had been given more in the understanding of God than the rich merchant cities who had been so profligate and were chastised by Nebuchadnezzar and again by Alexander. And (3) opportunity, vv. 23–24, especially since it was in Jesus' hometown;

the people were proud of Him but refused to live by His teachings. Capernaum was exalted, like Babylon, in pride comparative to Lucifer (Isa. 14:13–15). Similar comparisons with Sodom are found in Old Testament passages (Deut. 32:32; Isa. 1:10; Ezek. 16:46–57).

We know nothing from the Gospels of Chorazin, an hour's journey north of Capernaum, and little of Bethsaida on the north coast by the west bank of the entry of the waters from Mt. Hermon that form the Jordan. Yet the passage indicates that Jesus had shared a significant ministry among the people of these cities. There is an account of the blind man who was healed at Bethsaida (Mark 8:22–26) with reference to Peter, Andrew, James, John, and Philip being from Bethsaida! The limited detail of ministry in this city reminds us of the words at the close of the Gospel of John, which say that so many things happened in His life and ministry that John didn't see the world as having enough space to contain all the books that could be written about Him. (John 21:25). The Gospel writers were in no way attempting to write exhaustive biographies of the life of Jesus, but were selecting the teachings and events that would convey a valid and adequate understanding of Jesus as the Son of God and Savior of the world. These selections, by the inspiration of the Spirit, adequately present the gospel, the kerygma.

THE MESSIANIC HERALD OF SALVATION

25 At that time Jesus answered and said, "I thank You, O Father, Lord of heaven and earth, because You have hidden these things from the wise and prudent and have revealed them to babes.

26 "Even so, Father, for so it seemed good in Your sight.

27 "All things have been delivered to Me by My Father, and no one knows the Son but the Father. Nor does anyone know the Father but the Son, and he to whom the Son wills to reveal Him.

28 "Come to me, all you who labor and are heavy laden, and I will give you rest.

29 "Take My yoke upon you and learn from Me, for I am gentle and lowly in heart, and you will find rest for your souls.

30 "For My yoke is easy and My burden is light."

Matt. 11:25–30

This is one of the rare occasions in the Gospels that gives us one of Jesus' prayers. Tasker says, "Here recorded is one of the most precious pieces of spiritual autobiography to be found in the Synoptic Gospels. It shows that the dominant characteristic of His Incarnate life was obedience to His Father's will."[7] In contrast to the unbelief which He judged in the preceding section, Jesus now affirms the nature of His messiahship and of His relationship to the Father. In verse 25 the word translated "thank" is the same word which is translated "confess," as is used of people confessing their sins. It means to "speak the same thing out of," a word which means that Jesus was in "full agreement with the Father" (see Luke 10:21-22).

There are basically three sayings in this passage dealing with (1) Jesus' reverence for God, vv. 25-26; (2) Jesus' relationship to God, v. 27; and (3) Jesus' rest in the will of God, vv. 28-30. Jesus interpreted His messianic role by His unique relation to the Father as God's Son. This is Jesus' first public mention of God as His Father, the reference in 10:32 having been made privately to His disciples. It is also one of the most striking claims to His Sonship found in this Gospel. On an occasion when I spoke in a high school assembly, I was asked by a young man, "Why all of this emphasis on confessing Christ? Aren't there other ways to get to God?" In response I asked of him, "And when you get to God whom do you expect to see?" And to his limited response I answered, "You will be meeting Jesus Himself!"

Also, in Matthew's account there is a significant identification of Jesus with Wisdom, as found in passages like Proverbs 8 where Wisdom speaks in the first person, or as the Logos, the Truth of God personified in Jesus, John 1:1-3. The heart of the passage is the unique gem of verse 27, asserting the disclosure of God in the Son and the Son's relationship with the Father. This should be compared with the great Christological passage of Philippians 2:5-11, Paul's expression of the remarkable nature of the Incarnation.

Three aspects of the passage may be further developed thematically. First, Jesus' prayer is a word of praise to God that He has shared the mysteries of knowledge about Himself and His grace in a manner which opens them to the unlearned. This is literally to the "immature," a contrast between His disciples and the learned people who were stumbling at His ministry. Second, God's pleasure is to reveal Himself in His Son, and what is promised to "the poor in spirit" in the Sermon on the Mount is here fulfilled as fact. Knowledge is not primarily an intellectual process (Amos 3:2; Gal. 4:9; 1 Cor. 8:2–3), for we only know God as He knows us. The Old Testament looks forward to the knowledge of God in the *eschaton* (Isa. 11:9; 52:6) as God reveals His own righteousness (Isa. 52:10; 56:1; Rom. 1:16–17). Jesus believed that, when the Baptist questioned and the people of His hometown doubted, only the Father truly knew His identity. And third, Jesus' rest is a yoke of wisdom that unites persons with Himself. He offers rest, for He is not only the bearer of the wisdom of God, He *is* that Wisdom. Such rest, as interpreted in Hebrews 4:1–11, is the singleness of relationship with Christ, the rest of knowing His provision as a completed salvation. Discipleship is thereby kept from being a legalistic striving and is instead a joyous fellowship.

There is a legend that Jesus, in the carpenter shop in Galilee, made the best yokes in all of Galilee. The yoke was tailor-made to fit each ox. Above the door may have been a sign which read, "My yokes fit well." And now, according to this legend, Jesus could have been illustrating from the carpenter's shop at Nazareth to say, "My yoke fits well." In this passage Jesus is saying, "Yoke yourself with me, for my task for you is shared and made easy and the burden is light." Handel incorporated this in the immortalized *Messiah* in a great chorus of praise, "His yoke is easy, His burden is light." This is the joyous word of salvation in contrast to a legalism that obscured the mercy of God.

THE MESSIAH AS LORD OF THE SABBATH

1 At that time Jesus went through the grainfields on the Sabbath. And His disciples were hungry, and began to pluck heads of grain and to eat.

2 But when the Pharisees saw it, they said to Him, "Look, Your disciples are doing what is not lawful to do on the Sabbath!"

3 But He said to them, "Have you not read what David did when he was hungry, he and those who were with him:

4 "how he entered the house of God and ate the showbread which was not lawful for him to eat, nor for those who were with him, but only for the priests?

5 "Or have you not read in the law that on the

Sabbath the priests in the temple profane the Sabbath, and are blameless?

6 "But I say to you that in this place there is One greater than the temple.

7 "But if you had known what this means, *'I desire mercy and not sacrifice,'* you would not have condemned the guiltless.

8 "For the Son of Man is Lord even of the Sabbath."

Matt. 12:1–8

The deepest aspects of a person's character are often revealed under stress. In chapter 12 a series of happenings placed Jesus in situations of stress, revealing His integrity, convictions, and personal discipline. When good confronts evil, the result is an increase of defensiveness which actually increases the expression of evil to its own ruin by extreme exposure. The strategy of the good is to "overcome evil with good," but at times this victory may mean the increased expression of evil until its own inadequacy is exposed. Evil is not so much a power against the good as it is a perversion of the good, until the good has been altered to serve wrong ends.

Jesus' conflict with His opponents maintained the integrity of His mission but also exposed the inadequacy of their position in relation to the purposes of God. One cause of clash between Jesus and the Pharisees was their legalism, the keeping of laws as ends in themselves. Value was sought in the legalistic act rather than in the sense of fidelity to God. Jesus reminded them of the meaning of the prophetic word which they failed to understand: "For I desired mercy, and not sacrifice; and the knowledge of God more than burnt-offerings" (Hos. 6:6, KJV).

The interchange regarding the Sabbath was precipitated by the disciples' acts of plucking and eating some heads of grain as they walked through the fields. Matthew adds the note that the disciples were hungry. Walking along the path through the fields, they rubbed the grain out in their hands and ate. But the Jewish community had extensive laws forbidding work on the Sabbath and this act violated their laws. These laws included forbidding a man to spit on the ground on the Sabbath lest he rub it with his sandal and role up a ball of dirt, which would be plowing. Another forbade a woman to look in the mirror on the Sabbath lest she see a hair on her face and be tempted to pull it!

In answer to the Pharisees' charge that the disciples had violated the Sabbath rules, Jesus lifted two illustrations from their religious history and rites. First is the illustration from David's experience: fleeing from Saul, and being hungry, he entered the tabernacle and ate "the bread of Presence," which was only to be eaten by the priests. Following this reference to David, the highest person in their national history, He turned to the temple, the highest level of sanctity in their religious life. He pointed to the temple priests who were breaking the code by their work, yet who were blameless.

Having answered with illustrations impossible for the Pharisees to refute, Jesus then made two major affirmations about Himself. In Mark's account Jesus emphasized God's purpose in mercy, "The Sabbath was made for man, and not man for the Sabbath" (Mark 2:27). But Matthew shows Jesus as Lord of the Sabbath. Jesus attacked the two highest religious rites: first, He attacked temple dominance in their worship, of which Jesus says, *'I say to you that in this place there is One greater than the temple.'* Second, he attacked legalistic Sabbath observance with the words, *"For the Son of Man is Lord even of the Sabbath."* As greater than the Temple and as Lord of the Sabbath, Jesus is the ultimate authority regarding service and worship in the will of God. This offers Christological principles for our theological reflection.

The principles of Jesus stand in remarkable contrast to the picayunish way in which the Pharisees interpreted the acts of the disciples; they were plucking the grain—reaping; they were rubbing out the heads in their hands—threshing; and they were blowing the chaff from the kernels—winnowing! But Jesus gave a New Interpretation of Law, stressing the God-intended values of Sabbath renewal.

An outline for this section could be (1) conflict about the Sabbath, vv. 1–2; (2) considerations of the Sabbath, vv. 3–6; and (3) Christ the Lord of the Sabbath, vv. 7–8. The conclusion places mercy above ritual, and love above law. The larger passage from verse 1 through verse 14 expresses the Messiah as Liberator: (1) the denunciation, vv. 1–2; (2) the declaration, v. 8; and (3) the demonstration, vv. 9–14. Jesus showed us that human need takes precedence over rites, codes, or cultural taboos.

THE MESSIAH'S ACTION AS LORD OF THE SABBATH

9 And when He had departed from there, He went into their synagogue.

10 And behold, there was a man who had a withered hand. And they asked Him, saying, "Is it lawful to heal on the Sabbath?"—that they might accuse Him.

11 And He said to them, "What man is there among you who has one sheep, and if it falls into a pit on the Sabbath, will not lay hold of it and lift it out?

12 "Of how much more value then is a man than a sheep? Therefore it is lawful to do good on the Sabbath."

13 Then He said to the man, "Stretch out your hand." And he stretched it out, and it was restored as whole as the other.

14 Then the Pharisees went out and took counsel against Him, how they might destroy Him.

Matt. 12:9-14

The miracle of healing the withered hand is the Lord's answer to His critics. With the charge of Sabbath violation on the part of His disciples, Jesus extended His teaching by decisive action of His own. He deliberately performed a healing on the Sabbath and that in their very synagogue! Sometimes we find it easier to defend others in their decisions than to act ourselves and become personally accountable. This story appears also in Mark 3 and Luke 6, emphasizing the intrigue of the Pharisees and indicating the growing opposition and hostility toward the Person and ministry of Christ. Matthew says Jesus went "into *their* synagogue," identifying His movement as a separate one. The synagogue was in Galilee, probably in Capernaum, His home city. Jesus may well have known the man with the withered hand and placed Himself where this activity could take place with the symbolism that He intended.

The Pharisees' question as to whether it was lawful to heal on the Sabbath is interpreted by Matthew as having a wrong motive. They wanted to charge Jesus with violation of the Sabbath law. The man's problem did not demand immediate attention; it would remain relatively unchanged by another day. But Jesus met the challenge of His opposition. We are told nothing about the man in the Gospels. However, in the noncanonical Gospel According to the Hebrews, we are told that the man requested Jesus to heal him. He is reported to have said, "I was a stone mason, seeking my living with my hands. I pray you, Jesus, to give me back my health, so that I shall not need to beg for food in shame." True or not, it is clear in the account that Jesus looked on the man with compassion while the scribes and

Pharisees were not concerned about the man but about the minutiae of their regulations. They either took the initiative with their question or they intruded into the conversation between the man and Jesus and asked Jesus whether it was lawful to heal on the Sabbath. Jesus responded by a question that appealed to their materialistic interests and which had a provision in the Law: the right to rescue a sheep which had fallen into a pit on the Sabbath. Their laws at least permitted laying planks for the animal to get out. His argument is clear: of how much more value a man is than a sheep. *"Therefore it is lawful to do good on the Sabbath."*

In a deliberate act with no reference in Matthew to the man's faith, Jesus performed a gift of healing. But there was no movement of work on Jesus' part, for with only a word He made the man whole. In doing so He demonstrated the grace of God which wills our wholeness, a basic purpose of Sabbath! He disappointed His enemies by leaving them without an actual charge against Him of His working. By the gift of health He gave the man His freedom and His dignity among men. Such freedom places men under the obligation to love, thereby avoiding irresponsibility. The story does not follow the man, but follows the Pharisees who condemned Jesus for healing without labor, and went out themselves on the Sabbath and plotted to destroy Jesus. This emphasizes the seriousness of the conflict and the sharp difference between their position and that of Jesus.

One might develop a message from this section on the theme of Sabbath good and draw from the Old Testament the purposes of the Sabbath for human renewal, of the Jubilee or Sabbath of Sabbaths for release and equalization. This is beautifully demonstrated in Jesus' acts of renewal in giving the man his health. Or one can develop a message on the intrigue of the religious: (1) the attitude that accuses, v. 10; (2) the answer that acquits, vv. 11–12; (3) the act of mercy, v. 13; and (4) the actions of self-defense, v. 14. Our responsibility, when guided by love, is greater than that imposed by any set of laws. In Jesus we discover that when *agapē* comes in conflict with Torah, *agapē* is always first.

THE MESSIAH AS THE SERVANT OF THE LORD

15 But when Jesus knew it, He withdrew from there; and great multitudes followed Him, and He healed them all.

16 And He warned them not to make Him known,
17 that it might be fulfilled which was spoken by
Isaiah the prophet, saying:
18 *"Behold, My Servant whom I have chosen,*
   My Beloved in whom My soul is well pleased;
   I will put My Spirit upon Him,
   And He will declare justice to the Gentiles.
19 *He will not quarrel nor cry out,*
   Nor will anyone hear His voice in the streets.
20 *A bruised reed He will not break,*
   And smoking flax He will not quench,
   Till He sends forth justice to victory.
21 *And in His name Gentiles will trust."*

Matt. 12:15-21

Jesus was courageous but not careless. Knowing the Pharisees were plotting to destroy Him, He withdrew from premature confrontation. This was not only a sound political course of action but was good psychology. On many occasions an issue can be dealt with better after a time of emotional adjustment and creative distance. Jesus was not afraid to face adversity, as seen in His actions in the preceding story. Mark says that when He commanded the man to stand forth in their midst, He had looked around on them with anger at their hardness before acting in healing mercy. But, when he faced adversity, we see (1) His awareness—He knew what they were plotting; (2) His adjustment—He withdrew for space; (3) His action as before—He didn't alter His program in surrender; and (4) His anonymity—He didn't call undue attention to Himself (vv. 15–16).

With this background we are presented with the Ideal Servant as Messiah. Matthew shows that Jesus' conception of messiahship was radically different from that of the conventional expectation. The quotation from Isaiah 42:1–4 is the longest in the Gospel! The form of the source is not known, for it differs from the Hebrew and from the Septuagint, meaning that it may have been taken from the Targum. Clearly a messianic passage, it beautifully presents the Servant of God prior to the Passion of Christ as the Suffering Servant. A remarkable aspect of the quotation is the reference to the Gentiles, extending God's grace beyond the borders of the ethnic community of Jewry. For the Gentiles in the crowds, this was a word of grace. But this is to be seen as a direct answer to the bigotry of the Pharisees.

The Servant Chosen of God is introduced with poetic beauty and redemptive meaning: (1) the Holy Spirit rests creatively upon Him, v. 18; (2) the hope of all nations is centered in Him, vv. 18c, 21; (3) the helpfulness of grace characterizes His ministry, vv. 19–20. His work is characterized by (1) His bringing justice to all men; as Amos cried, "Let justice roll down like waters and righteousness like an ever-flowing stream" (5:24, NASB); (2) His modesty, for He will not stir up discontent among the people; (3) His compassion; He will respect even the smallest element of faith, for He will not break the bruised reed nor quench the smoking flax. He opens the invitation of grace to all people.

THE MESSIAH VERSUS BEELZEBUB

22 Then one was brought to Him who was demon-possessed, blind and mute; and He healed him, so that the blind and mute man both spoke and saw.

23 And all the multitudes were amazed and said, "Could this be the Son of David?"

24 But when the Pharisees heard it they said, "This fellow does not cast out demons except by Beelzebub, the ruler of the demons."

25 And Jesus knew their thoughts and said to them: "Every kingdom divided against itself is brought to desolation, and every city or house divided against itself will not stand.

26 "And if Satan casts out Satan, he is divided against himself. How then will his kingdom stand?

27 "And if I cast out demons by Beelzebub, by whom do your sons cast them out? Therefore they will be your judges.

28 "But if I cast out demons by the Spirit of God, then the kingdom of God has come to you.

29 "Or else how can one enter a strong man's house and plunder his goods, unless he first binds the strong man? And then he will plunder his house.

30 "He who is not with Me is against Me, and he who does not gather with Me scatters abroad.

Matt. 12:22–30

From the temptation in the wilderness and throughout His ministry, Jesus was in conflict with satanic influences. The confrontations with demon-possessed persons provided settings in which this conflict was made evident. While Jesus had defeated Satan in the wilderness temptation, a fact to which he alludes in this section as His having entered the strong man's house, the conflict continued, for He *will plunder his house"* (v. 29). The section reaches its climax with the affirmation introduced in verse 28, that the coming of the Kingdom is happening in the acts of God's Spirit. According to Gustav Aulen, this passage is the basis for a very significant interpretation of the atonement as Christ's victory over Satan. And for at least one thousand years of church history this was regarded as the classical view of the atonement.

The healing of a man who was both blind and mute because of demon possession offers a vivid illustration of the nature of Satan's work which limited one by blindness and bound one with the inability to communicate. The story simply tells us that Jesus healed him with little attention to the actual miracle. It focuses instead on the comments of the people as to whether Jesus might actually be the Son of David! Faith is beginning to dawn. Even though Jesus did not fit their picture of the coming Son of David, His deeds were of such power and nature that they had some stirrings of an awakening of faith.

The scribes and Pharisees were prejudiced and offered an answer which placed Jesus in league with the prince of devils. The word "Beelzebub" is derived from 2 Kings 1:2 in reference to the god of Ekron, a word meaning "exalted lord." But the biblical writers made the term Beelzebub, "lord of dung" or "lord of the flies" to show their contempt. Here the Pharisees used this contemptuous insult in saying that Jesus cast out demons by the power of Beelzebub, prince of demons.

Jesus responded with a series of logical arguments. First, if He were casting out demons by the help of the ruler of demons then the demonic kingdom was self-destructing. Second, the Jews themselves practiced exorcism and so they must be succeeding by demonic power, hence they were condemning themselves. And third, if He were casting out demons, which they had admitted by their statement, then it must be evidence that He had entered the strong man's house and defeated the strong man! It is Jesus' defeat of Satan in the wilderness through His authority as God's Son which enabled Him to cast out demons with a word. His authority and method stood in contrast to the extensive and strange exercises of the Jewish exorcists.

Two other concepts call for attention in the concluding verses of this section. The first is that in Jesus' acts the Kingdom of God had come to them. Matthew used the term "kingdom of heaven" more frequently while the other Gospel writers used the expression "kingdom of God." According to Caird, the kingdom of God and the kingdom of heaven are one and the same. The kingdom of God exists wherever God reigns, and the kingdom of heaven exists where heaven reigns, with "Heaven" as simply a title for God (as in Luke 15:18). Jesus was not talking of the church which, following Pentecost, actually became the visible expression of Kingdom reality, but of the Kingdom which comes and will ultimately come in its fullness. The second concept is the necessity to make our decision in relation to Christ. We must be either for Him or against Him, but not neutral. There are only two kingdoms, the Kingdom of God and the kingdom of darkness. This is the "sword of division" spoken of in 10:34. In context, Jesus' reply draws a clear line of distinction; those not with Him are against Him. It is a statement of awareness but also of judgment.

An outline for this section could include four aspects: (1) the charge is designed to refute His identity as "Son of David," vv. 23–24; (2) the critique shows the impossibility of a divided kingdom, vv. 25–27; (3) the coming of the Kingdom of God is happening in the works of God's Spirit, v. 28; and (4) the commitment regarding Jesus and His claims is inescapable, v. 30.

THE MESSIAH PROSCRIBES FORGIVENESS

31 "Therefore I say to you, every sin and blasphemy
will be forgiven men, but the blasphemy against the
Holy Spirit will not be forgiven men.
32 "And whoever speaks a word against the Son
of Man, it will be forgiven him; but whoever speaks
against the Holy Spirit, it will not be forgiven him,
either in this age or in the age to come.

Matt. 12:31–32

The expression of God's grace is a love which forgives sin, a love which reaches beyond the issue to the person and releases that person in mercy. The heart of the gospel is that "God so loved the world, that He gave His only begotten Son, that whosoever believeth in him should not perish, but have everlasting life" (John 3:16, KJV). And this grace of forgiveness is known fully in the Christ who is God's extension of forgiving grace, the Christ who absorbed man's hostility and sin to share the costliness of redemptive love. But if one completely rejects what God is doing by His Spirit in and through Christ and despises His Word, such a person places himself outside of the avenue to forgiveness. In Numbers 15:31 we read, "Because he hath despised the word of the Lord, and hath broken his commandment, that soul shall be utterly cut off" (KJV). So here, Jesus says that those who blaspheme the Holy Spirit are, in so doing, severing themselves from the only power that can bring them to repentance, to the forgiving grace of God. Forgiveness is always in relationship, it is not a package that one can get and run off with. Consequently, forgiveness cannot be known if one is closing his life to God.

Jesus said that persons may not fully understand the man Jesus of Nazareth and, out of ignorance, may speak critically of what He was doing and yet have forgiveness. But where the truth of God comes through by the illumination of the Holy Spirit and men reject that truth, they place themselves beyond pardon. While some interpret this "unpardonable sin" as an act of attributing the work of the Spirit to Satan, it is much more an attitude than a single act; it is a state of willful sin. It is an attitude that closes one's mind and conscience to the convictions of the Spirit until the conscience becomes so hardened that the one voice which calls to God, the voice of the Spirit, can no longer get through. Such are then beyond pardon, beyond hearing the call to pardon. Barnes interprets this as follows: "He that speaks against me as a man of Nazareth, that speaks contemptuously of my humble birth, etc., may be pardoned; but he that reproaches my divine nature, charging me with being in league with Satan, and blaspheming the power of God manifestly displayed by Me, can never obtain forgiveness." This sin is not simply an act which makes God so disgusted that He cuts one off, but rather is a sin which so changes the person's stance toward God that the one places himself outside of the experience of pardon—forever.

For those who are worried about their having committed the unpardonable sin, the very fact of conviction is evidence that the Spirit is still being heard in His conviction. Also, the mention of an unpardonable sin implies the pardonable; the latter being those rejections of Jesus' claims without the blasphemous attitude of complete defiance of the Spirit's illumination of the truth and call of Christ. The following points are submitted as a possible outline for this passage: (1) the unpardonable sin is the complete rejection of the Holy Spirit; (2) the unpardonable sin means refusing the realization that He alone could bring us to pardon; and (3) the unpardonable sin has eternal consequences, vv. 31–32.

THE MESSIAH'S CONTRAST BETWEEN GOOD AND EVIL

33 "Either make the tree good and its fruit good, or else make the tree bad and its fruit bad; for a tree is known by its fruit.

34 "O brood of vipers! How can you, being evil, speak good things? For out of the abundance of the heart the mouth speaks.

35 "A good man out of the good treasure of his heart brings forth good things; and an evil man out of the evil treasure brings forth evil things.

36 "But I say to you that for every idle word men may speak, they will give account of it in the day of judgment.

37 "For by your words you will be justified, and by your words you will be condemned."

Matt. 12:33–37

In context, this section is an elaboration on the issue just preceding. The Pharisees had uttered some terrible words about Jesus and His work and Jesus is holding these persons responsible for what they have said. In so doing He points specifically to the way in which one's words express the nature of the inner person—attitudes, preferences, thoughts, and ambitions. The key is in the sentence, *"Out of the abundance of the heart the mouth speaks."* We discover the character of a person by the words or conversation which express the inner life. Ultimately, our judgment will be on the basis of our own words, a disclosure that will either lead to our being justified or being condemned.

A message from this passage on the Integrity of Personhood could include these concepts: (1) wholeness begins with integrity at the basic levels of life, vv. 33–34; (2) works express the inner harmony of character and choices, v. 35; and (3) words as well as deeds express where we actually stand, vv. 36–37. Words spoken prematurely cause

160

extended damage. Harsh words wound; critical words destroy. Once words are spoken they cannot be recalled and we cannot be free from the responsibility of having made the statement. One of the awesome things about being human beings is that we will be in all eternity the persons who have done and said what we have done and said today. Who does not need God's forgiving grace? Of this James wrote; "But the tongue can no man tame; it is an unruly evil, full of deadly poison" (3:8, KJV). Yet, while this passage is something of an analytical judgment, there is an answer to this problem in Paul's teaching of "bringing every thought into captivity to the obedience of Christ" (2 Cor. 10:5).

THE MESSIANIC SIGN

38 Then some of the scribes and Pharisees answered, saying, "Teacher, we want to see a sign from You."
39 But He answered and said to them, "An evil and adulterous generation seeks after a sign, and no sign will be given to it except the sign of the prophet Jonah.
40 "For as Jonah was three days and three nights in the belly of the great fish, so will the Son of Man be three days and three nights in the heart of the earth.
41 "The men of Nineveh will rise in the judgment with this generation and condemn it, because they repented at the preaching of Jonah; and indeed a greater than Jonah is here.
42 "The queen of the South will rise up in the judgment with this generation and condemn it, for she came from the ends of the earth to hear the wisdom of Solomon; and indeed a greater than Solomon is here.

Matt. 12:38–42

The request for a sign on the part of the scribes and Pharisees was no doubt in self-defense. If this event followed close upon the preceding ones in this section, their defensiveness becomes even more apparent. The "sign" that they wanted was something other than the evidence of the exorcisms and healings Jesus was performing. In 16:1 they again ask specifically for "a sign from heaven." But Jesus maintains the same posture as He had when answering John the Baptist's question. The deeds and words that accompanied His ministry were sufficient to bring persons to faith. He stated in reply that it is "an evil and adulterous generation" that seeks after a sign. The literalist always needs the letter rather than the Spirit to show him the will of God.

Paul wrote that "the Jews require a sign" (1 Cor. 1:22, KJV), something that was characteristic of their history. But signs did not replace the impact of the prophetic Word, nor the meaning of the presence of the prophet who had demonstrated integrity and fidelity to God. Jesus said, *"No sign will be given . . . except the sign of the prophet Jonah."* The presence of Jonah in Nineveh was God's sign to the Ninevites. This statement introduces a question in that Luke makes no mention of three days and nights in the belly of the fish, but rather that Jonah was a sign to the Ninevites. This may emphasize the presence and preaching of Jonah as the sign (Luke 11:30). But Matthew makes specific mention of Jonah having been three days and three nights in the belly of the fish, interpreting the sign as Jesus' coming death, burial and resurrection. The point is, evidently, that Jonah himself was God's sign to Nineveh and his words were God's message. The statement in Matthew implies, as Tasker says, that as Jonah was for three days in living death and was delivered by God to go to preach in Nineveh as a sign of God's concern for them, so the death and resurrection of Christ would be the ultimate sign of God's grace in redemption.[8]

Jesus was saying, "I am God's sign among you." Nineveh recognized God's word in Jonah and repented. The Queen of Sheba recognized God's wisdom in Solomon and came from the farther-known regions to hear him. Jesus stands as God's sign, saying that *"a greater than Jonah is here,"* and again, *"a greater than Solomon is here,"* as He had said that He is Lord of the Sabbath and again that "a greater than the Temple is here." The people are called to recognize God's ultimate Word in Him. In John 7:52 the Pharisees said, "Out of Galilee ariseth no prophet" (KJV). But Jonah had come from Galilee! This may have been the sign of Jonah which Jesus meant.

THE MESSIAH POINTS BEYOND EXORCISM

43 "When an unclean spirit goes out of a man, he
goes through dry places, seeking rest, and finds none.

44 "Then he says, 'I will return to my house from which I came.' And when he comes, he finds it empty, swept, and put in order.

45 "Then he goes and takes with him seven other spirits more wicked than himself, and they enter and dwell there; and the last state of that man is worse than the first. So it also will be with this wicked generation."

Matt. 12:43–45

This strange parable is a conclusion for the sections dealing with Beelzebub and the teachings which were designed to call persons to repentance and faith. It is not just release but re-creation and renewal that Jesus brings. The individual in the parable is typical of an entire generation (v. 43). Incomplete repentance is man's desire for release from guilt without full participation in the Kingdom (vv. 44–45a). Insincere faith or incomplete faith is worse than having never started in the way of truth, for such then know enough about God to know how to resist His claims and harden themselves against Him.

The story of one exorcised of an evil spirit but who failed to place positive obedience at the center of his life is illustrative of one for whom religion is basically negative. The way of victorious Christian living is not to stand with one's attention on sin, fighting it, but to turn one's back on sin and become engaged in positive actions of righteousness. Sin is always a perversion of the good, the cheaper route of something better, and we overcome sin by choosing the better. Jesus calls us to the actions of the Kingdom—to seek first the Kingdom of God and His righteousness, and the other benefits will follow.

THE MESSIAH'S TRUE FAMILY

46 While He was still talking to the multitudes, behold, His mother and His brothers stood outside, seeking to speak with Him.

47 Then one said to Him, "Look, Your mother and

Your brothers are standing outside, seeking to speak
with You."

48 But He answered and said to the one who told
Him, "Who is My mother and who are My brothers?"

49 And He stretched out His hand toward His
disciples and said, "Here are My mother and My
brothers!

50 "For whoever does the will of My Father who
is in heaven is My brother and sister and mother."

Matt. 12:46–50

Spiritual relationships are the most high and most holy of life.
When family ties have the spiritual dimension there is no richer fellowship. But when family ties do not have the spiritual dimension
we find that the deeper meanings of fellowship are found beyond
the family. Even in Jesus' family, one of the things He had to face
was that His own brothers and sisters had a problem believing in
Him (John 7:5) and some of His relatives and friends thought that
He had gone mad (Mark 3:21).

Jesus' mother and brothers stood outside of the house and called
for Him. He met their request with a reproof, assuring His hearers
that He had come for all men. While born of a woman, He was
"not on that account more nearly united to her than to all those
who are united to Him by the Spirit, nor bound to regard the call
of earthly relations so much as the welfare of those whom He came
to teach and to save."[9] It is to be noted that while using the term
"brother," Jesus never used the designation "father" for an earthly
relationship.

Jesus' references to the Ninevites and to the Queen of Sheba had
introduced the Gentiles into the stream of God's saving acts, demonstrating that faith transcends ethnic heritage. Now in this incident
Jesus demonstrates that faith transcends family heritage. The family
of faith becomes our primary relationship in the will of God, one
which is neither superseded nor excluded by that of blood. This emphasis can be presented by the following points: (1) our family ties
are not enough to separate us from the evil generation, vv. 46–47;
(2) our family relation is not to supersede nor exclude the relation
of faith, vv. 48–49; and (3) the family of God is a relation of faith-
deed in the will of God, v. 50.

This section closes with the remarkable word of grace in which
Jesus includes in His family *"whoever does the will of my Father who is in*

heaven"! This word expresses the disciple's relationship with the Father but is also an identification with the disciples as brothers. In this light the writer of Hebrews refers to Jesus as saying, "I will declare thy name unto my brethren, in the midst of the church will I sing praise unto thee" (Heb. 2:12, KJV).

NOTES

1. Hans Stier, *Reden Jesu*, p. 355.
2. Alford, *The Greek New Testament*, 1:102.
3. Tasker, *The Gospel According to St. Matthew*, p. 108.
4. Yoder, *The Politics of Jesus*, p. 109.
5. Ibid.
6. Barclay, *The Gospel of Matthew*, 2:7
7. Tasker, *The Gospel According to St. Matthew*, p. 121.
8. Ibid., p. 131.
9. Alford, *The Greek New Testament*, 1:135.

CHAPTER FIVE

The Parables of the King

Matthew 13:1–58

Jesus was a master of the short story. His parables, amazing exercises of storytelling, are some of His unique ways of communicating. This chapter is "book three" in the series of five "books" of Matthew's compilation of the teachings of Christ. This chapter is a collection of seven parables, all interpreting the Kingdom of heaven. Jesus' parables may be divided into three categories: parables of assurance, which would include most of these as well as those in Mark 4:26–29 and Luke 11:5–8; 18:2–8; parables of gospel, as in chapter 21 and Luke 15 and 16; and parables of the *Parousia* as in chapter 25 and in Mark 13.

Interfacing Matthew with Mark and Luke, we discover that two of the parables in this section appear in all three: the sower (Mark 4:1–9, 13–20; Luke 8:5–15) and the mustard seed (Mark 4:30–32, Luke 13:18–19). One parable is found also in Luke, the leaven (Luke 13:20–21). But four of the seven are found only here in Matthew: the tares, the hidden treasure, the pearl of great price, and the dragnet.

The parable is a short story, not an allegory, and as such it is told to convey one basic point. When interpreting a parable we should look for that basic point and not try to hang truths on every detail of the story as though it were allegorical. Furthermore, its interpretation calls for a careful and correct understanding of the culture and language in which it was given, as they condition the meaning of the story. We should also bear in mind that a parable is a story to be heard; it is not a manuscript to be studied, and hearing it we discern the punch line of the story more readily. We should avoid adding meanings to details which are provided to accentuate the point the storyteller is making. Jesus' stories were the way in which He called people to the concrete situation rather than to abstract concepts. Jesus was interested in people in real life, in showing such people how to "seek first" the Kingdom of God.

But stories have a way of separating people. Some hear and some do not; that is, some catch the meaning and some miss it. Jesus chose the parable as a teaching method, a strategy by which He separated those who were honest and sincere about understanding the Kingdom from those who were only curious or were critical of his ministry.

THE PARABLE OF THE SOWER

1 The same day Jesus went out of the house and sat by the seaside.

2 And great multitudes were gathered together to Him, so that He got into a boat and sat; and the whole multitude stood on the shore.

3 And He spoke many things to them in parables, saying: "Behold, a sower went out to sow.

4 "And as he sowed, some seed fell by the wayside; and the birds came and devoured them.

5 "Some fell on stony places, where they did not have much earth; and they immediately sprang up because they had no depth of earth.

6 "But when the sun was up they were scorched, and because they had no root they withered away.

7 "And some fell among thorns, and the thorns sprang up and choked them.

8 "But others fell on good ground and yielded a crop: some a hundredfold, some sixty, some thirty.

9 "He who has ears to hear, let him hear!"

Matt. 13:1–9

The structure of verse 1 implies that Jesus was at home in Capernaum. The structure here is similar to that of Mark 4:1–2, presenting Jesus getting into a boat and teaching the crowd which stood on the shore. Capernaum itself was only a few hundred yards from the shore. Pressed by the crowd, Jesus apparently walked down to Peter's fishing dock and had the disciples move out on the water to give Him a unique setting from which to teach.

Matthew says that Jesus *"spoke many things to them in parables,"* implying that He is selecting from Jesus' teachings the few which he presents. In this sense the parable has a twofold historical setting; the first is the concrete situation in the activity of Jesus, and the second is, as Jeremias puts it, that the parables "went on to live in the primitive church."[1]

This story is called the parable of the sower and yet the interpretation usually focuses on the hearer, on the preparation of the soil. We shall stay primarily with the sower as Jesus tells the story. As the sower casts the seed evenly over the ground, some falls on the paths which passed through the fields for the travelers; some fell where the underlying limestone rocks were near the surface, limiting the amount of soil for plant growth; some fell where cultivation had not destroyed the roots of thistles, and wire grass would grow rapidly and choke out the grain; but some fell on good ground and yielded a good crop of varying density. From the perspective of the sower, this story is understood as the risk of sowing, but with the assurance that much of the seed would bear a harvest. The sower goes on, undaunted by the areas of inadequate soil, fully expecting a harvest from the good soil.

The intent of the story may have been primarily to encourage the disciples, as they saw the Master as the sower. He knew what He was doing and knew what to expect. The interpretation expressed by Jesus later in this chapter expresses the sower's understanding of the soil, that is, the response of the hearer. To emphasize the sower is to focus on the message of the Kingdom and primarily on Jesus as the Preacher of the Kingdom. It is a declaration that the messianic role, although having a small beginning, will nevertheless have its harvest.

THE PURPOSE OF PARABLES

10 And the disciples came and said to Him, "Why do You speak to them in parables?"

11 He answered and said to them, "Because it has been given to you to know the mysteries of the kingdom of heaven, but to them it has not been given.

12 "For whoever has, to him will be given, and he will have more abundance; but whoever does not have, even what he has will be taken away from him.

13 "Therefore I speak to them in parables, because seeing they do not see, and hearing they do not hear, nor do they understand.

14 "And in them the prophecy of Isaiah is fulfilled, which says:

'By hearing you will hear and shall not
    understand,
And seeing you will see and not perceive;
15 For the heart of this people has grown dull.
Their ears are hard of hearing,
And their eyes they have closed,
Lest they should see with their eyes,
Hear with their ears,
Should understand with their heart,
And should turn,
And I should heal them.'

16 "But blessed are your eyes for they see, and your ears for they hear;

17 "for assuredly, I say to you that many prophets and righteous men have desired to see those things which you see, and have not seen them, and to hear those things which you hear, and have not heard them.

Matt. 13:10–17

This is an intervening section and one of Matthew's significant contributions to the study of parables. He presents the disciples not as asking what the parable means but as asking why He was using parables! The teaching of the Sermon on the Mount had not been a series of parables, even granting the word-pictures and illustrations. The question is, why now? When the crowd is following and popularity with the masses is evident, why parables? Jesus answers, *"Because,"* a word that serves really as a colon: *"The secrets of the kingdom of heaven [have] been given to you"* (NIV), but not to them! This term, "secrets" corresponds to Paul's use of the word "mystery" in his letter to the Ephesians: "the mystery made known to me by revelation" (Eph. 3:3, NIV), and again, "This mystery is that through the Gospel the Gentiles are heirs together with Israel . . . sharers together with the promise in Christ Jesus" (Eph. 3:6).

The Old Testament reference Jesus gives from Isaiah 6:9–10 is the only quotation in Matthew which is actually from Jesus' mouth. Other such quotations are given by Matthew about Jesus, His deeds or His words. The quotation by Jesus is the only one in this Gospel that is actually in full agreement with the Septuagint. The abbreviated form given by Jesus in verse 13 precedes the actual quotation showing the hardness of heart closing people to God's purpose. The quotation shows what happens when people see but do not observe what is happening, when people hear but do not hearken. The concern of Jesus was that by hearing and seeing the Messiah they might turn to Him for blessing without actually understanding the true nature of what God was doing. Jesus' quotation was to say that the understanding of His hearers was dependent upon perceiving Him as Jesus the Messiah, and upon understanding the inbreaking of the Kingdom of God. Only as persons recognize this true messiahship can they believe and repent and enter the Kingdom. This difficult passage must be seen in direct relation to the veiling of the message, lest people affirm the Messiah and want to come into His Kingdom without sharing its true spiritual nature.

The Greek phrase beginning verse 16 should be translated, "as for you," making a special point of distinguishing the disciples. Matthew differs here from Mark and distinguishes between the disciples who can perceive and the general populace. The disciples may have "little faith" (8:26; 14:31; 16:8; 17:20) but Jesus honors what they have. The attention is focused upon hearing the Word of God, upon their unique privilege of hearing the Messiah. The prophets of the Old Testament had looked forward to the messianic presence, which was now fulfilled as Jesus' presence with the disciples. Later Peter wrote that "we have also a more sure word of prophecy" (2 Pet. 1:19 KJV), holding us accountable to understanding and to obeying His Word.

THE PARABLE OF THE SOWER EXPLAINED

18 "Therefore hear the parable of the sower:
19 "When anyone hears the word of the kingdom, and does not understand it, then the wicked one comes and snatches away what was sown in his heart. This is he who received seed by the wayside.
20 "But he who received the seed on stony places, this is he who hears the word and immediately receives it with joy;
21 "yet he has no root in himself, but endures only

for a while. For when tribulation or persecution arises
because of the word, immediately he stumbles.

22 "Now he who received seed among the thorns
is he who hears the word, and the cares of this world
and the deceitfulness of riches choke the word, and
he becomes unfruitful.

23 "But he who received seed on the good ground
is he who hears the word and understands it, who
indeed bears fruit and produces: some a hundredfold,
some sixty, some thirty."

Matt. 13:18–23

The designation "parable of the sower" places the emphasis on
Jesus as the Preacher of the Kingdom, yet the Preacher Himself draws
attention to the soils. It is the same sower and the same seed in all
four cases. The four types of soil represent four types of persons.
First are *the indifferent,* who allow the word to be lost from memory
while other things receive more attention on the beaten path of life.
Second are *the shallow,* who have hidden agendas and other priorities
which prevent in-depth understanding. Third are *the cluttered,* whose
lives are filled with the interests of this world and whose materialistic
ambitions choke out the convictions for the Kingdom. And fourth
are *the responsive,* who welcome the word, who hunger and thirst after
righteousness, who are longing for the meaning of a right purpose.

The parable shows that the sower expects fruit, knowing that the
variety of soils will determine His crop. The realism is further expressed in the recognition that in the good soil, among responsive
persons, there is still variation, yet with the variables there is the
harvest of faith. We keep on sowing the Word, believing that the
harvest will come; but recognizing the freedom of the hearer to be
open and responsive to grace or on the other hand to resist the Spirit.
And one who closes his mind to the truth begins a pattern which
makes it all the more difficult to ever hear that truth fully again.
As has been said, "No one turns his back on the light but what he
increases the darkness in his own soul."

THE PARABLE OF THE WHEAT AND THE TARES

24 Another parable He put forth to them, saying:
"The kingdom of heaven is like a man who sowed
good seed in his field;

25 "but while men slept, his enemy came and sowed tares among the wheat and went his way.

26 "But when the grain had sprouted and produced a crop, then the tares also appeared.

27 "So the servants of the owner came and said to him, 'Sir, did you not sow good seed in your field? How then does it have tares?'

28 "He said to them, 'An enemy has done this.' The servants said to him, 'Do you want us then to go and gather them up?'

29 "But he said, 'No, lest while you gather up the tares you also uproot the wheat with them.

30 'Let both grow together until the harvest, and at the time of harvest I will say to the reapers: First gather together the tares and bind them in bundles to burn them, but gather the wheat into my barn.' "

Matt. 13:24–30

There is a change in the introduction of the second and following parables from the first. Jesus now introduces the parable by saying, *"The kingdom of heaven is like. . . ."* The preceding parable stressed the sower's expectation of fruit, but this parable implies the question, "What of the plant that doesn't bear fruit?" Continuing the imagery of the preceding parable of the sower casting seed in the field, Jesus introduces some strange new features.

First, Jesus introduces an answer to the problem of evil by saying *"his enemy came and sowed tares among the wheat."* This was not an unheard-of illustration, for one of the acts of vengeance in tensions between farmers was the threat, "I'll sow weeds in your field." In fact, there were laws drawn up to prohibit this act. Second, Jesus rejected the idea of pulling up the tares (or darnel), saying that they were to be left alone until the harvest, i.e., the judgment. The wheat represents the disciples of Christ, the darnel represents the enemies of Christ in the world.

The judgment scene (v. 30) is of a harvest where servant labor, often of women, was engaged to sort out the tares. The darnel looked like wheat until it reached the stage where the heads showed the obvious difference. The gathering out of the tares first, then the wheat, does not sound like a "rapture" of the righteous. However, remember that we don't allegorize from every aspect of a parable but seek its main point. The powers of evil will do all they can to destroy the

Kingdom, but such will be fully exposed and dealt with at the final judgment.

A message from this parable on the Kingdom could emphasize several things: (1) no insulation, vv. 25–26; (2) no isolation, vv. 27–29, and (3) no indefiniteness, v. 30. The primary meaning has to do with the presence of the Kingdom amidst ambiguity.

Many interpreters have used this passage to support an open membership in the church, noting that Jesus left His circle open to include Judas as a tare. But this interpretation deserves more careful analysis which follows in the section where Jesus interprets His own parable (vv. 36–43). At this point we note the words of verse 29, *"No, lest while you gather up the tares you also uproot the wheat with them."* If the choice is between unresolved tension and a dishonest solution we should choose the tension.

THE PARABLE OF THE MUSTARD SEED

31 Another parable He put forth to them, saying:
"The kingdom of heaven is like a mustard seed, which
a man took and sowed in his field,
   32 "which indeed is the least of all the seeds; but
when it is grown it is greater than the herbs and
becomes a tree, so that the birds of the air come and
nest in its branches."

Matt. 13:31–32

This parable also appears in Mark (4:30–32) and in Luke (13:18–21). It is thought that the text in Matthew contains the material of Mark and of the theoretical manuscript Q, and should Q have been basically the Logia of Jesus compiled by Matthew prior to writing this Gospel, the theory is understandable. The account says that a man took the seed and sowed it in his garden or plot; a deliberate act with purpose. Since the mustard plant became one of the larger of the herbs, frequently as tall as twelve feet, it became a resting place for birds feeding on its seeds. Perhaps this suggests the purpose of the farmer in planting the seed. But Jesus' point is that from the smallest seed, with such an insignificant beginning, the plant becomes the greatest of the herbs and serves as an illustration of the Kingdom giving protection to many (see Dan. 4:9–18). The Kingdom, although having a very small beginning, seemingly insignificant in contrast to the popular messianic expectations, would become the greater expression of the "Sower's" purposive activity. The parable teaches that the Kingdom will grow inevitably to achieve results out of all proportion to its beginning.

THE PARABLE OF THE LEAVEN

> 33 Another parable He spoke to them: "The kingdom of heaven is like leaven, which a woman took and hid in three measures of meal till it was all leavened."
>
> *Matt. 13:33*

This parable is linked to the preceding one, and there is a movement in each from small to great. Again, the emphasis is on an insignificant beginning but a magnificent end. A woman may take three measures of meal for one of the larger bakings which would supply bread for family and guests, but using only a small lump of leaven. As it is mixed into this large amount of meal, it will work its way through the whole until all has been leavened. The Kingdom of God permeates the world, having its effect on all, influencing for the good even those who reject it. The rejecters' lot in life is improved, if in no other way than by needing to compete with something better! As the "salt of the earth" is interpreted by its enriching benefits, although not seen in and of itself when enriching the food, so leaven is not seen in itself in the loaf but works invisibly, making the bread rise. Yet, the results are visible, for we can see the bread rising!

Yeast is usually regarded as having negative overtones in Judaism. All leaven was to be removed from a home before the Passover lest it alter the special unleavened bread to be eaten at the Passover meal. However, this parable is not a study on the symbolism of leaven, but is a singular illustration that the Kingdom will penetrate and influence the world as effectively as yeast penetrates and transforms the flour into which it is placed. As in the preceding parables that show that since Jesus has come the field no longer stands empty, so it is shown here that since Jesus has come the dough is rising! God is at work as the primary Actor on the stage of history, permeating society with the influence of His grace.

This parable emphasizes the transforming power of the gospel of the Kingdom; it changes persons, social orders, economic relations, and primary loyalties. From the illustration of the way in which leaven moves from particle to particle, Plummer says, "That Kingdom in which the will of God is acknowledged until it becomes supreme is to spread from soul to soul until all are brought within His sovereignty."[2]

THE PARABLES IN PROPHECY

34 All these things Jesus spoke to the multitude in parables; and without a parable He did not speak to them,
35 that it might be fulfilled which was spoken by the prophet, saying:
"I will open My mouth in parables;
I will utter things which have been kept secret
from the foundation of the world."
Matt. 13:34–35

Matthew adds his own comment on Jesus' parables, stressing their use in speaking to the multitudes. The parable is spoken of as an enigmatic statement, which emphasizes that the use of parable was not a simple illustration but was to veil the truth from the insincere. The quotation itself is from Psalm 78:2, used by Matthew with the intent of relating Jesus' ministry to the Old Testament, to salvation history. The use of parables with the crowd stimulated their interaction, while the disciples either understood or asked for an interpretation. Parables permit the hearer a voluntary choice of identifying.

The quotation has a particularly positive note. Matthew's reference shows Jesus' parables as fulfilling the words of the psalmist. The prophetic word is looking forward to the time when the purpose of God, secret from the foundation of the world, will be fully known. Paul says in Ephesians 3:10 that God is making His purpose known to the principalities and powers in the heavenly realms by what He is doing through the church, and this purpose of God extends throughout history. Since God is not capricious, we can project an interpretation into the future on the basis of His acts in salvation history. In fact, as we read the Book of the Revelation, we see God with His arm outstretched toward the future, holding back the end until His purpose is completed!

THE PARABLE OF THE TARES EXPLAINED

36 Then Jesus sent the multitude away and went
into the house. And His disciples came to Him, saying,
"Explain to us the parable of the tares of the field."
37 He answered and said to them: "He who sows
the good seed is the Son of Man.
38 "The field is the world, the good seeds are the
sons of the kingdom, but the tares are the sons of
the wicked one.
39 "The enemy who sowed them is the devil, the
harvest is the end of the age, and the reapers are the
angels.
40 "Therefore as the tares are gathered and burned
in the fire, so it will be at the end of this age.
41 "The Son of Man will send out His angels, and
they will gather out of His kingdom all things that
offend, and those who practice lawlessness,
42 "and will cast them into the furnace of fire. There
will be wailing and gnashing of teeth.
43 "Then the righteous will shine forth as the sun
in the kingdom of their Father. He who has ears to
hear, let him hear!

Matt. 13:36–43

Jesus dismissed the multitude and closed His class for the day.
Having entered His house to be away from the crowd, He was alone
with the disciples. Fortunately for our understanding, they asked
Him to interpret the parable of the wheat and the tares. His answer
is clear and concise. The key to its meaning is in the seven terms
interpreted in verses 37–39: (1) the sower is the Son of Man, (2)
the field is the world, (3) the good seed means the children of the
Kingdom, (4) the tares are the sons of the wicked one, (5) the enemy
is the devil, (6) the harvest is the end of the age, and (7) the reapers
are the angels.

The meaning of the parable is that as the Son of Man introduces
the Kingdom of heaven into the world, the powers of evil will do
everything possible to resist the Kingdom. Ultimately, the Kingdom
will succeed. Special attention should be called to His statement that
the *field is the world,* not the church. This parable has often been used
to speak against a disciplined church, affirming that Jesus lets the
tares remain in the church until the final judgment. Such was the

position of Augustine, Luther, Calvin, and others who were defending a church-state, not a believers' church as separate in society. The radical Reformation of the sixteenth century called for an authentic church of believers answering to the mandate of Christ alone. The Anabaptists regarded the Constantinian State Church as a fallen church. The Reformers used this parable against the Anabaptists to justify a people's church where believers and unbelievers (or unconverted) shared together as wheat and tares. But Jesus said, *"The field is the world,"* not the church.

Jesus describes His own role at the end of the age in verse 41. The Messiah will be Judge, as foretold by John the Baptist, but Jesus places His action at the end of the age. This judgment is spoken of in Old Testament passages such as Zephaniah 1:2–6. The description, "the furnace of fire," is no doubt lifted from the apocalyptic language of Daniel (3:6), as is "the righteous will shine forth as the sun in the kingdom of their Father" (Dan. 12:3). Note the significant use of the two phrases, "of His kingdom," identifying it as a present reality at work in the world and "the kingdom of their Father," the eternal kingdom. This may best be understood by reading 1 Corinthians 15:24, in which Paul shows Christ as completing His Kingdom and turning it over to the Father as a *fait accompli,* a finished work.

THE PARABLE OF THE HIDDEN TREASURE

44 "Again, the kingdom of heaven is like treasure
hidden in a field, which, when a man found, he hid;
and for joy over it he goes and sells all that he has
and buys that field.

Matt. 13:44

This is the parable of great joy. The way of the Kingdom is the path of joy. Jeremias says that this is the main point of the parable: "The joy of the finder."[3] But in this short parable of one verse there is a remarkable message on salvation. There is (1) the discovery, (2) the response, and (3) the total commitment: selling all that one has in order to gain one treasure. His joy in the discovery of the Kingdom, the discovery of meaning, is so great that he cannot do other than to give up all else for the Kingdom. Such is the nature of full dedication to Christ, not a painful exercise of becoming religious, but a joyous relationship with the Redeemer.

Paul writes to the Romans, "I beseech you therefore, brethren, by the mercies of God, that you present your bodies a living sacrifice, holy and acceptable to God, which is your reasonable service" (Rom. 12:1). It is with joyous gratitude for His grace that we surrender all in order to share His life.

The setting of the parable was readily understood in Palestine. Many persons hid treasures, such as silver or jewels, in jars in the earth. In a land so often invaded by enemy forces, the safest thing to do with one's treasures was to bury them and flee and, on returning dig them up. Consequently, jars of treasure were lost, their burial unknown to others.

The picture is of a day-laborer who made the overwhelming discovery of a treasure buried in a field. Wisely he refrained from passing the information to others and arranged the purchase of the field to secure the treasure. Eduard Schweizer adds an interesting note concerning a lost opportunity, in that the son sold the field not knowing his father had buried a treasure there.[4] This homiletical note is permissible in applying the impact of the parable in preaching, but it is not the point of the parable. The focus is on the man who discovered the treasure of truth and was so enriched by joy as to pay any price to secure it for himself.

THE PARABLE OF THE PEARL OF GREAT PRICE

45 "Again, the kingdom of heaven is like a merchant seeking beautiful pearls,
46 "who, when he had found one pearl of great price, went and sold all that he had and bought it.
Matt. 13:45–46

This very brief parable is an illustration that in finding the most precious reality, one will pay any price, readily make any sacrifice to obtain its benefits. In the former parable, the man working in the field happened to come upon the treasure and responded in joy. In this parable the merchant was searching for the treasure, a conscious quest, and finding the pearl of great price, cries "Eureka"; "I've found it!"

The parable tells us that the merchant sold all he owned to secure the pearl. This concept is the same in both of these parables: the willingness to surrender all to gain the valued goal. An outline could be: (1) the unique magnificence of the object, (2) the unequivocal action, and (3) the unprecedented gain. The action of the Kingdom of heaven creates the response actions of men. And actions which involve the larger social order are still actions which are very personal. As Carl F. H. Henry has said, "Christian experience is always personal but it is never private."

THE PARABLE OF THE DRAGNET

> 47 "Again, the kingdom of heaven is like a dragnet that was cast into the sea and gathered some of every kind,
>
> 48 "which, when it was full, they drew to shore; and they sat down and gathered the good into vessels, but threw the bad away.
>
> 49 "So it will be at the end of the age. The angels will come forth, separate the wicked from among the just,
>
> 50 "and cast them into the furnace of fire. There will be wailing and gnashing of teeth."
>
> 51 Jesus said to them, "Have you understood all these things?" They said to Him, "Yes, Lord."
>
> 52 Then He said to them, "Therefore every scribe instructed concerning the kingdom of heaven is like a householder who brings out of his treasure things new and old."
>
> *Matt. 13:47–52*

This parable, like the one of the wheat and tares, avoids a separatism which prevents the people of God from associating with the people of the world. We are to be in the world but not of the world. The parable is not dealing with any transition from good to bad, or bad to good, but speaks to the fact that both exist together in the same world. Jesus is not creating a sectarian Israel to stand over against the rest of the world. Just as He ate with publicans and sinners, so His disciples will move among people who disbelieve. The dragnet, unlike the parable of the wheat and tares, permits the picture of variety among the evil. Men are all alike sinners, but not sinners alike.

The illustration of the dragnet was taken from everyday life, and Jesus' description from the several nets used in fishing. The casting net was thrown from above, weighted with lead weights, while the dragnet was pulled by the boats, gathering all in its path. Jesus' parable uses the latter. The Kingdom of heaven is as a net cast across the world, being pulled toward the final reckoning. At the judgment the division will happen; the angels, as God's agents, will separate the evil to destruction and the just to eternal life. We are not to be deceived by the good and bad existing together in the same culture, nor are we to execute the judgment of God. The apostles cast the net but the angels separate the fish. Plummer says, "It is difficult to believe that Christ would have given these interpretations . . . if there were no such beings as Angels."[5]

Here again the question is whether the dragnet is the church. The answer is that the parable refers to the world as the scene of Kingdom activity. The church came into being as the fellowship of the covenant community in society, a witness of the Kingdom. But the movement of the Kingdom is larger than the fellowship of believers. The dragnet is the total impact of the Kingdom in society, in the world, influencing people for God. Many will benefit from the grace of God and His Kingdom action in the world who do not identify with Him by faith and partake of the fellowship of His people.

Jesus concludes this parable with a reference that projects back over the whole series (vv. 51–52). He asked the disciples whether they understood all of this teaching and they answered, "Yes." To this He responded by laying upon them the responsible mission of becoming teachers who could now, as instructed in the Kingdom, share things new and old. A suggested outline for these two verses would be: (1) Christianity is to be understood to be experienced, v. 51; (2) the community of disciples is to become the carrier of the good news, v. 52a; and (3) the communication of the Kingdom will interpret old and new in proper relationship, v. 52b. When we come to Christ we do not forget all of the old in our lives, but the new reinterprets the old. The gifts and aptitudes known before conversion become resources in the new life. Learning from the Master Teacher enriches us to be our best in His Kingdom.

THE MASTER REJECTED AT NAZARETH

53 And it came to pass, when Jesus had finished these parables, that He departed from there.

54 And when He had come to His own country,
He taught them in their synagogue, so that they were
astonished and said, "Where did this Man get this
wisdom and these mighty works?

55 "Is this not the carpenter's son? Is not His mother
called Mary? And His brothers James, Joses, Simon,
and Judas?

56 "And His sisters, are they not all with us? Where
then did this Man get all these things?"

57 And they were offended at Him. But Jesus said
to them, "A prophet is not without honor except in
his own country and in his own house."

58 And He did not do many mighty works there
because of their unbelief.

Matt. 13:53–58

The formula of transition from this "third book" of Matthew is
found in verse 53. The break introduces His return to visit His former
home. We may ask, "Why did Jesus go back to Nazareth?" He had
moved from there to Capernaum, avoiding the necessity of explaining
to people who knew Him as the carpenter the reasons for His new
role or of giving an account for His wisdom. But having just addressed
the crowds in a series of parables designed to keep them from insights
beyond the level to which they were prepared to move, His thoughts
must have turned to people whom He knew in Nazareth who were
limited in understanding Him. His return was to affirm His people,
His old friends. They were persons with whom He had associated,
and with whom he had done business as a carpenter. His return
was to share with them the same evidence of His messianic role
which He was sharing elsewhere.

Returning to Nazareth, He went to their synagogue and taught
them. This was the accepted manner for one who had something
to say. Here in the synagogue, the leaders of the community engaged
in dialogue. Confronted by His wisdom and message, they took offense that He would instruct them, no doubt remembering that, as
a boy, He had been instructed by them. They did not recognize that
God had raised up a prophet in their midst. The very goal of their
faith was before them; the Messiah had come, but they didn't recognize Him!

Verses 55–56 speak of their knowledge about Jesus, yet knowing
about Him they didn't know *Him*. Tragically, people in religious systems often know a lot about God, but do not come to Him to let

God be God in their lives. It appears to be more comfortable to remain in control of one's own life and pay God some marginal respect than to move over and let Him on the throne of one's life. They knew about Jesus, "the carpenter," which perhaps suggests that He had carried on Joseph's work as the oldest son in the family. They knew Jesus' mother, Mary, and they knew His brothers, four of them, and at least two of His sisters. Mary's children numbered at least seven, suggesting that Joseph should not be pictured as an old man at Jesus' birth. Knowing these things, they judged Jesus by the measure, "He's one of that family," fitting Him into the mold of social stratification. "Logically" they asked, "Where did this man get all these things?" The wording, "this fellow," is an expression of contempt.

Here one is reminded of Kierkegaard's emphasis on God incognito in Jesus of Nazareth, preserving the step of faith. The evidence that Jesus provided in the human experience introduced the reality of the eternal realm. But the people at Nazareth did not take this step of faith. Jesus' answer was more mild than what we might expect. He did not upbraid them as He did Capernaum or Bethsaida, but commented, *"A prophet is not without honor except in his own country and in his own house."* The designation of Himself as prophet was enough and His withdrawal without deeds of miraculous healing was a judgment amidst their questions.

We should note that this was not a simple visit, for the use of the imperfect tense tells us that this was an extended ministry (v. 54). The basic question was, Whence this authority and power? (v. 56). Mark tells us that He only healed a few sick people, with no outstanding work, marveling at their unbelief. The latter suggests Jesus' own amazement that they were so prejudiced (Mark 6:1–6). Luke gives a longer account and reports His visit to Nazareth as following the wilderness temptation (Luke 4:16–30). In Luke's account Jesus added illustrations from the ministries of Elijah and Elisha to show that only people of faith receive from God. As Paul wrote, "The righteous will live by faith" (Rom. 1:17, NIV).

The work of Christ is limited by our unbelief. There is doubtless much that God would prefer to do for us and for society, but He limits His action to function where and when its results are recognized to be of God and not by our achievements. To say that God moves where it brings glory to Him is to recognize the integrity of His grace.

NOTES

1. Joachim Jeremias, *The Parables of Jesus* (London: SCM, 1963), p. 113.
2. Plummer, *An Exegetical Study on . . . Matthew*, p. 194.
3. Jeremias, *The Parables of Jesus*, p. 33.
4. Eduard Schweizer, *The Good News According to Matthew*, p. 312.
5. Plummer, *An Exegetical Study on . . . Matthew*, p. 198.

CHAPTER SIX

The Compassion of the King

Matthew 14:1—15:59

Having seen that Jesus used parables to make His message less obvious to the multitude, we might conclude that He was turning away from the crowd. But in this section Matthew records His compassion for the multitude, His acts of healing and the several occasions on which He fed the multitudes by a miraculous multiplication of loaves and fishes. Jesus regarded the crowd as sheep without a Shepherd.

Jesus personified the love of God, not only by His death at Calvary but by His deeds of compassion. Love means that one's life is intimately open to that of another. Love is caring and sharing, identifying with the person to achieve the other's wholeness and fulfillment. Love means participation, and as such it is never easy, it is costly. Jesus' love for the people at Nazareth cost Him, for it meant sharing at the expense of their rejection and contempt.

This section begins with the account of the death of John the Baptist. The martyrdom of John had actually happened earlier, because while Jesus was at Nazareth He heard of Herod's comments regarding rumors that Jesus, the miracle worker, might be John raised from the dead. Upon learning that He had the attention of Herod, Jesus withdrew from Nazareth, went to Galilee, and took a boat to a more secluded desert area to be away from Herod.

Matthew did not include the account of the death of John earlier, as several of the Gospel writers did, and so used this occasion to tell the story of John's execution. It is significant how much attention Matthew gives to John as the herald of the Messiah, concluding the Old Testament era with John standing on the threshold of the New.

Our thesis, that Matthew is dealing directly with *Heilsgeschichte,* is supported by these extensive references to John, to his role as a herald and his being a bridge from the Old Testament to the dawning of the New.

THE ACCOUNT OF JOHN THE BAPTIST'S MARTYRDOM

1 At that time Herod the tetrarch heard the report about Jesus

2 and said to his servants, "This is John the Baptist; he is risen from the dead, and therefore these powers are at work in him."

3 For Herod had laid hold of John and bound him, and put him in prison for the sake of Herodias, his brother Philip's wife.

4 For John had said to him, "It is not lawful for you to have her."

5 And although he wanted to put him to death, he feared the multitude because they counted him as a prophet.

6 But when Herod's birthday came, the daughter of Herodias danced before them and pleased Herod.

7 Therefore he promised with an oath to give her whatever she would ask.

8 And she, having been prompted by her mother, said, "Give me John the Baptist's head here on a platter."

9 And the king was sorry; nevertheless, because of the oaths and because of those who sat with him at the table, he commanded it to be given to her.

10 And he sent and beheaded John in prison.

11 And his head was brought on a platter and given to the girl, and she brought it to her mother.

12 And his disciples came and took away the body, buried it, and went and told Jesus.

Matt. 14:1–12

The immediate historical context for this section is Herod's having heard reports about Jesus (vv. 1–2). The story of John's death, which had happened earlier, is inserted by Matthew as a parenthesis. The flow of historical content goes from the end of verse 2 to verse 13.

The account explains Jesus' move to absent Himself from Herod's immediate region and to escape his dominion. Mark similarly reviews the story of John's death in the context of Herod's hearing of Jesus and from a troubled conscience wondering if John had been resurrected (Mark 6:14–29). Mark's account adds dramatic details missing from Matthew. Luke makes a very brief reference to this event (Luke 9:7–9), presenting Herod as hearing reports that Jesus is John raised from the dead and as being tormented by them. Herod said, "John I have beheaded, but who is this . . . ?" and Luke tells us "he sought to see Him." Jesus avoided the encounter.

The story of John's death is related from three scenes: the confrontation, the intrigue, and the execution. The confrontation, verses 4–5, is John's deliberate denunciation of Herod's immorality. Herod is called tetrarch, distinguishing him from Herod the Great, his father. The title "tetrarch" means ruler of a fourth part. When Herod the Great died, his kingdom was divided, two parts being given to Archelaus, one part to Antipas (this Herod) and one part to Philip. Herod Antipas was married to the daughter of Aretas, king of Syria (2 Cor. 11:32), but on a trip to Rome he seduced Herodias, the wife of his brother Philip, a wealthy private individual. He then divorced his own wife and took Herodias as his wife. John, the fearless prophet of God, was continually (imperfect tense) pointing this out to Herod, and calling for his repentance. Herod was guilty of breaking covenant with his wife, of breaking the marriage of his brother Philip, and of violating the Jewish law which forbids marrying one's sister-in-law.[1] Aretas made war against Herod in retaliation and heavily defeated him, causing many to suffer—a social problem which John didn't overlook.

Matthew does not report Herod's interest and sympathy for John as does Mark (6:20), but says that Herod arrested him because of Herodias, and wanted to kill him but feared to do so because the people regarded John as a prophet. In verse 9 Matthew does refer to Herod's having been sorry to give the order for John's execution, knowing that John was a righteous man.

John was imprisoned in a dungeon of Herod's fortress, Machaerus, to the east of the Dead Sea, at the northern end. The birthday party for Herod must have been held at the fortress, for upon Herod's oath the beheading of John immediately followed. The story reveals the conspiracy of Herodias, who wanted John out of the way and didn't see her weak husband acting to execute him. She arranged for her daughter Salome, probably sixteen or seventeen years old, to do the sensual dance of the veils before Herod. Enthralled, he offered her half of his kingdom if she but asked. To his amazement, she, prompted by Herodias, asked for the head of John on a plate. Although sorry, he was bound to the oath, and sent to have John beheaded. The prophet was sacrificed for a man's passion.

But removing the prophet didn't release Herod and Herodias from their problem. John's disciples buried his body, but his message lived on. When Caligula, Emperor of Rome, made Agrippa king, Herodias pressed Herod Antipas to go to Rome and buy the title and privilege of being king, but Caligula was told by Agrippa that their intrigue was subversive, and he banished Antipas to exile in Gaul where he and Herodias lived until his death. Caligula offered to spare Herodias, but she declined, saying it wasn't right that, having shared Herod's prosperity, she not share his misfortune.

JESUS' COMPASSION AND POWER

13 When Jesus heard it, He departed from there by boat to a deserted place by Himself. And when the multitudes heard it, they followed Him on foot from the cities.

14 And when Jesus went out He saw a great multitude; and He was moved with compassion for them, and healed their sick.

15 And when it was evening, His disciples came to Him, saying, "This is a deserted place, and the hour is already late. Send the multitudes away, that they may go into the villages and buy themselves food."

16 But Jesus said to them, "They do not need to go away. You give them something to eat."

17 And they said to Him, "We have here only five loaves and two fish."

18 He said, "Bring them here to Me."

19 And He commanded the multitudes to sit down on the grass. And He took the five loaves and the two fish, and looking up to heaven, He blessed and broke and gave the loaves to His disciples; and the disciples gave to the multitudes.

20 And they all ate and were filled, and they took up twelve baskets full of the fragments that remained.

21 And those who had eaten were about five
thousand men, besides women and children.

Matt. 14:13–21

The feeding of the five thousand was one of the more spectacular
miracles in the ministry of Christ. It was an occasion in which the
disciples overemphasized the problem and underemphasized the resources, for they underestimated the Master! Jesus had come to this
desert place to be alone with the disciples. They had just returned
from the mission to which Jesus had sent them, and they needed
time to process their experience (Mark 6:30–32). But as they crossed
near Bethsaida to a desert place on the other side of the bay, a large
crowd made its way around the bay and came to Jesus. Seeing them,
He was moved with compassion and extended His ministry to their
need, healing and teaching. At eventide the disciples urged Jesus to
send the multitude away so that they could get bread, probably at
Bethsaida.

Jesus amazed the disciples by saying, *"They do not need to go away.
You give them something to eat."* Upon their remonstrance that they had
only five loaves and two fish, Jesus said, "Bring them here to me."
We bring what we have to the Master, and He will bless it. A little
with God is more than much without Him. And yet they were staggered to look into the faces of five thousand men, plus women and
children, and then look at this little lunch basket! But one expectation
was that the Messiah, like Moses, would feed His people. This event
may be associated with the messianic banquet spoken of by Isaiah
(25:6).

In verse 19 we have the order of grace: He blessed; He gave to
the disciples; they gave to others. The Lord works through His disciples, through his church.[2] Reviewing the happening we recognize:
(1) the promise—they don't have to leave; (2) the commission—you
give them something; (3) the power—bring them to me; and (4) the
provision—they all ate. The conclusion is the abundance which satis-
fies, for there were twelve baskets full of fragments left over. The
word for "basket" here is *kophinos,* meaning a smaller wicker basket.
At the second feeding of four thousand the kind of basket was the
spuris, a larger basket. The point of reference here is that there was
more than enough.

This marks the climax of popular enthusiasm for Jesus, and of
the desire to make Him King. But Jesus was not a bread-King, and

according to John 6, Jesus followed up on this miracle by talking to the people about their need for spiritual sustenance. Jesus said, "I am the bread of life. He who comes to me shall never hunger, and he who believes in me shall never thirst" (John 6:35). And in answer to their unbelief, Jesus said, "I tell you the truth, unless you eat the flesh of the Son of Man and drink his blood, you have no life in you. Whoever eats my flesh and drinks my blood has eternal life, and I will raise him up at the last day. . . . Just as the living Father sent me and I live because of the Father, so the one who feeds on me will live because of me" (John 6:53–54, 57, NIV). As food sustains the energy of the body, so living by the energy of identification with Christ is the only sustenance of spiritual life.

JESUS' CONCERN FOR PRESENCE

22 And immediately Jesus made His disciples get into the boat and go before Him to the other side, while He sent the multitudes away.

23 And when He had sent the multitudes away, He went up on a mountain by Himself to pray. And when evening had come, He was alone there.

24 But the boat was now in the middle of the sea, tossed by the waves, for the wind was contrary.

25 And in the fourth watch of the night Jesus went to them, walking on the sea.

26 And when the disciples saw Him walking on the sea, they were troubled, saying, "It is a ghost!" And they cried out for fear.

27 But immediately Jesus spoke to them, saying, "Be of good cheer! It is I; do not be afraid."

28 And Peter answered Him and said, "Lord, if it is You, command me to come to You on the water."

29 And He said, "Come." And when Peter had come down out of the boat, he walked on the water to go to Jesus.

30 But when he saw that the wind was boisterous, he was afraid; and beginning to sink he cried out, saying, "Lord, save me!"

31 And immediately Jesus stretched out His hand and caught him, and said to him, "O you of little faith, why did you doubt?"

32 And when they got into the boat, the wind
ceased.

33 Then those who were in the boat came and
worshiped Him, saying, "Truly You are the Son of
God."

Matt. 14:22–33

There is a twofold concern for Jesus in this passage: to be in the
presence of His Father, and to be present with His disciples in distress.
Having dismissed the multitude, Jesus sent the disciples across the
bay in the boat. Matthew says, *"Jesus made His disciples get into the boat
and go before Him."* He must have given the impression that He would
walk to the other side of the bay. On their departure He went up
on the mountain slope to pray. As evening arrived He was alone
with God in prayer, while the disciples in the boat were caught in
a storm and driven with the wind. However, Jesus didn't act at once,
but continued in prayer, letting the disciples struggle, "laboriously
rowing," until the fourth watch, i.e., between 3:00 and 6:00 A.M.

Matthew says that in the fourth watch *"Jesus went to them"* (v. 25).
It should be noted that His walking on the sea was to get to the
disciples, to bring to them the reality of His presence. No matter
what the difficulties in our lives, Jesus comes to us in the stress.
His presence is our assurance. Not comprehending the reality of Jesus'
presence in their distress, the disciples misread Him to be a spirit
and cried out in fear. And into their fear and despair came the remarkable words, *"Be of good cheer! It is I; do not be afraid."* The Greek for "It
is I" reminds us of God's word to Moses, "I AM," that is, "I will
be what I will be." And Jesus stood there on the water, Sovereign
of creation, saying, "I will be what I will be," Lord in the storm.
From Mark we learn that Jesus appeared to be walking on by them,
having fulfilled His purpose of encouragement by His presence (Mark
6:45–52). But Matthew adds the account which Peter may have refrained from relating to Mark. Seeing Jesus walking by, Peter, the
realist, cries out, *"Lord, if it is You"*—he wanted to be sure, for he
knew the sea; he was a veteran fisherman, and no storm had ever
made him lose his senses—*"command me to come to You!"* And Jesus
said, *"Come."* Peter had his answer, and now it was a question of
faith![3]

It was Peter's move next. All that Peter had upon which to act
was the word "come." This is the ultimate test of faith, to move

on Jesus' word alone. And Peter stepped over the side of the boat to go to Jesus. We might ask, "Peter, how did you do it? Had you practiced, had you studied yoga, had you studied surface tension?" And Peter might have answered, "It was when I thought of surface tension that I began to sink!" Faith rivets its attention solely on the Master who says "Come."

We should avoid making this story allegorical. Schweizer falls into this trap in making the boat a symbol of community, Peter's act a symbol of the faith of the disciples, and Jesus' saving him as help in failure. The primary meaning is that Jesus as Lord of creation can be present in the lives of people in this material world.

As Jesus and Peter got into the boat, the wind ceased and the waves sank back to calmness, witnessing to the reality of the event that had just happened. The disciples fell before Him in worship, exclaiming, "Truly You are the Son of God." This miracle in nature should be seen as a part of the cosmic struggle between Jesus and the satanic in all its forms of evil. The confession by the disciples was a step toward the great confession made later by Peter, "Thou art the Christ, the Son of the living God" (16:16, KJV).

JESUS' MINISTRY AT GENNESARET

34 And when they had crossed over, they came to the land of Gennesaret.

35 And when the men of that place recognized Him, they sent out into all that surrounding region, brought to Him all who were sick,

36 and begged Him that they might only touch the hem of His garment. And as many as touched it were made perfectly well.

Matt. 14:34–36

Avoiding the western shore with its proximity to Herod, Jesus and the disciples came ashore at Gennesaret, not far from the region of Bethsaida. The crowd had dispersed, but the news of Jesus' presence in the region spread rapidly. Matthew says that when the men of the region recognized Jesus, they sent into all of the surrounding area for the sick and needy. This was a contrast to the attitude of the people of Nazareth. There He could do no mighty work because of their unbelief; here the people in need were sought out. Further indication of their faith was in their begging only to *"touch the hem of His garment"* for healing. This is reminiscent of the woman with the issue of blood. The word is a simple declaration: as many as touched His garment were made perfectly well. While Jesus had left the region of Herod's domain to avoid an untimely confrontation with him, in no way did He retreat from His ministry. In fact, His healing of the sick is seen here as a primary activity, and gains continued attention rather than the feeding of the multitude. Jesus is the compassionate Savior, touching people at their point of need. This was His conscious strategy of mission.

THE LAW AND JESUS' COMPASSION

1 Then the scribes and Pharisees who were from Jerusalem came to Jesus, saying,

2 "Why do Your disciples transgress the tradition of the elders? For they do not wash their hands when they eat bread."

3 But He answered and said to them, "Why do you also transgress the commandment of God because of your tradition?

4 "For God commanded, saying, *'Honor your father and your mother'*; and, *'He who curses father or mother, let him be put to death.'*

5 "But you say, 'Whoever says to his father or his mother, "Whatever you might be profited by me is a gift"—

6 'and does not honor his father or his mother, he will be free.' Thus you have made the commandment of God of no effect by your tradition.

7 "Hypocrites! Well did Isaiah prophesy about you, saying:

8 *This people draws near to Me with their mouth,*
   And honors Me with their lips,
   But their heart is far from Me.
9 *And in vain they worship Me,*
   Teaching as doctrines the commandments of
      men.'"

10 And He called the multitude and said to them, "Hear and understand:

11 "Not what goes into the mouth defiles a man; but what comes out of the mouth, this defiles a man."

12 Then His disciples came and said to Him, "Do
You know that the Pharisees were offended when they
heard this saying?"

13 But He answered and said, "Every plant which
My heavenly Father has not planted will be uprooted.

14 "Let them alone. They are blind leaders of the
blind. And if the blind leads the blind, both will fall
into a ditch."

15 Then Peter answered and said to Him, "Explain
this parable to us."

16 And Jesus said, "Are you also still without
understanding?

17 "Do you not yet understand that whatever enters
the mouth goes into the stomach and is eliminated?

18 "But those things which proceed out of the
mouth come from the heart, and they defile a man.

19 "For out of the heart proceed evil thoughts,
murders, adulteries, fornications, thefts, false witness,
blasphemies.

20 "These are the things which defile a man, but
to eat with unwashed hands does not defile a man."

Matt. 15:1–20

This entire section is in the mode of a disputation, for there are
questions and counterquestions. The hierarchy at Jerusalem was acting
through their scribes and Pharisees, who had come to Galilee with
the express purpose of refuting Jesus. As they accused the disciples
of transgressing *"the tradition of the elders,"* Jesus in turn accused them
of transgressing the commandments of God! Luther said, "He places
one wedge against the other and therewith drives the first back."
He exposed them for using the traditions of the elders to circumvent
the commandments of God (vv. 4–6). The leaders of the Great Synagogue enjoined three things: "Be deliberate in judgment; raise up
many disciples; and make a fence for the Law."[4]

The Pharisees' criticism had to do with ritual uncleanness, but Jesus'
criticism had to do with moral uncleanness. The commandments of
God required honoring one's father and mother, meaning to look
out for their well-being, and helping them financially. But the Pharisees had developed a program to amass economic wealth at the temple,
and permitted a churlish son to evade his duty to his parents by
saying that his gift was dedicated, that it belonged to the temple.
In so doing they emptied God's commandment of meaning. This use
of the term *corban* meant that the person refused to help his parents,

claiming all was dedicated to God. But Plummer adds a second meaning of *corban:* an oath in which a person might swear at the parents' request saying he could not help them; later if he repented and wanted to help, he was told by the scribes that what he swore, even in a fit of emotional passion, was forever binding. This is probably the meaning of Jesus' illustration.[5]

Jesus is pointed and fearless in His response. He doesn't back off a bit: "Hypocrites!" With this He quotes Isaiah's words of God's judgment on persons guilty of lip worship, of words without deeds, and/or words which actually excuse the deed. Religion, to perpetuate itself, has often developed "commandments of men" and presented them as though they were actually doctrines of God.

The next verses are an interpretation to the crowd of the issue raised by the Pharisees and scribes. Jesus said that defilement is of a moral nature; it is the perversions of the heart that defile a person's life. As the disciples informed Jesus that the Pharisees were offended, Jesus added to His denunciation: (1) they are not plantings in God's vineyard but are a wild thicket; (2) they are blind leaders of the blind; and (3) they face the judgment of God.

The section concludes with Peter's request for an interpretation of the parable on defilement. Jesus taught that ritual religion was never intended as an end in itself. Only acting contrary to God's will makes one unclean, and in so doing the issues of the heart, or seat of selfishness, are moral perversions. As Jeremiah said, "The heart is deceitful above all things, and desperately wicked, who can know it?" (Jer. 17:9, KJV). Origen interpreted Jesus to mean that eating with an unwashed heart defiles the man, and he applied this especially to "worthless reading," to intellectual food.[6]

The passage may be outlined: (1) the criticism by the Pharisees (vv. 1–2); (2) the cryptic rejoinder of Christ (vv. 3–6); (3) the condemnation of hypocrisy (vv. 7–9); (4) the interpretation of the interchange (vv. 10–11); and (5) the warning against pharisaical practice (vv. 12–20).

COMPASSION FOR A GENTILE

21 Then Jesus went out from there and departed
to the region of Tyre and Sidon.
22 And behold, a woman of Canaan came from that

region and cried out to Him, saying, "Have mercy on
me, O Lord, Son of David! My daughter is severely
demon-possessed."
23 But He answered her not a word. And His
disciples came and urged Him, saying, "Send her away,
for she cries out after us."
24 But He answered and said, "I was not sent except
to the lost sheep of the house of Israel."
25 Then she came and worshiped Him, saying,
"Lord, help me!"
26 But He answered and said, "It is not good to
take the children's bread and throw it to the little
dogs."
27 And she said, "True, Lord, yet even the little
dogs eat the crumbs which fall from their masters'
table."
28 Then Jesus answered and said to her, "O woman,
great is your faith! Let it be to you as you desire."
And her daughter was healed from that very hour.

Matt. 15:21–28

Perhaps to avoid further demands from the crowds and/or the
legalistic Pharisees, Jesus journeyed west toward the region of Tyre
and Sidon. Although a region not originally included in His ministry,
He went there to provide opportunity for persons to hear and respond.
In verse 22 we read that a Gentile woman, a woman of Canaan,
came to meet Him. Desperate, she was crying out for His help, addressing Him as Lord, and as Son of David. But Jesus ignored her,
and consequently she kept crying after His disciples. They were so
perturbed that they urged Jesus to send her away. But He answered
in a manner expressing the exclusiveness of the Jewish leaders with
whom He had just recently been in conversation—*"I was not sent except
to the lost sheep of the house of Israel."*

The scene changed when the woman came and worshiped Jesus,
making her entreaty. There are four interacting scenes in the account:
(1) her request, (2) His rejection, (3) her reaction, and (4) His response.
Jesus expressed the common Jewish attitude toward Gentiles, saying,
"It is not good to throw the children's bread to the little dogs." She
responded by saying in essence, "Yes, Master, what you say is true,
but the little dogs still eat the crumbs that fall from their master's
table." Even if she was not privileged to sit at Messiah's table, she
would be satisfied with the crumbs! Jesus responded, *"O woman, great*

is your faith! Let it be to you as you desire.'' And her daughter was healed. Her faith that moved beyond ethnic and cultural obstacles, bypassed the forms of ritual religion, and humbly confessed the Master's Lordship, received His grace.

COMPASSION ON THE MOUNT

29 And Jesus departed from there, came near to the Sea of Galilee, and went up on the mountain and sat down there.

30 And great multitudes came to Him, having with them those who were lame, blind, mute, maimed, and many others; and they laid them down at Jesus' feet, and He healed them.

31 So the multitude marveled when they saw the mute speaking, the maimed made whole, the lame walking, and the blind seeing; and they glorified the God of Israel.

Matt. 15:29–31

The tour into the region of Tyre and Sidon may have lasted several weeks, giving Jesus time with His disciples. From there He returned to the region of Galilee, as reported by Mark (7:31–8:9), evidently going to the east shore in the Hellenistic region. That this was a Gentile area is suggested by the words *''they glorified the God of Israel.''* It may well have been deliberate on the part of Jesus to follow His ministry to the Syrophoenician woman by going to the Decapolis.[7]

Having studied the Sermon on the Mount, we now have the healing on the Mount. Word is matched by deed throughout Jesus' ministry. In Acts 1:1–2 Luke writes "of all that Jesus began to do and to teach." The deed demonstrates the word, and the word interprets the deed. The deed authenticates the word and the word articulates the meaning of the deed. And yet, deeds of compassion need few words. The comparison with the Sermon on the Mount is suggested in the words of verse 29, that He "sat down there." This is the symbol of an official act of ministry. Matthew makes a point of the people coming to Him, of their bringing the sick, lame, and blind and placing them at His feet.

There is no other answer for our problems than to place them at the feet of Jesus. The feet that walked upon the water as Lord of creation are now symbolic of His power over creation to minister in compassion and wholeness (note Isa. 52:7).

JESUS' FEEDING OF THE FOUR THOUSAND

32 Then Jesus called His disciples to Him and said, "I have compassion on the multitude, because they have now continued with Me three days and have nothing to eat. And I do not want to send them away hungry, lest they faint on the way."

33 And His disciples said to Him, "Where could we get enough bread in the wilderness to fill such a great multitude?"

34 And Jesus said to them, "How many loaves do you have?" And they said, "Seven, and a few little fish."

35 And He commanded the multitude to sit down on the ground.

36 And He took the seven loaves and the fish, gave thanks, broke them, and gave them to His disciples; and the disciples gave to the multitude.

37 And they all ate and were filled; and they took up seven large baskets full of the broken pieces that were left.

38 And those who ate were four thousand men, besides women and children.

39 And He sent away the multitude, got into the boat, and came into the region of Magdala.

Matt. 15:32–39

A second feeding of the multitude happened in the wilderness of the Decapolis. That there were two different events is supported by the fact that Matthew and Mark both tell of the two occasions, and Jesus Himself referred later to two different feedings (Matt. 16:9–10). While Jesus was fulfilling in each a messianic expectation, and demonstrating His power over created things, the second feeding had a particular significance for Gentiles. Willard Swartley, in his excellent work on Mark, makes a point of the second act of Jesus pointing to His ministry being open to the Gentiles.[8]

In this account, Jesus Himself raised the question with the disciples about food for the multitude. They had been with Him for three days, and their bag lunches were gone. The disciples remonstrated by asking where they could find bread in the wilderness for such a crowd. But again Jesus asked what they had, and their reply was to play down even the little—seven loaves, and two "little" fish. But Jesus acted decisively, for His compassion was as great for this mixed multitude that included Gentiles as it had been for the previous crowd. The lesson of the Syrophoenician woman lived on!

As before, He asked the crowd to sit down, blessed the food they had, and gave to the disciples and they gave to the crowd. It is to be assumed that as the disciples broke off bread and passed it, that the miracle kept happening in their hands; the bread continued to be present! The stories of Elijah and the widow's meal (1 Kings 17:8–16), of the widow and two sons with the cruse of oil (2 Kings 4:1–7), and of Elisha feeding one hundred men with twenty loaves of barley (2 Kings 4:42–44) all come to mind. Here four thousand men, besides women and children, were fed. At the conclusion they filled seven large baskets with the broken pieces that were left. As mentioned earlier, the word for "basket" is different in this instance from chapter 14; this word, *spuris,* describes a very large basket, one such as was used to lower Paul from a window in the wall of Damascus (Acts 9:25). There was no doubt over the actual miracle of multiplying the food.

An outline for this passage could follow four points: (1) hopelessness, three days and no food; (2) helplessness, in the wilderness, for Moses and the Israelites, with no answer in sight; (3) hopefulness, in Jesus' compassion and request for the little that they had; and (4) helpfulness, as the disciples serve the Master in passing out what He had blessed. Again our Lord used His disciples to perform His ministry of compassion.

NOTES

1. Plummer, *An Exegetical Study on . . . Matthew,* p. 202.
2. Ibid., p. 204.
3. Ibid., p. 209, says the story is not an invention.
4. Ibid., p. 211.

5.   Ibid., pp. 211–12.

6.   Ibid., p. 214.

7.   John Charles Fenton, *Saint Matthew* (Philadelphia: Westminster Press, 1977), p. 257.

8.   Swartley, *Mark*, pp. 113–19.

CHAPTER SEVEN

The Confession of the King

Matthew 16:1—20:34

Step by step the progress in the Gospel of Matthew has led to a general recognition of Jesus as the Son of David, i.e., the Messiah. And interfacing this recognition is Jesus' teaching on the Kingdom of heaven, a very clear move on His part to help persons discover what kind of Kingdom the Messiah actually brings. But religious leaders in the large missed His message, being more concerned over legalistic observance of their tradition than about the new and unique thing happening among them in Jesus. And the political activists, the Zealots, missed His message because they could not understand a nonviolent revolutionary who would change society by a conversion of persons to the will and kingdom of God. But the disciples themselves had problems with the kind of messiahship Jesus was interpreting.

But for some, confronted with the quality of the mission and person of Christ, that faith would dawn was inevitable. People can't meet Jesus and be the same. And throughout the next major section of the Gospel there are numerous occasions on which people were led to confess Jesus as the Christ, the Son of God. This is not to say that they understood fully the impact of this awareness, but they were on the way, with Him. Also in this section we have the "fourth book" of Matthew, Jesus' discussion of the church (15:54–18:35).

DISTINGUISHING THE NEW COMMUNITY FROM RELIGIOUS LEGALISTS

1 And the Pharisees and Sadducees came, and testing Him asked that He would show them a sign from heaven.

200

2 He answered and said to them, "When it is evening you say, 'It will be fair weather, for the sky is red';

3 "and in the morning, 'It will be foul weather today, for the sky is red and threatening.' Hypocrites! You know how to discern the face of the sky, but you cannot discern the signs of the times.

4 "A wicked and adulterous generation seeks after a sign, and no sign will be given to it except the sign of the prophet Jonah." And He left them and departed.

5 And when His disciples had come to the other side, they had forgotten to take bread.

6 Then Jesus said to them, "Take heed and beware of the leaven of the Pharisees and of the Sadducees."

7 And they reasoned among themselves, saying, "It is because we have taken no bread."

8 But when Jesus perceived it, He said to them, "O you of little faith, why do you reason among yourselves because you have brought no bread?

9 "Do you not yet understand, or remember the five loaves of the five thousand and how many baskets you took up?

10 "Nor the seven loaves of the four thousand and how many large baskets you took up?

11 "How is it you do not understand that I did not speak to you concerning bread, but that you should beware of the leaven of the Pharisees and Sadducees?"

12 Then they understood that He did not tell them to beware of the leaven of bread, but of the doctrine of the Pharisees and Sadducees.

Matt. 16:1–12

Again the Pharisees and Sadducees asked a sign of Jesus, and being far from confessing Him as the Messiah, they asked for a sign from heaven. Interestingly, Jesus' answer was to point to the heavens! He said, you know how to read the sky for indications of weather, but you can't discern the signs of the times. They were skilled in religious knowledge, and yet "the fullness of the time had come" (Gal. 4:4), and they did not recognize God's acts in salvation history. Again Jesus called them hypocrites, saying that they read all of the signs but the important one. We still read the weather in this way, even though satellite pictures tell us much more, and more accurately. As a boy I learned the lines, "Red at night, sailor's delight; red in the morning, sailors take warning." Jesus was asking them to recognize the credibility of fulfilled prophecy happening before them.

Again He denounced the wickedness that sought a sign and ignored the meaning of His presence. No sign but that of the prophet Jonah would be given—that is, no sign but His presence announcing the Kingdom of heaven! And He left them and departed, refusing to waste time with their unbelief. As He went He admonished the disciples to beware of the leaven of the Pharisees and Sadducees. Having forgotten bread, they thought He was upbraiding them. He rebuked them for their little faith, their little discernment, calling attention to the two miracles of multiplying the loaves and fishes as though to say that a lack of bread is of little concern. Note this "rebuke," for Jesus rebuked the demonic and He rebuked the wind, and as Peter rejects the Passion announcement (16:23), Jesus rebuked him—reflecting His struggle with the tempter throughout His ministry.

The leaven of the Pharisees, against which He warned, was their doctrine.[1] Jesus was distinguishing between the New Community which He was creating and the Pharisees and Sadducees. He was creating a new Israel, not just reforming the old. The new wine had to be put in new wineskins. The legalistic traditions were not open to the new inbreaking of the rule of God.

PETER'S CONFESSION OF JESUS AS THE CHRIST

13 When Jesus came into the region of Caesarea Philippi, He asked His disciples, saying, "Who do men say that I, the Son of Man, am?"

14 And they said, "Some say John the Baptist, some Elijah, and others Jeremiah or one of the prophets."

15 He said to them, "But who do you say that I am?"

16 And Simon Peter answered and said, "You are the Christ, the Son of the living God."

17 And Jesus answered and said to him, "Blessed are you, Simon Bar-Jonah, for flesh and blood has not revealed this to you, but My Father who is in heaven.

18 "And I also say to you that you are Peter, and on this rock I will build My church, and the gates of Hades shall not prevail against it.

19 "And I will give you the keys of the kingdom of heaven, and whatever you bind on earth will be

bound in heaven, and whatever you loose on earth
will be loosed in heaven."
    20 Then He commanded His disciples that they
should tell no one that He was Jesus the Christ.

Matt. 16:13–20

Caesarea Philippi is about twenty-five miles north of Galilee; it
is not the Caesarea on the Mediterranean Coast. Near the base of
Mount Hermon, an ascent of about 1700 feet, it was a long trek
away. It was a border town where the people of Israel met the people
of the Gentile world, and a site of the worship of the idol Pan, the
so-called universal god, the most modern of heathen cults. In this
unique setting, where Judaism touched both the worship of nature
and the worship of man,[2] Jesus asked the question of His disciples,
"Who do men say that I, the Son of Man, am?" Their answer associated
Jesus with three great voices of salvation history: John the Baptist,
the herald of a new age; Jeremiah, the prophet of reform and hope;
and Elijah, the prophet of power and miracles. But none of these
witnesses of the past answered the question of the uniqueness of
Jesus and His presence before them.

Jesus then asked the disciples point-blank, *"Who do you say that I
am?"* Simon Peter gave the answer for himself and for all of the
disciples, *"Thou art the Christ, the Son of the living God"* (KJV). His confession
was a calm, calculated answer from the experiences in which God
had unfolded this revelation before them. It was not an answer given
in a euphoria after Jesus had walked on the water and calmed the
storm, when they had all said this (14:33), but was given in a calm
setting of deliberate response. Jesus answered, *"Blessed . . . son of Jonah"*—perhaps a name for John or a play on the sign of Jonah, but
which affirms above all that this insight was not of human origin
but by a disclosure from God, His Father. This confession marks a
turning point in the Gospel, for from this time Jesus began sharing
explicit detail of His coming Passion.

The three following verses of the section introduce a new element,
the church. This is the first use of the word "church" in the New
Testament. This word, *ekklēsia,* refers to an assembly of citizens regularly summoned, the "called-out ones," who were His official representatives. The church is not a building, nor a religious institution,
nor an ethnic group, but is the company of the committed, the covenant community where we are brothers and sisters in fellowship with
Christ. The church is people—the redeemed people of God. It is God's

primary program in the world, the visible expression of the rule of Christ, the voluntary association of those committed to Jesus as Lord.

Jesus announced His church in direct relation to Peter and his confession. The church is built on confessing people. The interpretation of the Kingdom of God is committed to such people, and the authority to structure its mission rests now upon such disciples of Christ. Jesus said, "You are *Petros* [Greek for Peter] and upon this *petra* [Greek for rock] I will build my church." The play on words appears as a significant identification, but Jesus spoke Aramaic, and the word *Cepha* would then be the same in both cases. The church will be built on such a confession as Peter had just made.[3] Further, Jesus stressed a course of action on the offense, not on the defensive. He would move in on a world that was so permeated with evil that it would reject Him, but the gates of hell would not stop Him, nor prevail against the planting of His church.

In verse 18 Jesus said, "My church," and followed this by giving the keys to Peter as a steward. The keys were normally in the hands of the teachers of the Law as they unlocked or interpreted God's Word, but these are now entrusted to Peter and to his associates. Significantly, the binding and loosing were exercised by Peter as he opened the door of the church to Gentiles (Acts 10:1–20). Verse 19 could be translated, "Whatever you bind on earth shall be having been bound in heaven"—holding us accountable, and relating us directly to the Head of the church. And this is the key for unity and effectiveness. I recall a missionary, touched by God in the East Africa Revival movement, saying, "If you keep the Head in its proper relationship to the body you won't be biting the little finger."

This matter of "binding and loosing" is developed in chapter 18 of Matthew, as the disciplinary function of the church. The only two uses of the term "church," *ekklēsia,* in the Gospels are the two associated with "binding and loosing." The new community is to be a responsible fellowship of regenerate people who hold one another accountable for their covenant with Christ. But, as Plummer says, it is "whatsoever" you shall bind, not "whomsoever" you shall bind.[4]

This section closes with Jesus' command to "tell no one"—this is inside information. The open word would come, but for the present they were to process this among themselves. We could outline this remarkable passage by five words: (1) the compassion, vv. 13–14; (2) the confrontation, v. 15; (3) the confession, v. 16; (4) the commendation, v. 17; and (5) the commission, vv. 18–20. (Compare Mark 8:27–30 and Luke 9:18–21.)

JESUS PREDICTS HIS PASSION

21 From that time on Jesus began to show to His disciples that He must go to Jerusalem, and suffer many things from the elders and chief priests and scribes, and be killed, and be raised again the third day.

22 Then Peter took Him aside and began to rebuke Him, saying, "Far be it from You, Lord; this shall not happen to You!"

23 But He turned and said to Peter, "Get behind Me, Satan! You are an offense to Me, for you are not mindful of the things of God, but the things of men."

Matt. 16:21–23

The church is built on the redemptive suffering of the Messiah. It is not an ethnic body, nor a political entity, nor a moralistic association, but a fellowship of the redeemed. Its lifestyle is correlated with Jesus' identity as the "crucified God," a stumbling block to the Jews and foolishness to the Greeks (1 Cor. 1:23). And its vitality will be in the fellowship of the risen Lord. Jesus followed the announcement that He will build His own assembly, His church, with the prediction of His death at Jerusalem and of His Resurrection. He had not shared this before, but Matthew says emphatically "from that time on" He kept interpreting it and preparing the disciples for His death and Resurrection (v. 21).

Peter took Jesus aside and rebuked Him. For Peter this prediction didn't fit his confession of Christ as God's Son. How could God permit such a thing to happen? Peter's words, no doubt well meant, caused Jesus to hear again the words of the tempter in the wilderness. His rebuke of Peter was in that light, for He addressed him as Satan, saying, "Get behind me, for you are an offense," a rock out of place! Peter was now a stumbling stone rather than a building stone. These words of Peter's were from human reasoning and not from God.

JESUS' CALL TO CROSS-BEARING DISCIPLESHIP

24 Then Jesus said to His disciples, "If anyone desires to come after Me, let him deny himself, take up his cross, and follow Me.

25 "For whoever desires to save his life will lose

it, and whoever loses his life for My sake will find it.

26 "For what is a man profited if he gains the whole world, and loses his own soul? Or what will a man give in exchange for his soul?

27 "For the Son of Man will come in the glory of His Father with His angels, and then He will reward each according to his works.

28 "Assuredly, I say to you, there are some standing here who shall not taste death till they see the Son of Man coming in His kingdom."

Matt. 16:24–28

Jesus calls His disciples to be suffering servants among men. The lifestyle of the new people of God, the church, is to be correlated with Christ in His suffering. The disciple is called to be a servant, to bear the identity of the cross in living for Christ and His Kingdom. Peter wrote later of our taking the "death route" saying, "He that hath suffered in the flesh hath ceased from sin; that he no longer should live the rest of his time in the flesh to the lusts of men, but to the will of God" (1 Pet. 4:1b–2, KJV). And Paul writes of our break with the old man, a break as decisive as death, and of the old man's being replaced by a new man (Col. 3:9–10). This break from the old life he calls the crucifixion of the old man. As we read in Romans 6:6, "Our old man is crucified by identification with Him, so that the sin-nature may be devitalized" (my translation). These references deal with the nature of the inner transformation wrought by the grace of Christ. But in this passage Jesus was expressing the nature of His calling to discipleship.

Discipleship, in the sphere of conduct, means saying no to the sinful ego; it means being prepared to suffer in the company of Christ; it means giving up selfish ambition and, in so doing, finding one's true self in the fellowship of Christ (vv. 24–25).

Discipleship, as in verse 24, can be expressed in three points: (1) making up one's mind; (2) giving up one's autonomy; and (3) taking up one's identity. An outline for the whole section includes four elements for discipleship: (1) partnership with Christ, v. 24; (2) priorities from the Person of Christ, v. 25; (3) perspectives from the judgment of Christ, v. 26; and (4) practices in the will of Christ, v. 27. Rather than to say, "He is happiest who possesses most," Jesus teaches that "He is happiest who is himself possessed by Christ."[5]

This section closes with Jesus' assurance for His disciples. The Kingdom is sure, and some of those hearing Him would live to see the Son of Man come in His Kingdom. This reference may have been to the disciples in anticipation of His resurrection and the new age of His Kingdom—a statement excluding Judas. This is the more likely interpretation rather than to see this as a reference to the *Parousia*.[6] There is the suggestion that He is alluding to the Transfiguration, in which the glory of His kingly identity was revealed, and that to only three of the disciples. But whichever was meant, the word was a deliberate note of assurance that His cause was not to end with the predicted Passion, but to reach its goal in the Resurrection.

JESUS' TRANSFIGURATION ON THE MOUNT

1 And after six days Jesus took Peter, James, and John his brother, brought them up on a high mountain by themselves,

2 and was transfigured before them. His face shone like the sun, and His clothes became as white as the light.

3 And behold, Moses and Elijah appeared to them, talking with Him.

4 Then Peter answered and said to Jesus, "Lord, it is good for us to be here; if You wish, let us make here three tabernacles: one for You, one for Moses, and one for Elijah."

5 While he was still speaking, behold, a bright cloud overshadowed them; and suddenly a voice came out of the cloud, saying, "This is My beloved Son, in whom I am well pleased. Hear Him!"

6 And when the disciples heard it, they fell on their faces and were greatly afraid.

7 And Jesus came and touched them and said, "Arise, and do not be afraid."

8 And when they had lifted up their eyes, they saw no one but Jesus only.

9 And as they came down from the mountain, Jesus commanded them, saying, "Tell the vision to no one until the Son of Man is risen from the dead."

10 And His disciples asked Him, saying, "Why then do the scribes say that Elijah must come first?"

11 And Jesus answered and said to them, "Elijah
truly is coming first and will restore all things.

12 "But I say to you that Elijah has come already,
and they did not know him but did to him whatever
they wished. Likewise the Son of Man is also about
to suffer at their hands."

13 Then the disciples understood that He spoke to
them of John the Baptist.

Matt. 17:1–13

We have seen the Messiah identified as the Son of God (16:16–
17), the Messiah interpreted as the Suffering Savior (16:21); now the
Messiah is introduced as the glorified Son of the Father (17:1–5).
While each of the synoptic Gospels record that a week after Peter's
confession Jesus took three disciples onto the mountain to witness
His Transfiguration, Matthew seems to relate the scene to characteristics of Moses on Mount Sinai. Moses took Aaron, Nadab, and Abihu
with him; Jesus took Peter, James, and John. Moses saw the glory
of God, and his face shone from speaking with God; Jesus was transfigured with a glory not reflected, but authentically His own. A greater
than Moses had come, for as the writer to the Hebrews says, "Moses
was faithful as a servant *in* all God's house. . . . But Christ is faithful
as a son *over* God's house" (Heb. 3:5–6, NIV). At Sinai the divine
voice spoke from a cloud, and at the Transfiguration God spoke from
a cloud and the disciples fell on their faces in reverent fear.

This passage might be called "the glimpse of the kingdom." Willard
Swartley calls the Transfiguration "a preview of the Kingdom
power."[7] Matthew tells of the presence of Moses and Elijah, but
omits Luke's statement that they talked with Jesus "about his departure, which he was to bring to fulfillment at Jerusalem" (Luke 9:31,
NIV). Matthew does not interpret the significance of these particular
men, Moses having been the first great lawgiver and Elijah the first
great prophet in Israel. But Moses, Elijah, and Jesus are not equals,
for in Jesus revelation had reached its peak, and He was pronounced
by God as His Son.

The word for "transfigured" is the word "metamorphosis," from
the Greek root *morpha*, a word which means a change arising from
the essential nature of His person, not an external impression. Peter's
offer came as an outburst of enthusiasm, *"Lord, this is great! Let us
build three tabernacles."* Let us capture the moment, let us institutionalize
the happening, as we are so inclined to do with God's movements,
with revival and with movements of the Spirit among us. But before

Peter was finished expressing his plan, God pulled the rug out from under him! The Greek is emphatic in the word "suddenly" (literally "behold") a voice came from the cloud with the ultimate word, *"This is My beloved Son, in whom I am well-pleased. Hear Him!"* It was God's affirmation of Christ and God's mandate to Peter—*"You listen to Him."* No small wonder that the disciples fell on their faces in fear. We should here note some Old Testament accounts of reverent fear from visions of God: Isaiah 6:5, Ezekiel 1:28–2:1, and Daniel 8:17.

Years after the event, Peter wrote, "We . . . were eyewitnesses of His majesty. For He received from God the Father honor and glory when such a voice came to Him from the Excellent Glory: 'This is my beloved Son, in whom I am well-pleased.' And we heard this voice which came from heaven when we were with Him on the holy mountain" (2 Pet. 1:16–18). And as on the mount, when Jesus touched them and said, "Do not be afraid," and they looked up and saw none but Jesus only, so their proclamation announced only Him. Peter said, "There is none other name under heaven given among men, whereby we must be saved" (Acts 4:13, KJV).

The glimpse of His Kingdom can be outlined as follows: (1) it partakes of the glory of the eternal, v. 2; (2) it includes the sweep of salvation history, Law and Prophets, v. 3; (3) it is the extension of God's presence in Christ, vv. 4–5; (4) it is expressed only in and by Jesus Christ, vv. 6–8; and (5) it is secured by the suffering of Christ, vv. 9–13. This latter was clearly stated by Jesus as He asked the disciples not to tell the vision until after His Resurrection—the glory of the Transfiguration would then be witnessed by all of them in the risen Christ!

The conclusion of this section is an answer to the disciples' question as to why the scribes said that Elijah would first come. They had just seen Elijah. And the spirit of Elijah had been present in John, and he had been rejected. In fact, Jesus identified His own coming Passion as partaking of the same suffering as had been inflicted upon John. The disciples appear to have understood, and were able to "close that book" and accept the unique mission of John as fulfilled in announcing "The Lamb of God which taketh away the sin of the world."

THE HEALING OF THE EPILEPTIC BOY

14 And when they had come to the multitude, a
man came to Him, kneeling down to Him and saying,

15 "Lord, have mercy on my son, for he is an epileptic and suffers severely; for he often falls into the fire and often into the water.

16 "And I brought him to Your disciples, and they could not cure him."

17 Then Jesus answered and said, "O faithless and perverse generation, how long shall I be with you? How long shall I bear with you? Bring him here to Me."

18 And Jesus rebuked him, and the demon came out of him; and the child was cured from that very hour.

19 Then the disciples came to Jesus privately and said, "Why could we not cast him out?"

20 And Jesus said to them, "Because of your unbelief; for assuredly, I say to you, if you have faith as a mustard seed, you will say to this mountain, 'Move from here to there,' and it will move; and nothing will be impossible for you.

21 "However, this kind does not go out except by prayer and fasting."

Matt. 17:14–21

This remarkable story may well be an illustration of the failures of religious presumption. The disciples had earlier gone out on a mission for Christ, and returned with the report that even the demons were subject to them. But now, when a man brought his son to them for deliverance, they could not cast out the demon. When this was reported to Jesus, He simply said, *"Bring him to me."* His statement to the crowd was an exclamation of disappointment. We are not told of all that happened, but when the disciples asked Jesus the reason for their failure, He answered that it was because of their unbelief. And faith in Him, small as a grain of mustard seed but alive, will be honored to the extent of moving mountains. This word, "mountain" was a common Jewish metaphor for difficulty. Thus Jesus said, *"Nothing will be impossible for you."* He then added a conditioning element, *"This kind does not go out except by prayer and fasting."* (This sentence is thought to have been added from Mark 9:29, as it is not in Codex Sinaiticus, Codex Vaticanus and other manuscripts. But being in Mark, we recognize in it a word from Jesus.) Engaging spiritual powers calls for spiritual resources, not human presumption.

There is a lesson in this account as contrasted with the Transfiguration on the mountain. The mountain experience, with all its glory, had to be translated into the situation of human need. And this was the ultimate meaning of the Incarnation, as so magnificently expressed in Philippians 2:5–11. Paul says that Christ, who was in very nature God, became in very nature man, humbling Himself to be a servant, even to death on the cross. This is also the character of faith as a mustard seed, willing to die to itself to become a transformed plant. Thus we always move beyond ourselves to Him as we hear His words, *"Bring him to Me."* This faith will move mountains of difficulties, and life will always deal with possibilities.

The difference between Matthew's account and that of Mark may be explained by recognizing Peter as Mark's source. Peter, with his privilege of having been on the mount with Jesus, is considerate of the other nine disciples and does not emphasize to Mark their lack of faith. But Matthew, one of the nine, is just as honest and identifies their problem fully. Mark also expands the interaction with the crowd and religious leaders over the incident, as well as Jesus' words with the boy's father. The latter contain the striking interchange in which the father says, "If thou canst do any thing," with Jesus' reply, "If thou canst believe" (Mark 9:14–29, KJV).

An outline for this section could be: (1) the disciples' lack of kingdom power, vv. 14–16; (2) the disappointment in their lack of faith, v. 16; (3) the deliverance of the epileptic, v. 18; and (4) the discourse on the nature of faith, vv. 19–21.

JESUS AGAIN PREDICTS HIS PASSION

22 And while they were staying in Galilee, Jesus said to them, "The Son of Man is about to be betrayed into the hands of men,
23 "and they will kill Him, and the third day He will be raised up." And they were exceedingly sorrowful.

Matt. 17:22-23

From the region of Mount Hermon to the north, Jesus and the disciples returned to Galilee. This was a return to the dominion of Herod Antipas, and Mark tells us that they maintained secrecy (Mark 9:30–32). While there, preparing for the trip to Jerusalem for the

Passover, Jesus prepared them for what He knew was to happen. This is the second prediction of His coming Passion. But it contains an additional element: He will be betrayed. This was warning enough for the disciples, including Judas, to do some serious self-examination. *"They were exceedingly sorrowful"*—a sorrow which stayed with them from this time on. John especially addresses this, showing how Jesus' messages during the Passion week were designed to encourage them (John 16:1). In that context Jesus spoke further of the coming of the Holy Spirit once He entered His glory.

In this passage Jesus speaks of His betrayal, of His death, and of His Resurrection. The insertion of the reference to betrayal answered a very major question for the disciples. Was Jesus inviting death; did He have a martyr complex? But the reference to a betrayal, in the context of the open conflict with the scribes and Pharisees, made the disciples more aware of the deeper aspects of the conflict. The issue was between the Kingdom and will of God, personified in Jesus, and the coercive counterwill of man. Jesus didn't fit the mold of their religious system, and being a threat to them, He had to be destroyed. From this point on there are repeated references to conflicts over issues between the Kingdom of God and the kingdoms of the world. They are basically the ones introduced in the wilderness temptation: conflict over material and economic matters, conflict over social and cultic matters, and conflict over power and political matters. The clash led to the rejection of Jesus by all parties—the symbol that He died because of and on behalf of the sins of all of us.

JESUS AND PETER PAY THE TAX

24 And when they had come to Capernaum, those who received the temple tax came to Peter and said, "Does your Teacher not pay the temple tax?"

25 He said, "Yes." And when he had come into the house, Jesus anticipated him, saying, "What do you think, Simon? From whom do the kings of the earth take customs or taxes, from their own sons or from strangers?"

26 Peter said to Him, "From strangers." Jesus said to him, "Then the sons are free.

27 "Nevertheless, lest we offend them, go to the sea, cast in a hook, and take the fish that comes up

first. And when you have opened its mouth, you will
find a piece of money; take that and give it to them
for Me and you."

Matt. 17:24–27

Having just spoken of coming events of ultimate importance to
happen at Jerusalem, Jesus is now confronted with the trivia of tax
to support the temple. Having been away from His home area for
some time, those who collected the temple tax may have implied
in their question to Peter that Jesus was a tax-dodger. Peter, ready
to defend the Master, was quick to reply, *"Of course Jesus pays the tax!"*

The temple was the center of Jewish worship, and its maintenance
was costly. A tax was levied on every male Jew above nineteen,
consisting of the small amount of a *didrachma,* a half-shekel (Neh.
10:32). Since the didrachma was not in coinage, it was customary
for two persons to pay together and present a full shekel or a *slater.*
From verse 27 it appears that Jesus is telling Peter to pay the slater
for the two of them. This is not the tax paid to Rome, the question
about which is raised in another context. However, we should not
conclude that the temple tax had no political import, for the temple
had its guard and agents for coercive political life in the Jewish community.

Jesus "anticipated" Peter when they came into the house, possibly
Matthew's house, and took this as an occasion to teach the primacy
of the kingdom. This is the key element of the passage, that the
new community, the new Israel which Jesus was creating, was free
in the world, answering to its own king. The relationship with the
Messiah superseded the relationship to the temple, and God, as Sovereign King, Lord over the temple, does not exact payment from His
Son or the sons of the Kingdom (vv. 25–26). Nevertheless, Jesus did
not precipitate a crisis by effecting a break with the temple at this
point, and agreed to pay the tax. This break took on a different
character with the cleansing of the temple.

The miracle of Peter catching a fish and finding the slater for the
tax in its mouth is variously interpreted. Some see this as an expression
of Jesus' humor, Jesus perhaps not expecting Peter to carry it out
literally. But the fact that it is recorded as a directive and apparently
carried through in detail implies that Jesus intended payment to avoid
offense. By providing for the payment of the tax in this way, Jesus
took a course of action which made the payment inconsequential

rather than a rite of allegiance on His part to religious cultism. Only as we see the miracle in this manner is it free from the offense of Jesus' using His power for selfish advantage. Again, a greater than the temple is here, the One who is Lord over His house.

LIFE IN THE NEW COMMUNITY

1 At that time the disciples came to Jesus, saying, "Who then is greatest in the kingdom of heaven?"
2 And Jesus called a little child to Him, set him in the midst of them,
3 and said, "Assuredly, I say to you, unless you are converted and become as little children, you will by no means enter the kingdom of heaven.
4 "Therefore whoever humbles himself as this little child is the greatest in the kingdom of heaven.
5 "And whoever receives one little child like this in My name receives Me.

Matt. 18:1–5

Matthew now presents the "fourth book" of the collected teachings of Jesus. In this section Jesus discusses the character of the new community He is creating. The values of the kingdom of heaven are qualitatively different from the patterns of the world. This new society expresses new relationships made possible by relationship with Christ. Of this community as a gift of grace, Dietrich Bonhoeffer says that "community means that we always relate to one another in and through Christ."[8] That is, we don't relate as two alone but with the sense of His presence. Relating as two alone we often become guilty of intimidating, manipulating, coercing, and misusing others. As we relate in and through Christ, each one remains free, and is enabled to liberate the other person.

This chapter is a very important passage for Christian ethics. It presents qualities for the personal and social aspects of community life. Although the new Israel is not under the Law but under grace, this does not mean a "cheap grace" of carelessness, but the "costly grace" of full identification with Christ and His suffering love. The messianic community is a community of the redeemed, a fellowship of the forgiven; should we become unwilling to forgive, we have lost the *raison d'être* of the community of the Redeemer.

In the first section of the chapter Jesus engages the disciples on the question of greatness. Mark says Jesus asked the disciples regarding their conversation, exposing their argument over who would be the greatest in His Kingdom (Mark 9:33–37). Matthew is kind to the disciples in saying that they came to Jesus with the question. Jesus had earlier said of John that there was none greater, and yet the least in the Kingdom of heaven would be greater than he. The issue is now the character of greatness.

Jesus answered by calling a child to His knee, and used the child as an object-lesson. He informed them that one becomes a kingdom member only by being converted and becoming as a child, for such are great in kingdom terms. This statement is emphatic, its force being shown in the Greek by the use of the double negative. Note that He does not say "become as little children," but *be converted and become as little children.*" And Jesus had modeled the child-to-Father relationship, as His use of *Abba* in addressing God was unparalleled in Jewish literature. Jeremias comments, "If you do not learn to say Abba, you cannot enter the kingdom of God."[9]

Conversion is a change of direction. We have been going our own way, but in answer to His call of grace we turn and go His way. This is a total change: intellectual, psychological, ethical, and relational. Jesus calls it a new birth, a new beginning (John 3:3–5), the only way by which we participate in the kingdom of God (John's only use of the term 'kingdom of God'). To repent is to turn back in humility as a child, and to open one's self in childlike humility to receive from Him. Conversion is not simply "turning over a new leaf," nor is it reforming one's life, nor is it practicing religious rites, even the sacraments, but it is a turning to God Himself as we meet Him in Christ, to identify with Him as Savior/Lord, as our Redeemer and Master. To be converted is to take our place in humble relationship with the Master. He thereby changes us from being self-centered to being Christ-centered (Gal. 2:20).

THE GREATNESS THAT RESPECTS THE SMALL

6 "But whoever causes one of these little ones who believe in Me to sin, it would be better for him if a millstone were hung around his neck, and he were drowned in the depth of the sea.

215

7 "Woe to the world because of offenses! For
offenses must come, but woe to that man by whom
the offense comes!

8 "And if your hand or foot causes you to sin,
cut it off and cast it from you. It is better for you to
enter into life lame or maimed, rather than having two
hands or two feet to be cast into the everlasting fire.

9 "And if your eye causes you to sin, pluck it out
and cast it from you. It is better for you to enter into
life with one eye, rather than having two eyes to be
cast into hell fire.

Matt. 18:6–9

As God accepts us in our weakness, so we are to accept others
who appear smaller or weak. The Servant of God does not break
the bruised reed nor quench the smoking flax, nor do His disciples
minimize the childlike faith of simple folk. The emphasis here is
on care for the believer. This is the only verse in the synoptic Gospels
where the phrase "believe in me" is used. Jesus is referring to His
disciples, and warning that God's most stern judgment rests upon
those who cause others to sin. The millstone referred to here is not
the small one for household cooking, but the large ass-millstone used
at the mill. It is a word-picture, conveying a judgment without hope,
a casting into the open sea, illustrative of utter destruction.

The language in verses 7–9 is eschatological language. It refers to
the offender as partaking of the character of antichrist, and to the
choice between eternal life and eternal punishment.

Jesus' frequent references to hell or eternal punishment (each message in Matthew contains some such reference) use the language of
everlasting fire or hell fire. The language is figurative, focusing our
attention on the judgment of God. The description of hell, as the
Gehenna of fire, as outer darkness, as a bottomless pit, etc., conveys
the horrible prospect of passing from this life to the next without
God. Hell is the end of a Christless life! It is to go out into eternity
without God, to be lost and alone in the darkness of separation,
where there is no light, no love, no fellowship, no hope, no God.
And "forever," who can understand this expression? "Oh eternity,
how long, how long art thou? Let thine ages tramp, thy cycles roll;
Thou can'st not silver the locks of God, nor scar the walls of hell,
Oh eternity, how long art Thou?"

THE GREATNESS THAT SEEKS THE LOST

10 "Take heed that you do not despise one of these little ones, for I say to you that in heaven their angels always see the face of My Father who is in heaven.

11 "For the Son of Man has come to save that which was lost.

12 "What do you think? If a man has a hundred sheep, and one of them goes astray, does he not leave the ninety-nine and go to the mountains to seek the one that is straying?

13 "And if he should find it, assuredly, I say to you, he rejoices more over that sheep than over the ninety-nine that did not go astray.

14 "Even so it is not the will of your Father who is in heaven that one of these little ones should perish.

Matt. 18:10–14

No one is inconsequential or unimportant. Every person counts with God. His care is equally sincere for all, and He operates without respect of persons. Here again Jesus refers to *"one of these little ones."* Do not despise or be condescending toward any. And uniquely Jesus refers to that phenomenon which the church has come to call "guardian angels," saying that the spiritual counterparts of each of the children have access to the presence of God in heaven. This is an insight into divine providence which we accept with gratitude, but of which we know little. One of the recent books on the theme of angels is the work by Billy Graham, a practical study for the encouragement of Christians.[10]

The story of the lost sheep is one of the more readily understood of Jesus' parables. In the Judean hills it was easy for a sheep to stray and become lost. When the shepherd put the sheep in the cote at night he counted them. A sheep missing sent the shepherd on his way to track it down and bring it back to the fold. Matthew gives us this story to illustrate God's love for a single person. Jesus was referring to one from His community who may stray away. The focus of Matthew is on our responsibility to go after the brother who is straying. In Luke the emphasis is on Jesus receiving sinners (Luke 15:3–7).

God's universal sovereignty is stressed by reference to the angels of His presence. In His compassion, He doesn't want any to be lost. The scene is of God going after His people like a shepherd, or of Christ as the Good Shepherd (John 10:1–18). This concern for the erring is different from the rabbinical attitude which represented God as being happier over a righteous man than over a sinner who repents. But Jesus said it is not the will of God that even one little one should perish. This is the model for our mission of love as disciples.

THE GREATNESS THAT DISCIPLINES TO REINSTATE

15 "Moreover if your brother sins against you, go and tell him his fault between you and him alone. If he hears you, you have gained your brother.

16 "But if he will not hear you, then take with you one or two more, that *'by the mouth of two or three witnesses every word may be established.'*

17 "And if he refuses to hear them, tell it to the church. But if he refuses even to hear the church, let him be to you like a heathen and a tax collector.

18 "Assuredly, I say to you, whatever you bind on earth will be bound in heaven, and whatever you loose on earth will be loosed in heaven.

19 "Again I say to you that if two of you agree on earth concerning anything that they ask, it will be done for them by My Father who is in heaven.

20 "For where two or three are gathered together in My name, there I am in the midst of them."

Matt. 18:15–20

The Christian community must know how to deal with failure. As forgiven people the fellowship is the expression of our common commitment to Christ, not our perfection. We don't have to be perfect to be good. Being converted or born from above is only a beginning; we are on the way with Jesus, we are in the process of maturing as we walk in the Spirit. And a part of maturity is to be tested. The writer of Hebrews says of Jesus, "Yet learned he obedience by the things which he suffered; and being made perfect, he became the author of eternal salvation" (Heb. 5:8–9, KJV). This reference is to a maturing process in the life of Jesus, a maturity which came as He made right decisions. In contrast, the first Adam failed and never reached maturity, for having been created innocent Adam and Eve were given opportunity to make right decisions and go on to maturity, but they failed. The writer to the Hebrews admonishes us, "Let us go on to perfection" (6:1).

This passage outlines the pattern of reconciliation when a *"brother sins against you."* For the Jews the neighbor was one who shared nationality (See Lev. 19:17–18); a brother was one who shared religion. When there is a fault between brothers, Jesus holds the disciples sinned against responsible to initiate action for restoration. His asking for a spirit of forgiveness stands in contrast to retaliation. This calls for deliberate action rather than a defensive attitude which would belittle the brother before others in the community. And the goal is to win and reinstate the erring brother into fellowship. This discipline is taught by the Apostle Paul in the Letters to the Corinthians: discipline is seen in 1 Corinthians chapter 5, and the restoration in 2 Corinthians chapter 2. Paul's approach is to confront the person, to call for repentance, and to extend forgiveness.

In this passage Jesus outlined a clear three-step procedure to reinstate the erring. First, go to him alone and discuss the fault. This enables you to respect the ego needs and honor of another, rather than to embarrass him before others. If he responds affirmatively you have gained your brother. This step also preserves confidentiality. Second, if he will not hear you, *"take with you one or two more"* persons and try again. The presence of several other brothers or sisters adds witnesses but also protects the sinner in the negotiations, lest your demands for correction are misguided or excessive. This preserves openness in the process. And third, if the offender will not hear the several persons in step two, then take the issue to the congregation. If the offender will not hear the church, then he is to be excommunicated and regarded as a sinner, for he is deliberately choosing to remain in his sin. The third step is the binding and loosing process of the church. It is not done simply by the leaders as authority figures, for the entire community is responsible to act and maintain a disciplined church. There are two reasons for discipline: one, for the sake of the erring person in that his brothers and sisters care enough to help him to correction, holding him accountable to his commitments; and two, for the sake of the integrity of the church and its witness as the community of Christ.

The question of the nature of the disciplined church and the use of the "ban" or excommunication was a basic issue in the sixteenth-century Reformation. The Anabaptists, who broke from Zwingli in January of 1525 and started a Free Church, had already in 1524 made this a prominent issue. Much later John Calvin, although differing with the Anabaptists, added to the life of the Reformed Church the doctrine of "Fencing the Lord's Table." Through the centuries this concern has been a part of great spiritual movements such as the Wesleyan revival, East African revival, and Keswick, and it remains an essential characteristic of the people of God. We could say, where there is no discipline there is no true church.[11]

John H. Yoder points out that binding and loosing, mentioned in both passages in the Gospels where the Greek word *ekklēsia* ("church") is used, is the act which makes the church actually the church. It is the function in which we recognize Christ in our midst, in which the work of the Spirit is evident in His guidance, and it is the act which enables men to speak to each other in God's name. Yoder says, "It gives more authority to the church than does Rome, trusts more to the Holy Spirit than does pentecostalism, has more respect for the individual than humanism, makes moral standards more binding than puritanism, is more open to the given situation than the 'new morality.' If practiced it would change the life of churches more fundamentally than has yet been suggested by the currently popular discussions of changing church structures."[12]

The procedure is clearly stated. If your brother sins against you, you ("A") go to him ("B"), taking the initiative, respecting confidentiality. If "B" does not hear "A", then "A" takes with him "C" and possibly "D", to avoid rationalization and irresponsibility, as well as to help "A" and "B" to each hear the other correctly. If reconciliation happens, "B" has been brought back correctly. But if "B" is still unrepentant, then the matter is shared with the *ekklēsia*, "E" to "Z", and the congregation (not just the leaders) hold "B" accountable for covenant openness. In the process the injured brother must have an attitude of forgiveness and of covenant love. And so with the church: each should be more concerned for the erring person than they are about the issue. And conversation must involve "B" directly, not be about "B" between "A" and "C" apart from what they also share openly with "B". A failure to confront and to help "B" make corrections is a failure to love.

The last verses of this section relate Jesus as Head of the body in a direct way to this exercise of discipline. In verse 18 He emphasizes the direct relationship between the binding and loosing in heaven.

This is placed in context by the risen Christ in John 20:23, where the "binding and loosing" are an extension of the work of the Spirit. In verse 19 Jesus stresses the necessity of community, for two agreeing is the evidence of functioning as disciples, not as individualists. We have a promise of His presence where only two or three gather in His name (v. 20). This is not only presence but authority, for He remains the one authority in the community of disciples. And the New Testament has various references to the power of His presence (John 14:12–14; Acts 4:9–12; 1 Cor. 5:3–4; and Rev. 1). In Revelation 1, John's vision is of Jesus, Lord of the church, among the candlesticks, symbolizing His presence amidst the congregations.

THE GREATNESS OF FORGIVENESS

21 Then Peter came to Him and said, "Lord, how often shall my brother sin against me, and I forgive him? Up to seven times?"

22 Jesus said to him, "I do not say to you, up to seven times, but up to seventy times seven.

23 "Therefore the kingdom of heaven is like a certain king who wanted to settle accounts with his servants.

24 "And when he had begun to settle accounts, one was brought to him who owed him ten thousand talents.

25 "But inasmuch as he was not able to pay, his master commanded that he, his wife and children, and all that he had be sold, and payment be made.

26 "The servant therefore fell down before him, saying, 'Master, have patience with me, and I will pay you all.'

27 "Then the master of that servant was moved with compassion, released him, and forgave him the debt.

28 "But the same servant went out and found one of his fellow servants who owed him a hundred denarii; and he laid hands on him and took him by the throat, saying, 'Pay me what you owe!'

29 "So his fellow servant fell down at his feet and begged him, saying, 'Have patience with me, and I will pay you all.'

30 "And he would not, but went and threw him into prison till he should pay the debt.

31 "So when his fellow servants saw what had been done, they were very grieved, and came and told their master all that had been done.

32 "Then his master, after he had called him, said to him, 'O you wicked servant! I forgave you all that debt because you begged me.

33 'Should you not also have had compassion on your fellow servant, just as I had pity on you?'

34 "And his master was angry and delivered him to the torturers until he should pay all that was due him.

35 "So My heavenly Father also will do to you if each of you, from his heart, does not forgive his brother his trespasses."

Matt. 18:21–35

The nature of forgiveness is a most profound aspect of reconciling grace. Forgiveness is never easy; it is hard. It is the most difficult thing in the universe. Forgiveness means that the forgiving person as the innocent one resolves his own wrath over the sin of the guilty one and lets the guilty one go free. To forgive means that one genuinely loves, and this love can move beyond the issue to the person, and that one cares more about the person than about what he or she has done. Forgiveness liberates. Forgiveness frees the person for the options of living. Our refusal to forgive is a power play that limits the offender, that holds the guilty "under one's thumb," or power. But such forgiveness is always in relationship, hence the condition of repentance. It is not a package that one accepts and runs away with. It is only known in reconciliation.

Following a sermon which I had preached in a meeting in western Pennsylvania, a gracious lawyer thanked me for the message, but then added, "I'm not a Christian; I've never accepted this idea of the innocent suffering for the guilty, this blood religion." I said, "Sir, I'm very sorry for you, for you can't have a happy marriage, or a happy family, or any lasting friendships in your social relations." He responded with, "And why not?" To this I replied, "Because you are not an angel, and you make mistakes, and as you make mistakes the only way in which people can keep on accepting you is if they, as innocent, will forgive your guilt and accept you. But

you just told me that you don't believe in the innocent suffering
for the guilty!" He was honest enough to say he would think this
over. And he came back to the next meeting when I preached on
the Cross, which showed in Jesus' death the depth of God's forgiveness as He absorbed His own wrath on our sin by His love and
extended forgiveness.

This is the remarkable truth of this story. Matthew says Peter
asked how often we should forgive. In his question he goes beyond
the rabbinic rule of three times and extends it to seven. But Jesus
answered, *"Not seven, but seventy times seven."*[13] Jesus taught that forgiveness is qualitative, not quantitative. And that forgiveness takes the
place of revenge. A man in Christ never reaches the limits of love
(Rom. 13:8). The following points express the teaching of the twofold
illustration or parable, and we state them first, then examine the
details of the parable. (1) Forgiveness creates the deepest awareness
of sin: we can't change the facts. (2) Forgiveness costs the innocent
one, for he resolves the problem in love. (3) Forgiveness conditions
one to forgive others for he is forever accountable for his privilege
of freedom.

The statement, "The Kingdom of heaven is like . . ." sets the parable in the context of Divine grace. A king, settling accounts with
his servants, found one servant owing ten thousand talents. The
amount is so great that there is no conceivable way in which he
could pay. This is the equivalent of at least twelve million dollars
in our currency. It was fifty million denarii, and one denarii was a
normal daily wage. Herod's annual income was only nine hundred
talents. The tax on Galilee and Perea together was only two hundred
talents, and this man owed ten thousand! Jesus is illustrating our
debt to God as totally beyond our payment.

The king decided to collect what he could, and ordered the man
and his family to be sold (see Josh. 7; 2 Kings 4:1). But the man
fell on his face and entreated the king for patience, promising to
pay everything. With this attitude toward the impossible, the king
had compassion on him and forgave him the debt. Forgiveness was
because of his attitude, not his ability. In view of the interpretation
given earlier of the meaning of forgiveness, we note that the guilty
man was liberated, and the innocent person, the King, paid the debt,
for He crossed ten thousand talents off of his accounts! This is Jesus'
illustration of forgiveness.

But human nature is inclined to resent rather than to release, to be demanding rather than to forgive. And Jesus adds a sequel to the story. The forgiven man, who should have lived accountably in gratitude for his freedom, went out and met a man who owed him a relatively small sum. The figure was one hundred denarii, about twenty dollars, 500,000 times less than the forgiven man's debt; but even so he demanded payment. He took him by the throat, throttled or strangled him, demanding the money. His debtor now fell at his feet, begged for patience as he had, promised to "pay all" with the same words the forgiven man had used in his own desperation. But he would not extend patience, and threw the man in prison until the debt should be paid. The behavior was so scandalous that his fellow servants were shocked at his injustice and reported it. The king called him in, and placed his condemnation in the form of a question—*"I forgave you all that debt because you begged me; should you not also have had compassion . . .?"* The king was angry, and measuring judgment by the same measure in which the man had treated his debtor, delivered him to the tortures of prison until he should pay.

The punch line is, so will my heavenly Father do if you forgive not. This is not a legalism, but states the expectation of responsible persons whose moral sense of responsibility will call them to express the forgiveness towards others that they have experienced from God. "Blessed is he whose transgression is forgiven, whose sin is covered. Blessed is the man unto whom the Lord imputeth not iniquity, and in whose spirit there is no guile" (Ps. 32:1–2, KJV). Our joy in this gift of grace keeps us from ever holding it to ourselves. This is illustrated by David having longed for a drink of water from the well at Bethlehem, whereupon three of his men risked their lives and broke through the ranks of the Philistines and brought him a drink. He said, in effect, "I cannot drink it; it is the price of blood," and he poured it out as an offering to God (1 Chron. 11:16–19). It is this awareness of the cost of our own forgiveness that keeps us from audacity in relation to those we are called upon to forgive. We only extend God's forgiveness. Thus Matthew concludes the "fourth book" of Jesus' teachings.

THE GREATNESS OF THE MARRIAGE COVENANT

> 1 And it came to pass, when Jesus had finished these sayings, He departed from Galilee and came to the region of Judea beyond the Jordan.

2 And great multitudes followed Him, and He healed them there.

3 The Pharisees also came to Him, testing Him, and saying to Him, "Is it lawful for a man to divorce his wife for just any reason?"

4 And He answered and said to them, "Have you not read that He who made them at the beginning *'made them male and female,'*

5 "and said, *'For this reason a man shall leave his father and mother and be joined to his wife, and the two shall become one flesh'*?

6 "So then they are no longer two but one flesh. Therefore what God has joined together, let not man divide."

7 They said to Him, "Why then did Moses command to give a certificate of divorce, and to put her away?"

8 He said to them, "Moses, because of the hardness of your hearts, permitted you to divorce your wives, but from the beginning it was not so.

9 "And I say to you, whoever divorces his wife, except for sexual immorality, and marries another, commits adultery; and whoever marries her who is divorced commits adultery."

10 His disciples said to Him, "If such is the case of the man with his wife, it is better not to marry."

11 But He said to them, "All men cannot accept this saying, but only those to whom it has been given:

12 "for there are some eunuchs who were born thus from their mother's womb, and there are some eunuchs who were made eunuchs by men, and there are eunuchs who have made themselves eunuchs for the kingdom of heaven's sake. He who is able to accept it, let him accept it."

13 Then little children were brought to Him that He might put His hands on them and pray, but the disciples rebuked them.

14 But Jesus said, "Let the little children come to Me, and do not forbid them; for of such is the kingdom of heaven."

15 And He laid His hands on them and departed from there.

Matt. 19:1–15

Another unit of sayings having been completed, Matthew now presents the trip to Jerusalem, by way of the region beyond Jordan. There was nothing secret or easy about the trip, for great crowds followed Him. He was ministering to their needs with deeds of healing, and the Pharisees came looking for Him. Their purpose, as Matthew says in verse 3, was to trap Jesus. His wit and wisdom, as well as His knowledge and interpretation, had always defeated them, but like the wolf pack they were (although in sheep's clothing), they kept nipping at His flank. Theirs was not a head-on confrontation about his messiahship, but a barrage of questions related to issues that represented their own concerns.

The passage deals with marriage and divorce, with sexual abstinence or celibacy, and with the beauty of children and family. Jesus had taught in the Sermon on the Mount regarding the God-given covenant of love and the sanctity of the marriage relationship as indissoluble. But here, the question is raised in a manner designed to trap Him between two schools of thought. In regard to a man's divorcing his wife this is focused by the phrase *"for just any reason."* The question was not on the legitimacy of divorce; they assumed this. Rather it was on the easy policy of the Hillel school. Hillel, the grandfather of Gamaliel who was the famous teacher of Saul of Tarsus, was a gracious and diplomatic person who sought the easier course of action in resolving problems. The opposing school of Shammai was much more strict, interpreting the Law with rigor. The Pharisees sought to trap Jesus between the two, and at first glance, it appears that He had identified with the school of Shammai. But a further analysis shows how that Jesus avoided the trap by going back beyond Hillel and Shammai, back before the Law which they were interpreting, appealing to the order of creation.

Jesus emphasized God's act of creating male and female in and for community, for the covenant of love. He emphasized their unique equality and oneness in the marriage covenant, for a man leaves his parental line and forms a new union with his wife, and the two become one flesh. Recognizing God's act of making two to be one, man is not to sever what God has joined. Consequently, all divorce is sin. Confronted by this argument, they responded defensively with, *"Why then did Moses command . . . ?"* Jesus responded in a twofold way: first, Moses permitted a compromise because of hard and sinful hearts; and second, from the beginning God's will continues not to be so (the verb being in the perfect tense means that a past action continues to the present).

Jesus states His position briefly and explicitly in verse 9. For anyone to break a marriage covenant, except where that covenant is already being disregarded by immoral living, and to marry another is to commit adultery, is to break covenant; and anyone who marries a woman so disregarded by her husband shares the act of adultery or covenant-breaking. The emphasis of Jesus is primarily on the integrity of persons in covenant. His disciples, not the Pharisees, now reveal their social conditioning, that it appears that a man entering marriage covenant is bound to a relation from which he should prefer to be free! And Jesus said in essence that marriage or celibacy should be seen as a matter of vocation, or calling. Some are called as disciples to share the covenant of marriage, and some are called as disciples to be celibate. This is set in the context of the Kingdom of heaven, and Jesus Himself is the model of the celibate life for the work of the Kingdom (see 1 Cor. 7–9).

A fitting sequel is that little children were brought to Jesus at this point, that He might lay His hands on them in blessing and pray for them. At the remonstrance of the disciples Jesus was indignant, an expression nowhere else used of Him.[14] Jesus said, *"Let the little children come to Me, and do not forbid them; for of such is the kingdom of heaven."* Such warm words for the little ones related Jesus meaningfully to family. He closed this intended trap with a witness of blessing on the offspring of marriage. This sanctified marriage and lifted it above the selfish and sensual shuffling that was evident in the practice of divorce at whim.

The Greatness of Eternal Life

16 And behold, one came and said to Him, "Good Teacher, what good thing shall I do that I may have eternal life?"

17 And He said to him, "Why do you call Me good? No one is good but One, that is, God. But if you want to enter into life, keep the commandments."

18 He said to Him, "Which ones?" Jesus said, " *'You shall not murder,' 'You shall not commit adultery,' 'You shall not steal,' 'You shall not bear false witness,'*

19 *'Honor your father and your mother,'* and, *'You shall love your neighbor as yourself.'"*

20 The young man said to Him, "All these things I have kept from my youth. What do I still lack?"

> 21 Jesus said to him, "If you want to be perfect,
> go, sell what you have and give to the poor, and you
> will have treasure in heaven; and come, follow Me."
> 22 But when the young man heard that saying, he
> went away sorrowful, for he had great possessions.
>
> *Matt. 19:16–22*

This story, known as the story of the Rich Young Ruler, is a story on the "Cost of Discipleship." In Bonhoeffer's stimulating book by that title, this account is used as his basis for outlining the call and cost of following Jesus. Some persons have seen in Matthew 19 a counsel of perfection, of absolute chastity, complete poverty, and unreserved obedience. But just as the passage on chastity (vv. 10–12) cannot be pressed to mean an ideal of asceticism, this section can hardly be made to teach a complete renunciation of possessions. Jesus spoke to this man at the particular point of his need. As in the case of Nicodemus, Jesus spoke of his need that something be done "to him" by God beyond what he had thought he was doing for God; he needed to be born from above. And Jesus did not say to Nicodemus, *"Go and sell what you have and give to the poor,"* as though this were a universal formula; rather he spoke to his problem of legalism, of do-it-yourself religion. Here, for the rich young ruler, the issue was the idolizing of wealth and a lack of compassion for the needy, and Jesus addressed his problem directly. And our problem of materialism needs a similar direct word. Let us not try to dodge the implications of this passage. This account calls for a commitment to reject secular materialism, whether it be Marxist or capitalist.

The story is found in Mark 10:17–22 and in Luke 18:18–30. Matthew tells us in verse 20 that the man was young. From the several accounts we learn that he was an earnest man—*"he came running to Jesus"*; he was respectful—*"he kneeled to him"*; he was interested in eternal life; he was religious in practice, having kept the commandments from a lad; and he was interested in finding peace—*"What lack I yet?"* But when Jesus asked him to practice His claims, to let God actually be God in his life, he couldn't surrender the control of his life to God.

In Matthew's account the young man said, *"Good teacher, what good thing shall I do . . . ?"* Jesus responded, *"Why do you call Me good?"* The emphasis is on "Me." His comment that only God is good moves the man's thought from his standards to the divine standard. Jesus' counsel was to keep the commandments. It was as though He said, begin with what you know, begin where you are, and begin by acting in obedience.

Matthew says the young man asked, "Which?" Perhaps this was to justify himself, or to focus the issue more academically. Jesus' response outlines God's injunction against killing, adultery, stealing, false witness, and focuses his duty to parents. But omitting reference to covetousness, Jesus added the summary of the second table of the Law by the positive note, *"Love your neighbor as yourself."* Affirming his religious practice, knowing that he is yet without joy and meaning in life, the young man asked, *"What do I still lack?"* Here Jesus met him at the point of his idolatry—he had held things as more important than the will of God. It is covetousness, as Paul says, which is idolatry. Jesus answered, *"If you want to be perfect [complete], go, sell what you have and give to the poor."* But the young man failed to obey. In Bonhoeffer's words, "Only he who obeys truly believes, and only he who believes truly obeys."

The story illustrates the meaning of eternal life as the quality of life with God. The emphasis on "eternal" is not so much on time as on the quality of life that partakes of God's love and purpose. And the conclusion to which Jesus moved the conversation was to show that one cannot share God's love without loving his neighbor as himself. This story lends itself to a variety of homiletical approaches. One suggestion is that the encounter of the rich ruler with the Master involved (1) the most serious question, v. 16; (2) the most specific answer, v. 21; and (3) the most searching decision, v. 22.

The Cost of Entering the Kingdom

23 Then Jesus said to His disciples, "Assuredly, I say to you that it is hard for a rich man to enter the kingdom of heaven.

24 "And again I say to you, it is easier for a camel to go through the eye of a needle than for a rich man to enter the kingdom of God."

25 When His disciples heard it, they were exceedingly amazed, saying, "Who then can be saved?"

26 But Jesus looked at them and said to them, "With men this is impossible, but with God all things are possible."

27 Then Peter answered and said to Him, "See, we have left all and followed You. Therefore what shall we have?"

28 And Jesus said to them, "Assuredly, I say to you, that in the regeneration, when the Son of Man sits on the throne of His glory, you who have followed Me will also sit on twelve thrones, judging the twelve tribes of Israel.

29 "And everyone who has left houses or brothers or sisters or father or mother or wife or children or lands, for My name's sake, shall receive a hundredfold and inherit everlasting life.

30 "But many who are first will be last, and the last first."

Matt. 19:23–30

Jesus' words in this section should be read as relating to our present life, showing that eternal life begins now in its quality. This suggests that verse 23 could be paraphrased, "It is hard for a rich man to become involved in the kingdom of heaven now!" This is because of the priorities that govern the rich man's life. It is difficult for him to hear Jesus' words, "Seek ye first the kingdom of God and His righteousness."

The hyperbole in verse 24 is not to be interpreted as though the needle's eye were the narrow opening in the city gate, to let a man through but not a camel after the gate was closed, nor is it to change the word "camel" to mean a "rope." Jesus actually meant a sewing needle and a camel, contrasting the smallest of artificial apertures with the largest beast of burden in Palestine. This rendered the illustration to be interpreted in verse 26, *"With men this is impossible, but with God all things are possible."* Further, we can paraphrase "rich man" to mean "man of privilege" in our application, for riches are not all material. It may be easier for a camel to go through the eye of a needle than for a professor, a doctor, a lawyer, a bishop, a nurse, a teacher, a businessman, etc., to get involved in the kingdom of heaven now! In any position of privilege there is the danger that the status and power become primary. In T.S. Eliot's play *Murder in the Cathedral* there is the line, "They who serve the greater cause have the greater danger of the cause serving them."

Peter's words may appear presumptuous, but Jesus doesn't rebuke him; rather He answers him. Peter said "we" have left all, to which

Jesus answered specifically, referring to the disciples, *"you who have followed me."* This passage contains a striking reference to the new creation, the throne of the Son of Man, the judgment seat, as spoken of later in Matthew 25:31. Jesus said that His disciples will participate in the judgment, perhaps the basis for Paul's statement about the participation of Christians in the judgment (1 Cor. 6:2, cf. Dan. 7:22). The symbolism of the twelve tribes of Israel is to emphasize God's covenant people, and this new Israel will sit in judgment upon those whose unbelief and legalism kept them from entering the covenant. Thus Jesus concludes, *"Many who are first will be last, and the last first,"* perhaps as an answer to Peter's remark. Not only would His immediate disciples receive God's reward, but latecomers into the Kingdom of God will be treated equally in God's grace and inherit eternal life. God remains faithful to His own promises and actions. History is not meaningless confusion, for God is the main Actor on the stage of history, and He will secure its ultimate completion.

THE GREATNESS OF GOD'S GRACE

1 "For the kingdom of heaven is like a man who is a landowner who went out early in the morning to hire laborers for his vineyard.

2 "And when he had agreed with the laborers for a denarius a day, he sent them into his vineyard.

3 "And he went out about the third hour and saw others standing idle in the marketplace,

4 "and said to them, 'You also go into the vineyard, and whatever is right I will give you.' And they went.

5 "Again he went out about the sixth and the ninth hour, and did likewise.

6 "And about the eleventh hour he went out and found others standing idle, and said to them, 'Why have you been standing here idle all day?'

7 "They said to him, 'Because no one hired us.' He said to them, 'You also go into the vineyard, and whatever is right you will receive.'

8 "So when evening had come, the owner of the vineyard said to his steward, 'Call the laborers and give them their wages, beginning with the last to the first.'

9 "And when those came who were hired about the eleventh hour, they each received a denarius.

10 "But when the first came, they supposed that they would receive more; and they likewise each received a denarius.

11 "And when they had received it, they murmured against the landowner,

12 "saying, 'These last men have worked but one hour, and you made them equal to us who have borne the burden and the heat of the day.'

13 "But he answered one of them and said, 'Friend, I am doing you no wrong. Did you not agree with me for a denarius?

14 'Take what is yours and go your way. I want to give to this last man the same as to you.

15 'Is it not lawful for me to do what I want with my own things? Or is your eye evil because I am good?'

16 "So the last will be first, and the first last. For many are called, but few chosen."

Matt. 20:1–16

This is a unique parable of the Kingdom of God, presenting the nature of God's grace. The story appears to further answer Peter's question as to what the disciples would receive by leaving all to follow. The employer illustrates the acts of God, sending laborers into his vineyard all through the day as he finds them unemployed in the marketplace. At the end of the day he paid the last first, an aspect of the story arranged for emphasis. Jewish Law required that payment be made when the day ended (Lev. 19:13), so that the family could eat. The employer had agreed with the earlier laborers for the full day's wages of one denarius. But he gave those who came in the last hour the same wage! His compassion recognized that it took just as much bread to feed their families as it did the families of those who had worked the whole day.

The conclusion in verse 16 is a statement of unexpected generosity. This is the emphasis to which the story progresses. This final statement is similar to the concluding statement of the preceding section (19:30), but with the additional sentence, *"Many are called, but few are chosen."* A pattern of picking up at the end of a section the idea from its introduction can be found eleven times in this Gospel. While the concluding sentence is not in many of the ancient manuscripts, if we see it as Matthew's statement, it emphasizes a distinction between the calling of all of the workers and of the chosen ones who sensed the meaning of grace.

Grace is God's graciousness, His steadfast love and mercy extended to all alike. The story illustrates that not all respond alike to His goodness, but some compare and evaluate their own "goodness" and thereby fail to understand God's graciousness. The fact that all of us alike are sinners places us together without distinction or degrees of need for God's gracious acceptance. Equal pay for unequal work was totally unexpected, and regarded by the laborers as unacceptable. While this story answered Peter's question, it also answered the murmurings of the Pharisees over Jesus' act of accepting tax collectors and prostitutes into the Kingdom. The words, *"You have made them equal to us"* (v. 12) reflects this idea. The story of the two prodigal sons in Luke 15:11–32 is similar, for the prodigal in attitude could not respect the grace of the father in accepting the prodigal of waste.

In verse 13 the employer answered one of the persons who complained, using the word, "friend," an expression used three times in Matthew by Jesus, and in each case the person is in the wrong (see 22:12 and 26:50). His answer was that the employer had paid according to the agreement and his generosity was not cause for jealousy among others.

There is a story in the Talmud which is similar but with a very different conclusion. I share it here to emphasize the contrast with Jesus' teaching on the grace of God. A distinguished scholar, Rabbi Bun bar 'H'ijja died at an early age in A.D. 325, on the same day his son was born, who was subsequently known as Rabbi Bun II. At his funeral his former teachers gathered to pay tribute, and Rabbi Zera gave the funeral oration in the form of a parable. Life is like a king who hired a great number of laborers; two hours later he inspected and saw one who surpassed the others. He took him by the hand and walked up and down with him until evening. When the laborers came for their wages, each received the same, upon which the others murmured, saying, "We worked all day, while this man worked only two hours and you have paid him a full wage." But the king said, "I haven't wronged you. He has done more in two hours than you have done during the whole day." Rabbi Bun had done more in his twenty-five years than many achieved in a longer life span. The point is valid, but quite different from Jesus' emphasis in the parable of God's grace.

It is never easy to outline a parable. The points lifted from the story must support and clarify its primary intent, and they must move to that conclusion. (1) The calling to service is in direct relation to the need; (2) the reward for service is a gracious meeting of our needs; and (3) the integrity of service will respect the integrity of grace in meeting needs equally.

JESUS PREDICTS HIS DEATH
AND RESURRECTION A THIRD TIME

17 And Jesus, going up to Jerusalem, took the twelve disciples aside on the road and said to them,

18 "Behold, we are going up to Jerusalem, and the Son of Man will be betrayed to the chief priests and to the scribes; and they will condemn Him to death,

19 "and deliver Him to the Gentiles to mock and to scourge and to crucify. And the third day He will rise again."

Matt. 20:17–19

The death of Christ was not an accident; it was an achievement. The confrontation with "the principalities and powers" was inevitable and Jesus knew this. His going to Jerusalem was consciously a part of God's movement in history to confront man with the clarity that would expose man's rebellion and express God's redemption. And the struggle was intense for Jesus, suggested in this section by the emphatic statement, *"Behold, we are going up to Jerusalem."* While they were on the way to Jerusalem, Matthew says, Jesus took the disciples away from the crowd and sought to condition them for the events that would happen. He announced a third time His suffering which would transpire.

This third prediction is found also in Mark 10:32–34 and Luke 18:31–34. Jesus adds progressively new dimensions to the information. He had previously predicted His death and Resurrection, then in the second reference He added the factor of betrayal, and here He added His knowledge that He would be turned over to the Gentiles to be mocked, scourged, and crucified. This prediction was to help prepare the disciples in understanding and in hope. The reference to the Resurrection accompanied the announcement in each instance. But referring to crucifixion added both horror and humiliation. In the Law the reference to one hanged on a tree as accursed (Deut. 21:23) was interpreted following the Resurrection to say that Jesus

234

was made a curse in the place of the sinner (Acts 3:15; 4:10; 5:30; Gal. 3:13; 2 Cor. 5:21). But the hope was in His Resurrection and our assurance is in His victory, for Paul says, He was "delivered up because of our offenses, and was raised again because of our justification" (Rom. 4:25).

THE TRUE GREATNESS OF SERVICE

20 Then the mother of Zebedee's sons came to Him with her sons, kneeling down and asking something from Him.

21 And He said to her, "What do you wish?" She said to Him, "Grant that these two sons of mine may sit, one on Your right hand and the other on the left, in Your kingdom."

22 But Jesus answered and said, "You do not know what you ask. Are you able to drink the cup that I am about to drink, and be baptized with the baptism that I am baptized with?" They said to Him, "We are able."

23 And He said to them, "You shall indeed drink My cup, and be baptized with the baptism that I am baptized with; but to sit on My right hand and on My left is not Mine to give, but it is for those for whom it is prepared by My Father."

24 And when the ten heard it, they were moved with indignation against the two brothers.

25 But Jesus called them to Himself and said, "You know that the rulers of the Gentiles lord it over them, and those who are great exercise authority over them.

26 "Yet it shall not be so among you; but whoever desires to become great among you, let him be your servant.

27 "And whoever desires to be first among you, let him be your slave—

28 "just as the Son of Man did not come to be served, but to serve, and to give His life a ransom for many."

Matt. 20:20–28

The request for position exposes the nature of selfish ambition. The disciples' interest is on status and power, not on empathy and participation in the suffering of Christ which He had just discussed. The account is the same as that in Mark 10:35–45, except that in Mark it was the two brothers who had made the request, while in Matthew they were with their mother, who approached Jesus. Jesus' acceptance of women in His company as disciples is evidenced in his acceptance of her words of request as openly as of the men's. The conversation that followed emphasized the cost to the disciples in participating fully with Him in His mission. Their sitting to His right and left in His Kingdom suggests some understanding of the messianic banquet (Matt. 19:28). Here He would share His victory with His disciples.

The cup of suffering and the baptism of martyrdom are referred to in the response of Jesus (vv. 22–23). To share His mission is to share its cost. With limited understanding they said, *"We are able."* Jesus did not rebuke them for their presumption, but predicted that they would share martyrdom for the will and work of God. The reference that it is the Father's role to grant Kingdom positions was an affirmation of the Kingdom of God and its place in salvation history. There is some evidence that the disciples are disturbed over Jesus' description of His role as that of the Suffering Servant. The difference in perspective had led to Peter's rebuking Jesus following his confession. This difference of lifestyle may be the basic element that led Judas to betray his Lord.

The reference to the indignation of the ten toward *"the two brothers"* reflects their kinship, possibly the language of community, perhaps the language of the early church at the time in which Matthew was writing. We might also interpret the reaction as a projection of their own ambition in their feelings against the two, for the two may simply have asked that which was in the heart of each of the disciples as they argued about who would be the greatest. This was the occasion for Jesus to teach the meaning of true greatness, in contrast to the characteristics of the leaders of society when power corrupts.

The contrast between the approach of rulers among Gentiles and the way for the disciples of Christ is expressed forcibly in verses 25–27. Jesus climaxes the point by an interpretation of His own mission. To be truly great is to serve. To be in first place in the work of God is to become a servant for the enrichment of others. In his stimulating work on 1 Corinthians 13, Lewis Smedes distinguishes the acts of love as servant love and collegial love. Servant love is personal power used to help a weaker person. Collegial love is personal power used to help a peer or colleague. Both expressions are positions of service to the other, but collegial love may be the more difficult because it is affirming a competitor. Jesus illustrates His meaning by identifying His own role, and adds another dimension to the understanding of His death on the cross.

The Christology of verse 28 is a model for service and an expression of the meaning of Christ's death. Jesus' life and death expressed the principles of divine love as a model for His disciples (1 Pet. 2:21–24). But there is an additional element. His ultimate service was in giving His life as a ransom for many. Again we call attention to the great Christological passage of Philippians 2:5–8: "Christ Jesus, who, being in the form of God . . . emptied Himself by . . . coming in the likeness of men. . . . He humbled Himself and became obedient to the point of death." The words in verse 28, "a ransom for many," translate *lutron anti pollon;* Christ was to die "in the place of," *anti,* not "instead of," which would have been meant had Matthew used *huper.* The meaning is the idea of substitution. The word *lutron* occurs nowhere else in the New Testament except in the cognate word *antilutron* (1 Tim. 2:6). This word was used in the Greek world of the first century as "the purchase money for the manumitting of slaves." Its Hebrew equivalent, *kapher,* meant something for the purpose of deliverance or redemption. Vincent Taylor says, "It is a metaphor used in order to say something forcibly."[15] The statement is a direct reference to the Suffering Servant of Isaiah 53, including the words "By his knowledge shall my righteous servant justify many; for he shall bear their iniquities" (53:11, KJV; see also Ps. 49:7–8).

In light of the teaching of chapter 18 on forgiveness it is not necessary to ask the question, "To whom was the ransom paid?" The emphasis is on the expiation, the deliverance, the release into freedom, not on a purchase from the kingdom of darkness. Paul does use the idea of purchase, but in the sense of our belonging to God who has redeemed us: "What? know ye not that your body is the temple of the Holy Ghost, which is in you, which ye have of God, and ye are not your own? For ye are bought with a price: therefore glorify God in your body, and in your spirit, which are God's" (1 Cor. 6:19–20, KJV). An Old Testament illustration is the redemption of the eldest sons of the Israelites, spared in Egypt by the blood on the door when the eldest sons of the Egyptians died. After the Israelites were in the wilderness, God "sold them their sons" by trading them for the

Levites, who from that day onward belonged to God (Num. 3:11–51).

GREAT COMPASSION

29 And as they departed from Jericho, a great multitude followed Him.

30 And behold, two blind men sitting by the road, when they heard that Jesus was passing by, cried out, saying, "Have mercy on us, O Lord, Son of David!"

31 And the multitude rebuked them, that they should be quiet. But they cried out all the more, saying, "Have mercy on us, O Lord, Son of David!"

32 And Jesus stood still and called them, and said, "What do you want Me to do for you?"

33 They said to Him, "Lord, we want our eyes opened."

34 So Jesus had compassion on them and touched their eyes. And immediately their eyes received sight, and they followed Him.

Matt. 20:29–34

This is the last episode of compassionate healing before Jesus entered Jerusalem. Matthew refers to two blind men, while Mark and Luke mention only one blind beggar (Mark 10:46–52; Luke 18:35–43). It may well be that Peter, in recounting the story for Mark, only mentioned the one man who may have been known to him or known in the early church.

As Jesus left Jericho on the way to Jerusalem, the blind men kept calling out to Him and the crowd tried to silence them. But Jesus stopped the whole procession to pay attention to these men in need. In fact, He called them to Himself and asked what they wanted of Him. Their request was immediate, *"We want our eyes opened."* Tasker says that an Old Syriac version adds the words, "and that we may see Thee."[16] With compassion Jesus touched their eyes with healing, and immediately they were able to see. Matthew says simply, *"they followed Him."*

A theme can be developed from the perspective of the blind men who needed a touch from the Master: (1) we see the awakening of faith, (vv. 30–31); (2) we recognize the asking of faith, (v. 33); (3) we hear the answer of faith, (v. 34a); and (4) we rejoice in the response of faith, (v. 34b). The messianic significance of this miracle is its fulfillment of Isaiah's prediction (29:18–19).

The story is told of a poet and an artist viewing a painting by Nicolas Poussin, the French master. The picture represented the healing of the blind man at Jericho. The artist asked the poet to relate what he saw as the most remarkable thing in the painting. The poet responded by noting the excellent presentation of the figure of Christ, of the grouping of the people, and the expressions on their faces. But the artist pointed to the corner of the canvas where the painter had pictured a discarded cane lying on the steps of a house, and said, "Now, look! The blind man sat on those steps with his cane in hand. But when he heard that Jesus was passing by, he was so sure that he would be healed that he let the cane lie there and he went to Jesus fully expecting to see!"

NOTES

1. Plummer interprets the leaven as evil influence. *An Exegetical Study on . . . Matthew,* p. 222.

2. Ibid., p. 224.

3. See Plummer's excellent treatment of Peter's confession, ibid., pp. 227–229.

4. Ibid., p. 231.

5. Ibid., p. 235.

6. Ibid., p. 237.

7. Swartley, *Mark,* p. 155.

8. Dietrich Bonhoeffer, *Life Together* (New York: Harper & Bros., 1954), pp. 21–25.

9. Jeremias, *The Parables of Jesus,* p. 191.

10. Billy Graham, *Angels* (Garden City, NY: Doubleday, 1975).

11. See Marlin Jeschke's significant work, *Discipling the Brother* (Scottdale, PA: Herald Press, 1972).

12. Yoder, in *Concern* 14 (February, 1969): 2.

13. See my brother David Augsburger's book, *The Freedom of Forgiveness* (Chicago: Moody Press, 1973).

14. Plummer, *An Exegetical Study on . . . Matthew,* p. 262.

15. Vincent Taylor, *Jesus and His Sacrifice* (London: Macmillan and Co., 1933), p. 104.

16. Tasker, *The Gospel According to St. Matthew,* p. 196.

CHAPTER EIGHT

The Presentation of the King

Matthew 21:1—23:39

This section deals with the presentation of Jesus to the Jerusalem community. Matthew has given primary attention to Jesus' ministry in Galilee and the surrounding regions. Now he presents Jesus as the gentle King coming to Jerusalem. He basically follows the outline of Mark. It is evident from Matthew's account that Jesus went up to Jerusalem as the Messiah, although messiahship was known only to Himself and His little band of followers. Of this T. W. Manson says that He went up "to claim His Kingdom, which is the Kingdom of God, to call men to enter the Kingdom, to break their allegiance to the kingdoms of the world, and to bring them to their one true loyalty and their only true peace, all this lies behind the resolve to go to Jerusalem."[1] As Messiah He would lead a nonviolent revolution, not a nationalist insurrection against Rome, but a religious rebellion against everything inconsistent with complete allegiance to the heavenly King. This included an attack against the institutions that hindered people from entering the Kingdom.

"The Messianic entry into Jerusalem does not stand alone," says Manson. "It is a piece with the denunciation of Pharisaism and the cleansing of the Temple. He flings down the challenge to the civil power, to the priesthood, and to the party of the Scribes and Pharisees: and He does it with the sure knowledge that He will be rejected by the elders and priests and the scribes and be handed over to the Gentile power for death."[2]

This larger section deals with the cleansing of the temple steeped in mercenary greed, with merchandise cluttering the court intended for Gentile worship. It includes the curse upon the fig tree as an

240

illustration of judgment upon fruitlessness. It includes three parables that appear to follow the order of the coming trial. There are lessons in them concerning John, Jesus, and the disciples. In the climax Jesus warned Israel that they were on trial (22:11–46), and then pronounced woe on their leaders (23:1–32), with their "sentence" following (23:33–36), and the execution of it predicted (23:37–24:2)!

We should also note that Jesus left the city of Jerusalem at the end of this section much as Ezekiel pictured the glory of God leaving the city (Ezek. 11:23–24). What is presented in the next section (chap. 24) of the coming of the Son of Man in glory is also in harmony with Ezekiel's scene of the glory of God coming back to Jerusalem (Ezek. 43).

JESUS' ENTRY INTO JERUSALEM

1 And when they drew near to Jerusalem, and came to Bethphage, at the Mount of Olives, then Jesus sent two disciples,

2 saying to them, "Go into the village opposite you, and immediately you will find a donkey tied, and a colt with her. Loose them and bring them to Me.

3 "And if anyone says anything to you, you shall say, 'The Lord has need of them,' and immediately he will send them."

4 All this was done that it might be fulfilled which was spoken by the prophet, saying:

5 *"Tell the daughter of Zion,*
'Behold, your King is coming to you,
Humble, and sitting on a donkey,
And a colt, the foal of a donkey.' "

6 And the disciples went and did as Jesus commanded them.

7 And they brought the donkey and the colt, laid their clothes on them, and set Him thereon.

8 And a very great multitude spread their garments on the road; others cut down branches from the trees and spread them on the road.

9 And the multitudes who went before and those who followed cried out, saying:

"Hosanna to the Son of David!
'Blessed is He who comes in the name of the
LORD!'
Hosanna in the highest!"
10 And when He had come into Jerusalem, all the
city was moved, saying, "Who is this?"
11 And the multitudes said, "This is Jesus, the
prophet from Nazareth of Galilee."
Matt. 21:1–11

The Triumphal Entry, as it is called, occurred on Sunday of Passion week. All four Gospels record this occasion and its significance. Having come to Bethphage, "house of figs," about two miles outside of Jerusalem, it appears that Jesus stayed at the home of Mary, Martha, and Lazarus for several days over the Sabbath. He sent two of His disciples into the city to find a donkey with a colt, and to bring the animals to Him. Matthew sees this as fulfilling Zechariah 9:9, *"Tell the daughter of Zion, 'Behold, your King is coming to you, humble, and sitting on a donkey, and a colt, the foal of a donkey.'"* The disciples went out, found the animals, and brought them to Jesus. Interestingly, Mark has one animal (Mark 11:1–10), while Matthew has the two. This may be either Matthew's literalism from the Hebrew prophet's poetic word, or probably that the donkey was necessary to bring the unbroken colt.

Jesus entered Jerusalem not on a white charger, but on a lowly beast of burden, not on a horse as a symbol of power, but on a colt of an ass as a symbol of humility. He is the peaceful King of the people of God, not a revolutionary with political interest (Isa. 11:1–2). Note the care with which Matthew stresses identity: the identity of the location, the identity of a colt rather than a white charger, the identity with Old Testament prophecy (vv. 4–5), the identity in the cry of the crowd (Ps. 118:26), and the identity as the prophet from Nazareth (v. 11). Also note that the Messiah is referred to by use of the Old Testament quotation as a King (v. 5), with further reference to Him as the Son of David (v. 9). A great part of the multitude (literal translation) spread their garments in the way and placed branches from trees before Him in expression of royal honor (see 2 Kings 9:13). *Hosanna* is a shout of praise in Matthew, while in Mark the word is one sentence which means "save now" (Ps. 118:25). The shout is followed by the designation "Son of David," and the messianic reference that Jesus is Jehovah's representative (v. 9).

The whole city was "shaken" by His entry. The extent of this influence is shown in a comment by Barclay, who says that thirty years later a Roman governor found that at the Passover the number of lambs slain was nearly a quarter of a million; and recognizing that Jewish practice suggests ten persons for each lamb, there would then have been two and a half million people crowding Jerusalem for the Passover.[3] But Jeremias says the population of Jerusalem was approximately 30,000, with around 125,000 pilgrims, making something over 150,000.[4] Whatever the size, this was the auspicious time for the presentation of the King! But when the city officials asked who this person was riding into Jerusalem with such acclamation, the crowd did not answer, "Son of David," but modestly said, *"The prophet from Nazareth of Galilee."*

Many messages have been presented from this beautiful passage, and one hesitates to offer another outline. One could read the account in relation to Psalm 24:7–10, with the emphasis on the King of Glory: (1) the King comes in peace; (2) the King is acclaimed by the people; and (3) the King is crowned with praise. This is the inauguration of the Prince of Peace as King of kings.

JESUS CLEANSES THE TEMPLE

12 And Jesus went into the temple of God and drove out all those who bought and sold in the temple, and overturned the tables of the moneychangers and the seats of those who sold doves.

13 And He said to them, "It is written, *'My house shall be called a house of prayer,'* but you have made it a *'den of thieves.'"*

14 And the blind and the lame came to Him in the temple, and He healed them.

15 But when the chief priests and scribes saw the wonderful things that He did, and the children crying out in the temple and saying, "Hosanna to the Son of David!" they were indignant

16 and said to Him, "Do You hear what these are saying?" And Jesus said to them, "Yes. Have you never

read, *'Out of the mouth of babes and nursing infants*
You have perfected praise'?"
17 And He left them and went out of the city to
Bethany, and He lodged there.

Matt. 21:12–17

This passage is a judgment on cultism in Israel. Just as Jesus announced earlier that He is Lord of the Sabbath, so here He makes
clear that He is Lord of the temple. It is evident that a greater than
the temple is here! The cleansing challenged the economic, political,
and religious powers of the Jewish leaders. There is special reference
to *"the seats of those who sold doves,"* the offering for the poor, and specific
reference to the tables of the moneychangers in the court of the
Gentiles. Swartley says, "If you want to see Jesus go into action,
just cheat the poor and squeeze out the Gentiles!"[5] In Jesus' action
He was setting new rules for the temple or calling Israel to recognize
its true intent. His quotation is from Jeremiah's famous "Temple
Sermon" (chap. 7), and the leaders to whom Jesus spoke well understood it.

Some interpreters have used this passage about Jesus' anger at the
misuse of the temple and His actions in cleansing it to justify the
use of violence. It should be noted that of the four Gospel writers,
only John says anything about Jesus making a scourge of small cords,
and in speaking of how He used it, John says, "He drove them all
out of the temple, with the sheep and the oxen, and poured out
the changers' money and overturned the tables" (John 2:15). There
is no evidence that He laid the whip on any person. But that He
confronted them forcefully, yes; that He was revolutionary and took
decisive action, yes; but that He did violence to any man in terms
of physical hurt, no.

Matthew records that the blind and the lame came to Jesus in
the temple and He healed them. The children, seeing the wonderful
things He was doing, recognized the true expression of God's grace
and broke out in praise again, *"Hosanna to the Son of David."* The chief
priests and scribes had gathered, and asked Jesus if He was hearing
what the children were saying of Him. Jesus quoted Psalm 8:2 as
indication that this was perfect praise. In the face of the unbelief
of the religious leaders He left the temple and returned to Bethany
as His temporary home.

The cleansing of the temple can be applied to the cleansing that the presence of Christ brings into our lives, or into our religious institutionalism. In context, it was a judgment upon cultism in Israel. The passage contains (1) the exposure of religious cultism (vv. 12–13); (2) the expression of God's grace (v. 14); and (3) the ecstasy of praise (vv. 15–17). In developing an interpretation, special note should be made of Malachi 3.

CURSING THE FRUITLESS FIG TREE

18 Now in the morning, as He returned to the city, He was hungry.

19 And when He saw a fig tree by the road, He came to it and found nothing on it but leaves, and said to it, "Let no fruit grow on you anymore forever." And immediately the fig tree withered away.

20 And when the disciples saw it, they marveled, saying, "How did the fig tree wither away so soon?"

21 Jesus answered and said to them, "Assuredly, I say to you, if you have faith and do not doubt, you will not only do this which was done to the fig tree, but also if you say to this mountain, 'Be removed and be cast into the sea,' it will be done.

22 "And all things, whatever you ask in prayer, believing, you will receive."

Matt. 21:18–22

The inauguration of the King in chapter 21 has at least five relationships: to the populace (21:1–11), to the religious system (21:12–22), to authority (21:23–27), to obedience (21:28–32), and to faithfulness (21:33–46). The curse upon the fruitless fig tree is an object lesson in the account, almost like an exclamation point. Jesus had just confronted the system of the temple orders and "left them," having performed a messianic act and having been rejected by the very persons who should have seen in Him their Messiah. But audaciously they regarded His confrontation and the praise of the people as "drops of water on a hot stone."

He returned to Bethany for the night, but evidently spent the next nights on the Mount of Olives, no doubt by an olive press called Gethsemane. As Jesus returned to Jerusalem the morning after the temple episode, He noticed a fig tree near the road. Being hungry,

He went to it for some refreshment and found nothing but leaves. He cursed the tree, saying *"Let no fruit grow on thee henceforth for ever"* (kjv). Mark places the story prior to the cleansing of the temple, and thereby has the disciples notice on the day following that the tree is withered. Matthew telescopes the events together, and says *"presently the fig tree withered away"* (kjv). Swartley says, "The point of the fig tree account is not Jesus' vendetta against fig trees, fruit or no fruit, out of season or in, but that the doom and destiny of the fig tree casts its shadow over the temple."[6] It illustrated the Jewish nation which held out a promise of spiritual fruit before the world, but when Jesus came to their temple He found the very court which was to be open to the Gentile world cluttered with activity but with no spiritual vitality.

As the disciples observed the fig tree wither, they were so impressed with Jesus' authority over nature that they missed the parabolic meaning of His act. Upon their comment He ignored the meaning of the fruit missing from the tree and from Israel, and gave the disciples a lesson on faith. The fruit of grace in their lives will be the faith to cope with insurmountable difficulties, described metaphorically as "mountains." The incident is symbolic of God's curse upon the fruitless Israel, as the cleansing of the temple was a symbolic act, showing the emptiness of forms of piety with no fruit.

The lesson of the withered fig tree can be developed around several points: (1) there is no fruit when we are in unbelief (vv. 18–19); (2) there is no future of meaning when we are disapproved by God (vv. 19b–20); but (3) there is no failure when we pray believing (vv. 21–22). There is a contrast between fruitlessness with no faith, and the fruitfulness of faith.

Jesus' Authority

23 And when He had come into the temple, the chief priests and the elders of the people came to Him as He was teaching, and said, "By what authority are You doing these things? And who gave You this authority?"

24 And Jesus answered and said to them, "I also will ask you one thing, which if you tell Me, I likewise will tell you by what authority I do these things:

> 25 "The baptism of John, where was it from? From
> heaven or from men?" And they reasoned among
> themselves, saying, "If we say, 'From heaven,' He will
> say to us, 'Why then did you not believe him?'
> 26 "But if we say, 'From men,' we fear the
> multitude, for all count John as a prophet."
> 27 And they answered Jesus and said, "We do not
> know." And He said to them, "Neither will I tell you
> by what authority I do these things.
>
> *Matt. 21:23–27*

The authority figures of the temple challenged Jesus' authority.
We begin a series of parables and discourses of our Lord with His
enemies which express His anger at their hypocrisy. Three groups
accosted Jesus as He taught in the temple: the chief priests, the scribes,
and the elders of the people. This included the representatives of
the congregation, the exponents of the written and oral traditions,
and the spiritual hierarchy. The question of Jesus' authority to do
"these things" no doubt included the act of cleansing the temple, His
triumphal entry, and His teachings. By their authority as the Sanhedrin, they could destroy Him; but His authority could redeem them
from sin if they could but believe!

Jesus responded with a counterquestion asking their perception
of the role of John. His messianic role was related directly to John
as the forerunner. With this question He was not dodging the issue
but was setting it in the context of salvation history. They understood,
and discussed how to answer, but being exposed by either answer,
they backed off and said, *"We don't know."* Jesus had outwitted them,
and said, *"Neither will I answer."*

The outline of the passage is simple: (1) the question, (2) the counterquestion, and (3) the draw! Compare Mark 11:27–33 and Luke
20:1–8. Note that Matthew adds the reference to Jesus' teaching in
the temple, laying claim to the temple for God, having driven out
the programs that perverted its meaning.

THE PARABLE OF THE TWO SONS

> 28 "But what do you think? A man had two sons,
> and he came to the first and said, 'Son, go work today
> in my vineyard.'

29 "He answered and said, 'I will not,' but afterward he regretted it and went.

30 "And he came to the second and said likewise. And he answered and said, 'I go, sir,' and he did not go.

31 "Which of the two did the will of his father?" They said to Him, "The first." Jesus said to them, "Assuredly, I say to you that tax collectors and harlots enter the kingdom of God before you.

32 "For John came to you in the way of righteousness, and you did not believe him; but tax collectors and harlots believed him; and when you saw it, you did not afterward regret it that you might believe him.

Matt. 21:28–32

This story is an exposure of the failure of the religious leaders, and has a positive message that the Kingdom of God is open to all who are prepared to enter. It is found only in Matthew. The two sons illustrate two groups of persons. The first son said he would not go and work. Afterward he changed his mind and went—illustrative of the publicans and sinners who, being far from righteous, repented at John's preaching. The second son represented the professed religious people who enthusiastically said they would work, but never went. The word translated "regretted" in verse 29 is a form of the word *metamelomai* which means "after-care," not the word *metanoia* meaning a deep repentance. It relates to the last part of verse 32, for the religious leaders saw others changing and entering the Kingdom, but they had no "after-care" to change their attitude toward John's ministry.

Persons who have said no can change their minds and do God's will. Gordon Allport has said, "One's intentions for the future have more power to shape his life than the experiences of the past." Persons who say yes but do not obey God's will have missed the meaning of the Kingdom. Jesus said, "Not every one that saith unto Me, Lord, Lord, shall enter into the kingdom of heaven; but he that doeth the will of my Father which is in heaven" (Matt. 7:21, KJV). Persons who hear Jesus and follow as disciples, regardless of their past failures, share the Kingdom of God. The judgment is upon those who say "Yes, yes" intellectually but do not identify (see Jer. 7).

This is one of ten parables that show God's mercy for sinners.

The others are the physician (9:12), the two debtors (Luke 7:41–43), the guests at table (22:1–10), the prodigal sons (Luke 15:11–32), the lost sheep (18:12–14), the lost drachma (Luke 15:8–10), the good employer (20:1–15), the Pharisee and publican (Luke 18:9–14), and the father and child (7:9–11).

THE PARABLE OF THE WICKED VINEDRESSERS

33 "Hear another parable: There was a certain landowner who planted a vineyard, set a hedge around it, dug a winepress in it, and built a tower. And he leased it to vinedressers and went into a far country.

34 "And when the time for fruit drew near, he sent his servants to the vinedressers, that they might receive the fruit of it.

35 "And the vinedressers took his servants, beat one, killed one, and stoned another.

36 "Again he sent other servants, more than the first, and they did likewise to them.

37 "But last of all he sent his son to them, saying, 'They will respect my son.'

38 "But when the vinedressers saw the son, they said among themselves, 'This is the heir. Come, let us kill him and seize his inheritance.'

39 "And they caught him, cast him out of the vineyard, and killed him.

40 "Therefore, when the owner of the vineyard comes, what will he do to those vinedressers?"

41 They said to Him, "He will miserably destroy those wicked men, and lease his vineyard to other vinedressers who will render to him the fruits in their seasons."

42 Jesus said to them, "Did you never read in the Scriptures:
'The stone which the builders rejected
Has become the chief cornerstone.
This was the LORD's doing,
And it is marvelous in our eyes'?

43 "Therefore I say to you, the kingdom of God will be taken from you and given to a nation bearing the fruits of it.

44 "And whoever falls on this stone will be broken; but on whomever it falls, it will grind him to powder."

45 And when the chief priests and Pharisees had heard His parables, they perceived that He was speaking of them.

46 But when they sought to lay hands on Him, they feared the multitudes, because they took Him for a prophet.

Matt. 21:33–46

Matthew's words, *"Hear another parable,"* relate this parable to the preceding one, placing it as the second of a trilogy. Spoken to the same audience, it is given in the nature of an allegory. The story focuses on their rejection of Jesus Himself, as the preceding parable had focused on their rejection of the messianic mission of John the Baptist. In the story, the vineyard is Israel (the same language is found in Isa. 5:1–2); the owner is God; the tenant-farmers are the religious leaders; the servants sent to receive the fruit are the prophets of the Old Testament; and the son is Jesus the Messiah. Some scholars see this allegorical use of a story as interpolation made later by the early church. However, in context the sequence makes the interpretation as Jesus' story appropriate. At the end of the parable His question is answered by the hearers, and His response is to apply the story to their unbelief.

There is no explanation of the death of the son in the story, only that the tenant-farmers killed him outright. (1) There is affirmation on Jesus' part that His position is superior to that of the prophets; (2) there is consciousness of a unique relation of sonship; (3) there is the conviction that He was sent from God as the final envoy; (4) there is recognition that rejection and death await Him, and this rejection clearly involves the judgment of Israel. This section is uniquely expressive of the mission of the Messiah as Suffering Servant.

In Matthew's account the chief priests and Pharisees expressed their own condemnation. Jesus' quotation from Psalm 118:22–23 is a reference relating to His place in the construction of the New People of God. (Note especially Eph. 2:11–22; 1 Pet. 2:4–5). With their rejection of God's Messiah-Son, Jesus said the kingdom of God would be taken from them and offered to a people who would bear the fruit of the Kingdom (Mal. 1:11). Verse 44 is missing in a number of older manuscripts; however, it recalls the words of Daniel 2:44–45, where the stone cut out without hands strikes the kingdoms of power and breaks them to pieces. The religious leaders understood His reference to them, and desired to lay hands on Him, but did not because of the multitude. The parable is a moving story about "how open minds close": those who had searched for truth were now closed to it.

THE PARABLE OF THE WEDDING GUEST

1 And Jesus answered and spoke to them again by parables and said:

2 "The kingdom of heaven is like a certain king who arranged a marriage for his son,

3 "and sent out his servants to call those who were invited to the wedding; and they were not willing to come.

4 "Again, he sent out other servants, saying, 'Tell those who are invited: See, I have prepared my dinner; my oxen and fattened cattle are killed, and all things are ready. Come to the wedding.'

5 "But they made light of it and went their ways, one to his own farm, another to his business.

6 "And the rest seized his servants, treated them spitefully, and killed them.

7 "But when the king heard about it, he was furious. And he sent out his armies, destroyed those murderers, and burned up their city.

8 "Then he said to his servants, 'The wedding is ready, but those who were invited were not worthy.

9 'Therefore go into the highways, and as many as you find, invite to the wedding.'

10 "So those servants went out into the highways and gathered together all whom they found, both bad and good. And the wedding hall was filled with guests.

11 "But when the king came in to see the guests, he saw a man there who did not have on a wedding garment.

12 "And he said to him, 'Friend, how did you come in here without a wedding garment?' And he was speechless.

13 "Then the king said to the servants, 'Bind him
hand and foot, take him away, and cast him into outer
darkness; there will be weeping and gnashing of teeth.'
   14 "For many are called, but few are chosen."

Matt. 22:1–14

This third parable of the trilogy is a further answer to the religious
leaders. Some commentators see this parable as parallel to another
version in Luke 14:16–24. But as Tasker says, the differences are as
numerous as the agreements.[7] Using the same theme, Jesus presented
different applications. In this account Jesus exposed the indifference
of the religious leaders, emphasizing the King's invitation to persons
other than those originally invited. The wedding feast calls to mind
both the eschatological feast associated with the messianic triumph—
the marriage supper of the Lamb (Rev. 19:7–9)—and the deep relational meaning of Ephesians 5:25–27.

There are three divisions to the story: (1) the invitation is rejected
by many (vv. 1–7); (2) the invitation is extended to strangers (vv.
8–9); and (3) the invited persons are still expected to be properly
considerate (vv. 10–14). The first section is illustrative of Jewish people
who were repeatedly invited by the call of God's gospel, but who
would not come. They even destroyed the messengers who brought
the invitation. The second section introduces the act of God in turning
from the Jewish in-group to invite the Gentiles, the strangers. And
the third section is actually another parable, making this a double-
edged statement, which perhaps accounts for verse 1 where Matthew
says Jesus spoke to them again by parables (plural). This section
has to do with our appropriate response to God's gracious call.

The wedding garment is symbolic of a totally new mode of existence. This man sat at the wedding banquet but his heart was not
there. In courtesy the host did not partake of the meal but appeared
among the guests during the meal. The soiled garments of this guest
were an insult to the host, especially since in God's grace the wedding
garment is provided. For God clothes the redeemed (see Zech. 3:1–
4; Isa. 61:10; Rev. 3:4–5, 18). God rejects those who try to enter the
Kingdom without doing the will of the King. They are cast into
outer darkness, the state of the lost who have turned their backs
on God. Perhaps in adding this second aspect of the parables Jesus
had Judas in mind. To address him as "friend" is to use the same
word that Jesus used in the garden when He addressed Judas. One

can be called to the messianic feast (v. 14) but not be among the chosen who identify with the Son.

JESUS ON PAYING TAXES TO CAESAR

15 Then the Pharisees went and took counsel how they might entangle Him in His talk.

16 And they sent out to Him their disciples with the Herodians, saying, "Teacher, we know that You are true and teach the way of God in truth; nor do You care about anyone, for You do not regard the person of men.

17 "Tell us therefore, what do You think? Is it lawful to pay taxes to Caesar, or not?"

18 But Jesus perceived their wickedness, and said, "Why do you test Me, you hypocrites?

19 "Show Me the tax money." And they brought Him a denarius.

20 And He said to them, "Whose image and inscription is this?"

21 They said to Him, "Caesar's." Then He said to them, "Render therefore to Caesar the things that are Caesar's, and to God the things that are God's."

22 When they had heard these words, they marveled, and left Him and went their way.

Matt. 22:15–22

The presentation of the King continues, and we move from the relation of grace to His relation to earthly powers. Matthew moves from the political to the theological (Resurrection), then to the pragmatic (the Law and love), and finally to the eschatological messianic expectation. The conclusion of this section will introduce the fifth of the so-called "five books" of Matthew dealing with eschatological perspectives.

This chapter is not a series of unrelated questions. There is movement toward the climax of messianic identity and authority. There is contrast between Jesus' emphasis on love and the power play of the leaders. They understood the intent of Jesus' teaching in the temple, and took deliberate counsel as to how to trap Him. Having decided on the best trap, they sent their disciples with the Herodians. The latter were Herod's men and representative of Rome, sent to make the trap more effective with both parties present. The two parties had different views on the issue. What strange bedfellows antagonists make when they have a common enemy! They introduced the question with ingratiating words of flattery, words true in themselves, that Jesus was an honest teacher of the ways of God without respect of persons. Their question was held to admit only a yes or a no answer. *"Is it lawful to pay taxes to Caesar, or not?"* Their question, *"What do you think?"* may have been mockery, as this was a phrase often used by Jesus. But Jesus perceived their purpose, and said bluntly, *"You hypocrites, why do you test Me?"*

Persons who want a yes or no answer should be aware that many things are not that simple. A Mennonite church leader was once asked for a yes or no answer, which he said he would give if the questioner would answer his question with yes or no. Upon acquiescence he asked, "Have you stopped beating your wife?" Either answer would incriminate.

Jesus shrewdly asked them to show Him the tax money. They brought Him the denarius. When He asked about the image on the coin, He was told that it was Caesar's. As the rabbis said, "Wherever any king's money is current, there that king is lord." Jesus convicted them by the simple fact that they were using it. His answer was not to "give" tribute to Caesar, but to "give back" to Caesar what belongs to him and at the same time to give to God what belongs to Him! To pay taxes for the benefits received from earthly powers should be a reminder of greater dues owed to God. Jesus' answer emphasized the positive, *"to God the things which are God's."* He rejected the Zealot's revolutionary position against Rome, but rejected as well any surrender of man's primary relation to God, man's greater obligation.

The early church faced this issue in the crucial demands of Emperor worship. They met these demands by declaring, "Caesar is not Lord; Jesus is Lord." Consequently, many were martyred, as was Polycarp, disciple and successor of John the beloved, who said, "Eighty and six years have I served Him, and He has done me no wrong; how then can I deny my King and my God?" The issue of what is Caesar's and what is God's has continued to confront the church. Clearly our first loyalty is to God. In the passage we do not give taxes, we pay them, or in Jesus' words, we *"give back to Caesar what is Caesar's."* But we must ask, How does knowing what is God's determine our response to Caesar when Caesar asks for our lives in military participation against the will of God, or when Caesar imposes a specific military tax to destroy our fellow man? Can one abdicate his moral responsibility and assign it to the State? Who will answer to God, the State, or each one of us who shall "give account of himself to God" (Rom. 14:12)?

JESUS ON THE RESURRECTION

23 The same day the Sadducees, who say there is no resurrection, came to Him and asked Him,

24 saying: "Teacher, Moses said that if a man dies, having no children, his brother shall marry his wife and raise up offspring for his brother.

25 "Now there were with us seven brothers. And the first died after he had married, and having no offspring, left his wife to his brother.

26 "Likewise the second also, and the third, even to the seventh.

27 "And last of all the woman died also.

28 "Therefore, in the resurrection, whose wife of the seven will she be? For they all had her."

29 Jesus answered and said to them, "You are mistaken, not knowing the Scriptures nor the power of God.

30 "For in the resurrection they neither marry nor are given in marriage, but are like the angels of God in heaven.

31 "But concerning the resurrection of the dead, have you not read what was spoken to you by God, saying,

32 *I am the God of Abraham, the God of Isaac, and the God of Jacob*'? God is not the God of the dead, but of the living."

33 And when the multitudes heard this, they were astonished at His teaching.

Matt. 22:23–33

The next trap was set by the party of the Sadducees. Matthew says it was on the same day as the previous interchange. Behind the scenes these two enemy groups had probably plotted together to trap Jesus. Or, the Sadducees, having seen the Pharisees and Herodians routed, wanted to show their superiority on theological matters. Using the illustration of Levirate marriage (where a man's brother is required to marry the widow and bring up children to his brother's name and inheritance), they wanted to discredit Jesus as a theologian and make the doctrine of the resurrection as held by orthodox Pharisees look absurd. The illustration is a notable hypothesis of a woman married in sequence to seven brothers in order to obtain a physical descendant. The problem of a resurrection was that she would be faced with seven husbands!

Jesus' answer is also classic: *"You know neither the Scriptures nor the power of God."* The question is irrelevant once it is recognized that the eternal world is not material. Jesus exposes their limited view of reality and their materialism which believed in neither angels, nor spirit, nor resurrection (Acts 23:8). Furthermore, neither heaven nor angels are characterized by sexuality but by fellowship. But the climax is Jesus' interpretation of the theology of the resurrection by asserting that God is not the God of the dead but of the living. The word of Jehovah to Moses is the basis for this assertion, for Abraham, Isaac, and Jacob had been dead for centuries when God affirmed that He is the God of these patriarchs. They had quoted Moses to Jesus, and He quoted him back, emphasizing that this word was spoken to them (v. 32). The crowd was astonished, probably hearing for the first time that the Law itself held the seeds of immortality and the hope of the resurrection.

The passage emphasizes belief in resurrection, built on the following points: (1) the statement of their position—the case of the hardy woman (vv. 23–27); (2) the character of life beyond life—fellowship beyond sexual association (vv. 28–30); (3) the assurance that God is the God of the living (vv. 31–33).

JESUS' REPLY CONCERNING THE GREAT COMMANDMENT

34 But when the Pharisees heard that He had put the Sadducees to silence, they gathered together.

35 Then one of them, who was a lawyer, asked Him a question, testing Him, and saying,

36 "Teacher, which is the great commandment in the law?"

37 Jesus said to him, *"'You shall love the LORD your*

God with all your heart, with all your soul, and with all your mind.'

38 "This is the first and great commandment.

39 "And the second is like it: *'You shall love your neighbor as yourself.'*

40 "On these two commandments hang all the Law and the Prophets."

Matt. 22:34–40

The Pharisees, having been defeated, were delighted that Jesus had silenced (literally, "muzzled") the Sadducees. Matthew now shows the Pharisees regrouping for another attack. This picture is described in Psalm 2:2, "The rulers take counsel together, against the Lord, and against his anointed." One of the group served as a spokesman. The word *nomikos,* translated "lawyer," means one trained in the Law, a scribe. The question is again to test Jesus, seeking an answer that would indict Him for blasphemy. The scribes said there were 613 laws, with 248 being affirmative and 365 being negative. Some even argued that the commandment to wear fringes on the garments was the greatest of the 613! This helps us to recognize the test to which they presumed they were subjecting Him.

A professor of Law at the school of Shammai addressed Jesus as professor, teacher. We do not have the tone of his voice and thus we don't know whether it was with respect or sarcasm. The account is related differently than by Luke (10:25–28) and does not include the well-known story of the Good Samaritan. In Luke's account, Jesus answered the lawyer's attempt to justify himself with an amazing conclusion. He turned the lawyer's question upside down. The question is not, "Who is my neighbor?" but a new question, "Are you willing to be a neighbor?"

In Matthew Jesus answered the scribe, as is the case in Mark (12:28–34), by quoting the Shema from Deuteronomy 6:5. This passage was quoted twice daily by faithful Jews. The commandment is to love God with every faculty of one's personality, unreservedly. But a second commandment is a corollary of the first, *"Love your neighbor as yourself."* In these statements the definite article is absent (vv. 38–39), meaning "a" first and great commandment, and "a" second of like character. On these two, Jesus said, every other principle of the Law has its base. Jesus was probably the first professor to draw together in this way the two passages, Deuteronomy 6:5 and Leviticus

19:18, thereby introducing the scribe to a new hermeneutic of love over law.

The contrast is seen between Pharisaic legalism and the ethic of love for God and one's neighbor. By fusing the two commandments, Jesus showed the way to fulfill the first, for it is in loving the neighbor whom we have seen that we express our participation in love for God whom we have not seen (1 John 4:20). All of the Law is fulfilled by these two commandments. Like the two hinges on a door, so the two belong together as the New Law, the new commandment. The order is significant, first the opening of one's life to God, followed by the opening of one's life to his neighbor. To love is to open one's life intimately to that of another. To open one's life to God means to open one's heart or affection to Him, to open one's soul or ambition to Him, to open one's mind or attitudes to Him, to open one's strength or activity to Him, and to open one's self to what God is doing in the neighbor, be he friend or enemy! This is the righteousness that exceeds the righteousness of the scribes and Pharisees (Matt. 5:20).

JESUS' QUESTION ON MESSIAHSHIP

41 While the Pharisees were gathered together, Jesus asked them,

42 saying, "What do you think about the Christ? Whose Son is He?" They said to Him, "The Son of David."

43 He said to them, "How then does David in the Spirit call Him 'Lord,' saying:

44 'The LORD said to my Lord,
"Sit at My right hand,
Till I make Your enemies Your footstool" '?

45 "If David then calls Him 'Lord,' how is He his Son?"

46 And no one was able to answer Him a word, nor from that day on did anyone dare ask Him any more questions.

Matt. 22:41–46

Jesus followed with a question to the Pharisees, *"while they were still gathered around Him"* (Knox's translation). Mark makes the point that this was while Jesus was teaching in the temple. To His question,

"Whose son is the Christ, the Messiah?" the Pharisees responded, *"The Son of David."* Jesus immediately quoted a passage in which David himself acknowledged the Messiah as Lord (Ps. 110:1). Then Jesus asked, *"If David calls Him 'Lord,' how is He his Son?"* We should note that Jesus said David made this statement *"in the Spirit"* (v. 43), a direct reference to the Spirit's inspiration of the psalmist in writing. Further, for David to call Him "Lord" means that the Son of David is not to be equated with David's military career; He can be a Messiah of peace and reconciliation, the Suffering Servant of Isaiah 53. As Filson says, "This passage shows Jesus declaring the freedom of the Messiah to establish the Kingdom by another path than the political and military methods of David."[8] In the face of such wisdom the religious leaders left off, not daring to risk another public debate.

The messianic role of Christ is seen in this passage with five important implications: (1) Jesus' hermeneutic enabled Him to find the predictions of His career in the Old Testament suggesting a christological hermeneutic for us; (2) Jesus was not involved in the literary and historical problems with which scholarship wrestles today, but simply considered Psalm 110:1 as David's Psalm, affirming the role of the Spirit in the inspiration of Scripture; (3) Jesus' interpretation, which connected Lord with Messiah, presents the messianic fulfillment as the Lordship of Christ in His church; (4) Jesus explained His messiahship by His unique link with God; (5) Jesus' triumph and exaltation were an integral part of the messianic hope.

JESUS JUDGES THE FALSE LEADERS

1 Then Jesus spoke to the multitudes and to His disciples,

2 saying, "The scribes and the Pharisees sit in Moses' seat.

3 "Therefore whatever they tell you to observe, that observe and do, but do not do according to their works; for they say, and do not do.

4 "For they bind heavy burdens, hard to bear, and lay them on men's shoulders; but they themselves will not move them with one of their fingers.

5 "But all their works they do to be seen by men. They make their phylacteries broad and enlarge the borders of their garments.

6 "They love the best places at feasts, the best seats in the synagogues,

7 "greetings in the marketplaces, and to be called by men, 'Rabbi, Rabbi.'

8 "But you, do not be called 'Rabbi'; for One is your Teacher, the Christ, and you are all brethren.

9 "And do not call anyone on earth your father; for One is your Father, He who is in heaven.

10 "And do not be called teachers; for One is your Teacher, the Christ.

11 "But he who is greatest among you shall be your servant.

12 "And whoever exalts himself will be abased, and he who humbles himself will be exalted.

13 "But woe to you, scribes and Pharisees, hypocrites! For you shut up the kingdom of heaven against men; for you neither go in yourselves, nor do you allow those who are entering to go in.

14 "Woe to you, scribes and Pharisees, hypocrites! For you devour widows' houses, and for a pretense make long prayers. Therefore you will receive greater condemnation.

15 "Woe to you, scribes and Pharisees, hypocrites! For you go about on land and sea to make one proselyte, and when he is made, you make him twice as much a son of hell as yourselves.

16 "Woe to you, blind guides, who say, 'Whoever swears by the temple, it is nothing; but whoever swears by the gold of the temple, he is obligated.'

17 "Fools and blind! For which is greater, the gold or the temple that sanctifies the gold?

18 "And, 'Whoever swears by the altar, it is nothing; but whoever swears by the gift that is on it, he is obligated.'

19 "Fools and blind! For which is greater, the gift or the altar that sanctifies the gift?

20 "Therefore he who swears by the altar, swears by it and by all things on it.

21 "And he who swears by the temple, swears by it and by Him who dwells in it.

22 "And he who swears by heaven, swears by the throne of God and by Him who sits on it.

23 "Woe to you, scribes and Pharisees, hypocrites! For you pay tithe of mint and anise and cummin, and

have neglected the weightier matters of the law: justice and mercy and faith. These you ought to have done, without leaving the others undone.

24 "Blind guides, who strain out a gnat and swallow a camel!

25 "Woe to you, scribes and Pharisees, hypocrites! For you cleanse the outside of the cup and the dish, but inside they are full of extortion and self-indulgence.

26 "Blind Pharisee, first cleanse the inside of the cup and dish, that the outside of them may be clean also.

27 "Woe to you, scribes and Pharisees, hypocrites! For you are like whitewashed tombs which indeed appear beautiful outwardly, but inside are full of dead men's bones and all uncleanness.

28 "Even so you also outwardly appear righteous to men, but inside you are full of hypocrisy and lawlessness.

29 "Woe to you, scribes and Pharisees, hypocrites! Because you build the tombs of the prophets and adorn the monuments of the righteous,

30 "and say, 'If we had lived in the days of our fathers, we would not have been partakers with them in the blood of the prophets.'

31 "Therefore you are witnesses against yourselves that you are sons of those who murdered the prophets.

32 "Fill up, then, the measure of your fathers' guilt.

33 "Serpents, brood of vipers! How can you escape the condemnation of hell?

34 "Therefore, indeed, I send you prophets, wise men, and scribes: some of them you will kill and crucify; and some of them you will scourge in your synagogues and persecute from city to city,

35 "that on you may come all the righteous blood shed on the earth, from the blood of righteous Abel to the blood of Zechariah, son of Berechiah, whom you killed between the temple and the altar.

36 "Assuredly, I say to you, all these things will come on this generation.

Matt. 23:1–36

The content of this passage concluded Jesus' public ministry, and also His interchange with the scribes and Pharisees. The passage begins with a message to the crowd about the scribes and Pharisees, exposing them as the false shepherds spoken of by the prophets (Jer. 23; Ezek. 22–23; Amos 7; Zech. 13; Zeph. 3). He exposed them in the Sermon on the Mount as well in His warning about false prophets (7:15–20). He then addressed the leaders directly, and completely unmasked them before the multitude. The seven woes stand in a contrasting relation to the statements of blessing in the first seven Beatitudes. It should be noted that with the "five book" approach to Matthew this section introduces the "fifth book," dealing with eschatological matters which take seriously the judgment of God.

Some have proposed that chapter 23 of Matthew did not come from Jesus, but was added at a later time. Others see this section as Matthew's compilation of sayings expressed by Jesus at various times in His ministry. Others see these sayings as inconsistent with the loving nature of the Christ and cannot believe that He uttered such sharp words. However, for several reasons this section should be accepted as the words of Jesus, as a summation of His interaction with the scribes and Pharisees. *First,* they fit as a response to the hypocritical questioning that was meant to trap Him rather than to hear Him. *Second,* they are expressions of judgment upon unbelief, consistent with the integrity of Jesus' role as Messiah, evidenced in His judgments upon Tyre and Sidon, and Bethsaida and Capernaum. This confrontation held them accountable, since they had been visited by God's messianic Son. *Third,* these statements help us to see Jesus as an authentic person, able to confront unbelief, able to have anger without doing violence to persons, able to be honest with His feelings, rather than to represent love as something spineless. And *fourth,* this passage is needed to give us a full picture of the integrity of Jesus' ministry. He held these religious leaders responsible for their claims in leadership, and accountable to God for integrity in executing their claim of being called.

Jesus' message to the crowd concerning the Pharisees opens this section (vv. 1–12). In a matter-of-fact statement Jesus said they occupy Moses' seat; they are the legal experts and exponents of the Law; and Jesus affirmed respect for their role in representing the Law, but said the people were to avoid following the practice of the leaders who failed to interface word and deed. The commendation was for their representation of Moses. But Jesus qualified their leadership by several observations: *first,* they multiplied commands upon individuals which they themselves would not practice; *second,* they practiced their religious traditions for the recognition they received of men;

third, they had respect of person, for they loved chief places in the assembly and wanted to be greeted with honor in society. Jesus condemned their status-seeking, and contrasted their practice with the New Community that He was creating. The New People of God have one Teacher, the Christ; one level, all are brethren; one Father before whom all bow, the Father in heaven; and one measure of greatness, that of being servants who humble themselves in service. This is a remarkable outline of worship and relationship in the *ekklēsia,* among those called by Christ to be His disciples.

The next unit contains the woes against false teachers. There are eight woes in the AV, but since verse 14 is not found in many ancient texts most scholars omit it and list seven woes. We will combine the statement in verse 14 with the preceding, and deal with seven pronouncements of "woe." An Old Testament example of this prophetic pattern of woe upon the erring is found in Isaiah 5:8–23. The word "woe" could be translated "alas," rendering the "woes" as lamentations. Such a translation interprets them as expressions of compassionate weeping rather than hard denunciations, and also relates the "woes of lament" directly to what follows in the lamentation of Jesus over Jerusalem.

Pharisaic hyprocrisy was exposed by Jesus in the manner by which it was being expressed. First, the legal experts had removed the keys of the Kingdom, and neither entered the kingdom themselves nor assisted others to enter (vv. 13–14). Second, in spreading their influence among the Hellenistic world (the Gentiles), they insisted that all converts live by the laws as they interpreted them, and thereby they perverted rather than converted people (v. 15). Third, their hair-splitting distinctions as to which oaths were binding perverted the understanding of God and man's relationship to Him as the Creator and Governor of the universe (vv. 16–22). Fourth, their lack in understanding the will of God was expressed in caring about the trivia of ritual practices and minimizing the great moral precepts meant to be practiced: justice, mercy, and faith (vv. 23–24). Fifth, the scrupulous attention to the externals of religion led to a disregard of inner perversions (vv. 25–26). Sixth, the outward conformity of appearance to be seen of men often concealed the inner corruption of moral defilement (vv. 27–28). Seventh, in relating to the heritage of the religious community, they had copied the worst traits of their fathers, while seeking to disclaim responsibility for the sins of their fathers (vv. 29–31).

Attention should be given to Jesus' emphasis on justice, mercy and faith (v. 23). Justice is honest diligence in doing what is right and fair. Mercy is active kindness to everyone in need. And faith here means faithfulness: consistent integrity in dealing with others. There is cutting humor in the statement that they strain out a gnat and swallow a camel!

Jesus' words contain scalding irony, in verse 32; the scribes and Pharisees were acting in a manner that "filled to the full" the pattern of their fathers (see Acts 7:52). In some manuscripts the word is in the future tense, a sad prediction: "you will fill up." As an answer to their need, Jesus said that He was sending them true prophets, apostles as the sent ones of His new order. He placed the apostles alongside the Old Testament prophets. Persecuted and killed, they would be regarded as the foundation of the New People of God, and of the New Age (see Eph. 2:19–22). But for the false prophets or leaders there is the judgment of God upon all unbelief, from the death of Abel at the hand of Cain to the last martyr in the Hebrew Bible (2 Chron. 24:20–22). The identification of Zechariah leaves some unanswered questions, but the point is clear.

Attention should be called again to a comparison of the Beatitudes with these contrasting statements of woe. These pronouncements of judgment are for the very opposite behavior from that which Jesus declared to be blessed. The first beatitude, in which Jesus blessed the poor in spirit, is in contrast with the Pharisees' attitude of power in controlling the keys of the kingdom. The seventh, in which Jesus blessed peacemakers, is contrasted with their sharing the tradition of their fathers in killing the righteous. There is an evident contrast in the others in the series as well.

Jesus' Lament Over Jerusalem

37 "O Jerusalem, Jerusalem, the one who kills the prophets and stones those who are sent to her! How often I wanted to gather your children together, as a hen gathers her chicks under her wings, and you were not willing!

38 "See! Your house is left to you desolate;

39 "for I say to you, you shall see Me no more till you say, *'Blessed is He who comes in the name of the Lord!'"*

Matt. 23:37–39

This passage has the same words as in the Luke account (13:34–35); therefore it is thought to have come from Q, the earlier source. But Matthew's inclusion of the lament is definitely to show that the prophecy of Jesus was not given in a spirit of vindictiveness. His lament over Jerusalem frames the laments of "woe" in love. In lamenting the faithlessness of His countrymen in not reaching their destiny, He transfers their rejection of the prophets to Himself. He wept over Jerusalem; He would have gathered them like a hen gathers chicks under her wings. He no doubt was recalling Isaiah 31:5, where Yahweh of hosts overshadows Jerusalem to protect her. *"But you were not willing"* is a sad statement of judgment given at the very time that Jesus was leaving the temple.

This scene reminds us of Ezekiel's picture of the glory of God leaving the temple (Ezek. 11:23). God became concretely real on earth in Jesus. God took the initiative in coming (John 1:14) but, as in Jeremiah 7, Jerusalem refused the grace of God (Jer. 7:25–27). Now Jesus said in essence that God has forsaken the temple which they had desecrated and abandoned it and them to Judgment. Jesus said that they would not see Him again until He returned in His glory, fulfilling the prophecies of Psalm 118:26. This is still to come, for following His Resurrection Jesus only appeared to disciples who believed in Him. But the unbelievers will see Him for "at the name of Jesus every knee [shall] bow . . . and . . . every tongue [shall] confess that Jesus Christ is Lord, to the glory of God the Father" (Phil. 2:10–11).

NOTES

1. Manson, *The Teaching of Jesus,* p. 208.
2. Ibid., pp. 208–209.
3. Barclay, *The Gospel of Matthew,* 1:262.
4. Joachim Jeremias, *The Eucharistic Words of Jesus* (Philadelphia: Fortress Press, 1964), p. 42.
5. Swartley, *Mark,* p. 170.
6. Ibid.
7. Tasker, *The Gospel According to St. Matthew,* p. 206.
8. Floyd Filson, *A Commentary on the Gospel According to Matthew* (London: Adam & Charles Black, 1960), p. 223.

CHAPTER NINE

The Predictions of the King

Matthew 24:1—25:46

Eschatology is the prophetic interpretation of the purpose of history, of end-time events and of the goal of history. In the Judaic-Christian faith, history is going somewhere because God is acting in history. The scope of salvation history moves to its *telos*, its completion, its culmination as we know history. As Christians we believe that history does not contain its own fulfillment, but that God as the main Actor on the stage of time will bring it to a victorious climax. He will triumph over all adversity and achieve the ultimate goal of the work of redemption. He chose to participate in man's dilemma by becoming concrete in Jesus the Christ. He reconciled us to Himself through the cross, and by the redemption of the cross brings us into the experience of grace. Jesus, as the Divine Agent of our redemption, has the ultimate purpose of completing a Kingdom which He will inevitably turn over to the Father (1 Cor. 15:24–28).

Any discussion of future events calls for humility and caution on the part of theologians. Our Master Himself said that He didn't know the day or the hour of His return, a statement which brings into judgment all date-setters. We are deluged with persons who, as Vernard Eller says, want to "sell tickets to the battle of Armageddon"[1] rather than humbly to obey His words to "occupy until He comes." A theology of hope, to use Moltmann's term, believes in the fulfillment of Jesus' promise to return and lives in that hope. Hope is the freedom to live openly in the world. We learn from the past and take our cues from the future as we live by His promise. To live effectively in a modern world we must beware of unexamined presuppositions, we must avoid a purely scientific view of life, and we must live by faith in the word of Christ and His victory as risen Lord.

This section contains and draws together Jesus' positive teachings about eschatology. A key statement is 24:36, *"of that day and hour no one knows, no, not even the angels of heaven, but My Father only."* Jesus emphasized the importance of preparedness, of watchfulness. He placed most of His emphasis on this faithfulness by a series of three very important parables.

The opening section is difficult for a number of reasons. First of all, we are not certain of the order in which Jesus answered the questions of the disciples, whether in the order raised, or with the last question answered first. Further, we are not certain whether Jesus answered in a systematic sequence or by statments interfaced with each other. Nor are we certain as to all of the factors that influenced Matthew as he arranged the materials of the passage. We can assume that this Gospel was written before the destruction of Jerusalem in A.D. 70, probably in the very late 60s, for it presents Jesus' statements without any reflection on that event as past or current history. There are hermeneutical problems in a passage like this because of various eschatological views that affect our reading: premillennial, amillennial, postmillennial, transmillennial, etc.

In fairness to the reader, it should be stated that the writer's premillennial conditioning has been modified into a view that I call transmillennialism.[2] I have created this word to mean something more than is commonly meant by the term *millennium.* This reign of Christ will include both the earth and the heavens and will fulfill Paul's teaching in Romans 8:19–25. By this is meant that, as with the premillennial view, a final culmination or *telos* issuing in an actualization of the Kingdom will be literally fulfilled, but it will not be limited to an earthly form. It is described in Revelation 20 as the ultimate actualization of the extension of Christ's victory with its cosmic significance, a victory we will share as we live and reign with Him. With this interpretation the approach to this passage will express exegesis that expects a literal fulfillment.

JESUS PREDICTS THE DESTRUCTION OF THE TEMPLE

1 And Jesus went out and departed from the
temple, and His disciples came to Him to show Him
the buildings of the temple.

2 And Jesus said to them, "Do you not see all these
things? Assuredly, I say to you, not one stone shall
be left here upon another that shall not be thrown
down."

Matt. 24:1–2

These verses follow immediately upon Jesus' judgment of religious
leaders, His lament over Jerusalem, and His departure from the temple.
His seven woes were pealed out like thunder, and His declaration
that their house was left desolate was like a bolt of lightning. But
upon leaving, the disciples, like tourists, were exclaiming over the
magnificence of the temple. Jesus addressed them with words that
made clear that His earlier statements in the temple were not just
passing comments. His words carried utmost gravity, for in verse 2,
the "Assuredly, I say to you" is most emphatic.

The sight of the temple at Jerusalem was one of the more outstanding sights in the ancient world. It was built of white marble and
plated with gold. It shone in the sunlight so that a person could
hardly look at it. For the pilgrim to Jerusalem, to come to Mount
Zion was an impressive call to reverence and worship. Some of the
temple's large supporting stones were forty feet in length and weighed
one hundred tons. The cutting and moving of these colossal stones
remains a mystery of ancient engineering. I have stood in amazement
before such stones at Balbeck in Lebanon, as well as at the excavations
by the temple area in Jerusalem. And the disciples, several of whom
were rural fisherman from Galilee, were duly amazed and impressed
by the majesty of the temple. But Jesus predicted its complete destruction, for the end of Jewish temple cultism was at hand. The New
Temple of "living stones" was yet to come. The people of God would
be the temple of His presence, no matter where they met. And the
disciples, of course, asked the question, "When?"

JESUS DISCUSSES THE END OF THE AGE

3 And as He sat on the Mount of Olives, the
disciples came to Him privately, saying, "Tell us, when
will these things be? And what will be the sign of
Your coming, and of the end of the age?"
4 And Jesus answered and said to them: "Take heed
that no one deceives you.

5 "For many will come in My name, saying, 'I am the Christ,' and will deceive many.

6 "And you will hear of wars and rumors of wars. See that you are not troubled; for all these things must come to pass, but the end is not yet.

7 "For nation will rise against nation, and kingdom against kingdom. And there will be famines, pestilences, and earthquakes in various places.

8 "All these are the beginning of sorrows.

9 "Then they will deliver you up to tribulation and kill you, and you will be hated by all nations for My name's sake.

10 "And then many will be offended, betray one another, and hate one another.

11 "And many false prophets will rise and deceive many.

12 "And because lawlessness will abound, the love of many will grow cold.

13 "But he who endures to the end will be saved.

14 "And this gospel of the kingdom will be preached in all the world as a witness to all the nations, and then the end will come.

Matt. 24:3–14

As Jesus sat on the Mount of Olives, the disciples asked what appear to have been three questions: *"When will these things be? . . . what will be the sign of Your coming and of the end of the age?"* Jesus answered but Matthew does not tell us in what order (v. 4). A careful reading of the chapter may suggest that Jesus answered the last question first. The disciples themselves had a limited understanding of eschatology, and thus their questions were limited. Jesus had new insight to share, and we have the first use of the term *parousia,* a word used only in this chapter in the Gospels (vv. 3, 27, 37, 39). Bear in mind also the difficulties for Jesus to interpret for them a scope of history that included the near and far aspects, the near destruction of Jerusalem, and the more distant end of the age. Even more difficult was His placing in context the future coming of the Son of Man as the culmination of a redemptive mission which was going to reach its climax in the crucifixion and Resurrection of the Messiah only a few days hence! The treatment in Matthew 24 is a masterpiece of restraint as well as an outline of the steps to the goal of salvation history, the eternal presence of God with His people.

In verses 5 to 14 Jesus warned the disciples to be careful lest they be deceived. This was a concern lest they confuse the destruction of Jerusalem in their near future with the ultimate judgment in the distant future. The disciples should not mistake cataclysmic events such as wars, earthquakes, and famines as indications that the end of the age was upon them. Such happenings are but the birth pangs of the ultimate fulfillment of the Kingdom. He next warned the disciples that secular catastrophes would come, but even they do not announce the end of history (vv. 9–13). Such will involve the world's persecution of the church, the pressures which cause brother to betray brother, defection from the church, false prophets deceiving many, and lawlessness which undermines the freedom of true love for God. Yet Jesus' words of encouragement are that *"he who endures to the end will be saved."* This reference corresponds with the statements to the churches of Asia Minor, "To him that overcometh will I grant to sit with me in my throne" (Rev. 3:21, KJV; see also 2:17, 26; 3:5, 12).

The end of the age will not come, as Jesus stated explicitly, until the gospel of the Kingdom has been preached as a witness to the nations (v. 14). This is a reference to worldwide evangelism—the proclamation of the Kingdom of heaven to the Gentiles, to the nations of the world. Significantly, all four Gospel writers affirm that Jesus spoke of this worldwide ministry. It is consistent with His redemptive mission to have picked up their last question regarding the end of the age and answer it first. This vision of the global nature of His redemptive mission holds the other matters in perspective.

JESUS FORETELLS THE COMING TRIBULATION

15 "Therefore when you see the *'abomination of desolation,'* spoken of by Daniel the prophet, standing in the holy place" (whoever reads, let him understand),

16 "then let those who are in Judea flee to the mountains.

17 "Let him who is on the housetop not come down to take anything out of his house.

18 "And let him who is in the field not go back to get his clothes.

19 "And woe to those who are pregnant and to those with nursing babies in those days!

20 "But pray that your flight not be in winter or on the Sabbath.

21 "For then there will be great tribulation, such as has not been since the beginning of the world to this time, no, nor ever shall be.

22 "And unless those days were shortened, no flesh would be saved; but for the elect's sake those days will be shortened.

23 "Then if anyone says to you, 'Look, here is the Christ!' or 'There!' do not believe it.

24 "For false christs and false prophets will arise and show great signs and wonders so as to deceive, if possible, even the elect.

25 "See, I have told you beforehand.

26 "Therefore if they say to you, 'Look, He is in the desert!' do not go out; or 'Look, He is in the inner rooms!' do not believe it.

27 "For as the lightning comes from the east and flashes to the west, so also will the coming of the Son of Man be.

28 "For wherever the carcass is, there the eagles will be gathered together.

Matt. 24:15-28

In this section the debatable question is whether Jesus is referring to the destruction of Jerusalem or to the coming of Christ. He may well be referring to both, with the near fulfillment being the destruction of Jerusalem in A.D. 70 under Titus, and the far fulfillment being the tribulation of the end times and His coming. However, in the suggested order in which we see Jesus answering the disciples' questions, it appears that He was referring to the fall of Jerusalem, to the end of one era and the beginning of another. The statements in verses 15 through 20 are related specifically to the A.D. 70 experience. The abomination of desolation (Dan. 11:31), as when Antiochus Epiphanes desecrated the temple by offering sacrifice to the pagan god Zeus, was predicted to reoccur. Jesus' prediction had a near fulfillment with the sack of Jerusalem by Titus, but Paul suggests a future fulfillment (2 Thess. 2:2-4). Josephus relates the horrors of the siege, of famine so severe that a woman ate her newborn child, of the death of over a million persons, of the crucifixion of hundreds, of 100,000 sold into slavery—a tribulation such as had not been seen before. The outline Jesus gave helped Christian Jews to escape the siege, and some fled to the Trans-jordan town of Pella. It appears in Daniel that the prophet was speaking of a tribulation at the end of the age. Jesus would appear to have supported this in verses 21–22; however, the references in verses 23 and following see history extending beyond this tribulation with false christs and false prophets working wonders to deceive.

The thrust of the last part of this section is a call to faithfulness to Jesus Christ as Lord, to refrain from following the false messiahs that will arise in each generation, and to await His coming with faith. To make the distinction clear, Jesus described His coming as lightning in contrast to the emergence of false christs; for as lightning is sudden and illuminates everything, so it will be with the coming of Christ. The closing statement in verse 28 pictures the eagles or vultures gathering at the carcasses, symbolic of the death and decay of the old age as it gave way to the new. The lifeless corpse of Judaism attracts the carrion eagles of Rome. This suggests that when the world has become rotten with evil, the Son of Man will come in judgment.

Jesus' Affirmation of His Coming

29 "Immediately after the tribulation of those days the sun will be darkened, and the moon will not give its light; the stars will fall from heaven, and the powers of the heavens will be shaken.

30 "And then the sign of the Son of Man will appear in heaven, and then all the tribes of the earth will mourn, and they will see the Son of Man coming on the clouds of heaven with power and great glory.

31 "And He will send His angels with a great sound of a trumpet, and they will gather together His elect from the four winds, from one end of heaven to the other.

Matt. 24:29–31

Jesus said that immediately after the tribulation the powers of the universe will be shaken. The descriptive language of verse 29 is frequently used in the Old Testament to describe chaos and judgment, war and devastation, the end of an era or rule. Hence it could mean primarily the ending of the old age and the inauguration of the new. This is eschatological language associated in the Old Testament with the coming of the messianic age (Isa. 13:10; Ezek. 32:7–8; Joel 2:31). The quotation by Peter of the Joel passage in connection with the day of Pentecost provides one indication that this eschatological language is related to the inauguration of the messianic era.

In verse 30 Jesus speaks of the *"sign of the Son of Man"* appearing in heaven. On the several occasions in which the Pharisees had asked for a sign, Jesus had said there will be no sign given except that of the prophet Jonah, the sign of the presence of the Prophet. This is the sign of His rule. It is possible that, if the preceding verse is symbolic language of the passing of the old order, the "sign" is a sign of the Son of Man being in heaven, enthroned, expressed by His rule which took the form of Lordship in and through the church which He inaugurated at Pentecost. This would place a space between the "sign" and the coming on the clouds of heaven. And then when He appears on the clouds of heaven with power and glory, the tribes of the earth will mourn (Zech. 12:10–12).

The section closes with a specific reference to the great judgment associated with the coming of the Lord. The sound of the trumpet is the note of victory; the King is reigning. He sends His angels to gather His elect from the four corners of the earth (Jer. 6:1; Isa. 18:3). This must be at the time of His coming, after the gospel has been preached to the ends of the earth. Herein is the completion of His Kingdom which He will deliver to the Father (Rev. 11:15; 1 Cor. 15:24).

The Parable of the Fig Tree

32 "Now learn this parable from the fig tree: When its branch has already become tender and puts forth leaves, you know that summer is near.

33 "So you also, when you see all these things, know that it is near, even at the doors.

34 "Assuredly, I say to you, this generation will by no means pass away till all these things are fulfilled.

35 "Heaven and earth will pass away, but My words will by no means pass away.

Matt. 24:32–35

This parable may be in direct relation to the destruction of Jerusalem, a flashback to the main issue in this section. This is suggested by what appears to be a transition in verse 36 to "that day," meaning the *Parousia.* If the verse is applied to the *Parousia,* it is a simple assertion of the certainty of the coming of the Son of Man. When the fig tree buds, even before the leaves are open, it is evident that summer is near. So when these things happen we know that "it" is near; the event is near. The same emphasis is found in Mark 13:28-31, with a similar impression that the parable is a summation of what had preceded. The budding of the fig tree in spring came at the time just before the barley harvest. The first sheaf was offered the day following the Passover.

In verse 34 we have the phrase, *"this generation shall not pass"* (KJV) until all is fulfilled. This had primary reference to the disciples and to the immediate events before them. The fall of Jerusalem was the type of the antitype, the harvest of God. Some date-setters have predicted the return of Christ in a given "generational period" when these things are interpreted as happening. But if the phrase is to be related to the *Parousia,* we should recognize that the word "generation" is also used for a people, and is not tied to a particular period of time. In 23:36 it appears that by "generation" Jesus meant the people of Israel, so here the reference could mean that in spite of the great tribulation predicted, this people will continue as a people until the fulfillment of history. The presence of the Jewish people scattered throughout the world is a continuing sermon to the nations about Yahweh, about salvation history. Jesus affirmed that His words will be standing when the present order of the universe is gone, just as He had affirmed previously the eternal quality of the words of God (Matt. 5:18).

JESUS' EXHORTATION TO WATCHFULNESS

36 "But of that day and hour no one knows, no, not even the angels of heaven, but My Father only.

37 "But as the days of Noah were, so also will the coming of the Son of Man be.

38 "For as in the days before the flood, they were eating and drinking, marrying and giving in marriage, until the day that Noah entered the ark,

39 "and did not know until the flood came and took them all away, so also will the coming of the Son of Man be.

40 "Then two men will be in the field: one will be taken and the other left.

41 "Two women will be grinding at the mill: one will be taken and the other left.

42 "Watch therefore, for you do not know what hour your Lord is coming.

43 "But know this, that if the master of the house had known what hour the thief would come, he would have watched and not allowed his house to be broken into.

44 "Therefore you also be ready, for the Son of Man is coming at an hour when you do not expect Him.

Matt. 24:36–44

While Jesus was certain of His return, He didn't know the exact time. Consequently, His primary emphasis was on watchfulness. This section is a call for faithfulness as we live in hope. Our motivation in the service of Christ is a meaningful relation with Him, not a fear of the end and a resultant artificial approach to life. Jesus calls us to be disciples in the world, to serve in the world, to evangelize the world—not to stand apart waiting for His coming. The section tells us that: (1) no one knows the time of His Coming; (2) no specific signs mark out the time (vv. 37–39); and (3) no change of involvements in the necessary pursuits of life are to preempt the final separation (vv. 40–44). The emphasis in this last section is on preparedness, for although we associate freely in society we have a different relation than the rest of society to the Master. There will be a division coming for *"one will be taken and the other left."* While this is often spoken of as the "rapture," the thrust is to insure our being ready for His coming, for Jesus said He is *"coming at an hour when you do not expect Him!"*

The reference to "the days of Noah" call for comment. Jesus' point is that life went on as always. There was no sign other than the preaching of Noah for the 120 years while he was building the ark, when suddenly the flood came. From this reference we note that God waited patiently for 120 years for people to repent, but there was no change, and He was morally free to bring the flood of judgment without someone answering back to say that if He had only waited a bit longer they could have repented. Similarly, we ask the question,

275

"When can Jesus come and bring an end without people answering back that if He had only waited they too could have been saved?" From this reference we can theorize that He is waiting until humanity has so tied the affairs of this world into knots that to wait longer would not make a difference. One aspect of this impasse may be that we have entered the nuclear age, and the world now has over 50,000 nuclear warheads, sufficient to blow the whole world up fifty times over! But God, the main Actor in salvation history, is holding back the end, pressing it back in His love and patience desiring that all should be saved and "come to the knowledge of the truth" (1 Tim. 2:4).

This section concludes with the mini-parable of the burglar (24:43). There are five parables of the *Parousia;* the other four include the parable of the ten virgins (25:1–13), the parable of the porter (Mark 13:34–37), the parable of the servants (24:45–51), and the parable of talents (25:14–30). The emphasis of this mini-parable is on watchfulness, for the householder is to watch lest his house be plundered. In Luke's presentation (12:31–40) there is the added warning against piling up riches which can only be plundered. Watchfulness means that each day has Christological significance for the disciple!

Jesus' Parable on Faithful Stewards

45 "Who then is a faithful and wise servant whom his master made ruler over his household, to give them food in due season?

46 "Blessed is that servant whom his master, when he comes, will find so doing.

47 "Assuredly, I say to you that he will make him ruler over all his goods.

48 "But if that evil servant says in his heart, 'My master is delaying his coming,'

49 "and begins to beat his fellow servants, and to eat and drink with the drunkards,

50 "the master of that servant will come on a day when he is not looking for him and at an hour that he is not aware of,

51 "and will cut him in two, and will appoint him his portion with the hypocrites; there will be weeping and gnashing of teeth."

Matt. 24:45–51

The disciples are likened to servants made responsible for others during their Master's absence. The story implies knowledge on the part of Jesus that His *Parousia* would be at some distant time. Those who have been left in charge by their Lord, in positions of responsibility, must be continuously faithful. Jesus was entrusting His mission and His church to their care and to ours. He asked His disciples to be faithful to Him and to the nature of His kingdom. On the other hand, the evil servant, who uses the privileges of leadership in the church for personal power and status, manipulating persons who are his brothers, will be held accountable and answerable to the Lord of the church!

The contrast between the faithful and unfaithful is shown by their function in the community of believers as well as by the sentence in their judgment. The faithful servant is elevated; the unfaithful servant is punished with the hypocrites. The judgment corresponds to the other descriptions of ultimate separation from God. The expression "weeping and gnashing of teeth" is found seven times in the New Testament. The characteristics of unfaithfulness are (1) being presumptuous, (2) being coercive, and (3) being profligate. To such the coming of Christ will be like a thief in the night (1 Thess. 5:4), at a time unannounced. Our service shall be from love and reverence for Christ, not from schemes for selfish advantage.

JESUS' PARABLE OF THE TEN VIRGINS

1 "Then the kingdom of heaven shall be likened to ten virgins who took their lamps and went out to meet the bridegroom.

2 "And five of them were wise, and five were foolish.

3 "Those who were foolish took their lamps and took no oil with them,

4 "but the wise took oil in their vessels with their lamps.

5 "But while the bridegroom tarried, they all slumbered and slept.

6 "And at midnight there was a cry made: 'Behold, the bridegroom is coming; go out to meet him!'

7 "Then all those virgins arose and trimmed their lamps.

8 "And the foolish said to the wise, 'Give us some of your oil, for our lamps are going out.'

9 "But the wise answered, saying, 'No, lest there not be enough for us and you; but go rather to those who sell, and buy for yourselves.'

10 "And while they went to buy, the bridegroom came, and those who were ready went in with him to the wedding; and the door was shut.

11 "Afterward the other virgins came also, saying, 'Lord, Lord, open to us!'

12 "But he answered and said, 'Assuredly, I say to you, I do not know you.'

13 "Watch therefore, for you know neither the day nor the hour in which the Son of Man is coming.

Matt. 25:1–13

This parable compares the Kingdom of heaven to a wedding. The introductive dative should be translated, "It is the case with," which means the Kingdom is not compared to the ten virgins as such but to the wedding. The ceremony reaches its climax with the coming of the bridegroom, a scene that regularly happened in Palestinian villages and was well understood by Jesus' hearers. Jewish marriage had three stages: the engagement, the betrothal, and the marriage. This story is of the third stage where the bridegroom goes to the home of the bride to bring her to his own home in marriage. It is this event that takes place in the parable, and the ten virgins are friends who join the celebration. It was customary for girls to keep the bride company as they waited for the bridegroom, and to dance along the road with their torches in celebration. In this parable the ten virgins are described as being of two kinds: five being wise and bringing oil in addition to their torches, and five being foolish who had no supply of oil.

During the long vigil they all slept, but at midnight the joyous cry rang out, *"The bridegroom is coming!"* The watchfulness is in their being prepared; the fact that all slept as they waited is irrelevant. The unprepared could not borrow from the prepared, and so the prepared went with the bride and groom to the wedding celebration while the foolish went to secure oil. Upon their return they found the door shut, and in response to their entreaty, they were rejected by the bridegroom, who said, *"I do not know you."* Three of the saddest sayings in the parables of Jesus are found here: (1) *"Our lamps are* gone out"; (2) *"The door was shut"*; and (3) *"I do not know you."* This is illustrative of God's judgment which is unequivocal and irreversible. We cannot know Christian assurance without the Spirit (illustrated by the oil), and we cannot succeed on borrowed religion.

But the story has its conclusion in verse 13; the command is for vigilance. Jesus says, "Watch," that is, be prepared. This parable is in direct relation to the preceding one, emphasizing the call to faithful obedience to the Master. In developing a message from this passage we could well relate the interpretation to the scene in Revelation 19:1–9. The Christian community asks itself, "What does it mean to wait for our Lord's coming?" And our Lord gives the answer—faithfulness. (See also 2 Thess. 2:2; 3:11–12.)

JESUS' PARABLE OF THE TALENTS

14 "For the kingdom of heaven is like a man traveling into a far country, who called his own servants and delivered his goods to them.

15 "And to one he gave five talents, to another two, and to another one, to each according to his own ability; and right away he went on a journey.

16 "Then he who had received the five talents went and traded with them, and made another five talents.

17 "And likewise he who had received two gained two more also.

18 "But he who had received one went and dug in the ground, and hid his master's money.

19 "After a long time the master of those servants came and settled accounts with them.

20 "And so he who had received five talents came and brought five other talents, saying, 'Master, you delivered to me five talents; look, I have gained five more talents besides them.'

21 "His master said to him, 'Well done, good and faithful servant; you have been faithful over a few things, I will make you ruler over many things. Enter into the joy of your master.'

22 "He also who had received two talents came and said, 'Master, you delivered to me two talents; look, I have gained two more talents besides them.'

23 "His master said to him, 'Well done, good and

faithful servant; you have been faithful over a few things, I will make you ruler over many things. Enter into the joy of your master.'

24 "Then he who had received the one talent came and said, 'Master, I knew you to be a hard man, reaping where you have not sown, and gathering where you have not scattered seed.

25 'And I was afraid, and went and hid your talent in the ground. Look, there you have what is yours.'

26 "But his master answered and said to him, 'You wicked and slothful servant, you knew that I reap where I did not sow, and gather where I have not scattered seed.

27 'Therefore you ought to have put my money with the bankers, and then at my coming I would have received back my own with interest.

28 'Therefore take the talent from him, and give it to him who has ten talents.

29 'For to everyone who has, more will be given, and he will have abundance; but from him who does not have will be taken away even what he has.

30 'And cast the unprofitable servant into the outer darkness. There will be weeping and gnashing of teeth.'

Matt. 25:14–30

This parable focuses primarily upon the useless servant. Gifts that are not used are lost. The title "talents" is unfortunate, in that in our language we use the word "talent" to refer to natural aptitudes or abilitites that people have. The talent in this story was a weight, and its value depended on whether the object weighed was copper, silver, or gold. In the story, talents were given to the several men according to their "abilities" (v. 15). It would be best to interpret the talents as opportunities. And in the parable each of the men is given opportunity according to ability and is expected to serve faithfully. This is a parable on responsibility.

There is a story that Archelaus went to Rome (4 B.C.) to get his kingship over Judea confirmed. A party of fifty Jews went as an embassy to Rome to resist the appointment, but did not succeed. The revenge he inflicted upon the Jews after his return was not soon forgotten. Such a story supplies emotional background for the weight of this illustration. But in Jesus' story, the issue is not revenge but accountability. The gift and the responsibility were commensurate. The men who had received five and two talents respectively took risks; they applied themselves actively in their responsibility. But the unfaithful servant thought only of himself and his security, risked nothing, and achieved nothing.

On the Master's return there is an accounting from each. The two servants, representing faithful disciples, had transformed privilege into action. The response of the Master carries the note of eschatological joy; the *"good and faithful"* servants enter the joy of their Master. But as soon as the unfaithful servant opens his mouth, it is evident that he was not interested in his Lord's cause or advantage but rather in saving his own skin. One who cannot venture his own person cannot take risks for the sake of his Lord! He was judged according to his conduct. What was given was taken away, "For whosoever shall save his life shall lose it. . . ." The story closes with the language of destruction in outer darkness—the symbol of the anguish of ultimate separation.

As one of the *Parousia* parables, this is a striking lesson on our responsibility. A possible but simple outline follows: The Master (1) entrusted responsibility to his servants; (2) increased responsibility for faithfulness; (3) judged inexcusable irresponsibility. (See Rom. 2 on God's judgment.)

Jesus' Ultimate Judgment of the Nations

31 "When the Son of Man comes in His glory, and all the holy angels with Him, then He will sit on the throne of His glory.

32 "And all the nations will be gathered before Him, and He will separate them one from another, as a shepherd divides his sheep from the goats.

33 "And He will set the sheep on His right hand, but the goats on the left.

34 "Then the King will say to those on His right hand, 'Come, you blessed of My Father, inherit the kingdom prepared for you from the foundation of the world:

35 'for I was hungry and you gave Me food; I was thirsty and you gave Me drink; I was a stranger and you took Me in;

36 'I was naked and you clothed Me; I was sick
and you visited Me; I was in prison and you came
to Me.'

37 "Then the righteous will answer Him, saying,
'Lord, when did we see You hungry and feed You,
or thirsty and give You drink?

38 'When did we see You a stranger and take You
in, or naked and clothe You?

39 'Or when did we see You sick, or in prison, and
come to see You?'

40 "And the King will answer and say to them,
'Assuredly, I say to you, inasmuch as you have done
it to one of the least of these My brethren, you have
done it to Me.'

41 "Then He will also say to those on the left hand,
'Depart from Me, you cursed, into the everlasting fire
prepared for the devil and his angels:

42 'for I was hungry and you gave Me no food; I
was thirsty and you gave Me no drink;

43 'I was a stranger and you did not take Me in,
naked and you did not clothe Me, sick and in prison
and you did not visit Me.'

44 "Then they will also answer Him, saying, 'Lord,
when did we see You hungry or thirsty or a stranger
or naked or sick or in prison, and did not minister to
You?'

45 "Then He will answer them, saying, 'Assuredly,
I say to you, inasmuch as you did not do it to one
of the least of these, you did not do it to Me.'

46 "And these will go away into everlasting
punishment, but the righteous into eternal life."

Matt. 25:31–46

This section, if it is a parable, is one of the most vivid of Jesus'
stories. The intent of the passage is to provide a description of the
Last Judgment. Since it begins with a straightforward statement, rather
than "the kingdom of heaven is like . . ." it would not appear to
be a parable. But it follows the *Parousia* parables as a concluding and
fitting climax. The Son of Man is shown coming in glory, sitting
on the throne of His glory. The role of the Messiah as Judge is a
designation without parallel in the perceptions of Judaism.

The judgment is all-inclusive, for all nations are literally "herded" before Him. The word-picture was understood in the Middle East, for shepherds tended sheep and goats together. The parable uses the sheep as symbolic of the good people, and the goats as symbolic of the evil. The statement that He will separate "them" (masculine), means people, not nations (which would be neuter).

The judgment is interpretive, for in this outline we discover the expectation of God. In verse 31 the reference to Christ's enthronement shows that He now refers to Himself as King. The phrase *"inherit the kingdom prepared for you from the foundation of the world"* is an affirmation of both the place of the Kingdom in salvation history and the fact that there is more to come than what we know at present. Significantly, the Person we will encounter at the Last Judgment is Jesus Christ Himself (Rom. 14:10; 2 Cor. 5:10; 1 Cor. 4:4–5). Eduard Schweizer, referring to 1 Corinthians 15:28, comments that Jesus "will subordinate Himself totally to God that God may be all in all, maintains the truth that in Jesus we encounter none other than God."[3]

The judgment is an indictment of the church for its lack of social involvement as Kingdom members. Jesus taught that love for God is evidenced by love for our neighbor, that knowing God's forgiveness will lead us to share mercy, and that experiencing God's love we will, as a consequence, extend that love. In the pronouncement upon the sheep (vv. 35–40), it appears that the righteous answer is innocent surprise, as though they had been doing these things out of the inner transformation of grace without being legalistically bound to do so. And in the judgment upon the unrighteous, the King lists the very same things with the addition of one word, "not," for they had failed to respond to the needs of humanity around them.

The judgment identifies Christ with the needy, so that a deed of love to *"one of the least of these, My brethren"* is a deed of love for Christ (v. 40). And in verse 45 the failure of the unrighteous to serve *"one of the least of these"* was a failure in relation to Christ. The words in verse 40, *"My brethren"* are missing in verse 45, perhaps suggesting that Jesus identified with the righteous ones as His brethren. Some commentators take this as a reference to the treatment of His brethren the Jews, and see this judgment of the nations as a decision as to which of these nations enter the millennium, the sheep nations being accepted and the goat nations rejected. There appears to be no evidence of this in the passage when read by itself, and such an interpretation comes from reading it in relation to a pattern of prophetic interpretation developed from other passages. David Ewert says the meaning can hardly be referring to entry into the millennium as the outcome is either "eternal life" or "eternal punishment."[4]

The judgment identifies sins of omission as most serious. All one needs to do to miss out on God's grace is to ignore Him. "All that needs to happen for evil to triumph is for good people to do nothing!" We saw this same sin of omission in the *Parousia* parables; the foolish virgins neglected to bring oil, the unfaithful servant was rejected for doing nothing, and those on the left hand are rejected for failing to minister to the needy about them. The passage emphasizes that the gospel always has social implications, even though not all social service has the gospel. The story of the Good Samaritan is the classic illustration of Christian social action.

Spending a sabbatical in Basel, Switzerland, my wife and I visited St. Martin's Church, and were impressed by the sculpture on the front wall depicting Martin of Tours, a Roman soldier with Christian faith. One cold winter day, entering a city, he was stopped by a beggar asking for alms. Having no money, Martin took off his coat, cut it in two, and gave half to the beggar. That night he had a dream of heaven, and Jesus was wearing half of a Roman soldier's coat. An angel asked Him, "Master, why are you wearing that battered old cloak?" And Jesus answered, "My servant Martin gave it to me."

Today, in many parts of the world, the Christian church is seeking to meet human need "in the name of Christ." In 1974 the United Nations reported more than 460 million people as permanently hungry. In 1980 the World Bank estimated that more than one billion people, nearly one quarter of the world's population, suffer from malnutrition. Over 900 million people subsist on annual incomes of less than 200 dollars per year. The reality of hunger and the social needs of the Third World, especially, call the Christian church to the deeds of love that care and share. A ministry of relief, of food and clothing, of education and medicine, or agricultural development, and of social enrichment is an authentic witness of the gospel. One can hardly expect persons to hear a word about salvation unless they see the saving deed of love, for empty stomachs lead to emptying thoughts. Throughout the Gospel of Matthew Jesus' ministry related time for the deed of love with time given to teaching. We are called to interface deed and word in our mission. This now concludes "book five" of Jesus' teachings in Matthew.

NOTES

1. Vernard Eller, *The Most Revealing Book of the Bible* (Grand Rapids: Eerdmans, 1974), p. 151.

2. Paul Erb, *Bible Prophecy* (Scottdale, PA: Herald Press, 1978), p. 109.

3. Eduard Schweizer, *The Good News According to Matthew*, p. 482.

4. David Ewert, *And Then Comes the End* (Scottdale, PA: Herald Press, 1980), p. 107.

CHAPTER TEN

The Passion of the King

Matthew 26:1—27:66

In the passion narrative it is clear that Jesus had a theology of the atonement. Having finished His sayings to the public, Jesus now addressed His disciples in a more private manner. Here He predicted His betrayal and crucifixion for the fourth time (26:2). There was no surprise in this for Jesus. Vincent Taylor sees in this statement the evidence of Jesus' theory of the atonement, for "to Him the cross was not an enigma, but a highway of conscious Messianic purpose."[1] In a review of Jesus' Passion sayings, "The truth slowly emerges that a study of the life of Jesus which does not find in it a theology in solution, is self-condemned. This is the lesson of the failure of the Liberal-Critical School to estimate the Person of Jesus."[2]

The passion narrative basically follows Mark, but there are minor points of agreement with Luke, and substantial agreement with John, suggesting an oral tradition running parallel. There is in Matthew a clear sense of theological purpose, emphasizing Jesus' mastery of the situation, and the fulfillment of both the prophet's predictions and of Jesus' own sayings. There are factors unique to Matthew's account: the contrast between Jesus and Barabbas; the fact that the Passion convulsed the earth and caused the dead to rise, marking the end of the old world and the beginning of God's new age; the rending of the temple curtain, symbolizing a split with Judaism; the Passion as the suffering of the righteous; the Resurrection as the enthronement of Jesus as Lord of the universe; and the commissioning of His disciples.

THE PLOT TO KILL JESUS

1 And it came to pass, when Jesus had finished all these sayings, that He said to His disciples,

2 "You know that after two days is the Passover, and the Son of Man will be betrayed to be crucified."

3 Then the chief priests, the scribes, and the elders of the people assembled together at the palace of the high priest, who was called Caiaphas,

4 and plotted that they might take Jesus by trickery and kill Him.

5 But they said, "Not during the feast, lest there be an uproar among the people."

Matt. 26:1-5

This fourth prediction associates the death of Jesus with the Passover by identifying Him with the Paschal Lamb. The Son of Man is now seen as a sacrifice (1 Cor. 5:7; 2 Cor. 5:20–21; Mark 15:25, 42; John 19:36). It was arranged by the official religious and political body, the Sanhedrin, as they plotted Jesus' death. The reference to the elders of the people is a symbol of how the leadership tied the whole populace into the event, even though verse 5 gives evidence that the people were still supporting Jesus.

A survey of the Passion sayings shows that Jesus spoke of His death at least twelve times before it happened. They are as follows: (1) His reference to the Bridegroom being removed, 9:15; (2) His statement at Peter's confession, 16:21–24; (3) His sayings on the suffering of the Son of Man, 17:22–23; (4) His sayings following the Transfiguration, 17:9–12; (5) His saying about the cup, 20:22; (6) the ransom passage, 20:28; (7) the parable of the vineyard, 21:33–45; (8) the statement at His anointing, 26:12; (9) His prophecy of betrayal, 26:21; (10) His sayings at the Last Supper, 26:26–29; (11) the sayings about the Shepherd, 26:31; and (12) His sayings in Gethsemane, 26:39–44. Five of these sayings are in the present section of our study.

JESUS ANOINTED AT BETHANY

6 Now when Jesus was in Bethany at the house of Simon the leper,

7 a woman came to Him having an alabaster flask
of very costly fragrant oil, and she poured it on His
head as He sat at the table.

8 But when His disciples saw it, they were
indignant, saying, "To what purpose is this waste?

9 "For this fragrant oil might have been sold for
much and given to the poor."

10 But when Jesus was aware of it, He said to them,
"Why do you trouble the woman? For she has done
a good work for Me.

11 "For you have the poor with you always, but
Me you do not have always.

12 "For in pouring this fragrant oil on My body,
she did it for My burial.

13 "Assuredly, I say to you, wherever this gospel
is preached in the whole world, what this woman has
done will also be told as a memorial to her."

Matt. 26:6–13

Matthew's account of the woman coming to Jesus at Bethany to
anoint Him is told in a somewhat abbreviated form by comparison
with Mark (14:3–9). This same Mary had sat at Jesus' feet on an
earlier occasion, and had learned of His compassion for people which
led to His suffering (Luke 10:42). The anointing is not to be confused
with the one recorded in Luke 7:36–50, but is the same as the one
in John 12:3. It seems that Matthew places this story in clear relief
as a contrast to the treachery of one of the twelve. Jesus was at the
house of Simon the leper, a man whom He had cleansed and with
whom He shared friendship. The woman came with a vial of very
expensive perfume, an alabaster flask of fragrant oil, and poured it
on the head of Jesus. Shackled by their materialism, and probably
stirred by Judas' murmuring, the disciples complained at the waste,
saying that this could have been sold and given to the poor.

Jesus' response was threefold: first, the word which liberated the
woman: *"Why do you trouble the woman?"*; second, the word that placed
service in relation to worship: *"You have the poor with you always, but
Me you do not have always"*; and third, the word of good news to the
world: *"Wherever this gospel is preached in the whole world. . . ."* Jesus' reference to this being preparation for His burial is evidence of His
awareness of what was happening in relation to Himself; and He

commended her deed, for it corresponded to Jewish belief that anointing a dead body was regarded as a "good deed." The note in verse 13 is that the gospel is good news for the world. Jesus included the woman and her deed in the story, and spoke of a memorial to her rather than to Himself!

Judas' Negotiation to Betray Jesus

14 Then one of the twelve, called Judas Iscariot, went to the chief priests
15 and said, "What are you willing to give me if I deliver Him to you?" And they counted out to him thirty pieces of silver.
16 And from that time he sought opportunity to betray Him.

Matt. 26:14–16

Judas' act is in vivid contrast to the act of Mary. Matthew says that he actually went to the chief priests and asked what they would give him to betray Jesus. As Swartley points out, Jesus' death was one of betrayal: first by Judas, second by the Jews to the Romans, third by Pilate to death. The same Greek word for "betray" *(paradidomi)* is used in all ten instances in Mark in relation to Christ's being "delivered over" and is an indication that "no one is guiltless."[3]

According to John, Judas was greedy (John 12:6) and went to the Jewish leaders with mercenary interests. There are many questions as to why Judas acted in this way. He probably expected the messianic Kingdom in a nationalistic way. Being disappointed when it became clear that Jesus was not a violent revolutionary, Judas took things into his own hands to try to force Jesus to act with His amazing power. This may account for his being willing to sell his Master for such a paltry sum. If his goal was to force Jesus to act for the defence of His kingly claims, any sum was adequate to get the wheels turning. At least the sum is so small that it appears the ultimate insult. The thirty pieces of silver were approximately $21.60, the price that the Law required as payment for a slave killed by an ox (Exod. 21:32). A similar reference in Zechariah 11:12 is held to have messianic connotations. Having made his decision against Jesus and

His interpretation of the Suffering Servant, Judas sought opportunity from that time on to betray Him.

JESUS CELEBRATES THE PASSOVER

17 Now on the first day of the Feast of the Unleavened Bread the disciples came to Jesus, saying to Him, "Where do You want us to prepare for You to eat the Passover?"
18 And He said, "Go into the city to a certain man, and say to him, 'The Teacher says: My time is at hand; I will keep the Passover at your house with My disciples.' "
19 And the disciples did as Jesus had directed them; and they prepared the Passover.
20 Now when evening had come, He sat down with the twelve.
21 And as they were eating, He said, "Assuredly, I say to you, one of you will betray Me."
22 And they were exceedingly sorrowful, and each of them began to say to Him, "Lord, is it I?"
23 And He answered and said, "He who dipped his hand with Me in the dish will betray Me.
24 "The Son of Man goes as it is written of Him, but woe to that man by whom the Son of Man is betrayed! It would have been good for that man if he had not been born."
25 Then Judas, who was betraying Him, answered and said, "Rabbi, is it I?" He said to him, "You have said it."

Matt. 26:17–25

Jesus had probably eaten a Passover meal before with His disciples. Every year it was observed in commemoration that the Israelites' sons had been saved by the sprinkling of blood the night the Egyptian firstborn were slain (Exod. 12:12–14). The custom was for a family to kill the lamb around three o'clock in the afternoon and prepare the meal which was to be eaten between six o'clock and midnight. It is thought that Jesus held His meal the day before the Passover. It appears that because this Passover fell on the Sabbath, some chose to eat the meal on Thursday, to avoid work on the Sabbath day.[4]

This timing would place His death on the thirteenth day of Nisan, the day of the preparation for the eating of the lamb on that evening. Josephus indicates that by this time the Feast of Unleavened Bread (Lev. 23:5-6) was a name given to the whole period: "We celebrate for eight days the feast called that of unleavened bread."[5] Jesus especially desired to eat this particular Passover with His disciples, His last one with them. As a part of the meal He instituted what we know as the Last Supper, or Lord's Supper (Luke 22:15-20).

Jesus had in mind using the house of a disciple or friend in Jerusalem, as He sent two of His disciples to prepare the Passover (v. 18). In Mark and Luke the account is told with more detail. Jesus sent the two disciples with instructions that they would meet a man carrying a pitcher of water. They were to follow him to the house of his master. They were to ask him for the use of his house for their Master to observe the Passover. We can conclude that by such directions Jesus outfoxed Judas who was seeking a time and place to betray Him. From these directions Judas would not have known the particular place where Jesus would observe the Passover!

The disciples made the arrangements, preparing the traditional meal. At the appropriate time later in the evening, Jesus came with the other disciples and reclined at the meal with His twelve. (Jeremias says that in the custom of this time as they sat to eat, reclining was a symbol of freedom.) The very solemn announcement that the betrayal of Jesus would come by one of His own disciples was a shattering blow. One after the other they put the question to Him, *"Lord, is it I?"* Matthew suggests that Judas waited to speak until last, and then adjusted his question to be, *"Teacher, it isn't I, is it?"* The other disciples addressed Jesus as "Lord," but Judas addressed Him as "Rabbi." Evidently he had been so cunning that not even the other eleven disciples suspected that he was guilty. In verse 23 Jesus said, *"He who dipped his hand with Me in the dish will betray Me,"* and John says that Jesus dipped a morsel of bread and gave it to Judas, designating him as the betrayer (John 13:26-30). Matthew emphasizes the seriousness of Judas' deed and Jesus' words of judgment being a warning to him. But in the context of salvation history, the Son of Man went as it had been written. This is to say that Judas in his unbelief served God's purpose. Barth says of Israel that in its unbelief it serves God's purposes. Israel's unbelief has served to open the gospel to the larger world, and by their presence as Jews scattered throughout the world they are an unspoken sermon about Yahweh.

JESUS INSTITUTES THE LORD'S SUPPER

26 And as they were eating, Jesus took bread,
blessed it and broke it, and gave it to the disciples
and said, "Take, eat; this is My body."
27 And He took the cup, and gave thanks, and gave
it to them, saying, "All of you drink from it.
28 "For this is My blood of the new covenant, which
is shed for many for the remission of sins.
29 "But I say to you, I will not drink of this fruit
of the vine from now on until that day when I drink
it new with you in My Father's kingdom."
30 And when they had sung a hymn, they went
out to the Mount of Olives.

Matt. 26:26–30

Following the meal Jesus instituted the Lord's Supper, variously
called the Eucharist, the Sacrament of Communion, or the Covenant
Meal. Different views of the sacraments have divided the church
through the centuries. Questions have been raised whether the emblems actually are or become the very body and blood of Jesus,
whether they are a means of dispensing grace, or whether they are
only a symbol or witness to grace. Today the ecumenical movement
is calling particular attention to the sacraments as that element in
the church through which the "apostolic succession" comes to all
Christians in the church universal. For those of us who hold what
has been called a "low view" of the sacraments, the Lord's Supper
is seen much more as a Covenant Meal, *"the new covenant in His blood,"*
to be observed in faith and hope *"until He comes."* This is a more
relational than ritualistic approach.

Jesus took bread, blessed it, and broke it. This was hardly the
traditional Jewish "grace" at the beginning of the meal, for this prayer
would have been prayed earlier: "Blessed art Thou, O Lord, King
of the Universe, who bringest forth bread from the earth." Jesus
emphasized what was to follow by praying a specific prayer of blessing
for the bread, identifying it as His body, and passing it to His disciples.
This reference to the bread as His body and the later designation
of the church as the Body of Christ stand in direct relationship. Next
He took the cup *"and gave thanks,"* an awesome thing, for He well
understood it to symbolize His own death. He referred to the cup
as *"My blood of the new covenant,"* a covenant to the death, His blood

292

being *"shed for many for the remission of sins."* This reference calls our attention to Isaiah 53:12 as well as to Exodus 24:8. This emphasis holding together covenant and forgiveness of sins is also seen in the prophecy of Jeremiah 31:34 (see Isa. 42:6; 49:7–8).

A point not to be overlooked is the implication of the fact that Jesus was sitting there in His body with blood in His veins when He said, *"This is my body . . . this is my blood."* His declarations were symbolizing that He gave Himself to the death for His people! The new covenant would carry the meaning of the cross. As He gave Himself to the death for us, we are to pledge ourselves to the death for Him. Partaking of the Lord's Supper is not just a memorial, it is a commitment to share His suffering love *"until He comes."*

There was a horror of drinking blood in the Jewish community and Jesus did not ask the disciples to drink blood but to drink the wine as a symbol of His blood. Jeremias says that wine was only drunk on festive occasions; otherwise it was used in everyday life for medicinal purposes. (It is only twice reported that Jesus drank wine at festive meals: Matt. 11:16–19; John 2:1–11.)[6] Back of this lies the symbolic history of instituting covenant (Exod. 24:1–11, see also Zech. 9:11–12). The statement in verse 29 was His note of victory, of assurance; it symbolized the coming "communion of the Kingdom of God" (see Isa. 25:6; 32:2, Hab. 3:17). As to the meaning of the blood in salvation history, A. W. Meyer says, "The atonement through the death of Jesus is at any rate the necessary premise of even the symbolical interpretation of the Lord's Supper. With every attempt to explain away the atoning death, the supper becomes utterly unintelligible."[7]

Matthew alone reports that they sang a hymn before departing the upper room for the Mount of Olives. It was the normal procedure to conclude the Passover with the recitation of the second half of the Hallel, called *himnon,*[8] taken from Psalms 115–118. It was also required that when the Passover was eaten in Jerusalem, the rest of the night should be spent in a prescribed area. The Mount of Olives was within that area. As they walked from the upper room down the stone steps which led to Gethsemane, they passed very close by the House of Caiaphas the High Priest who would condemn Jesus later that night, and the place where Peter would deny his Lord. Perhaps it was as they walked past it that Jesus uttered the prediction of Peter's denial.

An outline for this section could be (1) a covenant to the death, (2) a covenant of forgiveness, and (3) a covenant of hope.

JESUS PREDICTS PETER'S DENIAL

31 Then Jesus said to them, "All of you will be made to stumble because of Me this night, for it is written:
'I will strike the Shepherd,
And the sheep of the flock will be scattered.'
32 "But after I have been raised, I will go before you to Galilee."
33 Peter answered and said to Him, "Even if all shall be made to stumble because of You, yet I will never be made to stumble."
34 Jesus said to him, "Assuredly, I say to you that this night, before the rooster crows, you will deny Me three times."
35 Peter said to Him, "Even if I have to die with You, yet I will not deny You!" And so said all the disciples.

Matt. 26:31–35

Luke tells us that Jesus was accustomed to go to the Mount of Olives, and this is the destination to which He led the disciples. As they walked, Jesus said, *"All of you will be made to stumble (skandalizō) because of Me this night."* Matthew is the only writer who uses the expression "because of Me." They would become disheartened and scattered, for He as their Shepherd would be smitten and they as His little flock would be scattered (a quotation from Zech. 13:7). But note Jesus' expression of faith, "But after I have been raised, I will go before you into Galilee!" This statement was especially appropriate for Peter who was later restored at Galilee (John 21:15–19). Jesus approached His death believing His Father's Word that He would raise Him up in three days. Paul wrote "Concerning his Son Jesus Christ our Lord, which was made of the seed of David according to the flesh; and declared to be the Son of God with power, according to the spirit of holiness, by the resurrection from the dead" (Rom. 1:3–4, KJV).

Peter's self-confidence became presumption when he said that even if all of the other disciples stumbled, he would not. Jesus said, "Before the rooster crows, you will deny Me three times," but Peter was so cocksure of himself that he said even if it came to death he would not deny Him. In the spirit of Peter's boldness, all of the disciples echoed the same commitment.

Before moving to the Garden of Gethsemane in Matthew's account, we should note that only John records the act of Jesus washing the feet of the disciples (John 13:1–14), the lengthy and beautiful discussions regarding discipleship (13:31–14:31), the lesson about abiding in Him (15:1–25), teachings on the Holy Spirit (15:26–16:33), and the very meaningful High Priestly Prayer (chap. 17).

The passage shows that (1) Jesus anticipated the disciples' failure; (2) Jesus affirmed His victory; and (3) Jesus acknowledged their limitations. A covenant-pledge to the death could not be kept without a full experience of His victory and grace.

JESUS' PRAYER IN THE GARDEN

36 Then Jesus came with them to a place called Gethsemane, and said to the disciples, "Sit here while I go and pray over there."

37 And He took with Him Peter and the two sons of Zebedee, and He began to be sorrowful and deeply distressed.

38 Then He said to them, "My soul is exceedingly sorrowful, even to death. Stay here and watch with Me."

39 And He went a little farther, fell on His face, and prayed, saying, "O My Father, if it is possible, let this cup pass from Me; nevertheless, not as I will, but as You will."

40 And He came to the disciples, found them asleep, and said to Peter, "What, could you not watch with Me one hour?

41 "Watch and pray, lest you enter into temptation. The spirit indeed is willing, but the flesh is weak."

42 He went away again a second time and prayed, saying, "O My Father, if this cup may not pass away from Me unless I drink it, Your will be done."

43 And He came and found them asleep again, for their eyes were heavy.

44 And He left them, went away again, and prayed
the third time, saying the same words.

45 Then He came to His disciples and said to them,
"Sleep on now and take your rest. Behold, the hour
is at hand, and the Son of Man is being betrayed into
the hands of sinners.

46 "Rise, let us be going. See, he who betrays Me
is at hand."

Matt. 26:36–46

Jesus led His disciples to a place called Gethsemane, meaning "oil-
press." Here He would wrestle in prayer over the test before Him
to be prepared in His spirit to meet His enemies. Leaving eight of
His disciples to wait, He took the three—Peter, James, and John—
as a small "inner circle" to be close to Him in His anguish. He shared
with them the deep sorrow that was affecting Him, an anguish so
intense and so exhausting to empathize with that they went to sleep.
This account, while a historical document, cannot be read as a simple
historical record, for no one witnessed or heard the prayers of the
Master. It may well be autobiographical material that He shared with
them following His resurrection. It is a moving account of Jesus'
separation from His disciples at the fiercest point of His temptation,
alone in His humanity. In verse 41 the statement *"The spirit indeed is
willing, but the flesh is weak"* is no doubt a reference to Himself. He
was ready to do the Father's will, but was wrestling with the limitations of humanness.

The three prayers are interfaced with His coming to the disciples
for emotional support, only to find them sleeping. The first time
He reproved them; the second time He seems to have left them asleep,
for their eyes were heavy. Luke says they were sleeping for sorrow,
worn out by His agony (Luke 22:45).

The more important thing is the spirit of His prayers. His words
"Abba Father" express the closest relationship with the Father as He
submitted to the divine will. His will and the Father's will were
one in relation to His Passion. And further, He accepted the fact
that He must drink the cup alone and fulfill salvation history. The
cup was the wrath of God upon the world's sin (Isa. 51:22), the
horror of the cross. This was the act of entering into the depth-
encounter between God and hostile humanity that placed upon Him
the "iniquity of us all" (Isa. 53:4–6, NIV). He would "taste death for

everyone" (Heb. 2:9). The first prayer was a surrender, *"As you will."* The second and the third were supplications, *"Your will be done."* The prayer incorporates the petition of "The Lord's Prayer" in the words, *"Thy will be done . . ."* and according to the letter to the Hebrews, His prayer was heard (Heb. 5:7). This faith enabled Jesus to say, "The cup which my Father hath given me, shall I not drink it?" (John 18:11, KJV).

Having been heard by the Father and strengthened by angelic presence, Jesus returned to the disciples with a victorious spirit. He was composed and ready to meet the mob that was already on the way. His words *"sleep on now"* could be translated to say, "It is all right now for you to sleep if you can." We do not know the space of time between this statement and the next, when He said that the hour had come, that the Son of Man was even then being betrayed, that they should rise and join Him in meeting the betrayer. On a clear night with the full moon of the Passover season, Jesus could easily have seen the mob coming down the hill from the house of Caiaphas and up the western slope of the Mount of Olives to where He was standing by the olive press.

JESUS IS BETRAYED AND ARRESTED

47 And while He was still speaking, behold, Judas, one of the twelve, with a great multitude with swords and clubs, came from the chief priests and elders of the people.

48 Now he who was betraying Him had given them a sign, saying, "Whomever I kiss, He is the One; seize Him."

49 And immediately he went up to Jesus and said, "Greetings, Rabbi!" and kissed Him.

50 And Jesus said to him, "Friend, why have you come?" Then they came and laid hands on Jesus and took Him.

51 And, suddenly, one of those who were with Jesus stretched out his hand and drew his sword, struck the servant of the high priest, and cut off his ear.

52 Then Jesus said to him, "Put your sword in its place, for all who take the sword will perish by the sword.

53 "Or do you think that I cannot now pray to My
Father, and He will provide Me with more than twelve
legions of angels?

54 "How then will the Scriptures be fulfilled, that
it must be thus?"

55 In that hour Jesus said to the multitudes, "Have
you come out, as against a robber, with swords and
clubs to take Me? I sat daily with you, teaching in
the temple, and you did not seize Me.

56 "But all this was done that the Scriptures of the
prophets might be fulfilled." Then all the disciples
forsook Him and fled.

Matt. 26:47–56

Again Matthew's account follows that of Mark. The one exception
is that Mark includes the account of a young man in the garden
who fled naked when the soldiers attempted to take him as well—
perhaps a reference to John Mark himself! John adds the detail that
the crowd fell to the ground at Jesus' words, a demonstration of
power that could well have permitted His escape. All of the Gospel
writers report that Judas, the betrayer, was with the crowd, but this
was no surprise to Jesus. Since this motley crowd was not of the
people who attended Jesus' teachings, Judas needed to identify Him
for them, and he had given them a sign. Jesus would not give the
Pharisees a sign of His messianic kingship, but Judas dared to give
them a sign to betray Him! Judas said, *"Hail, Rabbi,"* a greeting which
meant "rejoice" or "I'm glad to see you," an especially inappropriate
word. Thereupon he kissed Jesus, the compound word implying that
he kissed Him much. Jesus' response was *"Friend,"* comrade or com-
panion. The angels must have leaned over the battlements of heaven
and applauded Jesus at that moment. To greet the betrayer with a
word of friendship was to say, "Judas, I haven't changed; you are
the one who is changing, but the door of grace is still open."

Jesus' words *"Why have you come?"* must mean, "Enough hypocritical
fawning; do that for which you have come." In the movement of
the mob to take Jesus, one of the disciples (who John said was Peter)
drew his sword and struck at the servant of the high priest and cut
off his ear. Jesus rebuked Peter with a statement that lives on as
something of a "categorical imperative": *"All who take the sword will
perish by the sword."* It was said in a context in which the use of violence
would normally have been expected. But Jesus lived the way of nonvi-

olence; He believed in the active power of love and gave His life rather than defend Himself. The note in verse 53 shows that both Jesus' love for God and His faith in God were genuine. A Roman legion was six thousand soldiers, and Jesus said that His Father could readily have provided Him with twelve such legions if He would but have asked it!

We might well ask why Peter had a sword. We find in Luke 22:34–38 that Jesus had responded to Peter's boast that he would die for Him by asking how many swords they had. When they answered that they had two, Jesus said, "It is enough." This could not have meant enough for armed conflict. It may have been an expression which meant "enough of that." But more likely He meant that it was enough to fulfill the scripture that upon His arrest "He was numbered with the transgressors" (Luke 22:37 and Isa. 53:12).

Jesus made a special point in verse 54 of the fulfillment of Scripture even in the small details. He chided the mob for not taking Him in the temple where He had taught openly rather than sneaking out to the Mount of Olives at night when the public wouldn't be witness. Matthew records that all of the disciples now forsook Him. We have thus moved in salvation history from national Israel, to the smaller faithful Israel, to the small group known as the remnant, to the lone Suffering Servant! The passage deals with (1) Judas' betrayal of the Master, (2) Peter's rebuke by the Master, and (3) the mob's exposure by the Master.

Jesus' words, *"Put away your sword"* (TLB), make it incorrect to follow Luther's interpretation that Jesus approved the use of the sword. Jesus is the prototype of His followers who renounce violence. His access to power was not used for His own self-interest. Rather He lived by the authority of Scripture and its fulfillment.

JESUS FACES THE SANHEDRIN

57 And those who had laid hold of Jesus led Him away to Caiaphas the high priest, where the scribes and the elders were assembled.

58 But Peter followed Him at a distance to the high priest's courtyard. And he went in and sat with the servants to see the end.

59 Now the chief priests, the elders, and all the

council sought false testimony against Jesus to put Him
to death,

60 but found none. Even though many false
witnesses came forward, still they found none. But
at last two false witnesses came forward

61 and said, "This fellow said, 'I am able to destroy
the temple of God and to build it in three days.' "

62 And the high priest arose and said to Him, "Do
You answer nothing? What is it these men testify
against You?"

63 But Jesus kept silent. And the high priest
answered and said to Him, "I adjure You by the living
God that You tell us if You are the Christ, the Son
of God."

64 Jesus said to him, "It is as you said. Nevertheless,
I say to you, hereafter you will see the Son of Man
sitting at the right hand of the Power, and coming
on the clouds of heaven."

65 Then the high priest tore his clothes, saying, "He
has spoken blasphemy! What further need do we have
of witnesses? Look, now you have heard His
blasphemy!

66 "What do you think?" They answered and said,
"He is guilty of death."

67 Then they spat in His face and beat Him; and
others struck Him with the palms of their hands,

68 saying, "Prophesy to us, You Christ! Who is the
one who struck You?"

Matt. 26:57–68

From Matthew's account we learn that the Sanhedrin was already
in session, waiting for Jesus to be brought before them. The verb
in verse 59, being in the imperfect tense, means that they had sought
for some time to gain evidence that would provide a charge against
Jesus. What Caiaphas needed was two witnesses who agreed, false
or not. Finally they found two who both said, *"This fellow said, 'I am
able to destroy the temple of God and to build it in three days.' "* But Mark
says that even these didn't agree (Mark 14:58–59). John points out
that Jesus had made a statement early in His ministry that if they
destroyed "this temple" meaning His body, He would raise it up in
three days (John 2:19).

Matthew, in verse 58, says that Peter followed at a distance, and
sat in the courtyard with the servants. John adds an interesting note

that a disciple known to Caiaphas, evidently John himself, had entry into the house. He went out and brought Peter in. At least we give these disciples credit for following. Peter's despair is evident in the words that he *"sat with the servants to see the end."*

When Jesus expressed no words of defense, Caiaphas attacked Him in open hostility. Earlier, apparently as an attempt to be diplomatic, he had asked Jesus about His disciples and of His doctrine (John 18:19) and Jesus had answered briefly. But, in the face of false charges before Caiaphas, Jesus refused to defend Himself. Then, openly hostile, Caiaphas forced His hand by saying, *"I adjure You by the living God that You tell us if You are the Christ, the Son of God."* The Mishna[9] says that all are bound to answer this famous Oath of Testimony of the Hebrew Constitution. Jesus answered, *"I AM,"* or *"It is as you said."* The high priest is face to face with the divine Epiphany. Jesus underscored His answer with the messianic mystery, *"You will see the Son of Man sitting at the right hand of the Power, and coming on the clouds of heaven."* This messianic picture from Daniel 7:13–14 was known and unmistakable to the high priest. Jesus' response *"It is as you said"* is the traditional form in which a cultivated Jew responded to a question of grave import, courtesy forbidding a direct yes or no. There is no question that Jesus' answer was understood.

Caiaphas had what he wanted. When it appeared that the trial was breaking down, he had conceived an expedient but illegal approach: to apply the Oath of Testimony to which even silence was an unforgiveable offense. Now Caiaphas shouted, "Blasphemy!" and tore his clothes, a symbolic expression of horror, after which he called for the verdict. The Sanhedrin cried out, *"He is guilty of death."* (We learn elsewhere that Joseph of Arimathea and Nicodemus had refrained from participation in this meeting; see Luke 23:51 and John 7:50–52.) The power struggle condemned Jesus, for Caiaphas knew that the coming of the Messiah would preempt his own position as arbiter of the national fortunes. And he, with the other members of the Sanhedrin, watched while the guards manhandled Jesus, mocking Him and buffeting Him with their fists.

Studies have shown that the trial of Jesus was illegally conducted according to Jewish law. The Talmud says, "The Sanhedrin is to save, not to destroy life." The illegalities in the trial of Jesus were: (1) Capital crimes were to be tried during the daytime only. (2) They were not to be tried during festival times. (3) They were not to be dealt with at a single sitting of one day. (4) They were not to be tried with immediate appearances of witnesses for the prosecution, for this was a breach of law. (5) There was no precedent or a single evidence for a person claiming to be the Messiah being accused of blasphemy and being sentenced to death. (6) If a man stood accused of blasphemy in relation to the name of God, Jewish authorities could have him stoned, but they must hand him over to the governor. (7) The priests were to have judgment in the charge, but they presented Jesus to Pilate, making Him a political suspect in a strategy to rid themselves of the prophet of Nazareth. Yet they asked for the release of the political criminal Barabbas, who was guilty of the very thing they were attributing to Jesus. (8) The temple guard could not act for the high priest in an arrest charging blasphemy unless they themselves were witnesses to the blasphemy. Finally, (9) when witness breaks down, the accused could not be cross-examined by the judges.

PETER DENIES THE MASTER

69 Now Peter sat outside in the courtyard. And a servant girl came to him, saying, "You also were with Jesus of Galilee."

70 But he denied it before them all, saying, "I do not know what you are saying."

71 And when he had gone out to the entrance, another girl saw him and said to those who were there, "This fellow was also with Jesus of Nazareth."

72 And again he denied with an oath, "I do not know the Man!"

73 And after a while, those who stood by came to him and said to Peter, "Surely you also are one of them, because your speech betrays you."

74 Then he began to curse and swear, saying, "I do not know the Man!" And immediately a rooster crowed.

75 And Peter remembered the word of Jesus who had said to him, "Before the rooster crows, you will deny Me three times." And he went out and wept bitterly.

Matt. 26:69–75

All four Gospels relate Peter's act of disloyalty. The story of Peter's denial must have been handed down by Peter himself. Thereby Mark likely presented the story from Peter's account and/or preaching.

No doubt Peter told this to illustrate how completely Jesus forgives. The report that one of their number had been injured in the garden and that Jesus had healed him may have spread among the high priest's servants. Peter had followed at a distance, had gained entrance into the courtyard, and sat with the servants to see how things would end.

The first approach to Peter was by a servant girl who identified him as one of the followers of Jesus from Galilee. Peter denied that her statement had any merit. After he had withdrawn from the group and had gone out to the entrance, a second servant girl identified him. Again he denied it with an oath for emphasis, saying specifically that he did not know Jesus. This denial was a step further in his negative statements. A while later, some of the servants accused him on the grounds that his Galilean accent gave him away. He now increased the cursing and swearing, doubtless words that confirmed their judgment of him, saying that he didn't know Jesus. At that moment the cock crowed and Peter remembered. Luke adds that "the Lord turned and looked at Peter" (Luke 22:61). Under a deep sense of conviction and remorse, Peter staggered out into the night, weeping bitterly about his failure. This "godly sorrow" led to repentance. In Mark's account of the Resurrection, the angel at the tomb told the women to tell Christ's disciples "and Peter" that He would meet them in Galilee (Mark 16:7). This special reference to Peter, the back-slidden disciple, is a warm note of compassionate caring.

A lesson on "The Disciple at a Distance" would show (1) denial as a dodge, v. 70; (2) denial as disassociation, v. 72; and (3) denial as defense, v. 73. Such a meditation should clarify why we make the mistakes of denying our Lord.

JESUS HANDED OVER TO PONTIUS PILATE

1 When morning came, all the chief priests and elders of the people took counsel against Jesus to put Him to death.
2 And when they had bound Him, they led Him away and delivered Him to Pontius Pilate the governor.

Matt. 27:1–2

The Sanhedrin held a second very brief meeting early in the morning. They had charged Jesus with blasphemy (26:65–66), but they needed a charge by which they could secure the death penalty by

Pilate. Matthew doesn't tell us what the additional charge was, but Luke gives us three elements of their charge before Pilate: (1) national subversive activity, (2) teaching against paying taxes to Rome, and (3) claiming to be a King, the Christ (Luke 23:2). This charge, according to Luke, followed their bringing Jesus out of the dungeon to Caiaphas' court, and then bringing Him a second time before their council for questioning and mocking. They fabricated the charges, giving them political meaning to influence Pilate's judgment, passed their own sentence on Him, and led Him away to Pilate. The Lord of the universe "came unto his own, and his own received him not" (John 1:11, KJV). He was examined before the representatives of justice in the courts of the nations, and rejected because they could not understand Him or His kingdom.

JUDAS SELF-DESTRUCTS

3 Then Judas, who had betrayed Him, when he saw that He had been condemned, felt remorse and brought back the thirty pieces of silver to the chief priests and elders,

4 saying, "I have sinned in that I have betrayed innocent blood." And they said, "What is that to us? You see to that!"

5 And he threw down the pieces of silver in the temple, departed, and went and hanged himself.

6 And the chief priests took the silver pieces and said, "It is not lawful to put them into the treasury, because they are the price of blood."

7 And they took counsel and bought with them the potter's field, to bury strangers in.

8 Therefore that field has been called the Field of Blood to this day.

9 Then was fulfilled what was spoken by Jeremiah the prophet, saying, *"And they took the thirty pieces of silver, the value of Him who was priced,* whom they of the children of Israel priced,

10 "and gave them for the potter's field, as the LORD directed me."

Matt. 27:3–10

Matthew interrupts the story of Jesus' trial to tell of Judas' reaction and death, as he had earlier inserted the account of Peter's denial into the trial. He is the only one of the Gospel writers to relate this account. It is referred to in Acts 1:18–20, which shows different aspects of the suicide. A third source of information from history is a reference by Papias of the second century. Matthew's word "then" suggests that it was after the Sanhedrin had sentenced Jesus to die that Judas was gripped with remorse. It can be surmised that Judas had never intended to betray Jesus to death, but to betray Him into the hands of His enemies as a strategy to force Him to demonstrate His power as the messianic King. If so, he had meant to force Jesus to come forth as conqueror, but instead he had prepared His way to the cross.

Judas took the thirty pieces of silver and went to the temple, to the chief priests and elders who were there on this holy day awaiting word from their colleagues of the trial of Jesus before Pilate. The word used here for "temple" specifies the inner court, not the temple court. Judas passed through the Gentile court, the women's court, and the main court of the Israelites, to the inner court of the priests. Here he cried out in remorse, *"I have sinned,"* only to be met with the words from so-called religious leaders that his guilt was nothing to them! He threw down the thirty pieces of silver and went out and hanged himself. Luke's account in Acts 1:18 shows us that this must have taken place on a tree by a cliff, with the result that either a broken limb or broken rope allowed his body to be broken on the rocks below.

The account has three emphases: (1) remorse changed Judas' regard for what had once been important to him, for he returned the thirty pieces of silver; (2) betrayal of the Lord was a betrayal of himself, and like Ahithophel who betrayed David (2 Sam. 15:12; 17:23), he hanged himself; and (3) the "blood money" left no one free to use it, for by their law it could only be used for strangers. Matthew reached for scriptural background for this act and grouped statements from Jeremiah (32:6–9) and Zechariah (11:12–13) as a word from the prophet Jeremiah, showing a purchase and a price at a time of national judgment. He related the Old Testament references to this ultimate expression of Israel's unbelief and rejection of the Word of God among them, their greater judgment.

Judas must have been a great man, talented, dedicated to his work, enterprising, careful in his role, for apparently he was respected by his associates. But, upon his failure, he tried to wipe up his footsteps, while Peter, upon his failure, wept bitterly with no excuse, dependent solely upon the grace of God. From Judas we learn (1) that one can act like a disciple and not be fully dedicated, (2) that the heart is deceptive and behavior can be rationalized, and (3) that associating with the people of God still leaves each individual the decision to choose to be godly.

JESUS FACES PILATE

11 And Jesus stood before the governor. And the governor asked Him, saying, "Are You the King of the Jews?" And Jesus said to him, "It is as you say."
12 And while He was being accused by the chief priests and elders, He answered nothing.
13 Then Pilate said to Him, "Do You not hear how many things they testify against You?"
14 And He answered him not one word, so that the governor marveled greatly.

Matt. 27:11–14

In Jesus' trial before Pilate, or mistrial as it should be called, there are five brief scenes: the accusation (vv. 11–14), the contrast with Barabbas (vv. 15–18), the interruption by Pilate's wife (v. 19), the question concerning Jesus (vv. 20–23), and Pilate's wash basin (vv. 24–26). Matthew omits the interlude before Herod (Luke 23:6–12). This section deals with the first scene, the accusation of Jesus as claiming to be a king, a claim that was against Rome. Pilate's question is in response to the Sanhedrin's charge (Luke 23:2–3). Jesus' answer was made with the same reserve and courtesy that he had shown before the Sanhedrin (26:64), yet it was clearly unambiguous. John shares a brief interchange between Jesus and Pilate which adds another dimension to Jesus' answer, for He confronted Pilate with a different understanding of kingship. Jesus said, "My kingdom is not of this world: if my kingdom were of this world, then would my servants fight, that I should not be delivered to the Jews: but now is my kingdom not from hence" (John 18:36, KJV). This is doubtless one of the more basic affirmations at the trial, the distinction between the Kingdom of God and the political kingdoms of this world. This distinction precipitates our theology of separation of church and state. Paul emphasizes this in Romans 13, seeing the work of God always on a level above the power of the state, for God ordains government.

The state is on another level, at best operating by God's providence, but on the basis of the franchise of the people.

Further charges were made against Jesus by the priests but Jesus did not answer them. Pilate was amazed at His poise, but evidently disappointed in His not having a defense that would allow him to release Jesus. He was aware that these leaders were envious of Jesus' popularity and were threatened by His success. In *The Grand Inquisitor*, Dostoevski has the ecclesiastical prelate asking the Christ to "get out" because He challenged the whole religious bureaucracy.

THE CHOICE BETWEEN JESUS AND BARABBAS

15 Now at the feast the governor was accustomed to releasing to the multitude one prisoner whom they wished.

16 And they had then a notorious prisoner called Barabbas.

17 Therefore, when they had gathered together, Pilate said to them, "Whom do you want me to release to you? Barabbas, or Jesus who is called Christ?"

18 For he knew that because of envy they had delivered Him.

19 While he was sitting on the judgment seat, his wife sent to him, saying, "Have nothing to do with that just Man, for I have suffered many things today in a dream because of Him."

20 But the chief priests and elders persuaded the multitudes that they should ask for Barabbas and destroy Jesus.

21 The governor answered and said to them, "Which of the two do you want me to release to you?" They said, "Barabbas!"

22 Pilate said to them, "What then shall I do with Jesus who is called Christ?" They all said to him, "Let Him be crucified!"

23 And the governor said, "Why, what evil has He done?" But they cried out all the more, saying, "Let Him be crucified!"

24 When Pilate saw that he could not prevail at all, but rather that a tumult was rising, he took water and washed his hands before the multitude, saying,

"I am innocent of the blood of this just Person. You
see to it."

25 And all the people answered and said, "His blood
be on us and on our children."

26 Then he released Barabbas to them; but when
he had scourged Jesus, he delivered Him to be crucified.

Matt. 27:15–26

Pilate is called the governor, the Latin word being "procurator,"
the person sent by Rome to keep order in Judea. The Jews did not
like Pilate because of the manner in which he disregarded their religious rites. He had deliberately brought the Roman ensigns to the
temple and had placed the Roman eagle there as a symbol of the
sovereignty of Rome. Josephus relates that he then went off to Caesarea to his summer quarters by the sea, to be surprised by five thousand Jewish men who came to petition him to remove the symbols.
Calling in his militia, he was further surprised to see these Jewish
men bow to the ground and bare their necks, saying, "You can cut
off our heads, but don't desecrate our Temple." Pilate backed off.
Now he was caught between the pressure of the Jewish Sanhedrin
and the position of Rome on seeking justice. As a way out, Pilate
proposed a trade. If they were concerned to not have their relation
with Rome threatened by an insurrectionist, he would substitute an
actual insurrectionist, Barabbas, arrested for the very crime which
they were attributing to Jesus. Following a Roman custom, he offered
to release one of the two as a goodwill gesture accompanying this
high feast occasion. He was again thwarted in his maneuvering, for
after he had conferred with the leaders of the Jews (v. 17), they
immediately incited the crowd to ask for Barabbas (vv. 20–23). Pilate
subsequently released Barabbas and delivered Jesus to be crucified.
Note that the name *Bar-abbas* means "son of a Father." The Jews
would have been conscious of the play on words in light of Jesus'
claim.

Matthew alone records the incident of Pilate's wife having sent
him a message to avoid involvement with this *"just Man"* (v. 19).
Pilate had been called early to the judgment seat, and evidently his
wife awakened later from a horrible dream and sent a message at
once to him. Whether she had any contact with the disciples of Jesus
is unknown. Early tradition suggests that she later became a
Christian.[10]

This section concludes with Pilate's last act before sentencing Jesus being the farce of washing his hands. He tried to withdraw from moral responsibility for a sentence which he knew to be unjust. Beckoning for an attendant to bring a bronze basin and a bronze pitcher with water, he held his hands over the basin and washed them as the water was poured over them—a symbol to the Jews that he carried no responsibility for what they were doing. But one cannot be neutral in relation to God, and since He has come to us in Jesus one cannot be neutral in relation to Christ. I have frequently preached a sermon on "Decision between Two Wash Basins," contrasting Pilate's wash basin with the basin Jesus used in the upper room when He washed the disciples' feet. Using John 18:36 to set the stage, the points are as follows: (1) the setting of the basins is the concept of two kingdoms; (2) Pilate's wash basin is the modus operandi of the status-seeker; (3) Jesus' wash basin is the modus operandi of the servant of God.

JESUS IS MOCKED BY THE SOLDIERS

27 Then the soldiers of the governor took Jesus into the Praetorium and gathered the whole band of soldiers around Him.
28 And they stripped Him and put a scarlet robe on Him.
29 And when they had twisted a crown out of thorns, they put it on His head, and a reed in His right hand. And they bowed the knee before Him and mocked Him, saying, "Hail, King of the Jews!"
30 And they spat on Him, and took the reed and struck Him on the head.
31 And when they had mocked Him, they took the robe off Him, put His own clothes on Him, and led Him away to crucify Him.

Matt. 27:27–31

Our Lord was mocked by the Gentile soldiers. The rejection of Jesus was not only by the Jews but by all of mankind represented in Jew and Gentile. While preparation was being made for the crucifixion, the Roman maniple, about 200 men, took Jesus into the barracks at the Fortress of Antonia and began to mock Him. They stripped Him of His clothing and put a scarlet tunic on Him, a soldier's robe for the Prince of Peace. To further symbolize His kingship they put on His head a crown of woven thorns, and a "scepter" in His hand. Kneeling before Him, they mocked Him as the King of the Jews and insulted Him further by spitting in His face. John describes this as having transpired while Pilate was haggling with the Jewish leaders (John 19:1–12), and adds that Pilate had Him scourged, a custom in preparation for crucifixion.

The mockery was an exposure of the very opposite position from what Jesus actually represented. The scarlet military robe mocked the Prince of Peace. Their buffeting mocked His deeds of compassion. The symbols of kingship were a part of a game which the soldiers played called "king for a day," the symbols of which can still be seen scratched in the rocks in the excavations at the Fortress of Antonia. But the mockery of the King of kings will find further answer when "at the name of Jesus every knee should bow . . ." (Phil. 2:10–11).

Jesus Is Crucified

32 And as they came out, they found a man of Cyrene, Simon by name. Him they compelled to bear His cross.

33 And when they had come to a place called Golgotha, that is to say, the Place of a Skull,

34 they gave Him sour wine mingled with gall to drink. And when He had tasted it, He would not drink.

35 And they crucified Him, and divided His garments, casting lots, that it might be fulfilled which was spoken by the prophet:

"They divided My garments among them,
And for My clothing they cast lots."

36 And sitting down, they kept watch over Him there.

37 And they put up over His head the accusation written against Him:

THIS IS JESUS THE KING OF THE JEWS.

38 Then two robbers were crucified with Him, one on the right and another on the left.

39 And those who passed by blasphemed Him, wagging their heads

40 and saying, "You who destroy the temple and build it in three days, save Yourself! If You are the Son of God, come down from the cross."

41 Likewise the chief priests also, mocking with the scribes and elders, said,

42 "He saved others; Himself He cannot save. If He is the King of Israel, let Him now come down from the cross, and we will believe Him.

43 "He trusted in God; let Him deliver Him now if He will have Him; for He said, 'I am the Son of God.'"

44 Even the robbers who were crucified with Him reviled Him with the same thing.

Matt. 27:32–44

The horrible act of crucifixion was now underway. Pilate had Jesus scourged, a most terrible torture in which the prisoner was tied to a post with His back bent, and a whip with long leather thongs studded with sharp pieces of bone and pellets of lead was used. The pain was so severe that men died under it, or broke with loss of their senses. But Jesus retained His consciousness throughout. When presented to the people as a broken person He still retained His poise. John tells us that Jesus carried His own cross, perhaps the crossbar, as they started out of Jerusalem (John 19:17). But with His condition weakened from the torture, He stumbled under the load. The Synoptics tell us that the soldiers took a man from the crowd, a Cyrenian named Simon who was coming into the city from the country (according to Mark), and ordered him to carry Jesus' cross. Luke tells us that Jesus was composed sufficiently to address the women who were weeping as they followed Him, "Do not weep for me, but weep for yourselves and for your children . . ." announcing coming judgment upon Jerusalem (Luke 23:28–31). It is thought that this Simon became a Christian and that his two sons, Alexander and Rufus, became well-known Christians in Rome (Mark 15:21).

The Gospels all relate the crucifixion with a minimum of words. None go into the terrible description of a Roman crucifixion. The major question has to do with "Who is this Jesus?" And "Why did He have to die?" At Calvary something was happening to God by man, but something was also happening to man and for man by God. Both of these aspects need to be recognized for us to think adequately of the meaning of the cross. The historic fact is that "Christ died," and the theological significance is that "Christ died for our sins" (1 Cor. 15:3). This is the heart of the *kerygma*, of the good news of the gospel. The death of Jesus, set in the Passover week, emphasizes the expiatory nature of His sacrifice. The Hebrew word *kaphar* means to cover or wipe away, and when used in relation to God it means to forgive or purge away, a cleansing from sin (Lev. 16:30). C. H. Dodd says that Hellenistic Judaism, represented by the Septuagint, did not regard the cultus as a means of pacifying the displeasure of the Deity, but as a means of delivering man from sin.[11] The crucifixion of Jesus brought the interaction between God and man together, for here Jesus actualized the depth of God's love in absorbing man's hostility to the death and speaking back the word of grace. He "bore our sins in His own body on the tree" (1 Pet. 2:24).

The place of crucifixion was a skull-shaped hill called Golgotha. The soldiers, according to a custom of mercy, offered drugged wine to make the person more insensitive to the pain, but Jesus refused it. Some researchers suggest that the upright post was stationary and that the person was nailed through the hands to the crossbar and raised above the ground, somewhat higher than the height of a man, with the heels crossed and a nail thrust through them. Other descriptions suggest that the person was crucified by being nailed to the whole cross, which was then raised and planted.

Jesus was crucified about nine o'clock in the morning and died six hours later, at three o'clock in the afternoon, the time of the evening sacrifice. His agony was six hours long on the cross and yet short compared to the fact that at times crucified persons were still alive a second day. Matthew simply mentions the two thieves crucified with Jesus while Luke includes them in the story, reporting the faith-conversation of one (23:39–43).

Matthew tells of the soldiers parting His garments by lot. Each Jewish man wore five articles: shoes, turban, girdle, inner garment, and outer cloak. The soldiers, according to John 19:23–24, divided them four ways, casting lots on the Galilean's peasant tunic which was without seam. John was near the cross, and probably witnessed the scene. Matthew simply reports this as a fulfillment of the statement in Psalm 22:18. He alone adds that the soldiers sat down and kept watch over Him to thwart any attempts at interfering with Him.

The sentence of the crucified one was fixed to the cross above his head. The placing of the sign above Jesus' head suggests the form of the cross having been in the shape traditionally ascribed to it.

More significant is the statement Pilate wrote designating His crime: *"This is Jesus the King of the Jews."* John's account adds the words "of Nazareth" to the identification. He also writes that the chief priests went to Pilate to ask him to change the statement to read, "He said that He was the King of the Jews." Pilate, evidently fed up with their shenanigans, said, "What I have written I have written." The sign was no small placard, for the statement was written in Latin, in Greek, and in Hebrew, the languages of the political, the cultural, and the religious worlds of the day.

The mockery of Jesus expressed the unbelief of the people not directly involved in the scheme of the leaders. Matthew says that He was mocked by those passing by. Further, He was mocked by the Sanhedrin and by the two robbers. Matthew thereby shows the world's rejection of the Son of God, the fulfillment of Psalm 22:7–8. Note the intense form of the temptation for Jesus as He hung listening to their jeers: *"If you are the Son of God, come down." "Save Yourself." "He saved others; Himself He cannot save." "If He is the King of Israel, let Him now come down from the cross, and we will believe Him."* And the climax of it all was their reference to Jesus' claim to be *"the Son of God."* The accusations were in the large correct statements, and showed that they had heard Jesus' words but missed their truth. Matthew focuses on the mockery of the King, on the rejection of the Messiah. In J. S. Bach's *St. Matthew Passion,* the wild chorus of the scoffers ends with all eight parts singing in unison, "For he has said: I am the Son of God."

JESUS' DEATH ON THE CROSS

45 Now from the sixth hour until the ninth hour there was darkness over all the land.
46 And about the ninth hour Jesus cried out with a loud voice, saying, *"Eli, Eli, lama sabachthani?"* that is, *"My God, My God, why have You forsaken Me?"*
47 Some of those who stood there, when they heard that, said, "This Man is calling for Elijah!"
48 And immediately one of them ran, took a sponge and filled it with sour wine, put it on a reed, and gave it to Him to drink.
49 The rest said, "Let Him alone; let us see if Elijah will come to save Him."

50 Jesus, when He had cried out again with a loud voice, yielded up His spirit.

51 And behold, the curtain of the temple was torn in two from the top to the bottom; and the earth quaked, and the rocks were split,

52 and the graves were opened; and many bodies of the saints who had fallen asleep were raised;

53 and coming out of the graves after His resurrection, they went into the holy city and appeared to many.

54 Now when the centurion and those with him, who were guarding Jesus, saw the earthquake and the things that had happened, they feared greatly, saying, "Truly this was the Son of God!"

55 And many women who followed Jesus from Galilee, ministering to Him, were there looking on from afar,

56 among whom were Mary Magdalene, Mary the mother of James and Joses, and the mother of Zebedee's sons.

Matt. 27:45–56

The unusual phenomenon of darkness over the land from the sixth hour (noon) until the ninth hour (3:00 P.M.) was not an eclipse of the sun, for the moon was full at Passover time. It was God's act, and amidst the darkness as His time of death approached, Jesus cried with a loud voice, *"Eli, Eli lama sabachthani?" "My God, My God, why have You forsaken Me?"* The cry was interpreted by some of the crowd as having messianic connotations, that He was calling for Elijah! They ran to get vinegar for Him to drink to sustain Him till they could see if Elijah would come! But He cried again *"with a loud voice [and] yielded up His spirit."* In these last words Matthew presents Jesus as having given His life. Perhaps he was recalling Jesus' words, "The Son of man came not to be ministered unto, but to minister, and to give his life a ransom for many" (20:28, KJV).

We will look at this statement by Jesus in a later paragraph. Note how Matthew stressed the unusual phenomena which attended the death of Jesus. First, the curtain of the temple was torn in two from top to bottom, symbolizing that the old order had come to an end (Heb. 8:6–13). This curtain veiled the most holy place and hung before the place where the High Priest was offering the Paschal lamb. It was no small curtain, but was sixty feet long and thirty feet wide, woven a handbreadth thick of seventy-two plaits with twenty-four

threads each. Second, the earth quaked and the very rocks reeled
and shattered. Third, Matthew reports that graves were opened and
that after the Resurrection of Jesus, saints arose from these tombs
and appeared to people in the holy city. Following the occurrence
of darkness and the earthquake, the Roman centurion cried out in
awe, *"Truly this was the Son of God,"* or "a Son of God." The language
does not identify a full awareness but suggests that the Gentile centurion was transfixed with the certainty that Jesus was the very One
they had said in mockery that He was. It is of interest that this
centurion was probably quartered in the garrison at Caesarea where
Cornelius was stationed (Acts 10:1).

Matthew records only one of the seven sayings of Christ on the
cross, emphasizing that what was happening on the cross was affecting
God in heaven. Luke gives us the first two sayings: (1) Jesus' prayer
as they nailed Him to the cross, with the imperfect tense meaning
that He prayed it repeatedly, "Father, forgive them, for they do not
know what they do" (Luke 23:34); and (2) His words in response
to the faith of the repentant robber, "Today you will be with me
in Paradise" (Luke 23:43). John gives us the next two statements:
(3) Jesus' words to His mother Mary and to His disciple John, as
He looked out for His mother's care, "Woman, behold your son.
. . . Behold your mother" (John 19:26–27); and then, (4) His words
reflecting the depth of His physical suffering, "I thirst" (John 19:28).
The next statement is given us by Matthew in this passage (v. 46),
(5) "My God, My God, why. . . ?" Martin Luther, reading this statement, cried out, "God-forsaken of God, who can understand it?"
The poet Browning expressed it:

> Yea, once Emmanuel's Orphan cry
> His universe has shaken
> It went up single, echoless
> My God, I am forsaken,
> It went up from holy lips
> Amid His lost creation,
> That of those lost,
> No son should use
> Those words of desolation.

The last two statements are found in Luke and John respectively.
Jesus' words, (6) "Father, into your hands I commend my spirit"
(Luke 23:46), give evidence of His abiding and meaningful relation

with the Father. His last words, (7) "It is finished," meaning "completed," are a shout of victory: *"Tetelestai!"* "We've won!" (John 19:30). Isaiah 53 is finished, confirmed by 2 Corinthians 5:21. Jesus is the expiation for our sins.

The cry of Jesus found in Matthew was a statement of utter loneliness and desolation we cannot fathom. One interpretation has been to describe it as God's turning His back on the Son, while He poured out His wrath over our sins on Jesus. This is not an adequate representation of the Father, even though it does emphasize the cost to Jesus of substituting Himself for us. But to His last breath He was conscious that He was the well-beloved of the Father. Forgiveness, as we have noted in chapter 18, means that the innocent carries his own wrath over the sin against him. So here at Calvary, God in Christ is carrying His own wrath on our sin (2 Cor. 5:19). He carried it to the depth of death, suffering man's sin in the act of destroying Him, beyond which sin cannot go. The cry from the cross let the world know that suffering of this depth was happening to the Godhead. The full Godhead was involved in bearing the sin of the world at a cost so inconceivable as to mean the death of the Son of God. This cost affected the full trinitarian aspects of God: the Father suffering in giving His Son (John 3:16), the Son suffering in giving His life, and the Holy Spirit suffering in associating with the world's pain through the centuries.

Many issues important in a theology of the atonement are suggested in this Gospel account and have been unfolded throughout salvation history: (1) the representative character of Jesus' sacrifice for men; (2) the vicarious character of His suffering (Isa. 53:6); (3) the substitutionary element of bearing for another in forgiveness; (4) the penal nature of suffering, that God may be just in dealing with sinners (Rom. 3:23–26); (5) reconciliation in which God reconciles men to Himself by revealing His love for man and turning man to trust (Rom. 5:8); (6) the sacrificial principle in which Jesus in self-identification with sinners brought them to union with Himself (Rom. 6:1–6; Gal. 2:20); and (7) the emphasis on covenant, the new convenant in His blood, by which God's act of grace is met by our act of faith in worshipful identification with Him. There will always remain the element of mystery, but our faith holds that "the blood of Jesus Christ His Son cleanses us from all sin" (1 John 1:7).

Matthew concludes this section with a reference to the presence of many women who had followed Jesus from Galilee (vv. 55–56).

He gives specific names for three of them, but does not mention others further, including Jesus' mother, Mary. The reference identifies followers of Jesus who were near the cross. The presence of the women is in contrast to the scattering of the disciples. The only one of the twelve whom we know to have been present was John. The reference shows the faithfulness of the women, their presence and aid in removing the body for burial (v. 61), and their reason for coming to the tomb early on Easter morning (28:1).

JESUS' BURIAL IN JOSEPH'S TOMB

57 Now when evening had come, there came a rich man from Arimathea, named Joseph, who himself was also a disciple of Jesus.

58 He went to Pilate and asked for the body of Jesus. Then Pilate commanded the body to be given to him.

59 And when Joseph had taken the body, he wrapped it in a clean linen cloth,

60 and laid it in his own new tomb which he had hewn out of the rock; and he rolled a large stone against the door of the tomb and departed.

61 And Mary Magdalene was there, and the other Mary, sitting opposite the tomb.

Matt. 27:57-61

The prophet Isaiah said of the Suffering Servant, "He made his grave with the wicked, and with the rich in his death" (Isa. 53:9, KJV). Jesus had died between two robbers, given names in history as Zoathan (on His right) and Camma (on His left). The story of His burial brings in the rich, for it was Joseph of Arimathea, a wealthy man and a member of the council or of the Sanhedrin, who came to the fore and asked Pilate for Jesus' body. Joseph was a disciple of Jesus who had left the Sanhedrin when it became evident that they were set to destroy Jesus (Luke 23:51). His role of love was now needed. Jewish Law required that an executed person be buried the same day as executed. The Romans would have left Jesus' body for scavengers unless His relatives came and took it down. But they were in a difficult position, being from Galilee and owning no tomb in Jerusalem. So Joseph of Arimathea (a town between Jerusalem

and Joppa, about fifteen miles east of the latter) made his bold request
of Pilate for the body. Pilate, amazed that Jesus was already dead,
made inquiry to be certain, whereupon he gave the body to Joseph.

Joseph had prepared a new tomb in Jerusalem, no doubt due to
his move from Arimathea to the city of Jerusalem. It was to this
tomb that Joseph and his helpers (evidently including a number of
the women who followed Jesus) took the body. They wrapped it
in a clean linen cloth for a quick burial, since this was the evening
of the Passover. To make sure that no one disturbed the body, Joseph
rolled a great stone before the door of the tomb. This was actually
a style in which many tombs were built. They were often carved
out of the rock in the side of a hill, as were the tombs of the kings
in Jerusalem. There was a trench before the opening in which a stone,
like a round millstone, was rolled and firmly held and secured. At
least two Marys, one the Magdalene, and the other the mother of
James and Jesus, were near the tomb and watched Joseph bury the
body. Having been at the Garden Tomb by Gordon's Calvary on
numerous occasions, I have been moved by the meaning of the empty
tomb, rejoicing that Jesus arose. Whether this particular tomb was
the grave of Jesus or not, the site is a very characteristic example.

An interesting series of legends has grown up about Joseph.[12] A
very interesting one is that Joseph was Mary's uncle, thereby identifying him as a relative of Jesus. This includes a legend of Joseph taking
Jesus with him on a trip to England when He was a lad of about
twelve—a very unlikely account, but a legend that has been the basis
for poetry and fiction.

THE SANHEDRIN SET THEIR GUARD

62 Now the next day, which followed the Day of
Preparation, the chief priests and Pharisees gathered
together to Pilate,

63 saying, "Sir, we remember, while He was still
alive, how that deceiver said, 'After three days I will
rise.'

64 "Therefore command that the tomb be made
secure until the third day, lest His disciples come by
night, steal Him away, and say to the people, 'He has
risen from the dead.' So the last deception will be worse
than the first."

318

65 Pilate said to them, "You have a guard; go your
way, make it as secure as you know how."
66 So they went and made the tomb secure, sealing
the stone, and setting the guard.

Matt. 27:62–66

As Bornkamm says, "The Tomb makes the death official."[13] The
burial and sealing of the tomb by Joseph should have settled matters
for the public. But Matthew very carefully reports the actions of
the chief priests in asking for a guard, for they knew of Jesus' predictions that on the third day He would rise! At the time Matthew
wrote this Gospel, the story was being promoted by the Jews that
the disciples had stolen the body. Justin confirms the fact that the
Jewish people charged Jesus disciples with stealing the body and reporting Jesus to be alive. But Matthew's account shows the impossibility of this happening with the securely guarded tomb.

Note again that the chief priests knew of Jesus' prediction regarding
His Resurrection. They went to Pilate for a Roman guard, afraid of
the results if word ever got around that Jesus was alive. They had
a guard of their own (a temple guard), and Pilate gave them permission
to use it for this purpose. Matthew says that they sealed the stone
and set the guard. Pilate's words *"as secure as you know how"* sound
ironic. They had killed Jesus, and now they needed to seal His body
in the tomb. They did not realize that no tomb in the world could
hold the Son of God. He is Victor over death and the powers of
darkness.

NOTES

1. Taylor, *Jesus and His Sacrifice*, p. 272.
2. Ibid., pp. 272–273.
3. Swartley, *Mark*, p. 183.
4. Note Jeremias's extensive study of whether this was actually the Passover, or "Our Lord's Supper," and the problem of dating it in *The Eucharistic
Words of Jesus.*
5. Flavius Josephus, *Antiquities of the Jews*, 20 vols. (London: Shapira Vallentine & Co.), II, 15, p. 1.

6. Jeremias, *The Eucharistic Words of Jesus*, p. 52.

7. Taylor, *Jesus and His Sacrifice*, p. 142.

8. Jeremias, *The Eucharistic Words of Jesus*, p. 52.

9. The Mishna is the Jewish sourcebook of their official laws.

10. See H. V. Morton, *The Women of the Bible* (New York: Methuen, 1940), pp. 157–165.

11. C. H. Dodd, *The Bible and the Greeks*, 2nd ed. (Naperville, IL: Allenson, 1954), p. 93.

12. Several of these legends are reported in Barclay, *The Gospel of Matthew*, 1:410–412.

13. Gunther Bornkamm, *Jesus of Nazareth* (New York: Harper & Row, 1956), p. 168.

CHAPTER ELEVEN

The Victory of the King

Matthew 28:1-20

The story of Jesus does not end with His death; it begins a new chapter with His Resurrection. The writer of Acts referred to His former treatise being "of all that Jesus began both to do and teach" (Acts 1:1), setting the stage for a second treatise of all that Jesus continues to do and to teach through the Spirit. The crucified Lord is risen and back in business! His message is the same, for appearing to His followers over a forty-day period, He talked with them of the things pertaining to the Kingdom of God. The striking statement regarding the Resurrection is that "He . . . presented Himself alive after His suffering by many infallible proofs" (Acts 1:3).

The disciples, as He confronted them as the risen Lord and overcame their unbelief, became a new community. This community was now certain that, in the Resurrection of Christ, God had vindicated Jesus, who had been put to death as a rejected Person. By His Resurrection He is "declared to be the Son of God with power" (Rom. 1:4). They were absolutely convinced that He was present with them, Lord of the church, and Head of the church as His body. The Preacher of Nazareth now becomes Himself the content of the message of faith. Christ as Victor over death is also Victor over sin and the powers which caused His death. Bornkamm says, "Wherever there were early Christian witnesses and communities, and however varied their message and theology were, they are all united in believing and acknowledging the risen Lord."[1] And observing the consequences of this belief, he adds, "Just as certainly as—even in a completely historical sense— there would be no gospel, not one account, no letter in the New Testament, no faith, no Church, no worship, no prayer in Christendom to this day without the message of the resurrection of Christ, even so difficult and indeed impossible is it to gain a satisfactory idea of how the Easter events took place."[2]

From the Resurrection onward, the gospel that Jesus had preached became the gospel that was Jesus. The disciples now recognized that Jesus Christ came not only to preach a gospel but to be a gospel. The themes of their message were now: (1) the Messianic Age has come; (2) the gospel is the ministry, death, and Resurrection of the Messiah; (3) Jesus is now at God's right hand as Lord; (4) Jesus has verified His role by the outpouring of the Holy Spirit; (5) Jesus has created, and continues to create, a new community; and (6) Jesus will return as Judge. (See 1 Cor. 15:3–5; Gal. 3:1; 1 Cor. 1:23; Rom. 8:31–34, 2 Cor. 5:16.) As Ramsey says, for the first disciples the "Gospel without the resurrection was not merely a Gospel without its final chapter, it was not a Gospel at all. . . . His resurrection threw its own light backwards upon the death and the ministry that went before; it illuminated the paradoxes and disclosed the unity of His words and deeds."[3] The Resurrection answered the perplexity which earlier beset the disciples and gave them the key to understand the true role of the Messiah.

Both historically and theologically we regard the Resurrection as the ultimate interpretive event of Christology, for in the Resurrection His death is meaningful in its victory, and His ministry is confirmed as having introduced an actual Kingdom. From the Resurrection came Christian belief, Christian worship, and Christian preaching (see Rom. 4:24). The earthly ministry of Jesus becomes a part of the gospel, for the risen Christ extends the validity of His deeds and words. Rather than being a self-contained biography, His ministry becomes content expressing the gospel. For the Christian, Incarnation becomes resurrected Humanity! Christian Theism becomes Resurrection Theism. Christian ethics become Resurrection ethics, a walk in the Resurrection (Rom. 6:4, Col. 3:1–3).

But no one witnessed the actual Resurrection event. What happened was that various persons met the resurrected Christ. The story is told by them with reticence and awe. The disciples themselves had to be convinced of this awesome and stupendous fact. Their unbelief is itself evidence of the fact of the Resurrection, for it deletes the idea that they had hallucinations, or created a fiction of their own to perpetuate the cause of their slain leader. The fact that no human witnessed the resurrecting "process" itself preserves the nature of faith. Bornkamm says, "The event of Christ's resurrection from the dead, his life and his eternal reign, are things removed from historical scholarship. History cannot ascertain and establish conclusively the facts about them as it can with other events of the past. The last historical fact available to them is the Easter faith of the first disciples."[4] And Caird comments, "The first disciples did not come to believe in the resurrection as an event which happened to themselves, comparable with Gautama's illumination, but as an event which happened to Jesus."[5]

It should be noted that the variation in the accounts of the appearances of Jesus do not discredit the factual nature of the Resurrection. Rather they support the authentic character of each witness who tells of amazing encounters with the risen Christ from his own perspective. The accounts do not carry the imprint of biography but of *kerygma*, of telling the meaning of the Jesus story. An attempt to integrate the appearances into a consistent unit cannot be done without leaving some problems. However, the more probable sequence may have been as follows: (1) Jesus' appearance to Mary Magdalene at the tomb (Mark 16:9; John 20:11-18); (2) Jesus' appearance to the other women as they left the garden (Matt. 28:9-10); (3) Jesus' appearance at some point to Peter (Luke 24:34; 1 Cor. 15:5); (4) Jesus' appearance to the two on the Emmaus Road (Luke 24:13-35; Mark 16:12); (5) Jesus' appearance to the ten in Jerusalem (Luke 24:36; John 20:19-23); (6) Jesus' appearance to the eleven including Thomas (John 20:24-29; 1 Cor. 15:5; Mark 16:14); (7) Jesus' appearance to seven disciples at the sea of Tiberias (John 21); (8) Jesus' appearance to the eleven later in Galilee (Mark 16:7; Matt. 28:16-20); (9) Jesus' appearance to five hundred at once (1 Cor. 15:6); (10) Jesus' appearance to James (1 Cor. 15:7); (11) Jesus' appearance to all of the apostles (Luke 24:50; 1 Cor. 15:7; Acts 1:3-12); and (12) Jesus' appearance to Paul (1 Cor. 15:8). There are numerous unresolved problems in such an attempt at harmonizing the appearances reported.

JESUS IS RISEN

1 Now after the Sabbath, as the first day of the week began to dawn, Mary Magdalene and the other Mary came to see the tomb.
2 And behold, there was a great earthquake; for an angel of the Lord descended from heaven, and came and rolled back the stone from the door, and sat on it.

3 His countenance was like lightning, and his clothing as white as snow.

4 And the guards shook for fear of him and became like dead men.

5 And the angel answered and said to the women, "Do not be afraid, for I know that you seek Jesus who was crucified.

6 "He is not here! For He is risen as He said. Come, see the place where the Lord lay.

7 "And go quickly and tell His disciples that He is risen from the dead, and indeed He is going before you into Galilee; there you will see Him. Behold, I have told you."

8 And they departed quickly from the tomb with fear and great joy, and ran to bring His disciples word.

Matt. 28:1–8

Early on that morning following the Sabbath the most stupendous news began to permeate the world. Jesus is risen! All of the Gospel writers agree on the time and on the amazement with which the followers of Jesus are confronted with the evidence of the Resurrection. *"After the Sabbath,"* when it was permissible to be involved in work, very early in the morning as dawn was breaking, the women came to the tomb. They were especially anxious to perform the proper burial rites which they had not been able to do for the body of Jesus on the Sabbath evening of the crucifixion (Mark 16:1; Luke 24:1). Having witnessed the burial of Jesus, they were talking about the problem of removing the stone to gain access to the tomb (Mark 16:3). Apparently they were unaware that a guard had been posted after they had departed from the burial.

Matthew omits the detail relating to why the women came to the tomb early on Sunday morning, concentrating instead on the Resurrection and the miraculous things associated with it. In verse 2 he tells of a great earthquake accompanying the coming of the angel who rolled back the stone. The earthquake struck terror into the guards who shook with fear and *"became like dead men"* (v. 4). Those holding the dead a prisoner became as dead! Matthew describes the angel as removing the stone and sitting on it, giving evidence of the divine activity in the event unfolding before the witnesses. The appearance corresponded to Old Testament descriptions of heavenly visitors.

It has been said that the stone was not removed to let Jesus out but to let the women in. This theophany, the divine activity leading to the appearance of their Lord, was unexpected by the women and was so bewildering that they were confused. Evidently they ran to tell the disciples that the tomb was empty, prompting Peter and John to run immediately to the tomb (John 20:3–10). The women probably returned to see the tomb, and were slowly leaving, while Mary Magdalene lingered behind. She became the first one to see the risen Lord in the series of appearances which followed (John 20:11). The other women were second as they met Him while leaving the garden.

Matthew's selection of appearances very fittingly ties the women, who had observed the burial of Christ and had probably participated in removing the body from the cross, to the early visit to the tomb and the first appearances of the risen Lord. The angel told the women not to be afraid, then shared the exciting news: *"He is not here! For he is risen as He said"* (v. 6). He commissioned them to go and tell the other disciples that the risen Jesus was going before them to Galilee. This was a note of authenticity, indeed of historicity, in the identification of the risen Lord as the Jesus with whom they had associated. The angel had fulfilled his mission, signified by the finality of his words, *"Behold, I have told you,"* meaning literally, "This is what I had to tell you."

The verb used by Matthew may well have been a "prophetic present," meaning that He was going to precede them to Galilee. With both fear and great joy the women ran to tell the disciples. Matthew's reference to the promised appearances in Galilee, and in the conclusion of his Gospel the "Great Commission" given in Galilee, are selections emphasizing his interpretation of salvation history. The gospel is now to be shared with the nations; the message is for all the world. Matthew omitted Luke's reference to Jesus' appearances to the disciples in Jerusalem and of their gathering back in Jerusalem with the risen Christ leading them out of the city to the Mount of Olives, where He ascended (Luke 24:50–53; Acts 1:9–12).

JESUS APPEARS TO THE WOMEN

9 And as they went to tell His disciples, behold,
Jesus met them, saying, "Joy to you!" And they came
and held Him by the feet and worshiped Him.

> 10 Then Jesus said to them, "Do not be afraid. Go,
> tell My brethren to go to Galilee, and there they will
> see Me."
>
> *Matt. 28:9–10*

The first appearances of the risen Jesus were to the women who were among His disciples. John tells us that He appeared first to Mary (John 20:11–18), but Matthew tells of His confronting the women as a group as they hurried from the garden. Jesus' greeting was, *"Joy to you!"* or simply, "Hail," a greeting to which they had long been accustomed. The act of the women in holding Him by the feet was an expression of respect to a sovereign; it was their expression of submission to the risen Lord. His words were similar to the message from the angel: "Joy," "Don't be afraid," and *"Go, tell my brethren to go to Galilee, and there they will see Me."* It is significant that Jesus here used the expression *"My brethren,"* identifying a relationship with them similar to what He had expressed in the washing of their feet, and possibly identifying a larger circle than the immediate disciples. This expression could have included all persons attached to Him who were then in the environs of Jerusalem. Such a group, gathering to meet the risen Lord, could well have comprised the five hundred brethren to whom Paul refers (1 Cor. 15:6). Such varied appearances with varieties of witnesses provide evidence of the historicity of the Resurrection of Jesus of Nazareth.

This brief section speaks of Presence, of place, and of promise. To live in a world in which Jesus is risen means that (1) He is Lord, (2) He is contemporary, (3) He is inescapable!

While we can't prove the Resurrection any more than we can prove God, this belief is central to the Christian faith. We stand before the Thou of the Universe, the One who is wholly Other, but Who has come to us in Jesus. As Schweizer says, "If God had first to prove Himself in man's eyes He would no longer be God."[6] The fact is that a group of people were convinced that they had seen the risen Lord. It resulted in a terrified band of fugitives becoming messengers, with total disregard for danger to themselves as they spread the gospel of the risen Jesus throughout the world. The significance of the empty tomb to the whole event is that it is not immortality without a body that we affirm, but the bodily Resurrection of Jesus (Luke 24:39). As Calvin reminds us in emphasizing the Ascension, "Jesus Christ took humanity to heaven as the guarantee that you and I can be there some day."

In the past one hundred years the evidence for the bodily Resurrection of Christ has been subjected to historical criticism: (1) from Strauss, the appearances of Christ were recorded as visions of intense emotional ecstasy; (2) similarly, Dr. Streeter proposed a vision theory of God acting to communicate by "a telegram from heaven" that Jesus is alive and well; and (3) other interpretations represent the meaning of Jesus' continued life without the need for His resurrected body. As Bultmann has said, "All that historical criticism can establish is the fact that the first disciples came to believe in the resurrection."[7]

Our belief in His Resurrection is based on the evidence that the first disciples had: (1) the words of Jesus that He would rise, (2) the witness of angels at the tomb, (3) the empty tomb itself, (4) the appearances of Jesus to believers, (5) the transformation of the disciples, (6) the reaction of the opposition, (7) the commission to mission, (8) the existence of the gospel itself, (9) the fact that it was unexpected by the disciples and they became convinced, and (10) the existence of the church in spite of Jesus' death on Good Friday.

THE GUARDS BRIBED TO LIE

11 Now while they were going, behold, some of the guard came into the city and reported to the chief priests all the things that had happened.

12 And when they had assembled with the elders and taken counsel, they gave a large sum of money to the soldiers,

13 saying, "Tell them, 'His disciples came at night and stole Him away while we slept.'

14 "And if this comes to the governor's ears, we will appease him and make you secure."

15 So they took the money and did as they were instructed, and this saying is commonly reported among the Jews until this day.

Matt. 28:11–15

Matthew's account of the report of the guards to the Sanhedrin and their subsequent bribery is his answer to the report that the disciples had stolen the body. This report was still circulated among the Jewish community at the time Matthew was writing. His account also serves several other purposes: further evidence for belief in the Resurrection, and evidence of the unbelief and rejection of the Messiah on the part of the leaders of Israel. The Sanhedrin had seen to the crucifixion of Jesus, and now they were confronted with evidence of His Resurrection. They dealt with the report in the one manner which they understood: the use of money. The account says that the Sanhedrin assembled, deliberated, and gave "a large sum of money" to the soldiers to buy their services in perpetuating the story that the body of Jesus was stolen by disciples who fabricated the resurrection report to keep their cause alive. Note the problem in verse 13: the contradiction in that the soldiers slept and yet were supposedly able to witness what was to have happened while they slept. For guards to sleep on the job was to sign their own death warrant, and so the Sanhedrin promised that if this fault came to Pilate's ears, they would appease him. In verse 15 it is evident that the Jews and the Christians had, by the time of this writing, gone separate ways.

In reading the charge that the body was stolen by the disciples, we should note that the disciples would not have been so positive and bold, nor would they have paid the ultimate price of martyrdom for something they knew full well wasn't true. A review of the first seven chapters of the Acts gives abundant evidence of the disciples' witness to the Resurrection and to miracles attesting to the continuing power of the risen Christ. The poem "A Guard of the Sepulcher" is a graphic review of the unbelief of the guards.

> I was a Roman soldier in my prime;
> Now age is on me, and the yoke of time.
> I saw your risen Christ, for I am he
> Who reached the hyssop to Him on the tree,
> And I am one of two who watched beside
> The sepulcher of Him we crucified.
>
> All that last night I watched with sleepless eyes;
> Great stars arose and crept across the skies.
> The world was all too still for mortal rest,
> For pitiless thoughts were busy in the breast.
> The night was long, so long it seemed at last
> I had grown old and a long life had passed.

Far off, the hills of Moab, touched with light,
Were swimming in the hallow of the night.
I saw Jerusalem all wrapped in cloud,
Stretched like a dead thing folded in a shroud.

Once in the pause of our whispered talk
I heard a something on the garden walk
Perhaps it was a crisp leaf lightly stirred—
Perhaps the dream-note of a waking bird.
Then suddenly an angel, burning white,

Came down with earthquake in the breaking light.
And rolled the great stone from the sepulcher,
Mixing the morning with a scent of myrrh.
And lo, the Dead had risen with the day:
The man of Mystery had gone His way!

Years have I wandered, carrying my shame;
Now let the tooth of time eat out my name.
For we, who all the wonder might have told,
Kept silence, for our mouths were stopt with gold.[8]
                    Edwin Markham, 1852–1940

JESUS' GREAT COMMISSION

16 Then the eleven disciples went away into Galilee,
to the mountain which Jesus had appointed for them.

17 And when they saw Him, they worshiped Him;
but some doubted.

18 And Jesus came and spoke to them, saying, "All
authority has been given to Me in heaven and on earth.

19 "Go therefore and make disciples of all the
nations, baptizing them in the name of the Father and
of the Son and of the Holy Spirit,

20 "teaching them to observe all things whatever
I have commanded you; and behold, I am with you
always, even to the end of the age." Amen.

Matt. 28:16–20

The disciples journeyed to Galilee, an adequate experience of travel
to remove them from the conditioning that might have lead to imagi-
nary visions, and far enough removed from the events at Jerusalem
to give them some objectivity. They went to the mountain where

Jesus had appointed them, possibly the site where He had at the first called and commissioned them (chap. 10), but more likely to a mountain He had designated as a meeting place. No doubt other of His followers were present also, and this could have provided the occasion at which the larger group of over five hundred brethren met Him at one time (1 Cor. 15:6). Matthew says, *"When they saw Him, they worshiped,"* a statement suggestive for our own worship! His words *"they worshiped Him"* are also a tribute to Jesus Christ as Lord, as the Son of God. This is a transition from the preaching "of" Jesus to their new message of preaching Jesus. *"But some doubted,"* a phrase which actually has positive meaning in its negative expression, for the fact that some doubted makes the account much more believable.

The story of Thomas, in John 20, is a marvelous account of a movement from doubt to faith. When the other ten disciples told Thomas, "We have seen the Lord," he responded as any thinking man should, "Well, if you have seen Him, then I can see Him." Upon the appearance of Christ to Thomas, his reasonable response to evidence was the cry of faith, "My Lord and my God!" At this meeting with the disciples we have confrontation, worship, questions, and commission.

Jesus' statement *"All authority has been given to Me in heaven and on earth"* is a declaration of the ultimate victory of Christ. He is now the recipient of God's investiture of authority, that "in all things He may have the preeminence" (Col. 1:18). The word for "authority" is *exousia*, meaning Divine authorization. *"Go therefore,"* under this authority, is even better translated, "Therefore, while going in the world, make disciples." The emphasis in verse 19 is on "making disciples," this being the main verb of the verse; the others are subordinate: going, baptizing, teaching. The word for "disciple" is *mathēteuō*, meaning a follower, a learner. As disciples we are always identifying with and learning from the Christ. Note that now they are not sent "to the lost sheep of the house of Israel" but to the whole world, to all of the Gentiles, *ethna*, a universal mission of discipling. This is the beginning of Jesus' reign, the sign that the Son of Man is in heaven.

In the commission to baptize those who become disciples, Jesus institutes the "threefold formula." This is prior to the development of the doctrine of the Trinity in the early creeds, whether we regard it as expressed by Jesus Himself, or as written in this form later by Matthew. Accepting it as the form of Jesus' words of commission, it holds Father, Son and Holy Spirit together as three Persona by whom God encounters us in His love from all eternity and to all eternity. Matthew says we are to baptize *"in the name of . . . ,"* bringing persons into direct relation with God as we know Him: Creator, Redeemer, and Sanctifier. When we think Trinity we should think "Threeness," not a numerical or mathematical three; just as when we think of God as One we should think of "Oneness," not of a mathematical or numerical one.

The commission is to teach the believers or new disciples *"To observe all things whatever I have commanded you."* This statement is related directly to the content of Jesus' ministry. Salvation is not simply a pietistic experience of assurance that we are "justified by faith," or "forgiven," or "saved," but is the assurance of a saving relationship with Christ whom we confess as Lord and serve as Lord by following His teachings. This is a righteousness of relationship, a new life in which we walk with Christ (Phil. 3:9).

Matthew concludes the book with a most remarkable promise that Jesus would be with the disciples in the Spirit whom He would send from the Father, "until the consummation of the present age." This is the ultimate assurance for the disciple, the missioner of Christ; He is with us. David Livingstone, when asked what had sustained him in all of the perils of his pilgrimage in Africa, answered by quoting this verse. It is said that, when his wife died in Africa, he helped prepare her body for burial, helped make the coffin, helped lower it into the grave, and helped cover it with earth, then opened his New Testament and read this text, whereupon he said to his African associates, "Jesus Christ is too much of a Gentleman not to keep His word; let us get on with the task."

A profound but simple outline of the Great Commission could make use of the word "all": all authority . . . all nations . . . all things . . . and always.

The disciples returned to Jerusalem, as Jesus instructed, to await the Holy Spirit whom he had promised to send. Leading them out of the city across the Mount of Olives to the area of Bethany, He ascended to heaven. His first regal act at the right hand of the Father was to give the Holy Spirit to those who acknowledged Him as Lord. Matthew only refers to the Holy Spirit in the commission, but in so doing, he joins each of the other Gospel writers in some special reference to the Holy Spirit at the end of each one's particular Gospel.

Of the Ascension, Paul writes that He "gave gifts to men" for the building of the church (Eph. 4:8–12) and for its efficiency (1 Cor. 12).

Brunner has said, "The Church exists by mission as fire exists by burning." In the sixteenth century, the Reformers were so tied to a Constantinian State Church that they interpreted this passage as only for the first century. But the Anabaptist Believers' Church took this mandate with a seriousness that spread them across Europe in evangelism. One man converted to Christ by this movement, Leonhardt Dorfbrunner, an imperial knight, was after a few months ordained as an evangelist and in the four months from September 1527 to January 1528 (when he was burned at the stake) he had converted and baptized three thousand persons.

William Carey sought to get the North Hamptonshire Baptist Missionary Association to send him as a missionary to India. The leader of the meeting tugged at his coattails, and said, "Young man, sit down. When God wants to convert the heathen he will do it in His own time." But, after gathering the evidence of over three hundred Moravian missionaries at work and presenting this documentation to the Board, they changed their decision and sent him to India.

The Resurrection of Jesus Christ is not some aesthetic appreciation of the eternal dying and rebirth in nature around us. It is not an Easter celebration of the return of spring, nor is it the inner aspects of emotional renewal in the lives of the disciples. The New Testament Christians regarded themselves "as those who have been conquered, whose former lives and belief have come to nought. The men and women who encounter the risen Christ in the Easter stories have come to an end of their wisdom."[9] It is like the story of the men who met the Lord on the Emmaus road; they immediately returned and began to witness. The founding of the church in Jerusalem was not the work of Jesus on earth, but of the risen Lord. The statement in chapter 16 was pointing toward a future happening, "I will build My church, and the gates of Hades shall not prevail against it" (vv. 18–19). "The story of Pentecost shows that the resurrection and exaltation of Jesus and the sending of the Holy Spirit are inseparably bound together."[10]

The risen Christ is building His church, using us as His agents of reconciliation. We are ambassadors for Christ (2 Cor. 5:20), proxies for the Messiah, witnessing by deed and word to His saving grace. "For he is our peace, who hath made both one, and hath broken down the middle wall of partition between us; having abolished in his flesh the enmity, even the law of commandments contained in ordinances; for to make in Himself of twain one new man, so making peace; and that He might reconcile both unto God in one body by the cross, having slain the enmity thereby; and came and preached peace to you which were afar off, and to them that were nigh, for through Him we both have access by one Spirit unto the Father" (Eph. 2:14–18, KJV). "To Him be glory, in Christ Jesus, throughout all ages, world without end; amen!"

NOTES

1. Bornkamm, *Jesus of Nazareth*, p. 181.

2. Ibid., p. 187.

3. A. M. Ramsey, *The Resurrection of Christ* (Great Britian: Fontana Edition, 1961), p. 9.

4. Bornkamm, *Jesus of Nazareth*, p. 180.

5. C. B. Caird, *The Language and Imagery of the Bible* (London: Duckworth Press, 1980), p. 217.

6. Eduard Schweizer, *The Good News According to Matthew*, p. 520.

7. Rudolf Bultmann, *Kerygma and Myth* (New York: Harper & Row, Torchbooks), p. 41.

8. In George Stewart, ed., *Redemption: An Anthology of the Cross* (New York: Geo. H. Doran Co., 1927), pp. 162–163.

9. Bornkamm, *Jesus of Nazareth*, p. 184.

10. Ibid., p. 185.

Bibliography

Alford, Henry. *The Greek New Testament.* Vol. 1. *The Four Gospels.* Boston: Lee and Shepherd Pub., 1872.

Allen, W. C. *The International Critical Commentary.* London: Driver, Plummer and Baiggs. Edinburgh: T. & T. Clark, 1951.

Argyle, A. W. *The Gospel According to Matthew.* Cambridge: University Press, 1963.

Augsburger, David W. *The Freedom of Forgiveness, Seventy × Seven.* Chicago: Moody Press, 1973.

Augsburger, Myron S. *The Expanded Life.* Nashville: Abingdon, 1972.

——. *Principles of Biblical Interpretation in Mennonite Theology.* Scottdale, Pa: Herald Press, 1967.

Bacon, B. W. *Studies in Matthew.* New York: Henry Hold and Co., 1930.

Barclay, William. *The Gospel of Matthew.* 2 vols. Edinburgh: St. Andrew Press, 1963.

Bengel, J. A. *Gnomon of the New Testament.* Translated by James Bandinel. Edinburgh: T. & T. Clark, 1866.

Bonhoeffer, Dietrich. *The Cost of Discipleship.* New York: Macmillan Co., 1960.

——. *Life Together.* New York: Harper & Brothers, 1954.

Bornkamm, Gunther. *Jesus of Nazareth.* New York: Harper & Row, 1956.

Bornkamm, Gunther; Barth, G. and Held, H. J. *Tradition and Interpretation in Matthew.* Translated by P. Scott. Philadelphia: Westminster, 1963.

Bultmann, Rudolf. *Kerygma and Myth.* New York: Harper & Row, Torchbooks.

Caird, C. B. *The Language and Imagery of the Bible.* London: Duckworth Press, 1980.

Carr, A. *Cambridge Greek Testament: St. Matthew.* Cambridge: University Press, 1901.

Charles, Howard. *The Story of God and His People.* Scottdale, PA: Herald Press, 1969.

Cope, O. Lomor. *Matthew: A Scribe Trained for the Kingdom of Heaven,* Catholic Biblical Quarterly Monograph Series 5. Washington D.C.: Catholic Bible Institute Association of America, 1976.

Davies, W. D. *The Setting of the Sermon on the Mount.* Cambridge: University Press, 1964.

Dodd, C. H. *The Bible and the Greeks,* 2nd edition. Naperville, IL: Allenson, 1954.

——. *The Bible Today.* Cambridge: University Press, 1947.

——. *The Parables of the Kingdom.* New York: Scribner, 1961.

Earle, Ralph. *Matthew,* in *The Wesleyan Bible Commentary,* vol. 4. Edited by Charles W. Carter. Grand Rapids: Eerdmans, 1975.

Eller, Vernard. *The Most Revealing Book of the Bible: Making Sense out of Revelation.* Grand Rapids: Eerdmans 1974.

Erb, Paul. *Bible Prophecy.* Scottdale, PA: Herald Press, 1978.

Erdman, Charles. *Commentaries on the New Testament Books: Matthew.* Philadelphia: Westminster, 1920.

Eusebius. *Ecclesiastical History.* Translated by C. F. Cruse.

Ewert, David. *And Then Comes the End.* Scottdale, PA: Herald Press, 1980.

Fenton, John Charles. *Saint Matthew.* Philadelphia: Westminster Press, 1977.

BIBLIOGRAPHY

Filson, Floyd V. *A Commentary on the Gospel According to Matthew.* London: Adam & Charles Black, 1960.

Franzmann, Martin H. *Follow Me: Discipleship According to St. Matthew.* St. Louis, MO: Concordia Pub. House, 1961.

Goulder, M. D. *The Midrash and Lection in Matthew.* London: SPCK, 1974.

Graham, Billy. *Angels.* Garden City, NY: Doubleday, 1975.

Green, H. Benedict. *The Gospel According to Matthew.* New York: Oxford University Press, 1975.

Gundry, Robert H. *The Use of the Old Testament in St. Matthew's Gospel.* Leiden: E. J. Brill, 1967.

Hare, Douglas R. A. *The Theme of Jewish Persecution of Christians in the Gospel of St. Matthew,* Society for N.T. Studies, Monograph Series 6. Cambridge: University Press, 1967.

Hobbs, Herschel H. *An Exposition of the Four Gospels.* Grand Rapids: Baker, 1965.

————. *The Interpreter's Bible.* Edited by George Buttrick. 12 vols. Nashville: Abingdon, 1951–57.

Jeremias, Joachim. *The Eucharistic Words of Jesus.* Philadelphia: Fortress Press, 1964.

————. *The Parables of Jesus.* London: SCM, 1963.

Jeschke, Marlin. *Discipling the Brother.* Scottdale, PA: Herald Press, 1972.

Johnson, Marshall D. *The Purpose of the Biblical Genealogies,* Society for N.T. Studies Series 8. Cambridge: University Press, 1969.

Jones, E. Stanley. *The Christ of the Mount.* Nashville: Abingdon, 1966.

Jones, Martin Lloyd. *Studies in the Sermon on the Mount.* Grand Rapids: Eerdmans, 1974.

Josephus, Flavius. *Antiquities of the Jews.* London: Shapira Vallentine & Co.

Kik, Jacob Marcellus. *The Eschatology of Victory.* Nulley, NJ: Presbyterian & Reformed Pub. Co., 1971.

Kilpatrick, G. D. *The Origins of the Gospel According to St. Matthew.* Oxford: Clarendon Press, 1946.

Kingsbury, Jack Dean. *Matthew: Structure, Christology, Kingdom.* Philadelphia: Fortress Press, 1975.

————. *Proclamation Commentaries: Matthew.* Philadelphia: Fortress Press, 1977.

Kissinger, W. S. *The Parables of Jesus.* Metuchen, NJ: Scarecrow Press, 1979.

Knox, W. L. *Sources of the Synoptic Gospels.* Edited by H. Chadwick. Cambridge: University Press, 1953–57.

Küng, Hans. *On Being a Christian.* New York: Doubleday, 1976.

Kunkel, Fritz. *Creation Continues.* Waco, TX: Word Books, 1973.

Ladd, George Eldon. *New Testament Criticism.* Grand Rapids: Eerdmans, 1967.

Lederach, Paul M. *A Third Way.* Scottdale, PA: Herald Press, 1980.

Lindars, Barnabas. *New Testament Apologetic.* London: SCM Press, 1961.

————. *The Sayings of Jesus.* London: SCM Press, 1961.

Manson, T. W. *The Teaching of Jesus.* Cambridge: University Press, 1939.

Metzger, Bruce. *Historical and Literary Studies.* Grand Rapids: Eerdmans, 1968.

————. *The New Testament, Its Background, Growth and Content.* Nashville: Abingdon Press, 1965.

————. "The Sermon on the Mount: Aspects of Its Form and Content." *Central Baptist Seminary Journal* 1, no. 2 (October 1966).

————. "The Text of Matthew 1:16." in *Studies in the New Testament and Early Christian Literature.* Leiden: E. J. Brill, 1972.

Miller, John W. *The Christian Way*. Scottdale, PA: Herald Press, 1969.

Morrison, Frank. *Who Moved the Stone*. London: Faber Editions, 1967.

Morton, H. V. *The Women of the Bible*. New York: Methuen, 1940.

Niebuhr, Reinhold. *The Nature and Destiny of Man*. New York: Charles Scribner's Sons, 1949.

Parker, Joseph. *A Homiletical Analyses of the Gospel of Matthew*. London: Hodder and Stoughton, 1870.

Plummer, Alfred. *An Exegetical Study on the Gospel According to St. Matthew*. London: R. Scott, 1928.

Ramsey, A. M. *The Resurrection of Christ*. Great Britain: Fontana Edition, 1961.

Riesenfeld, H. *The Gospel Tradition and its Beginnings*. London: A. B. Mowbray, 1957.

Robinson, J. A. T. *Jesus and His Coming*. Philadelphia: Westminster, 1979.

————. *Relating the New Testament*. Philadelphia: Westminster, 1976.

Robinson, Theodore H. *The Gospel of Matthew*. Garden City, NY: Doubleday, 1928.

Saddler, M. F. *The Gospel According to Matthew*. London: George Bell & Sons, 1906.

Schweizer, Eduard. *The Good News According to Matthew*. Translated by David E. Green. London: SPCK, 1978.

Scofield, C. I. *The Scofield Reference Bible*. New York: Oxford University Press, 1945.

Simcox, Carroll E. *The First Gospel, Its Meaning and Message*. Greenwich, CN: Seabury Press, 1963.

Soggs, M. Jack. *Wisdon, Christology and Law in St. Matthew's Gospel*. Cambridge: Harvard University Press, 1970.

Stendahl, Krister. *The School of St. Matthew*. Upsala, 1954.

Stewart, George, ed. *Redemption: An Anthology of the Cross*. New York: Geo. H. Doran Co., 1927.

Stier, Hans. *Reden Jesu*.

Stonehouse, Ned B. *The Witness of Matthew and Mark to Christ*. Philadelphia: The Presbyterian Guardian, 1944.

Stott, John R. W. *Basic Introduction to the New Testament*. Grand Rapids: Eerdmans, 1979.

————. *Christian Counter-Culture*. Downers Grove, IL: InterVarsity Press, 1978.

Strecker, G. "The Concept of History in Matthew." *JAAR* 35 (1967).

Swartley, Willard M. *Mark: The Way for All Nations*. Scottdale, PA: Herald Press, 1979.

Tasker, R. B. G. *The Gospel According to St. Matthew*. Tyndale New Testament Commentary Series. Grand Rapids: Eerdmans, 1979.

Taylor, Vincent. *Jesus and His Sacrifice*. London: Macmillan and Co., 1933.

Trench, R. C. *Notes on the Parables of Our Lord*. London: Kegan, Paul, Trench, Trubner and Co. Ltd., 1902.

Vincent, Marvin R. *Word Studies in the New Testament*. Vol. 1. Grand Rapids: Eerdmans, 1977.

Walvoord, John F. *Matthew: Thy Kingdom Come*. Chicago: Moody Press, 1974.

Ward, Marcus. *The Gospel According to St. Matthew*. London: Epworth Press, 1961.

Wenger, John C. *God's Word Written*. Scottdale, PA: Herald Press, 1966.

White, R. E. O. *The Mind of Matthew*. Philadelphia: Westminster, 1973.

Wilckens, Ulrich. *Resurrection*. A. M. Stewart. Atlanta: John Knox Press, 1978.

Yoder, John Howard. *The Politics of Jesus*. Grand Rapids: Eerdmans, 1972.